PERFECT ME

Perfect Me

Beauty as an Ethical Ideal

Heather Widdows

PRINCETON UNIVERSITY PRESS

PRINCETON AND OXFORD

Copyright © 2018 by Princeton University Press

Published by Princeton University Press,
41 William Street, Princeton, New Jersey 08540

In the United Kingdom: Princeton University Press,
6 Oxford Street, Woodstock, Oxfordshire OX20 1TR

press.princeton.edu

All Rights Reserved

ISBN 978-0-691-16007-8

Library of Congress Control Number: 2017956005

British Library Cataloging-in-Publication Data is available

Editorial: Al Bertrand and Kristin Zodrow
Production Editorial: Debbie Tegarden
Jacket Design: Faceout Studio, Charles Brock
Jacket image courtesy of Liliya Rodnikova / Stocksy
Production: Jacquie Poirier
Publicity: Jodi Price
Copyeditor: Jay Boggis

This book has been composed in Adobe Text Pro and Gotham

Printed on acid-free paper. ∞

Printed in the United States of America

10 9 8 7 6 5 4 3 2 1

For Clara, my piece of perfect.

CONTENTS

ACKNOWLEDGMENTS

Perfect Me has been a personal rollercoaster as well as a professional one. Not only were the arguments I ended up making not those I intended to make, but working on the topic has challenged and changed my views in all kinds of ways. I began the book with something of a split personality. On feminist grounds I was highly critical of beauty norms, and I originally thought the answer could be found through revisionist second wave feminist accounts. I did hold the view that unrealistic and demanding beauty ideals were a way of perpetuating gender subordination; and one that was particularly pernicious as it made otherwise strong and independent women self-critical and vulnerable. As *Perfect Me* shows, I still endorse much of this critique, especially regarding the harms of demanding and unrealistic beauty ideals, but I now think something else far more nuanced, complicated, and interesting is going on. While I endorsed these second wave feminist accounts, something didn't ring true in my lived experience, both in my history with beauty practices and my experience as a woman and vocal feminist in philosophy. As *Perfect Me* progressed, I realized I had used beautifying and presenting as an obviously "made-up" woman to assert my identity and survive in philosophy. If women are not welcome in philosophy in general, women with strong northern accents, heels, eyeliner, and nail polish are even less welcome, and must be, self-evidently, not smart. But yet I have never forgone make-up; although before working on *Perfect Me* I would take my nail polish off before an interview or giving a paper. Working on *Perfect Me* made me reflect on this: why have I not thrown away my polish and paint? For a long time I couldn't answer this and struggled, as many feminists have, with what I saw as my hypocritical behavior. But working on *Perfect Me* has made me revisit the wisdom of simply refusing to beautify. If I am honest, I know it is not wholly harmful or imprisoning to engage in beauty practices, and in the very particular context of philosophy—male dominated but socially awkward—it has been a form of defiance (albeit in a very small way and I am not claiming this is a huge difference or discrimination). I am still working through this, but I think I have used powder, paint, leather, and heels to assert myself. In presenting my polished face and nails, I am a challenge. I unsettle and undermine the status quo. A woman like "that," like me, jars, doesn't fit, upsets. Just by being there I raise questions. This works less well as I age, and possibly I will end up conforming to a different philosophy norm; that of the eccentric. It has also likely made my life much harder than if I had I adopted the outward form of a serious philosopher. This is a small part of my own complex story with beauty, and as the beauty ideal embeds stories beauty will become more complex and more important. Beauty is not simple. It matters, and academics need to engage seriously and urgently. If we want to live in the world, understand the world, and ultimately change it, we need to start by taking seriously what actually matters to people, and beauty matters, and for many it matters consciously and continually.

At the beginning of the project, a close friend teased me that I had turned to beauty because I'd turned forty. Maybe it was that, or perhaps it was trying to bring up a daughter in a world of pink with occasional purple highlights. At the age of three, she had already been told she couldn't play in the playhouse as she was wearing trousers and therefore a boy. (Not a good moment.) This work has allowed me, somewhat, to square the circle between my northern upbringing in a broadly working class community (although my parents were decidedly middle class—with books; my dad had been to Cambridge!) with the elite community of philosophy to which I now belong. My best mate and I did lots of beautifying from the ages of ten onwards. We painted each other's nails, shopped for and shared clothes, and spent hours brushing and styling hair. She is still my best friend, godmother to my daughter, twice my bridesmaid, and we still shop for and swap clothes, do nails, and go on

Spa days (Spa days being a newer addition). I love this kind of beautifying, and I love seeing my friends beautiful, and take pride and joy in their beauty. For the record, I totally reject narratives that women are always in competition. Yet, despite these very positive experiences of beauty—and I still paint nails (of anyone) at every opportunity—I have experienced the changes in the demands of beauty with some horror. Horror at the rising minimal demands (body hair removal and Botox being very obvious examples), horror at the lengths we are willing to go to (rising requests for labiaplasty from girls as young as ten), and horror at how we have come to think of success in beauty as success nearly everywhere (academia being an unusual outlier). We are in the midst of an epidemic of anxiety and shame that is verging on despair, and we are calling this normal. In *Perfect Me* I seek to name these phenomena, to do justice to my experience of beautifying and my love of women while recognizing that beauty norms, even in their best form are problematic, and as they are emerging will be catastrophic.

Very many deserve thanks for their support of *Perfect Me.* First I thank the Leverhulme Trust who supported this project with a Major Research Fellowship, which provided the time and space that made the final writing of this book possible. Accordingly I would like to thank my referees for this project, Darrel Moellendorf, Anne Phillips, and Jenny Saul. I have admired Anne since I first picked up a feminist book, and it is a pleasure and a privilege to count her as a mentor. Darrel is a much valued collaborator and fellow traveler who, unlike many in global ethics and justice, has supported me in what some have regarded as a strange departure into beauty; And Jenny is in the vanguard of seeking to transform philosophy into a place less hostile for woman. I am exceptionally grateful to her. As well as the Leverhulme I would like to thank the AHRC who funded a Network Grant on the "Changing Requirements of Beauty" and the many academics, practitioners, and policy makers who participated in this project. I thank my academic partners on the Network Grant, Melanie Latham and Jean McHale, and most of all Fiona MacCallum, with whom I continue to run the Beauty Demands Blog and Network. In addition, she is a very dear and hugely valued friend, colleague, and critique. Thanks also go to the Nuffield Council on Bioethics, for being a partner in the Network Grant, and particularly to Catherine Joynson, Katharine Wright, and Kate Harvey whose contribution, especially but by no means exclusively to the Briefing Paper, was invaluable. Some of those I met on this project have become friends and collaborators, and are too many to mention. I single out just one, Debra Gimlin, who became in a very short space of time a close friend. Tragically, she died suddenly in 2017 and she is both a personal loss and a significant loss to beauty scholarship.

I thank Princeton University Press, particularly my editor Al Bertrand, for support on this project over the years, patience with some of my wilder ideas and concrete guidance. Thanks to the anonymous reviewers, whose careful reading and detailed comments were invaluable in revising, clarifying, and improving the manuscript. The latter part of my work on *Perfect Me* was concurrent with the work of the Nuffield Council on Bioethics' working party on the "Ethics of Cosmetic Procedures." Without exception I thank every member of the working party for their insights and support. From the Nuffield Council, of which I have been a member since 2014, I'd like to mention by name Simon Caney, Erica Haimes, Jonathan Montgomery, Tom Shakespeare, Hugh Whittall, and Paquita de Zulueta, as individuals I am particularly grateful to and indebted to. To the University of Birmingham I give thanks, especially to the philosophy department, a vibrant and dynamic department full of fabulous individuals. Those I owe a particular debt to are Nikk Effingham, Lisa Bortolotti, Iain Law, and the wonderful staff in Global Ethics: Herjeet Marway, Jonathan Parry, Wouter Peeters, Merten Reglitz, and Jeremy Williams.

I have benefited tremendously from the support, comradeship, and friendship of some remarkable women. I mention these in alphabetical order, as I had no idea how else to do it, but all of them have my respect, love, and gratitude: Clare Chambers, for her clarity, calmness and just being right so often; Monique Deveaux, for her determination, optimism, and thoughtfulness; Alison Jaggar, for her openness, extreme kindness, and dedication to truthfulness and accuracy; Serene Kadher, for her warmth, irreverence, and bravery; Jo Mowat, for her patience, love, and acceptance; Sheelagh McGuinness, for her care, activism, and brilliance; Nichola Rumsey, for her incredible wisdom, magnanimity and exuberance; Sigrid Sterckx, for her insight, her forthrightness, and her deep friendship.

Thanks to Helen Beebee, who could have been listed under remarkable women, but deserves a separate sentence. Without the intensive writing weeks with Helen I would not have finished *Perfect Me*, or at least not in the timescale I did. Eggs for breakfast, writing for eleven hours followed by '80s music, dinner and beer, and repeat, is a research recipe for success. I look forward to many more weeks of the same! Chris Wickham and Leslie Brubaker, and Leslie too could be in the remarkable woman section, for their friendship, advice, solidarity, food and wine. Simon and Laura, for 'family fun', laughter and acceptance. Clare Brice, my beautiful fab friend, for still being my best mate and putting up with me all these years!

Final thanks go to my mother, Gillian—whose nails I have yet to paint—for unfailing and indomitable support and love and who neither I nor my daughter would get through a week without. To my brother, Dominic, and family, who goes beyond the call of duty and actually reads my books (wow!). To my father, Kit, who I miss every day. To my brilliant and brave husband Matthew, who shares my northern roots, remembers my '80s hair, big hooped earrings, fishnets, and collar bones, and loves me as we both become fat, wrinkly, and saggy. Finally thanks to my daughter, Clara, to whom this book is dedicated. She is indeed my piece of perfect; irrespective.

PERFECT ME

Introduction

Beauty Matters

The beauty ideal is changing.* Beauty is becoming more important, and as it does so the beauty ideal is transforming into an ethical ideal. That appearance matters in a visual and virtual culture
should not be surprising. Yet the extent to which beauty matters,
defines meaning and identity, constructs the self, structures daily
practices, and against which individuals are valued (or not), is not
well recognized. Too often beauty is dismissed as trivial fluff,
changeable fashion, not a serious subject for academic—especially
philosophical—study nor, it is implied, is beauty something that serious people should take seriously. In *Perfect Me* I will show that
whatever else beauty may be, it is serious stuff. It profoundly shapes
our shared culture and individual practice, and is increasingly a dominant ethical ideal. Beauty matters to individuals—to real women
and increasingly men—as they navigate their lives. It matters because it makes lives go better or worse. It matters because it is
something that very many of us spend time and money striving for.

* The title of the introduction, as well as being a claim about beauty morally
mattering is a homage to Peggy Brand's *Beauty Matters* (Bloomington and Indianapolis: Indiana University Press, 2000).

It matters because the extent of the industries and infrastructure that are required to support the pursuit of the body beautiful is vast—from food to fashion, from basic grooming to cosmetic surgery. The lack of attention that moral philosophers have paid to the contemporary beauty ideal is surprising, as implied moral judgments and imperatives are ubiquitous in the beauty context: You *should* 'make the best of yourself', you're *worth* it, you *deserve* it and you *should not* 'let yourself go'. Consider possible readings of 'perfect me': an aspiration to become perfect; a statement about the nature of perfection; and a command, 'Perfect Me!', to be obeyed.

Beauty is a moral matter. In *Perfect Me* I will show how profoundly this is so. In so doing, I hope to encourage philosophers of all types to engage in this important debate, to contribute a philosophical voice to disciplines in which the beauty debate is raging, and to be of use to policy makers and practitioners as the ethical nature of the beauty ideal challenges their governance assumptions and proposed solutions. As an applied philosopher, I do not take a "one size fits all" theory "off the peg" and seek to apply it to beauty practices and the beauty ideal. Rather I work through the practices of beauty using the categories and arguments of moral philosophy. I have not sought to impose a theory on the data, but rather have taken the data seriously, especially that of women's lived experiences. I have sought to interpret it using the tools of my discipline, and the arguments are shaped and changed in response to the data.

The Arguments of *Perfect Me*

In *Perfect Me* I make four main arguments. First, the beauty ideal is a dominant and in some instances a predominant ethical ideal. It functions as an ethical ideal in that it sets ideal standards to aspire to and presents working towards such standards as a moral duty.[1] It provides a shared value framework against which individuals judge themselves morally good or bad. It is constitutive of identity and provides meaning and structure individually and collectively. Praise, blame, and reward are apportioned in accordance with it. Finally, engagement is virtuous, and failure is a moral vice engendering shame and disgust. It is important to note that my claim is that in practice the beauty ideal *is*, and *is functioning as*, an ethical ideal for very many people; though for some it remains a prudential ideal or mere social norm. It is not a claim that beauty *should* function in this way or that it is good for us that it does so. Indeed in *Perfect Me* I track the significant current and likely future harms that result from this manifestation of the beauty ideal; while also seeking to be true to the mixed nature of the ideal.

Second, the current beauty ideal is more dominant than previous ideals to the extent that, if trends continue, the ideal will be global. I argue that there is a convergence of current trends that results in a relatively narrow range of acceptable appearance norms for the face and the body. It is not simply an expansion of Western ideals, but a global mean, which is demanding of all racial groups. No racial group is good enough without "help" as all need to be changed or added to. Thus, all women, and increasingly men, need surgical and nonsurgical technical fixes, if they are to be "perfect", or just "good enough." Moreover, as it becomes more dominant, its ethical features become more pronounced making it harder to resist and reject.

Third, key to understanding the power of the beauty ideal is understanding the construction of the self under the ideal. I begin with feminist accounts of sexual objectification and self-objectification and develop these into an account of beauty objectification without sexual threat and that is separable from sexual desire. The aim of such an account is to establish the "to be looked at" nature of the self located in the body, but not just in the actual flawed body, but also in the transforming body, a body of potential and possibility, and the imagined body, full of promise. This self, while located in the body, is no passive self, but active, both subject and object, and, under the beauty ideal, the body is never mere body, but always full of potential. This understanding of the self helps to explain both the power of the beauty ideal as an ethical ideal, and why, despite the costs and harms of beauty, we continue to embrace and celebrate the ideal. This argument, undertaken primarily in chapters 7 and 8, is the heart of the book. The first argument (that the beauty ideal is an ethical ideal) and the final argument (about the limits of choice) only work if the claims about the nature and functioning of the self under the beauty ideal work. It is here that the claims are the most philosophical and, to my mind, the most significant.

Fourth, as individuals we do not choose our beauty ideals. Arguably, we choose the extent to which we conform to them, but the extent to which we can do this is limited by the dominance of the ideal. As the beauty ideal becomes more dominant, the ethical pressure to conform increases. Not conforming is "not an option," and previously extreme procedures, however defined, are normalized, and more practices are required to meet minimal standards of normal. Given this, to claim that engagement is simply individual choice is unsustainable and practices of informed consent are undermined. However, while individual approaches fail, so too do traditional responses of gendered exploitation, coercion, false consciousness, and adaptive preferences. None of these are sufficient to account for lived experience under the current beauty ideal. To understand the beauty ideal we need to recognize its ethical function and dominance. It cannot be dismissed as wholly harmful or as wholly benign, and it is too important to be left for individuals alone to choose.

The Structure of *Perfect Me*

The first two arguments are largely made in the first half of the book and the third and fourth in the second half; although in a real sense the book is a single argument that builds each subsequent claim on the previous claim. The first half of the book introduces and uses more empirical evidence to make its claims, while the second half is more theoretical and traditionally philosophical. Chapters 2 and 3 are particularly empirical, and those who are already familiar with this literature may wish to move quickly over these chapters. However, not only are these chapters necessary to set the scene and establish the ethical worries and provide the social and cultural contexts, but the more philosophical claims of the later chapters are also built upon these chapters. The arguments of *Perfect Me* span the literatures of cultural studies, psychology, and sociology, amongst others, as well as my own discipline of philosophy. Bringing these often isolated literatures into conversation not only allows me to build arguments about the nature of the beauty ideal, but also brings a philosophical voice to the table. My hope is that this voice not only makes a contribution and a distinctive claim about the moral nature of the beauty ideal, and illuminates the changing construct of the self under the beauty ideal. But also, and importantly, it begins a more multidisciplinary conversation. Too often scholars who are working on the same, or very similar issues, are working in isolated disciplinary silos which can result in self-referential conversations. Given that many of these scholars, doing great work in their own disciplines, in fact have very similar concerns to those working in other disciplines, albeit expressed in different terminology and understood in different frameworks, talking across disciplines and working together can only strengthen our understandings.

I will make the arguments of *Perfect Me* over the course of ten chapters. In the first chapter, 'A Duty to Be Beautiful?' I argue that the beauty ideal is increasingly presenting as and functioning as an ethical ideal for very many people. To make this argument, I outline the features of the contemporary beauty ideal, which we would standardly regard as features of an ethical ideal. First, and most importantly, for those who fall under it the beauty ideal provides a value framework against which individuals judge themselves, and others, as being good and bad. As such, the beauty ideal is functioning, for some, as their overarching moral framework, to which they must conform to think well of themselves irrespective of, and in addition to, other metrics by which they judge themselves. Second, the beauty ideal prescribes habits and practices around which daily life is structured and ordered; third, it constructs meaning and identity; fourth, failure invokes shame and disgust and fifth, and by no means least, it promises the goods of the good life. Further I set out a number of assumptions necessary to underpin this ideal: first, the body is malleable; second, body work is required; and third, power is internalized. The ethical nature of the ideal is the first reason that the beauty ideal is different from past beauty ideals.

In the next two chapters, "Life Is One Long Catwalk" and "A New (Miss) World Order?", I argue that the ideal is more dominant than previous ideals. In chapter 2, I argue that the beauty ideal applies to more types of women, potentially all women, whether in the public eye or not. That it applies for longer, starting as young as three and continuing past the menopause, and at times when it previously did not (such as in illness and pregnancy). It is not simply that more individuals happen to value appearance more, but that, as the dominance of the beauty ideal extends, so beauty becomes more valuable and valued. As an ethical ideal, which constructs selves and identities, and creates habits and practices, the beauty ideal becomes more dominant. In turn, the extended dominance contributes to its ethical function. In chapter 3 I argue that this dominance extends to the global. This is not a claim for a Western ideal, or for a single acceptable ideal, but rather a claim that local beauty ideals are converging, resulting in an increasingly narrow range of what is considered beautiful, or just good enough. While not all can engage, or afford to engage, this does not mean that they cannot aspire to engage. Poverty is no barrier to aspiration, and I use the evidence of engagement in affordable trends (such as seeking thinness or using skin-lightening cream) as indicating engagement and aspiration, and thus as supporting the global claim. I argue that extension of the scope, coupled with the ethical nature of the ideal, is transformative. As the ideal expands, there are fewer competitor and alternative ideals, from which both to challenge the dominant beauty ideal and to provide resources for alternative ideals. Moreover the ethical and the dominant aspects of the ideal are mutually reinforcing, and together they produce a greedy ideal. The dominance of the current ideal is the second reason the contemporary beauty ideal is different from past ideals.

In the next chapter, "Routine, Special, and Extreme," I move from the dominance of the ideal to the demands. I argue that incrementally, almost stealthily, the demands of beauty rise, and practices that were previously rare, occasional treats or exceptional measures, gradually become regarded as routine. In this chapter, I map the increasing demands of beauty focusing on supposedly routine practices; particularly body hair removal. I consider five possible criteria by which to define routine practices and argue that the only criterion that consistently holds is that of "required for minimal standards." However, such demands are not minimal and what falls under minimally required is changeable. I argue the collapsing of routine into minimal is convenient, even pernicious, and contributes to the ease with which demands rise along with the harms and costs. If the demands continue to rise along current trajectories, then the costs of beauty, in terms of time and money, as well as the harms of failing to measure up, such as self-loathing and anxiety, will also continue to rise. In the final section of the chapter, I explore what it means for an ideal to be increasingly demanding if such demands are often unrealistic and impossible to meet.

In chapter 5, "Perfectly Normal," I explore the normalization of more extreme practices and the way the language of normal is used in the beauty context. I argue that as practices are normalized minimal standards of beauty rise. This means that more is required just to be "good enough," which results in the narrowing of what is acceptable or normal and a parallel expansion of "abnormal." The gradual escalation, or ratcheting up, of the demands of beauty falls on all of us. As minimal standards rise, so the choices of some to engage eventually mean that all have less choice not to engage. I then consider how normal has been used in the beauty debate to justify practices and as a legitimizing language for engagement. I argue that the narratives of "to be normal" or "to be perfect," while apparently different, are ethically similar. These expressions serve the same function; they enable individuals to access practices in correct and context-appropriate ways. The rise in minimal demands coupled with the normalizing of once extreme practices is the third difference between the current beauty ideal and past ideals.

In chapter 6, "Hidden Costs and Guilty Pleasures," I map the harms and benefits, pleasures and pains, of beauty, focusing on the communal and social rather than the individual. This chapter sets the debate about dominance and demandingness in a wider context. Recognizing the social and communal costs and benefits is crucial, as focusing only, or even primarily, on the individual leads to policy and practice interventions that are, at best, partial and ineffective, and, at worst, counterproductive, contributing to the raising of minimal standards and the narrowing of normal. In this chapter, I touch on standard justice harms including costs to vulnerable others, costs of resource allocation and opportunity cost, and the harms of a toxic and discriminatory environment, and the benefits of social bonding and the loving touch.

In chapter 7, "My Body, Myself," I describe the self under the beauty ideal, in particular the imagined self, the end point of the ideal. I argue that the first stage in locating the self, in part, in the imagined self is locating the self in the body. To make this argument, I introduce traditional accounts of sexual objectification and self-objectification. I develop from such accounts an account of beauty objectification that does not imply sexual threat and is distanced from sexual desire. I argue that under the beauty ideal a person can be objectified and self-objectified, made an "object to be looked at," in whole or in part, and judged according to the beauty ideal without the primary consideration being sexual. Skin can be judged for its flawlessness and luminosity (or for wrinkles, spots and blemishes), legs for their length and lack of cellulite (or for their chunkiness and bumpiness), or the whole as a beautiful, ideal, and perfect (or ugly, flawed and downright imperfect).

In chapter 8, "I Will Be Worth It!" I develop the argument of chapter 7 and argue that objectification in beauty is not always reductive in the way that sexual objectification has been claimed to be. In beauty objectification, we are not reduced to a mere body, as the body we are identified with is not only our actual flawed and vulnerable body, but also our transforming and imagined body. Further, because our actual body is already, in part, our transforming body—and contains the promise of the imagined self—the actual body is a source of potential. This conception of the self helps to explain the continued power of the beauty ideal. I argue that the self under the beauty ideal is dual: negative and critical of the current self, and full of promise and possibility with regard to the future self. Likewise, the beauty ideal is dual: both demanding and rewarding. Accordingly, I argue that beauty objectification does not reduce to a mere body or deny subjectivity as, under the beauty ideal, we are both subject and object.

In "I'm Doing It for Me," I explore the chosen and required nature of the beauty ideal. I outline why choice is regarded as trumping in liberal frameworks. I argue that the "I'm doing it for me" narrative is the correct and acceptable discourse for engaging in beauty practices, and should not be taken at face value. I then argue that even on its own terms the liberal choice model is insufficient and informed consent undermined. However, while the choice-framework fails, I go on to argue that beauty choices are not desperate choices or coerced, nor are they instances of false consciousness or adaptive preference. I finish the chapter by mapping three consequences of ignoring communal critiques and adopting a liberal model of individual choice: first that it artificially polarizes actors into empowered agents or passive victims; second, that it silences debate and criticism; and third, that, despite claims to respect autonomy and empower the agent, the liberal choice model is ultimately victim-blaming.

In chapter 10, "More Pain, Who Gains?" I explore the traditional claim that beauty practices are for the benefit of men. In this chapter, I argue that traditional accounts of gendered exploitation are not sufficient to account for what is going on in the current context. The inequality, asymmetry and hierarchy, upon which exploitation arguments are premised is eroding in a context in which men are increasingly vulnerable to body dissatisfaction and increasingly engaging in beauty practices. Men's bodies are "to be looked at," as women's bodies have long been, and in some quarters men are equally subject to demanding and unrealistic appearance ideals. This is not to say that the male ideals are equivalent; in fact, important differences remain. Nonetheless, although differences persist, inequality is reducing on this axis, undermining arguments of gendered exploitation; although other harms, such as those deriving from binary and hypergendered norms, remain and even extend. I conclude that inequality and gendered exploitation are not the primary moral problems of the dominant beauty ideal. An equal, but equally demanding beauty ideal, would address some aspects of gender inequality, but still be morally troubling given the extent of the demands and the functioning of the beauty ideal as an ethical ideal.

The book finishes with a short conclusion: "Beauty without the Beast," in which I revisit the argument for a beauty ideal as an ethically, dominant, demanding, and increasingly global ideal. The power of the beauty ideal constructs and sustains the construct of the self of beauty objectification, which in turn helps to explain the continued and increasing adherence to the ideal. I finish by arguing that responses to the beauty ideal must recognize both the profound attraction of the ideal and the very real pleasures involved in its pursuit, as well as the significant, growing, and potentially catastrophic harms that attach to it. Ignoring the attractions of beauty leads to false theories and bad policy and practice. If the extensive and increasingly destructive harms of beauty are to be addressed, we must begin with an accurate picture of the beauty ideal and of why it matters so much to individuals. The harms of beauty, particularly the communal harms, are very real and, if current trends continue, will profoundly limit what human beings can be and do. I suggest that effective solutions must be positive, life-enhancing, celebratory, and communal; not divisive, critical, victim-blaming, or individual.

The Limits and Limitations of *Perfect Me*

Let me finish this short introduction with a number of caveats, explanations, and apologies.

First, while gender is primary in my analysis, I adopt an intersectional approach in which gender is simply one component in the analysis and one that cannot be divided from or separated from others; including, but not exclusively, those of race, religion, class, age, and sexuality. I have tried to find a balance between recognizing and respecting difference, and being able to make substantial and general critiques. As such I have used the category "women"— anathema to some—as a class term as the beauty ideal falls on those who present as, are perceived to be, or are situated as, women. Indeed, beautifying is one of the ways in which women are made women. In chapter 10, I argue that one of the pervasive harms of the beauty ideal is its heteronormativity and its hypergendering function. A function that is increasingly prominent and manifest in the emerging global ideal of women as "thin with curves" and in some dominant male ideals, most obviously the muscled man. Given this, the beauty ideal is experienced as gendering and gendered. Yet, there are no natural bodies, all bodies are constructed, and accordingly the category "women," as I use it, is not essentialist, nor is it intended to be exclusive or exclusionary. Rather it is a place holder for those who are made, and make themselves, women, and it is practical and political, intended to allow gender analysis that resonates in many different contexts, without trying to deny the difference of raced, sexed, and classed experience. I have sought to recognize the partial nature of my approach, and be attentive to difference, while still tracking shared experiences, communal patterns and structures. As such, and inevitably, I generalize, sometimes overgeneralize, and skip over important differences in order to make broad claims about the beauty ideal; claims that inevitably will fail in certain instances, but that nonetheless are revealing, particularly about general trends, patterns, and practices. Undoubtedly, my claims will be too general for some, particularly my claims for an emerging global ideal, and may seem presumptuous and highhanded. Also, undoubtedly, my claims will not be general enough for others, and I will be criticized for giving too much weight to the varieties of individual experience, particularly when it comes to the pleasures of beauty. To both groups I apologize, and both criticisms have truth in them. I am both overgeneral in a way that is unusual in social science disciplines and yet I seek to pay attention to actual lived experience and real-world evidence, which is unusual in my own discipline of moral philosophy.

My only defense is that only by ignoring certain differences can I track the emergence of what, I will argue, is a significant transformation in the nature, dominance, and demandingness of the beauty ideal. Moreover, as is clear throughout, my critique of the beauty ideal as an ethical ideal is not the whole story, not by any means, and the sustained accounts of the raced, classed, sexed, and gendered nature of beauty are also necessary. Many of these I refer to and draw on in *Perfect Me* others I have not used in this work, but they have informed my thinking in broad terms, and others I am yet to discover. A challenge throughout has been the vast amount of data on this topic from social science, science, policy makers, and practitioners; and more is published every day. My critique, from the perspective of moral philosophy, should be read as offering another voice to what is already a nuanced and developed debate, a debate that spans many disciplines (including but not limited to cultural studies, medicine, law, psychology, and sociology). My contribution is to highlight the ethical nature of the beauty ideal in the hope that this goes some way to explaining the continued and increasingly pronounced dominance of it. This ethical account runs alongside and complements other accounts, and only together can progress, in both understanding and social change, be made. Thus, while I take a particular approach, in order to uncover a distinctive and neglected ethical aspect of the beauty ideal, I endorse and embrace other approaches; all approaches uncover parts of the beauty puzzle. Although I have long been committed to multidisciplinarity, in this project more than any other I have become convinced that we need the insights of all disciplines, each revealing different aspects, to understand and address complex and pressing social and ethical issues. In short, I trust my commitment to intersectionality and multidisciplinarity is clear, and I celebrate the work of many scholars from across disciplines and am very grateful for their work.

A final point on gender is that, even though I touch on the hyper-gendering and binary nature of the beauty ideal, I do not discuss the challenges and resources of LGBTQ* activist and academic communities. This is not because I do not recognize their significance or importance in both theory and practice. On the contrary, I suspect that they may offer resources for resistance, challenge, and change which are so needed. At the outset of this project I intended to include far more of this debate. However, setting out the dominant beauty ideal and its ethical functioning proved too much material for one book. Hence, this remains a topic for future work, and perhaps in conjunction with others.

A similar omission is a discussion of the challenges of subcultures, such as body modification and body-building, as well as certain religious communities, which again I hope may provide resources to challenge and diversify the beauty ideal. The extent to which these are real alternatives or variations on a theme requires further research. For example, is strength and muscle display in body-building an alternative ideal, perhaps emphasizing the action and power of the body, or is it a version of firmness and, like the beauty ideal, "to be looked at"? Even supposedly hugely different communities that reject the display of the body are often more conforming than might be assumed; for instance, as will be discussed, focusing on the areas that can be seen (such as wearing visible rhinoplasty bandages). In addition, covered bodies can still aspire to the beauty ideal (in terms of thinness, smoothness, firmness, and youth), and there are modest, cute, and sexy variations of the beauty ideal; and such variations do not greatly challenge the demands of the ideal. The arguments about subcultures are complex and divergent; for instance, while lesbian culture can protect against the thin ideal, it can also mark nonconformity, which might or might not be problematic as the beauty ideal narrows.[2] Such divergence requires more attention than I could possibly have included in this work. This lack of discussion is an omission, but I hope not unforgivable given the breadth of the claims I am making. Again this is a hugely fruitful area for research, and I suspect such communities will be a place to start considering how to communally address the beauty ideal, the point where *Perfect Me* ends.

The final omission, and one that might be surprising, is the lack of sex in the book. Given the connections between sex and beauty ideals, for example, worries about the sexualization of young girls or the mainstreaming of porn as beauty becomes glamour, this omission may seem unforgivable. Again I had intended at the outset to address this question in detail, particularly the complex relationship between looking sexy and feeling sexy, and the fact that one might not entail the other. Further I had intended to consider phenomena such as the slut marches, as subcultures, which might provide, as other subcultures might, resources for resistance to the dominant beauty ideal and for diversification of the ideal. However, again this debate did not make it into the final draft, and is an argument for another day. This is because the arguments for beauty objectification, as opposed to sexual objectification, track differently to, and perhaps even in the opposite direction to, the arguments about sexualization and the mainstreaming of porn. That it is possible to separate beauty objectification from sexual objectification is a key claim of this book. However, this is only one aspect of the myriad claims that could, and should, be made about how sex and beauty do, and do not, connect. In addition it is not a claim that sexism is decreasing; if anything the opposite is true. Rather it is a claim that not all beautification is sexual, sexist, or about gender. These arguments I am keen to return to in future work, as if I am right about beauty objectification, then the challenge of how to address "hotness" as a requirement and whether it is about sex or beauty or both is left hanging.

Moving from omissions to a profound and heartfelt apology. *Perfect Me* is empirically informed throughout, but it is not empirically comprehensive. As a philosopher, I lack empirical training and expertise, but as an applied philosopher I seek to respond to lived experience as it actually is, rather than as we might wish it to be. Given this, even though I use empirical data in rather unscientific ways, the empirical data is crucial. I am sure that there are data I have not used, which I should have, and data I have used wrongly, either misinterpreted or failed to recognize its import. In addition, new data will have emerged since I submitted this manuscript in November 2016. Moreover, given my scattergun approach I am sure that evidence can be found to challenge and counter my claims. However, my hope is that such evidence, while complicating my claims and providing opportunities for future discussion, will not greatly damage my arguments in *Perfect Me*. I use empirical data in a broadly illustrative, rather than strictly scientific, way and have focused on general trends and patterns. I have sought to identify broad trends, and map the likely trajectory of such trends into the future, and as such, despite the problems of such data use in my discipline, and with profuse apologies to those in more data-savvy disciplines, I trust my data will do the limited job that is required and support the philosophical arguments of this work.

Finally a few words about what this book is and is not. Most important, as I will return to in chapter 6, *Perfect Me* is not an ethics of practices, but a book about the beauty ideal; its ethical nature, its dominance and demandingness, and the construction of the self under it. My book does not seek to endorse or condemn certain practices, nor does it suggest that individual women should or should not engage in such practices or should be, as individuals, praised or blamed for engagement or non-engagement. Indeed it rejects such tactics out of hand; as missing the power of the ethical nature of the ideal and the promise of the self under the beauty ideal. Throughout I have sought to be true to the evidence and to take seriously the extent of the dominance that the young particularly, but not exclusively, experience when it comes to managing their bodies and their selves. As such I have attempted to recognize the very real joys and benefits of beauty as well as the extreme and increasing demands of a dominant, ethical beauty ideal. I do not mean to underplay the extreme harms that attach to a dominant and demanding beauty ideal. The harms to individuals who engage, individuals who do not engage, and to us all are extensive and devastating, in ways that I will map. But the answer has to be communal not individual, to simply tell women not to engage is unrealistic and ineffective, and, as I will argue, profoundly unethical. This commitment not to blame individuals and to recognize the mixed nature of the ideal, while recognizing its ultimate harms, has led to a very different book from the one I first conceived. Initially I had thought that the crisis in body image and the increasing location of the self in the body could be addressed by revised and revived second wave feminist arguments; such as those of coercion, objectification, and gendered exploitation. However, as I worked on the topic and tried to make these arguments it became clear that even though they are hugely illuminating, they no longer work as explanatory frameworks. No longer do they speak to the experience of those who fall under the ideal, and it was not possible to explain this mismatch in lived experience away by pretending that such arguments were sufficient. While there are many harms of objectification and there are gendered harms attached to beautifying, there are also pleasures and benefits. Moreover, it is important to remember that one thing worse than locating the self in the body is locating the self in the mind and neglecting embodiment: a view my discipline of philosophy has a particularly shameful record in propagating (the ghost in the machine).

Human beings are more than bodies, something in an increasingly visual and virtual culture we are in danger of forgetting, but they are also more than disembodied minds, and this is just as important to remember as we confront the challenges of the beauty ideal. In *Perfect Me* I argue that the self is located in the body, although not reduced to the body. As embodied beings, appearance—beauty—should matter, but it should not be all that matters or what matters most. Beauty ideals should be broad, inclusive, diverse, and celebratory, not homogenous, demanding, dominant, and ultimately destructive and devastating. How we look should not be, as it increasingly is, our very selves.

1

A Duty to Be Beautiful?

In this chapter, I aim to show why the contemporary beauty ideal—
as it is emerging and in some instances already manifests—is an ethical ideal. That the beauty ideal is functioning as an ethical ideal is
the first core argument of the book and is necessary for all the claims
that follow. Beauty has long been connected to morality, both implicitly and explicitly. Beauty on the outside as representative of
beauty on the inside—think of paintings of the virtues as beautiful
women—and at times the two have been equated. For Plato, beauty
is the only spiritual thing we love by instinct, by nature, and it is
love of beauty that sets us on the moral path towards goodness and
moral virtue.[1] Conversely, ugliness and evil are equated. The link
between beauty and goodness (and ugliness and evil) is particularly
clear in the stories we tell our children where heroes and heroines
are young and beautiful and stepmothers, goblins, and ugly sisters
are, well, ugly. Disney exemplifies the paradigmatic equation of
beauty with goodness and without ambiguity or nuance. The outside must match the inside: the beast must become a beautiful
prince (he cannot remain a beast and be loved); the evil stepmother
must be punished for seeking to remain beautiful, for pretending to
be beautiful, or for trying to compete with, or steal beauty from,

the young.[2] Thus, goodness and beauty are, and have been, intimately acquainted, and often beauty is used symbolically to represent the good. How this equation manifests, and what it means, can be, and has been, very different. For example, while images of beautiful women might have represented the virtues, actual flesh and blood, particularly beautiful, women were regarded suspiciously and potentially as morally corrupting; the devil's gateway.[3] In contemporary culture, beauty, as will become abundantly clear, is physical, with particular attention on the naked body and the close-up face.

The assumption that the beautiful are morally good is not limited to fairy tales but is an assumption that continues to underpin our expectations of the beautiful. In this chapter, I will document some of the ways in which these assumptions are manifested in the contemporary context and unpick the ways in which the beauty ideal is, and is functioning (for some wholly and for most in part) as, an ethical ideal. Despite mantras such as "it's what's on the inside that counts" in an increasingly visual and virtual culture, and irrespective of whether we think this *should* be the case, often it is what is on "the outside" that counts. Judgments about the inside, about the person, are made on the evidence of the outside. Moreover, at times it is effectively *only* the outside that counts: what is inner is identified with and determined by the outer.[4] I argue that in such instances, beauty does not simply represent, but has *become* goodness. The symbolic nature of the relationship (where beauty signifies goodness) is broken: beauty is no longer a stand-in, or a place-holder, for goodness, but rather beauty *is* what is desired (for itself and for the goods that it is believed it will deliver). Beauty then becomes *the* (ethical) ideal to aspire to and strive for, as the song says it is "your duty to be beautiful, keep young and beautiful if you want to be loved." The song even instructs you how to attain this beauty: of the face ("don't fail to do your stuff, with a lot of power and a puff"), and the body ("if you're wise exercise all the fat off, take it off over here, over there").[5]

For some then beauty is what is desired for itself, beauty is the goal, the end point, the good, which is sought, striven for, and worked towards—the ideal. For others, beauty may be desired in part as a good itself and in part as a means to other goods, and some may not value beauty at all. For those who fall wholly under the beauty ideal, beauty functions unambiguously as an ethical ideal, as a primary value framework; and, as I will argue in the next chapter, more of us fall under the ideal and to a greater extent than previously. In this chapter, I aim to show that, and how, the contemporary ideal of beauty is becoming, and for some already is, an ethical ideal, an overarching moral framework. It provides an ideal to aspire to, and work towards, and individuals judge themselves and others successes or failures according to the extent they conform to it. Under such a framework attaining minimum (good enough) standards of beauty becomes effectively a (moral) duty, something that is required and necessary. As a value framework, the beauty ideal provides shared standards by which to apportion praise, blame, and reward, making beauty-success a moral virtue and beauty-failure a moral vice. As I will go on to show, increasingly beauty failure is regarded as a failure of the whole self, rather than a local failure. Thus, failure to measure up in beauty stakes is not minor or limited, but colors how the self is perceived across contexts. Finally, the beauty ideal is an ethical ideal in that it promises to deliver the goods of the good life. None of these arguments alone is sufficient to establish the beauty ideal as an ethical ideal, but they all point to the change in the status of the beauty ideal, and taken together they have significant weight. That the beauty ideal is an ethical ideal is further supported by claims in subsequent chapters about dominance, scope, and demandingness. As the ideal extends across domains, and in ways I will outline, the nature of the ideal transforms and the ethical nature embeds.

Perfect Is ...

Let me begin by sketching the features of the ideal, features that will be elaborated over subsequent chapters. At this point, my aim is not to defend the larger claim that beauty ideals are converging, but to broadly map the key features of the ideal. By using the language of "an" or "the" ideal I do not mean that there is just one possible "perfect," a detailed blueprint that must be conformed to in all aspects to be "good enough" or "perfect." There is not a single acceptable hair color, eye color, height, or weight. For instance, to be perfect we do not need to be exactly the same (say 5 foot 8, size 10, with long blond hair and blue eyes and a wide smile, or any other detailed and particular instance of "perfect"). We do not all have to be Barbie! Rather to be "perfect," "better," or just "good enough," we have to meet a number of broad requirements. The beauty ideal is not a single model, but a (relatively narrow) range of acceptable models. For example, size can vary, you can be tall or short, petite or Amazonian, but you must be some version of slim; hair style and hair color can vary, but some evidence of grooming is required; breast size can vary, but pertness is desirable across sizes; and so the list goes on. Further, some aspects are more important in certain contexts than others, and features of the beauty ideal can be traded off against each other. For example, while golden or bronze skin is generally desired, very light and very dark skin is no barrier to being beautiful if you have attained the other features of the ideal. In addition, some features of the ideal are more dominant in some places than others, as will become very clear when the global nature of the ideal is discussed. In sum then, the beauty ideal centers on the physical body and the face; beautiful bodies must be thin, perhaps with curves, and bodies and faces must be firm, smooth, and young.

To be perfect, or just to be good enough, you must meet minimal standards of the body beautiful sufficient to fall within the parameters of acceptable. If you fail to fall in this range, then you will be judged by others to have failed; and if you endorse the ideal, you may judge yourself to have failed—even regard yourself, your whole self, as a failure. I will argue in subsequent chapters that the range of what is acceptable is becoming narrower, increasingly homogenized, and globally aspired to. This narrowing of what is acceptable makes what is required to achieve minimal standards of acceptable appearance more demanding. Further, as the beauty ideal narrows, not conforming to such standards becomes less acceptable, and less possible in practice. So some divergence is possible, but divergence is less. There are fewer truly alternative beauty ideals, *and* there are fewer alternative nonbeauty ideals, making it less possible to dismiss, resist, or opt out of beauty ideals. That the beauty ideal is increasingly narrow, demanding, and dominant is relevant for the claim that beauty is an ethical ideal; most important is that as the scope of the ideal expands alternative ideals become rarer and more costly to adopt. Thus dominance supports the ethical claim, and in turn the ethical nature increases the dominance of the ideal.[6] Accordingly, the claim that the beauty ideal is an ethical ideal will be strengthened by the arguments of dominance, scope, and demandingness in subsequent chapters.

THIN AND SLIM

The primary feature of the dominant beauty ideal is that of thinness. Study after study suggests that women would choose to be thin in preference to almost anything else. For example, in a study of nearly 10000 women "89 percent of women ... experienced some form of weight-based dissatisfaction with the vast majority wanting to be thinner."[7] This is repeated in numerous studies; irrespective of size we want to be thinner, and believe we would be happier if we were. The thin ideal manifests in a number of ways. For some it is very thin (catwalk thin); for others it is slim with curves; for others it is athletic, buff, and strong. However, for all slimness in some form is crucial. And importantly for my claims the preference for thinness rather than fatness, is becoming global. Different local norms still exist—what is considered thin in one place may be positively chunky in another—but nearly everywhere relatively thinner figures are prized. We do not need to hold exactly the same ideal of thinness for the range of what is acceptable to be narrowing.[8] Of course, the trend may not continue, and current trajectories may reverse.[9] But, while I hope this will be the case, the current dominance of the thin ideal suggests this is unlikely.

For now I simply wish to note that all versions of the dominant beauty ideal—whether hourglass, thin with curves, athletic, 'model-thin' with 'thigh gaps' and so on—require thinness in at least some body parts. Most obviously, waists are required to be thin; "muffin tops" and "love handles" are not features of any version of thinness.[10] Women's magazines and fashion programs may remind us that Marilyn Monroe had a pot belly and curves, but these are curves within very narrow limits. Marilyn Monroe was never more than a UK size 12 (U.S. size 8 to 10), with a waist of between 22 and 24 inches; and at times she was considerably smaller. While this might be the fleshiest ideal of recent decades, it is far thinner than the average woman. Likewise, we are told not to worry about our burgeoning flesh; we are still attractive, as "real men like something to get hold of."[11] But these reassuring words belie, and in so-doing reinforce, the underlying message that thin is best. The reason that we need reassurance about our lack of thinness is because it is assumed that we will, and perhaps should, worry about it. The extent to which thinness is required and the fairly continual pressures to keep our flesh in check and our appetites under control, will be returned to, for now it is enough to note that being relatively thin or slim, is a key feature of the dominant beauty ideal.

FIRM AND BUFF

A second feature of the beauty ideal, and one that connects to thin, is firm. Firmness becomes more important in an increasingly visual culture in which the body, especially the naked body, is a predominant image. While, in some places the face matters more than the body, in all places it is the physical features that dominate. The body to which we should aspire is a certain type of body, it is young, firm, smooth, and thin; in parallel the ideal face is smooth, firm, sculpted, and young. This young, firm body is the body we continually see images of, and the average person in the United States sees around 3000 ads a day.[12] However attuned we are to the manipulation of advertising, we cannot but imbibe these images. While we may well be critical of them, they become, in one form or another, part of our own imaginings of what it is to be "good enough" or "perfect." Thinness alone is not enough—being scrawny and haggard is not desired—the body also needs to be firm, and increasingly "thinness with curves" is desired.[13] Large, or at least firm, breasts are desirable, but coupled with the thinness of a small waist. A large and shapely backside needs to be attached to long, slim legs. A large saggy, pockmarked, and cellulite-dimpled backside attached to "thunder thighs" and "cankles" is not ideal.[14] So it might be possible to escape the tyranny of thin if you are "shapely," but where you do have curves they must be firm: "Strong is the new sexy" we are told. The firm requirement does little to mitigate the demandingness of thinness. To be buff requires more effort than thinness alone. Curves cannot be lumpy, bumpy, or look like orange peel, and wobbles and jiggles are sources of shame. Thus while the addition of curves to the thin silhouette potentially expands the range of the beauty ideal, the firmness requirement can result in further demands. Firmness requires more work than simple thinness (although thinness alone is hugely demanding). Body work is required in one form or another: either by constant diet and exercise to build the right curves in the right places, or in the form of cosmetic surgery (for instance, breast or buttock implants on an otherwise thin frame).

Firmness as a feature of the beauty ideal highlights the materiality and physicality of the current beauty ideal. Primary is body shape and tone, and skin texture and tone. It is the physical body and it is physical features that matter. In many cultures naked bodies are increasingly on display, and as nakedness becomes normal, so increasing demands are being made of the naked (as well as the clothed) body.[15] This is significant in that a beauty ideal that is more focused on the shape of the naked body is largely immune to changing clothing fashions, and arguably in fashion, if not bodies, there is far more diversity than ever before. With a focus on the face and body there is less scope for artifice, concealment and theater (or at least such arts now move from clothes to the body). This is not to say that we do not still use clothes to enhance, to conceal, to hint at the beauty of what is underneath, and most of us are not routinely seen naked (though more of us are in person or in images), but nonetheless the ideal imagined self, the perfect me, is increasingly imagined naked. In cultures where the naked body, and flesh generally, is not publically on display the extent to which women attain firmness may be a private matter, and so arguably less important. By contrast, in the beach culture of Brazil, where near-naked bodies are on display, firmness may matter more. However, as the lines between private and public personas decrease, and selfies of the face, the body, and parts of the body are routinely posted or shared, the private may not stay private; as the rise in revenge porn suggests.[16] Even in covered cultures, firmness may matter, and the firmness of the body, may be hinted at in the small amount of flesh that is visible; and both Beirut and Iran, among others, have been termed the "world capital" of cosmetic surgery.[17] Moreover, firmness may be desired, and aspired to, even if not publically displayed. In chapter 3, I will argue that, despite the many global differences, firmness increasingly matters, although less in some contexts than others.

SMOOTH AND LUMINOUS

The third feature of the ideal is smoothness. Smoothness connects to firmness and being buff, and has also emerged in a context where the beauty ideal is focused on the physical face and body. As well as being firm, skin should also be smooth and luminous. It should not be blemished, pock-marked, or with uneven pigment (age-marks, blemishes, rosacea, veins, and even overly large pores should be erased or concealed).[18] The demand for smoothness, like firmness marks a difference from previous beauty ideals. For example, the attention to the texture of the skin is transformative. Rosalind Gill and Ana Elias use the word "forensic" to refer to the phenomenon of the increasing focus on microscopic flaws in the skin. This attention is encouraged by beauty ads and products that focus on pore texture and luminosity and by the increasing use of apps. As a result the "surveillant gaze" becomes more intense, "operating at ever finer-grained levels and with proliferating range of lenses that do not necessarily regard the outer membrane of the body—the skin—as their boundary."[19] The requirement for smoothness applies to the face and the body.

When it comes to the body, the smoothness requirement has resulted in the demand that bodies be hairless, and I argue in chapter 4 that the move to hairless bodies is a significant barometer for understanding the changing focus and increasing demands of the beauty ideal. Like firmness, the requirement for smoothness extends beyond past beauty ideals and applies to every inch of the body and the face. As visual and virtual culture expands and is more dominant, the contexts in which the beauty ideal applies multiply. We need to be smooth and luminous not just at key times (for example, when our picture is likely to be taken on holidays or at weddings), but increasingly all the time. Being captured on camera is now a possibility in almost any context, and the mere thought of our blemished or hairy skin captured, posted, and shared is enough to induce shame. Being "camera ready" is increasingly a requirement, and given that we can imagine ourselves (or our failings) being photographed in almost any context this demand is extensive. Finally, smoothness requires a certain type of skin, which is often connected to shade and tone, although in the beauty language not to color: this said in an individualist and supposedly race-blind beauty context undoubtedly the specter of racism and colorism remain. In chapter 3, I will return to this aspect of smoothness and suggest that the emerging global ideal endorses a golden or bronze skin tone, which tends to be lightened black skin or tanned white skin. For now it is enough to note that smoothness is a third feature of the beauty ideal.

YOUNG AND YOUTHFUL

The final key feature of the ideal that I wish to highlight is youth; a long-standing feature of all beauty ideals. Youth is perhaps what thinness, firmness, and smoothness are seeking, collectively, to create and emulate. Unlike some of the other features, where there is a range of options, the ideal permits very little deviation when it comes to youth. Quite simply, you should not look old. If there is a narrow range of beauty ideals when young, the range when old is tiny. Very few of us can emulate Helen Mirren, and be "gold not old"; despite the encouragement that "now is our golden age, be-cause, we're worth it."[20] There is remarkably little tolerance for, or acceptance of, aging bodies in general, and there are few excep-tions to the expectation that aging bodies should be hidden and regarded as falling below the ideal and even shameful. However, despite the lack of tolerance for aging bodies the beauty ideal now applies to older women, something that is a product, in part, of an increasingly visual culture, as well as a result of the technological possibilities that are accessible, affordable, and normalized. Youth then is the final key feature of the dominant ideal, and perhaps the least contested. Even the most relativist anthropologically minded among us will grant that youth is a global feature of beauty ideals.

In sum, and to caricature a little, the dominant beauty ideal is young, thin, firm, and smooth. It is not old, aging, pockmarked, blotchy, pot-bellied, muffin-topped, wobbly, wrinkly, bumpy, saggy, hairy, ill, decaying, or dying. This is a very broad brush picture of the beauty ideal, and there are many other features, or variations, as the beauty ideal is negotiated and manifested in context. I will develop these arguments over the course of the book.

An Ethical Ideal?

The claim that beauty is an ethical ideal is a straightforward claim that the beauty ideal is emerging as, and for some already is, effec-tively a moral ideal, a value framework. Moral frameworks pro-vide the background and contexts that determine the things, peo-ple, and qualities we value, respect, endorse, and promote; and they are action-guiding in that in striving to attain an ideal we act in ways designed to enable us to realize it. They provide shared stan-dards against which we judge our own (and others) success and failure, goodness and badness, and according to which we set our lives' priorities and goals. As such, they provide end points to strive for (the "good enough" or "perfect" me) and according to which we orientate the habits and practices of our daily lived existence. In the light of such ideals, we find, imbue and construct meaning, iden-tity, and our very selves.

BEAUTY SUCCESS IS MORAL SUCCESS

Many people judge themselves according to their success and failure in beauty terms. This is true of long-term goals. We view ourselves as successful when we have attained some aspect of our ideal; when we've reached our goal weight, filled our wrinkles, or firmed our thighs. It is also true of daily accomplishments. We feel good about ourselves if we have made it to the gym, stuck to the diet, or undergone (suffered through) some procedure. We are "good" when we do all kind of beauty-related actions: when we say "no thanks" to cake, chocolate, cheese, or carbs; force ourselves to go out for a run; or when we routinely remove make up, body brush, and perform the tasks of routine maintenance. The Bridget Jones daily count-up of calories, alcohol, and cigarettes is a caricature of a very familiar type of calculation that many of us make on a daily basis: "What have I eaten today?" is a value-laden question. We are "good" when we've resisted "bad" food (or food that is a "sin") and eaten "healthily" (by which we mean the right amount to become or to stay thin).[21] The same is true for exercise and the many other daily acts and tasks that contribute to attaining the beauty ideal. We must "make the most of ourselves" and will be chastised if we fail to "make an effort." Naomi Wolf, in her ground-breaking book *The Beauty Myth,* pointed towards the emergence of an ethical ideal when she speaks of a "moral imperative" to remove "lines so faint as to be non-existent to the human gaze."[22]

In order to claim that beauty is, for some, becoming an ethical ideal the good in question must be a moral good. For this to be the case, the beauty ideal must be the dominant ideal and beauty the overarching value framework such that not engaging in beauty activity is not merely a prudential failure, aesthetic failure, or failure to conform to some social norm (although it may be these too), but a moral failure. That beauty is the primary moral framework for some, and an increasingly dominant moral imperative for others, I argue is already the case. I do not endorse beauty as an ethical ideal, indeed much of my argument in *Perfect Me* focuses on the harms of such an ideal, rather I argue that we should recognize what is happening and part of this is an ethical turn. For very many of us, when we say we are "good" for engaging in beauty work we do mean that we are "morally good"; that these actions are good in themselves. The implication is that we have not merely done something good instrumentally (i.e., for a prudential reason such as for better health), but something good in general, something we value for, and believe is good, in itself, a moral good.

Success and failure when it comes to the body beautiful is not just aesthetic, but moral. It matters to our sense of self and to how good we believe ourselves—taken as a whole—to be. We see engagement in beauty practices and creating habits that we believe will bring us nearer to the beauty ideal as good in and of themselves, not just prudentially or to comply with a social norm, but intrinsically. Indeed often at a level of day-to-day practices success can *only* be moral—sticking to our calorie count for the day or making it to our exercise class has very little impact upon how we look, on the aesthetic. As Debra Gimlin notes, participating in exercise provides little actual physical change, so the change must be elsewhere.[23] For Gimlin too, the change is about renegotiating meanings of the self. For me, the renegotiation is overtly moral. While some beauty work does contribute to prudential goods (such as maintaining health by exercise), other beauty work improves appearance but does not contribute to other goods (from routine grooming to cosmetic surgery). Thus when we feel good for this engagement it can only be because we value attaining beauty as a good in itself: it is at this point where the beauty ideal tips into an ethical ideal and becomes an overarching moral framework. As we value beauty more and it becomes, for some, *the* most important value, we judge ourselves, our whole selves, as good or bad, failing or succeeding, as a person, according to the extent we attain the beauty ideal, or engage in habits and practices that make conformity with the beauty ideal more likely. Over the long term, inevitably and ultimately, we will fail aesthetically, we will wrinkle and sag, but morally we can succeed at the level of habits and practices, as we keep working on our bodies.[24] Reaching a desired goal is less important than striving for the goal, and, on a day-to-day basis, we can succeed. Indeed part of the reason that the beauty ideal can function as an ethical ideal is that daily achievements are attainable and embedded in lived experience and they deliver social rewards. These are moral rather than merely personal goals and activities. I could feel good about almost any personal achievement—finishing a paper as a good philosopher, tidying my kitchen as a good mother, and so on—and there may be moral aspects to these ideals. For instance, there is clearly a moral aspect to tidying the kitchen if this is part of striving for perfect motherhood by being perfectly caring and nurturing.

As the beauty ideal becomes more dominant, its ethical aspect increases, and beauty activity becomes required activity; less a personal preference and more an ethical duty. I will return to the mutually reinforcing nature of the ethical and dominant features of the ideal. For now, it is important to note two key things about the beauty ideal as an ethical ideal—rather than as a social norm, prudential ideal, or personal aspiration or commitment: First, that it is a *collective* ideal: a moral framework must be broadly shared. An ethical ideal cannot be a mere personal framework or be endorsed only by a small group (unless that group is wholly self-contained, which I will go on to argue is increasingly unlikely). In order to shape the expectations of what individuals can be and do ethical frameworks act as powerful constrainers and enablers and so must be broadly shared and endorsed. Second, as beauty functions as an ethical ideal it is more dominant and powerful than a mere prudential or social norm. To be sure, there may be sanctions and critique for rejecting social and prudential norms, but these do not carry the weight of the sanctions attached to transgressing ethical norms. To transgress a prudential or social norm is perhaps unwise, displaying bad judgment or poor taste, but it is not a definitive critique of the person, carrying not just disapproval, but disgust, disappointment, and distain. However, while ethical failure is regarded as more serious—by others and by the self—than mere prudential or social failure, the line between such failure is blurred. For some, failing to measure up in the beauty stakes may simply be prudential or social failure—failure to conform to social norms. Such failure may be costly, but it is not of the same order as moral failure. Indeed such failure may be deliberate rejection of social norms in a way that cannot be paralleled in the moral sphere. For others, failure in beauty is ethical, it is a failure not in just one domain, but a failure that colors all domains. To fail in this aspect is to *be a failure*, irrespective of success in other aspects. That beauty for some is a mere social norm which can be shrugged off obscures that it is functioning as an ethical ideal for others. Recognizing that beauty is tipping from a mere prudential and social norm into an ethical ideal, at least for some, is crucial to understanding the increasing dominance of the beauty ideal and why it is increasingly the central value framework for very many individuals.

That beauty is functioning as an ethical ideal—providing values and standards against which we judge ourselves and others morally good and bad—is particularly clear when we consider what it means to "fail." Beauty failure results in explicit moral judgments of culpability and responsibility, and, as such, beauty failures, for some, are effectively equivalent to moral vices. Beauty failure is not a local or partial failure, but a failure of the self, which invokes shame of the self.

The moral nature of beauty success and failure is hinted at in the language of beauty as employed by both women and the beauty business: be "your best self," "the best you can be," "it's still you, but the best version of you," "the real you." Language such as this directly invokes moral requirements and demands. You *should* strive for that best you; you *ought* to invest in yourself, because "you're worth it," "you deserve it," and "you owe it to yourself." The converse is also true. To fail to engage is to admit or accept that "you're not worth it." Piling on the pounds is not just aesthetic failure but a moral failure: "You let yourself go." If we unpack the implications of this the moral assumptions are clear: You *should* not have let yourself go, but more than this, it was morally bad, a failure in or of the self, and you *should* work to address your failure. Appearance becomes a proxy for, and intimation of, character and value—thinness and grooming shows competence and efficiency; it also shows respect (for the self and for others). Such judgments are routinely and constantly made, read directly from appearance, and are moral. Effectively they are character assessments of moral virtues and vices.

These views are commonly held—implicitly and explicitly—more strongly in some contexts than others. For instance, in her work on cosmetic surgery, which includes interviews with surgeons and those who have undergone procedures, Virginia Blum suggests that this position is manifested in at least some surgeon's views to the extent that "If you let yourself 'go' as it were, then you are not a fit, or normal, psychological subject. You lack self-esteem, you let yourself go to pieces, your paint chips, the signs of wear and tear remain unattended to. You might be cited. You might be fined. You might be condemned."[25] Such condemnation is moral, as it is about the person, the self, and evokes moral responses and implies moral failure. We have failed to respect ourselves and others, failed in our duty to make the most of ourselves, or at least to be "good enough." We are a *failure*.

The using of such moral language on its own is not enough to claim that the beauty ideal is a fully-fledged ethical ideal; however, it does suggest that there is something ethical and moral going on. I suggest that key here is not just the moral language—important as that is as indicator of the extent to which beauty matters—but what is implied by failure, and the extent and nature of condemnation and self-condemnation that attaches to failure. That this is moral is further shown by the shame and disgust that attach to body failures.

ASHAMED OF YOURSELF

Emotions and sanctions we standardly associate with moral failure are prevalent in the beauty context. "Letting yourself go" is morally bad, shameful and disgusting. Shame is doing the same work in accounts of beauty failure as in traditional accounts of moral failure—for example, shame from not being kind, truthful, or caring enough—this is again indicative of the ethical nature of the beauty ideal: you "*should not* have let yourself go" or "you *should* be *ashamed* to turn up looking like that" are similar to you "*should not* have lied" or "you *should* be *ashamed* to have cheated in that test." These are moral emotions, as the shame is global not local; it is not minor, but shame of the self. These statements are morally similar not merely linguistically similar. "You *should* have got pasta, it's better than the pizza" or "you *should* take that job, it's a good job" are not moral; they do not condemn or sanction. These are prudential or enhancing shoulds, they are not moral shoulds; shame and disgust do not attach to such shoulds. Not all beauty imperatives are moral ("you should get your hair cut like that. It will suit you" is not moral). The shoulds I am concerned with are moral shoulds: shoulds that condemn, sanction, and blame.

As highlighted in the previous section, there are no clear lines between ethical, prudential, and social ideals and norms in the beauty context. This said, while it might be difficult to distinguish between a demanding prudential or social norm and a moral norm at the point at which the prudential ideal tips into the ethical ideal, the difference between the two is clear at either end of the spectrum. To clarify this, we can consider the different contexts in which moral language is used and the difference between "an ethical edge" and a fully fledged ethical ideal. For example, you "ought" to practice your musical instrument or you "ought" to clean your bedroom are familiar uses of "ought" that carry an ethical edge.[26] Yet while these oughts might have some moral element, and perhaps imply some underlying moral vice, such as laziness or lack of respect, they do not imply transgression of an ethical ideal. While a failure to tidy the room might show laziness or even dirtiness, and this might be something to be morally ashamed of, it is a different order from the moral judgments and responses in beauty. For while the parent might think the child *should* tidy their bedroom, failure to do so is not global failure of personality or character, but only local failure. Failure is partial, in one domain, and not likely to be regarded as significant; annoying but not significant. Such failure does not define the child, it is not a judgment of how valuable she is as a person or indicative of how she should be judged in other contexts. There are instances where one could perhaps imagine cleanliness as an ethical ideal, a value-framework. For instance, in a puritan household where "cleanliness is next to godliness" untidiness might be a significant moral failing; marking the child as "sinful" or "bad" in a global sense that is defining of how the child is judged, but in most contexts such failure is not a moral failure. By contrast the beauty ideal is, for those who fall under it, the dominant value framework and as such judgments of "good" and "bad" map directly to "success" and "failure" as a person. They are defining of who one is across domains. That the beauty ideal is tipping from a partial, prudential, or social ideal is evident in the way that beauty failure is seen as a global failure of the self. As the ideal becomes more dominant, it is likely that the moral condemnation of "letting yourself go," and the resulting shame, will only increase.

Narratives of shame already appear across beauty practices; fat shaming being the most obvious example, but also when it comes to botched surgery, visible body hair, and aging.[27] And surgeons and doctors report that shame is a feature in the increasing requests for labiaplasty.[28] Shame attaches to all aspects of appearance, and being appropriately clothed was particularly important historically, since it demarcated status; including class, trade, religious and political affiliation, and so on. There are many contexts in which it is shameful to be inappropriately dressed—for instance, at a wedding or job interview—and some communities, particularly but not exclusively religious communities, police dress rigorously. However, arguably, fashion and clothing norms are becoming more diverse rather than less.[29] In an era of technological intervention, shame attaches more to the body than its clothing; shame of wrinkles, shame of bumpy noses, and shame of sagging jowls, shame, in general, of the imperfect and nonconforming body.

Fat shaming is a prominent form of beauty shame, and practices of fat shaming are common, and fatness is routinely treated as if it were a moral failure.[30] Despite the evidence that diets generally fail, obesity is regarded as the responsibility of the individual: weight loss is presented as possible with a little commitment, will-power, and dedication. This is not only true in pop culture, but in medical discourse.[31] However, while obesity offers a particularly good example of collective moral condemnation, it could be argued that this is (somewhat) complicated by the connections to health. Losing weight might be for health reasons rather than beauty reasons. However, while there may be some truth in this (and obesity does result in adverse health outcomes), the neat connection between weight and health has many critics.[32] Further, the moral condemnation leveled at obese individuals goes beyond what can be justified for health reasons. While smoking and drinking are sometimes treated as moral failings (implying a lack of will power or lack of self-respect), rather than just prudential failures, they are not routinely regarded as defining of the self and across contexts. They are not identities, in a way that fatness can be. For example, Clara Rice notes that for the women in her study "fat became an overriding identity during childhood" and often a "defining attribute they carry throughout their lives."[33] Fatness cannot be hidden. Thus, while health failures, like smoking, may carry moral sanction, sanctions for failing to live up to the demands of thinness are particularly vicious and a clear example of the tipping point between moral and prudential ideals.[34]

Negative moral properties, character traits, are attached to those who are fat, such as lazy, ill-disciplined, impulsive, stupid, slow, gross, and greedy.[35] Conversely positive moral properties are attached to those who are thin; such as disciplined, energetic, clever, in control, active, and hard working. This goes beyond health and into the moral arena and attaches moral values and character to body size; as Susan Orbach states, the aim is to "demonise fat while extolling thin as a new kind of morality."[36] This is a common view, one that crosses from popular talk of fat shaming into medical talk. For instance, the 2014 UK Chief Medical Officer's annual report on women's health speaks about obesity as a "national priority."[37] This was discussed in the media as "a war on fat." It is difficult to separate "the fat" from "the fat person." Such rhetoric is just as likely to lead to shame as to empower and inspire: it puts you at war with your own fat. Even if there are good reasons to worry about fat on health grounds, the disgust leveled at fat people, is not proportionate. It smacks of moral condemnation not prudential worry. The distinctively moral emotions of shame and disgust in beauty narratives further attest to the fact that the beauty ideal is functioning as an ethical ideal. When you fail at beauty, the criticism is moral: you should be ashamed of yourself.

SHARED EXPECTATIONS AND COMMUNAL NORMS

To claim that the beauty ideal functions as a moral ideal is to claim, for those who fall under it, that it is an ethical ideal, that it is defining of their self-identity and it colors how they see themselves across domains and irrespective of their success in other domains. It is a value framework according to which they judge themselves and others; it determines their aspirations and goals, and daily habits and activities are ordered around attaining the ideal. For some people it functions as the dominant moral ideal (their most important value framework); for many it functions as part of their value framework (not the most important ideal but still impinging on, and contributing to, their understandings of identity, success, and failure, and shaping some of their habits and practices); and some may even reject it, although, as I will argue in the next chapter, as the beauty ideal becomes more dominant rejection is more difficult. An important feature of recognizing that the beauty ideal is an ethical ideal is its shared nature. We not only judge ourselves "good" and "bad" according to the beauty ideal; we also judge others and do so collectively.

Importantly, as individuals we do not choose our beauty ideals. Arguably we choose the extent to which we conform to them, but the extent to which we can do this is limited by the dominance of the ideal. Further, I am increasingly skeptical that there are many women for whom the claim that the beauty ideal is a moral ideal does not strike a chord. Moreover, I suspect that those women who do succeed in rejecting and resisting the beauty ideal either do so at significant cost and some effort, or they are protected from the costs of nonconformity by membership in a community that endorses some other competing beauty ideal or other ideals that oppose the dominant beauty ideal. These communities are increasingly rare, and often privileged.

There may be enclaves of certain professions and ways of life where the demands of beauty do not apply—and where women do not suffer external costs for not conforming to the beauty ideal and where nonconformity may even be rewarded. For instance, academics often tell me (sometimes a little too smugly) that they never wear make-up, and cannot imagine why anyone would consider cosmetic surgery or straighten their hair or engage in other beautifying practices.[38] Underlying such statements is the implication that to engage in beauty practices is somehow beneath them, for lesser beings. However, often, such rejection of the beauty ideal is not the whole story. For example, they may reject make-up but diet obsessively, ostensibly for health reasons, but nonetheless they maintain a thin figure (and benefit from all the assumptions that go with thinness). Such behavior allows conforming to a key aspect of the beauty ideal while simultaneously dismissing it. Alternatively they may conform in settings "outside" academia (for instance, at special events) or over time, and under pressure from others. Even when such protestations are genuine, and adhered to consistently, rejection might not be the "pure" rejection it seems. For instance, the claim that beauty matters less in academia, because all are equal in the "life of the mind," is belied by the gender disparities in academia and the difficulty that women find succeeding in an overwhelmingly male environment (at least in some disciplines).[39] In addition, it ignores other hierarchies of power that a rejection of beauty invokes, particularly but not only, those of race and class. As Ruth Holliday and Jacqueline Sanchez Taylor note, the hierarchy of beauty has promoted certain types of beauty as true and natural (good) and other forms of beauty as false and artificial (bad).[40] Such categorizations are a means by which some groups distance themselves from others. In particular, middle-class white women assert their superiority over working class women and women of color.[41] Such a rejection of beauty is only possible in relatively privileged groups and is a form of demarcating "them" from "us"; an issue I will return to.

Even if such rejections are exactly what they are claimed to be, in these scenarios resistance to the beauty ideal is conscious. It is a public and political rejection of beauty as defining of the self; it is a form of protest and perhaps an overt attempt to promote alternative ideals. Accordingly, such rejection is a far cry from being immune to the demands of beauty. Indeed in such scenarios the beauty ideal *is* recognized as a powerful value framework, and it is rejected as being morally bad. Further, it is likely that even those in such communities feel themselves under pressure to conform to broader beauty norms at the same time as they are under pressure to conform to antibeauty norms. For example, pressures to make an effort for a wedding, or not to be the "embarrassing mum" at the school gates, fall on academics in their lives outside the university. As the beauty ideal becomes more dominant, such enclaves will be increasingly visible and unless insulated from the values of wider society, then it is likely—particularly as roles conflict—that many of those currently less vulnerable to the demands of beauty will become more vulnerable. In the face of such pressure, some may maintain their antibeauty stance, while others may find this increasingly difficult to do. It is likely that the more powerful the alternative ideal is the easier the position will be to maintain, making, say, religious communities that reject all aspects of the beauty ideal more likely to maintain this stance into the future, than communities where this rejection is important in only some aspects of their lives. Importantly, rejecting the beauty ideal is not individual but communal and is supported by the endorsement of alternative value frameworks that promote some antibeauty element in their ideals. To reject the ideal, we need to be supported and reassured by others like us. Such enclaves offer some resistance to the beauty ideal, but their rejection, and the moral judgment that goes with it, implicitly recognizes that the beauty ideal is a moral ideal and one they oppose by asserting conflicting values. Accordingly, such narratives of rejection do little to challenge the claim that the beauty ideal is an ethical ideal.

BEAUTY DELIVERS THE GOODS

The final argument I wish to make with regard to the beauty ideal functioning as an ethical ideal, is that it, like other moral ideals, purports to deliver the goods of the good life. For a moral ideal or value framework to be enforced, embedded, and lived by, it must deliver (or we must believe it will deliver). To be dominant we must believe that being righteous, honest, or kind (or any other construction of the morally virtuous life) will lead to success, that we will be well regarded by others and that we will benefit, flourish, from conforming to the ideal. For the beauty ideal to be an effective ideal—an ideal to live by—it must promise to deliver the goods of the good life: material goods, relational goods, lifestyle goods, and the elusive good of happiness. The beauty ideal does this, or at least it promises this. Essentially the message is that if you conform to the beauty ideal, become better (thinner, firmer, smoother, younger) you will be rewarded. The notion that the beauty ideal will deliver the goods of the good life is ubiquitous and ingrained. As Blum states, "that we're desperate to be seen as fit and energetic and young and attractive makes sense when we are told on so many tacit and overt levels that we will find neither work nor sexual partners without these attributes; moreover, we are fated to lose both if we don't retain at least the superficial vestiges of the original assets."[42] Alternatively as Susan Bordo states, "people *know* the routes to success in this culture—they are advertised widely enough—they are not "dopes" to pursue them."[43] Or in the words of a sixteen-year-old girl:

> I think people think oh I have to look like that because they think that they will have a perfect life as well. If I'm beautiful, if I'm attractive, if I'm skinny then everything else in my life has to come up as well, like my school grades will come up, I'll get a boyfriend, you know I'll have a great social life.[44]

That the beauty ideal is a worthwhile way to live from day to day, that there are engagement goods (of pleasure and achievement) is an argument I will return to. At this juncture, I simply wish to note that the beauty ideal does promise the goods of the good life and promotes behaviors that purport to deliver such goods. In so doing, it is both austere and indulgent. It requires hard work, effort, and striving, but it is also pleasurable, pampering, self-caring, and self-respecting. That the beauty ideal is pleasurable *and* demanding, and often concurrently, is a key feature of the ideal (an argument I will make in detail in chapters 7 and 8). Many beauty practices are *in themselves* pleasurable, and not just "worth it" for the goal. Some, of course, are not; body hair removal or cosmetic surgery are not pleasurable, but even practices not obviously pleasurable in themselves, can be pleasurable in the excitement and sense of purpose and control that they bring. For now I wish to focus on the external goods that the beauty ideal promises, both material and relational goods.

The first set of goods that the beauty ideal offers are material goods. And there is evidence that the beautiful do reap material benefits. That beauty pays off in terms of attaining work is attested to in many studies, and while empirical evidence for such claims, and perhaps for all claims in beauty, is contested there is evidence that beauty improves employability and salaries. For example, one study found attractive women had a call-back rate of 54 percent and attractive men of 47 percent (versus 7 percent for women and 26 percent for men who fell into the unattractive category).[45] In general, those who are attractive earn more, and those who are unattractive less. Hamermesh calculates that there is a "3 or 4 percent premium for good looking workers," and total gap of 12 to 13 percent between those who are unattractive and attractive.[46] Similarly, a recent large UK study suggested that tall men and slim women are significantly better paid than those who are not.[47] The headlines in the broadsheets were that annual income for men increased by £1600 a year for every 2.5 inches, and women genetically predicted to be two stone (twenty-eight pounds) heavier were "losing out" by £3000 a year, and if one stone heavier by £1500.[48] Even if we regard the causal genetic claims with some suspicion (especially when it comes to weight, which is strongly linked to socioeconomic factors and to possible discrimination and bias, something that the researchers themselves note), being tall as a man and being thin as a woman are likely to lead to some material benefit.

To recognize that rewards attach to beauty does not require the endorsement of an evolutionary view of beauty. The gains that accrue to thin women and tall men can be explained just as easily by reference to social and cultural preferences and, as beauty becomes an ethical ideal, to the endorsement of the pursuit of beauty as virtuous. Further, even if evolutionary accounts are correct, there are many instances when we seek to reject such hard-wired biases as immoral. The most common example is our preference for sameness, and the implications for race. We should be skeptical, for two reasons, of any account that presents what are (at least partially) constructed norms as natural, especially when this is taken to mean unchallengeable. First, constructions of beauty, particularly as they are manifested in beauty norms that define and demarcate masculine and feminine, are anything but natural, they are hyperconstructed, overwhelmingly instances of social construction. Second, even if they were natural, this would have no bearing on whether or not we should seek to emphasize or reduce the pressure of such norms.[49] However, for the purposes of recognizing beauty as an ethical ideal, it does not matter whether an evolutionary view is adopted or not. The fact that beauty is rewarded by material goods does not require an acceptance that such norms will or should continue to dominate. Even in the current context of a dominant beauty ideal, there is counter-evidence. For instance, beauty matters less when it comes to success over time, and there are professions where nonconformity to standard beauty ideals is required: for example, jockeys must be short and perhaps academic women should not obviously conform to the beauty ideal (with the exception of thinness) if they wish to be regarded as clever.[50] In sum, despite counter examples, those who conform to the beauty ideal, are likely to reap material rewards even, if the extent of these goods is often overestimated. As Nancy Etcoff states, "beauty conveys modest but real social and economic advantages and, equally important, ugliness leads to major social disadvantages and discrimination."[51] Again, I emphasize, I am not endorsing that this should be the case, nor do I subscribe to evolutionary views, though there is no barrier to endorsing that beauty is an ethical ideal for those who do. Rather the claim is that beauty currently does deliver some goods, though far fewer than it purports. Moreover, if trends continue, and we do not counter them, beauty is likely be increasingly valued and promoted as a route to economic success.

The second set of goods that the beauty ideal promises are relational goods, and it is these that are perhaps most commonly imagined to accrue to the beautiful. The promise is that as you approximate the ideal you will become more attractive and so lovable and loved. This is the trope of nearly all advertising, whether or not what is being sold is beauty related. The message is the same old message, be better and he'll love you more (and usually it is he, as in beauty discourse heteronormativity is pervasive).[52] Likewise, if you fail to take heed of these messages you are blamed for what befalls you: "no wonder he left, she let herself go!." The empirical evidence is again contested—both for methodological reasons, and with regard to the strength of the positive effects—nonetheless many psychological studies suggest that there is a correlation between being regarded as attractive and being treated more positively.[53] The "halo effect" is well documented and leads attractive individuals being assumed to have positive personality traits, such as friendliness, competence, and intelligence.[54] More than this, a recent study suggests that the more attractive not only benefit from being regarded more positively, but also that they are more accurately assessed.[55] This is in part because more attractive people are likely to provide better information about themselves (being confident in social situations and used to being well regarded), but also because more attention is paid to more attractive people. Even if other features are more important over the long term—in both employment and relationships—there is likely to be benefit from being well perceived initially. In addition, in a virtual world in which more relationships—both personal and professional—are transient, conducted over long distances, and often short-lived (characterized by short and multiple interactions rather than long relationships that continue over years), the value of first impressions is likely to become relatively more important.[56]

In some very real ways then, beauty does pay or is believed to pay, and not surprisingly "many are calculating that a freshly purchased face-lift or suctioning of fat through liposuction is the best route to improved lives, careers and relationships."[57] Being beautiful, or at least attractive enough to fall in the normal range, will deliver at least some of the goods of the good life. Whether or not it will deliver happiness is open to question, but the message that the beautiful will be happy (or at least more so than if they were not beautiful) is widely propagated and believed.[58] Again in making this claim I am not arguing that this has to be the case, or that it should be the case, nor am I disregarding the contrary evidence. Whether or not the ideal delivers is not what matters. What matters is that we believe it will. That we must continually strive for beauty is part of the logic of beauty as an ethical ideal—as it is for other successful ethical ideals. That perfection remains always beyond, something we have to strive for and can never attain, does not diminish the power of the ideal; indeed it may even strengthen it. Iris Murdoch argues, when considering the moral force of goodness, that perfection is always beyond, and out of reach and that this is crucial to the functioning of ethical ideals.[59] The beauty ideal is self-defeating over time—ultimately we all sag, wrinkle, and die—but nonetheless the ideal, like other ideals, provides meaning and identity. It gives us life goals to strive for and daily practices by which to structure our lives.

Three Assumptions of Makeover Culture

In the final section of this chapter, I will highlight the key assumptions that have emerged that are necessary for the beauty ideal to function as an ethical ideal: first. that the body is malleable; second, that "body work" is required; and third, that power is internalized, we self-monitor and self-discipline.

THE MALLEABLE BODY

The first underlying assumption of the contemporary ideal is the notion of the body as malleable. It is fluid, in flux, in Susan Bordo's words "plastic,"[60] in Alex Edmonds words the body is "malleable and perfectible material."[61] This view of the body is highlighted by many working in cultural critique, including, but not only, Meredith Jones, Rosalind Gill, Debra Gimiln, Cressida Heyes, and Diana

Meyers.[62] This is both obvious and necessary from the description of the beauty ideal as a moral ideal that is to be strived for and worked towards and that shapes habits and practices. It *must* be the case if you have a duty to improve the body that you must first believe that the body *can* be changed. [63]

This understanding of the body, and I will go on in later chapters to argue of the self, is a significant change in our understandings. The self is now embedded in, suffused through, and written on our bodies. Effectively the construction of the body as malleable and representative of, or equated with, our selves is so ubiquitous that it is taken for granted by those who fall under the ideal, and yet this has not yet been recognized as significant, nor has it been sufficiently interrogated.[64] As a result, like all effective ideals (and ideologies), that the body is malleable is assumed. To view the body in this way is regarded as obvious and natural. The more effective an ideology is the more invisible it becomes, the more its assumptions are taken for granted and regarded as natural (a process we will return to in chapter 5 when normalization is discussed). This function of ideals and ideologies, to normalize and naturalize, is true for the beauty ideal as it is for other successful ideals. Recognizing this is helpful for understanding the drivers for engaging in beauty practices at all, and the drive to engage maximally. In other words part of the reason we "choose" to spend ever more time "working on ourselves" and ever more money buying products that we hope will deliver the body beautiful is because the construction of the body as malleable, to be shaped, is embedded and assumed. That the body is malleable is a relatively new assumption.

BODY WORK

The second assumption—again hidden by the taken-for-granted nature of the beauty ideal—is the constant demandingness of the work involved in the project of creating the body beautiful. In chapter 4, I will consider the content of these demands. For now, what is important is that for the ideal to be a dominant moral ideal we have to believe that work on the body is work that matters, work we believe to be worth it. In short, we must buy it. We must believe that striving for beauty (whether interpreted as flat stomachs, thin thighs, pert breasts, or high and round buttocks) is something that we really want and are willing to work for. Hard work and commitment are required of us in the form of body work. "No pain, no gain" applies across practices: whether pumping iron, feeling the burn, plucking stray hairs or undergoing cosmetic surgery. That the body can—and *should*—change and that such body work will be rewarded is ubiquitous in what scholars often refer to as "*makeover culture.*"[65]

Cultural studies scholars emphasize this understanding of body, of which the "before" and "after" shots familiar from television, magazines and ads are emblematic. For example, Meredith Jones emphasizes that "in makeover culture the process of *becoming something better* is more important than achieving a static point of completion."[66] And more than this, "makeover culture is about industriousness and the display of labour."[67] The extent of what is required of us, just how much sweat, tears, and hard work are needed to attain a good enough, let alone perfect body (self), will become clear as the book progresses. Suffice to say at this juncture that the demands of beauty are significant for most of us and for some of us they are all-consuming. And some pay the ultimate price.[68] However, we do not often view the labor involved as demanding—as hard, time-consuming, constant, intensive, and often painful—but embrace it as positive, enjoyable, and always, "for ourselves." We are told "just do it," we owe it to ourselves, and we embrace the labor and the pain. The hard work serves to reinforce our belief that we are achieving our ends, that the transformation is working. The more we invest in the transformation, the more we identify with it, the harder we are likely to (willingly) work. The centrally funded health campaign, by "Sport England," aims to promote exercise amongst the whole of the population.[69] While some of its ads show women with nonideal body types engaging in exercise, a prominent ad is of women doing aerobics with the tag line "sweating like a pig; feeling like a fox." The message is clear. Pushing yourself is worth it because, so the assumption goes, it will pay dividends: You will become a "fox"! The more invested you are, the more you work; and the more you work, the more invested you are. And, as we shall discuss further in chapter 5, the more of us that engage in intensive body work the more we may all have to do so.

The beauty ideal is an ethical ideal, in part because it is where put our effort; and where we put our effort reveals what matters to us. We aim to *better* ourselves by improving our bodies. In our New Year's resolutions, we make promises to ourselves of very similar types—that we will eat better, drink less, lose weight, go to the gym three times a week, save for the operation, and so on—such resolutions focus on body work as a way to transform our selves and lifestyles. This is a new phenomenon; in previous generations it was not body work that we engaged in to improve ourselves but character work. An adolescent diary in 1892 reads: "Resolved, not to talk about myself or feelings. To think before speaking. To work seriously. To be self restrained in conversation and actions. Not to let my thoughts wander. To be dignified. Interest myself more in others."[70] Such aspirations could not be further from improvement under the beauty ideal. Our expectation is that hard work on the body will pay off—that it will result in a better us, by which we mean a better body; a better self. Of course, there comes a point where this is not the case. As Diana Meyers puts it:

> Bodies do not evolve forever. The fatal potentiality—vulnerability to accident and disease—dwells within every body. If one is not killed suddenly when one is young, one's body will deteriorate. It will require more attention all the time, and it will become stiff, brittle, and weak regardless of how much attention one lavishes on it. Then death comes.[71]

Nonetheless, a belief in body work continues over much of the lifespan. The body as the focus of effort when it comes to changing and improving the self, rather than the character or the mind, is a recent phenomenon, and without this underpinning assumption the beauty ideal could not be an ethical ideal. Later I will return to understandings of the self as such, but at this point I simply want to emphasize how deeply body work is valued.

DISCIPLINE AND POWER

The third assumption of the beauty ideal is that the ideal is not imposed or enforced externally; or at least that it need not be and it is often not. This is not to say, that there are no institutional requirements for beauty (for example, dress codes, height codes or even, though more controversially in contemporary contexts, weight codes)—there are.[72] But, for the most part, engagement in beauty practices and procedures is not enforced by the state or other powerful institutions. We are forced by law to do all kinds of things, but very few of these are beauty-related. Rather we tend, especially if we are uncorrupted by feminism, to articulate our engagement in beauty practices as if they were freely chosen, as if they were practices we wish to engage in. This does not mean that we do not sometimes feel they are burdensome (we often do) or that they are not sometimes done grudgingly (sometimes they are). But even when we say that we *have* to do something (such as diet for a wedding, shave before going to the swimming pool, or put on make-up before a big night out), we still tend to think of these practices as prima facie chosen, as things we could equally not do if we chose. This rhetoric of choice is dominant, and often unquestioningly assumed to be accurate, despite our feelings about *having* to do these things that belies the choice narrative.

How we understand the discourse of choice that surrounds beauty practices and the feelings of pressure to conform to the increasing demands of beauty is a central concern of this book. At this juncture, I simply want to highlight that however we explain the pressure that women undoubtedly feel (and women feel this pressure even if they do not find it burdensome, but embrace and revel in their beautifying), it cannot be explained by a top-down model. The locus of power when it comes to beauty is not the state or any of the usual agents of power that dominant, usually liberal, political structures recognize. As Clare Chambers convincingly argues, liberal theory struggles to recognize the injustices involved in compliance to social norms.[73] There is no agent of power, and although there are all kinds of beneficiaries of beauty practices, these do not track back neatly to identifiable individuals or groups. For instance, arguments that claim that beauty regimes are socially and structurally imposed upon women by men, and therefore men are the loci of power, are difficult to sustain in the contemporary context—an argument I will return to.

In an attempt to explain the power dynamics, many scholars from different philosophical traditions have turned to Foucault.[74] His notion of power is diversified, networked, and creative.[75] Unlike liberal theory, which valorizes and fetishizes free choice and struggles to recognize social, indirect, and structural power, Foucauldian approaches recognize the power of social construction to shape and constrain what we do. As Chambers states, "we do not have to be acting under the commands of a dictator to be acting in response to power."[76] We do not have to adopt a thoroughgoing Foucauldian approach, indeed Chambers does not, to recognize how useful this understanding of power is to help understand social pressures; and social pressures is a term I use throughout.[77] One single identifiable *source* of power, whether that be a dictator, a state, or a powerful group, is not necessary to recognize power in action. Power then is nebulous—everywhere and nowhere—but it is very real, felt, and experienced. Power understood in this way is internalized, rather than overt and external. In other words, at least in part, the pressure we feel to conform to the demands of beauty is pressure that we place on ourselves and is, in some sense, chosen by us. That power is internalized—rather than imposed by a clearly identified other—is the third underlying and prior assumption of the beauty ideal.

The classic example of this (again used by many scholars) comes from Foucault's description of Jeremy Bentham's self-policing of prisoners in the Panopticon. The Panopticon is a jail in which the cells are arranged in a circular form around a central guard pillar. Each wedge-shaped cell is visible from the guard tower in the center. The prisoner is fully visible, but does not know exactly when he is being watched. As a result, the prisoner begins to self-police, to behave *as if* he were being watched at all times. Importantly he exhibits behavior and engages in practices consistent with "watched" behavior to the extent that these become his normal behavior. The prisoner is disciplined not by the guards, but by self-surveillance. Likewise, by self-surveillance the woman polices her own compliance with beauty norms (and more critically than another would).

The notion of self-policing is explicitly assumed in much beauty advertising, and you are encouraged to imagine you are on display and, because of this, to self-police, self-monitor, and self-survey.[78] Chambers cites the Clarks ads for shoes that present "life as one long catwalk"—an ad that is credited with making Clarks fashionable—as embodying this. Numerous other examples immediately come to mind. According to this reading, "power is not a repressive force coming from outside the individual, constraining her actions, but a creative force manifested in the individual's everyday life."[79] Power and self-discipline understood in this way chime with the above discussion about women feeling that they have failed or succeeded (or that others have) according to the extent to which they have conformed to the ideal of beauty. Again, how we understand this pressure, and the extent to which conformity is chosen, will dominate the second half of the book. For now it is important to recognize that power under the beauty ideal is internalized. An ethical ideal that is not *owned* cannot function as an ethical ideal. For instance, if we turn to traditional ethical ideals, such as a commitment to truthfulness, beneficence, or goodness, they *have* to be internalized. You are not truthful if you only tell the truth when you are forced to by an external power, and similarly for goodness. This does not mean, in practice, that you will always succeed in living up to the ideal. People "cheat" at truthfulness (little white lies) while still endorsing the ideal of truthfulness. Similarly we can "cheat" at beauty—and we use this word often in the beauty context—when we eat that oh-so-tempting piece of cake or skip the gym—while still endorsing the ideal. As discussed in the last section, the fact that the ideal is unattainable is not in itself damaging to the ideal. All ideals are unattainable. We can never be perfectly good any more than we can be perfectly beautiful. But we can still strive and desire to be, and be ashamed of ourselves when we fail. Thus the third underpinning assumption is that power is internalized.

Conclusion

In this chapter, I have set out the key features of the beauty ideal: thinness, firmness, smoothness, and youth. I have argued that the dominant beauty ideal is an ethical ideal, because it provides a value framework against which individuals judge themselves, and others, good and bad; it sets long-term goals to aspire to and prescribes habits and practices around which daily life is structured and ordered; it constructs meaning and identity; failure invokes shame and disgust; and, by no means least, it promises the goods of the good life. Further I have claimed that a number of assumptions underpin this ideal: first, the body is malleable; second, body work is required and valued duty; and third, power is internalized. These assumptions are so embedded in contemporary culture that they appear normal and natural; however, they are significant, and transform understandings of the body and the self. Over the course of the next few chapters, I will argue that the contemporary beauty ideal is different from past beauty ideals in other ways too: that it applies to more, perhaps all, of us, for longer and is increasingly a global ideal; that it is increasingly demanding; and that it requires technological intervention to attain.

2

Life Is One Long Catwalk

In the last chapter, I argued that the current ideal of beauty, in contrast to previous beauty ideals, is functioning as an ethical ideal. While it may previously have been the case that some regarded beauty as their primary value framework, the ideal was not dominant and could not have functioned as a shared ethical ideal. Recognizing that appearance has always mattered to some individuals and groups is not equivalent to my claim that the beauty ideal is emerging as a dominant ethical ideal: a shared standard against which (moral) success and failure is judged, self-worth determined, and character imputed. This is different from previous beauty ideals, which were limited geographically, by economic and social status, by technical possibilities, or by other ethical ideals. If I am correct, extending the dominance of the beauty ideal transforms its nature. It is not simply that more individuals happen to value appearance more, but that, in the extension of the dominance of the beauty ideal, beauty becomes more valuable and valued. In this chapter, I will argue that the extension of the scope of the ideal makes it possible for the beauty ideal to become a dominant or predominant, rather than a subordinate, ideal. I will argue that the beauty ideal now applies to more types of women, for longer, and at times when it previously did not. Building on this increasing dominance I will then argue, in the next chapter, that the emerging beauty ideal is a global ideal: the second main argument of the book. A global beauty ideal is not just "more of the same," just another beauty ideal. There have been many beauty ideals, and some of them have been extremely demanding and overtly debilitating—think corsets and foot-binding—but there has never been a global beauty ideal. If the dominance strengthens the ethical aspect of the ideal, then the extension of scope is significant.

Difference and Dominance

It is, of course, the case that appearance has always mattered. Human beings as embodied beings have always sought to adorn and beautify themselves, to use their appearance to signal and to enhance status and power. A caricature of this view is that trying to be younger and more beautiful is a core human (animal) instinct, necessary for attracting a mate and delivering other goods. For example, adopting an evolutionary account, Etcoff argues that "good looks are a woman's most fungible asset, exchangeable for social position, money, even love."[1] In addition, women's appearance has also mattered for other reasons, as a carrier of community or religious value, signaling family honor or demarcating particular groups. Given that we have always sought to change, or enhance, appearance, you might wonder what is so different about the current beauty ideal. You might even argue that, compared to some beauty ideals, the current one is fairly benign.

However, the scope is significant. While some historical norms were exceptionally demanding for a small group of women, they were necessarily limited: first, they were limited geographically; second, they were limited within societies; third, they were limited by other ideals, thus while important, and for a small number of individuals perhaps defining, they did not function as shared ethical ideals. For example, practices such as foot-binding in China, corset-wearing in Europe, the use of white lead (from Roman to Elizabethan times) were practiced within certain local areas and by a relatively small proportion of the population. Such practices were not available to, or required of, the majority of women. This does not mean women not belonging to these elite and "privileged" segments of society did not beautify or spend time on their appearance, nor that they did not aspire to engage in these practices (presumably, given what we know about human beings in general, it is very likely that they did). But what it does mean is that these extremely excessive and costly beauty norms were limited. They were limited in terms of who actually engaged, and, and important, they were limited in that they were challenged by other appearance norms and ideals. Accordingly, they could not be regarded as natural and taken for granted as the current ideal increasingly is. In addition, because they only applied to a small stratum of a society, different and divergent beauty norms were evident *within* the society. Thus, while it might not have been an option for an actual aristocratic Chinese woman (or child as foot-binding is done to the young) not to have her feet bound or for an aristocratic Victorian women not to wear a corset, they did see women of other classes who did not; indeed suffragettes pointed to maids not wearing corsets to challenge such norms. In addition, the differences between beauty norms of different cultures was very striking, not only in terms of fashion, but there were also very real differences in terms of what body shape and facial features were regarded as beautiful. Moreover, beauty was often regarded as a relatively trivial pursuit, to be engaged in by those who lacked other, more important, pursuits.

The limited nature of previous beauty ideals ensured that there were obvious instances of divergent beauty norms, which even if not available to individual women (who could not change their particular place and status and so the beauty practices that were required of them as individuals), did provide a resource to challenge particular beauty ideals. The obvious existence of divergence provides a resource for change both because it shows that other beauty ideals are possible (so bringing into question the correctness of your own), and it makes it unlikely that beauty norms will be regarded as natural. This makes it less likely that beauty ideals can be elevated into ethical ideals. The more limited an ideal is, the more minor it will be. In previous times, beauty ideals may have been demanding, but they were not dominant, shared by all or most, and therefore, while conformity was socially required, they were not ethical ideals. In short, difference shows that other beauty norms are possible and challenges the ethical status of such norms. The assumption that beauty ideals are always varied and competing with each other underpins many dismissals of beauty, and beauty ideals, as *mere* matters of taste.

There are two ways in which beauty can be dismissed as mere taste: first, on the grounds that taste is always changing and second, because taste implies *mere* fashion; the implication is that beauty is trivial. Both of these arguments are challenged by a beauty ideal that is more dominant than previous beauty ideals. The argument that beauty is just a matter of taste relies on there being differences. However, in a context where divergence is less then not only do arguments from difference lose their basis, but the argument can be reversed and an opposite conclusion drawn. In a context of many competing beauty ideals, beauty is a matter of fashion, by definition fleeting, passing, and ever changing. But in a context where there are no competing ideals to serve as reminders of the limited nature of such ideals, or to provide resources to challenge and transform them, the dominant beauty ideal will further embed, and become continually more dominant, appear more natural, and gradually become more important to the extent that it becomes a key ethical ideal. I argue that beauty ideals are converging, and accordingly such ideals cease to be trivial and easily changeable and become dominant and constraining. If this is correct, then the claim that past beauty norms have been vastly divergent and subject to change, and so all future beauty norms will be, is a weak argument from which to challenge the current beauty ideal. If current beauty ideals are converging, and there is a trend towards a global norm, then it is less easy to dismiss beauty norms as matters of taste. Moreover, as the beauty ideal becomes narrower, more homogenous, and more dominant, it is harder to challenge by appeal to alternative and comparator ideals.

There are both stronger and weaker versions of the claim that the beauty ideal is more dominant and potentially a global ideal. The stronger version is that the beauty ideal now applies to all women (and increasingly men) and in all places—irrespective of profession and irrespective of the extent to which individual women value appearance. A weaker version is that it applies to more types of women and in more instances. Currently, I suggest, we are some-where between these two. The weaker version is certainly true, and the stronger version likely to become true—at least for women—if trends continue. The weaker version is sufficient to make the argu-ment that the expansion in scope of the ideal is transformative of the nature of the ideal (as long as the expansion can be evidenced and there is a clear trajectory towards a global ideal). While there are still alternative beauty ideals available within and between cul-tures, they are, in general, weaker, and the subcultures are more isolated, although there are places where they remain strong, and such cultures may well be important resources for resistance. Yet, while alternative ideals may offer some challenge to the beauty ideal, and provide some resources for resistance, in the face of a globally dominant ideal, such challenges are increasingly limited.[2] This read-ing of the expansion of the beauty ideal is open to dispute and con-testation; both regarding the extent of the expansion and regarding what this means for the nature of the ideal. My aim is to make at least a prima facie case that the ideal is more dominant and that this extension of scope matters. In the rest of the chapter, I will track this expansion of the ideal—from applying to some women and only some of the time, to all of us and increasingly all of the time.

Perfect in Public

First then, to claim that the beauty ideal applies to more *types* of women is relatively uncontroversial. I suggest that all women in the public sphere are subject to the beauty ideal. Moreover, they are subject to the ideal irrespective of why they are in the public eye and whether or not elements of the ideal are pertinent to the type of work they do.

Those who are most obviously in the public sphere and subject to the ideal are those classed as celebrities, or more affectionately "celebs." Who is a celeb is something of a movable feast; it certainly includes those who are in the "fame" business, for instance, movie and television actors, models, singers and (most) performers in general, royalty, and (to a slightly less extent than previously) aristocracy.[3] More controversially, but undeniably, celebs are also those who are "famous for being famous," and key routes to this are reality TV or prominence as a partner of a celeb, which then results in celebdom in your own right. Kim Kardashian is perhaps the first superceleb of this kind. She took her reality TV appearances and turned herself, her life, and her family into a dominant global brand.[4] Her sister Kylie Jenner is perhaps now outdoing her in influence, at least among younger girls; although she has some way to go to rival Kim's near 50 million twitter followers.[5] Reality TV stars come in different types with different levels of fame. Some are globally stratospheric, like Kim and Kylie, and some are national and local household names (in the UK *The Only Way is Essex (TOWIE)*, *Gordy Shore* and *Big Brother* come to mind), and some have only fifteen minutes of dubious fame. Most of those who appear on Reality TV do not make it to household name status and have to return to their previous lives. For every Jade Goodie, Megan McKenna, or Gemma Collins, there are others whose names only survive one program or series. In addition, there are fly-on-the-wall programs such as *The Real Housewives of Wherever*, to competition programs like *X Factor, America's Next Top Model (ANTM)* as well as topic-specific programs such as *Wife Swap*, the *Biggest Loser, Supernanny*, and *Embarrassing Bodies*, and of course there are also more traditional talk shows where people bear their souls for fifteen minutes of fame.

No one would argue that "celebs" do not fall under the beauty ideal. Indeed, the beauty ideal is *the* dominant ideal in this sector, and often success depends on approximating the ideal. Celebs and would-be celebs are judged when they put on weight, praised when they lose weight, vilified when they show body hair, wobbly flesh, cellulite, criticized when they show signs of aging, criticized for undergoing procedures to rectify these signs, and so on. [6] Of course, arguably these women (and men) sign up to living up to the ideal; indeed, doing so is a large part of what celebdom is, and they can struggle to be taken seriously on other grounds.[7]

That celebs must conform—or be vilified for failing to conform—to the beauty ideal is regarded as normal; part of the package. However, the ideal also applies to other women: for example, sportswomen. Sportswomen you might think should be judged on their bodies, but not obviously according to the beauty ideal. To be sure, some of the categories that sportswomen are judged by coincide with features of the beauty ideal, such as weight. For example, certain sports require low weights, such as long-distance running or gymnastics, and some even require the public recording of weight, such as some martial arts. However, while it might be reasonable for sportswomen to be judged on their bodies and for commentators and the public to have an interest in the eating habits and training regimes by which they hone their bodies to better perform, it is not obviously reasonable for sportswomen to be expected to conform to the beauty ideal. Indeed you might think, given the different types, sizes, and shapes of bodies required for different sports—broad shouldered for swimming, with visible muscle for some forms of athletics—that expectations that women also fit the beauty ideal would be self-defeating.

However, a quick look at the coverage of sportswomen suggests that they are not treated significantly differently from celebs. Media coverage and public expectations of sportswomen combine both celebration of athleticism and comments on the extent to which they conform to the beauty ideal.[8] A few examples are sufficient to show this. Jessica Ennis Hill, despite her significant sporting achievements, is often written about as if she was a standard celebrity and is described as a "pin-up."[9] Ennis has been a cover girl for *Cosmo* and *Marie Claire* and numerous nonfashion publications, and is the face of Olay.[10] Anna Kournikova never won a tournament, yet she was the highest-earning female tennis player, and she attained a significant amount of media coverage.[11] In contrast those who do not conform may suffer. The Williams sisters have been criticized in derogatory terms for being too muscular; and, this is compounded,

Shirley Tate argues, by dark skin.[12] And some sporting women may fail to secure the funding they need to compete, dismissed because they do not make the beauty grade, as in the case of a top Brazilian surfer, Silvana Lima.[13] The beauty ideal clearly applies to sportswomen. They are not treated only as athletes with bodies judged on athletic norms, but also judged according to the extent to which they conform to the beauty ideal. Indeed, Andrew Edgar argues, that the sports body with defined muscle is "aesthetically normative" and powerful, but that this must be sexualized in the female body.[14]

If we turn from women whose bodies are material to their performance in some form, to other women in the public eye, they too are judged according to the extent to which they conform. In the coverage of female politicians, including coverage on serious political programs, beauty-related issues (about weight, dress and hairstyle) are invariably raised. If what is at issue for such women is their competence to do their jobs, it is not clear why they should be judged according to the beauty ideal, or at least why it should be given such prominence. But these women too are judged, at least in part, according to their conformity to the beauty ideal. This can be seen clearly with a quick look at some prominent female politicians. The most famous female politician is Hillary Rodham Clinton. Clinton was the first female senator for New York, the third female secretary of state (following Madeleine Albright and Condoleeza Rice), and was nearly the first female president of the United States of America. Yet there must be as many column inches about her dress sense and hair style as there are about anything she ever did or said. This attention to female conformity to the beauty ideal is ubiquitous. The recent election of Teresa May as prime minister of the UK was covered with particular attention to her shoes.[15] Likewise, Nicola Sturgeon's style, or restyle, is credited as contributing to her success as the leader of the Scottish National Party.[16]

So ubiquitous is the beauty ideal that it now applies to all women in the public sphere. That this is the case is clear if we consider the type of women who might be least expected to fall under the beauty ideal. Academics might think themselves immune from the beauty ideal, but those who are visible are vilified for their appearance if they fail to conform. For example, the extent of the trolling that Mary Beard, professor of classics at Cambridge University, was subject to was so extreme it made headlines, and broadsheets discussed whether she was "too ugly for television."[17] If even professors of classics are judged according to the beauty ideal, then the beauty ideal is a shared and ubiquitous lens by which to judge all women in the public sphere.

Perfect in Private and Virtually

In an increasingly visual culture, the beauty ideal falls on private individuals too. In most walks of life appearance norms are not imposed, although there are expectations of certain body shapes and presentation standards in certain jobs and at certain events. While the days of airhostesses being weighed and measured are gone, there are many professions where looks overtly matter.[18] Even in professions where looks traditionally have not mattered they matter more; students rate not only teaching, but also their professor's "hotness" (by allotting chili peppers).[19] In all aspects of life, whether dropping kids off at school, or just seeing friends and family, we are expected to consider and monitor how we look. Indeed snaps of women going about their daily business are regular newspaper and magazine features, and there are countless social media ways in which to share what you're wearing today.[20] In our private lives—in person and virtually—we are expected to be, and expect ourselves to be, "camera ready."

That the visual is more important in a virtual world is not surprising. Many relationships are now wholly virtual, and even those that are not are more reliant on the visual.[21] In a culture where many of us do not live and work within groups of people who know us well, appearance is going to figure more highly than it did in less mobile cultures. In transitory relationships, first impressions are more dominant, and less often do we get past this stage. The visual and virtual nature of contemporary culture is more demanding the younger you are, and particularly significant is the extent to which you have embraced "selfie culture." The extent of selfie culture, es-

pecially for those of us who were teenagers before email, let alone
before social media, is staggering. Facebook alone has over 1.3 billion regular users, many of whom are young women, and over 10
million new photographs are uploaded to Facebook every hour.[22]
As well as Facebook, there are many other popular social media sites,
including Instagram, Snapchat, and MySpace, all of which are predominantly, and sometimes wholly, visual. It is hard to find global
figures, but over 90 percent of young women in the United States,
UK and Australia use social networking sites.[23] Given that internet
access, usually accessed by mobile phone, is globally growing—with
reportedly more mobile phones than flushing toilets in India—
there is no reason to suppose that this growth of visual and virtual
culture will not continue.[24] Not only can we retouch and remaster
the images we post and project, but the virtual self can be improved
and remade and the flaws of our actual body interrogated and exposed. Elias and Gill identify five types of appearance apps in the
many hundreds of beauty apps available: apps that teach technique,
that enhance selfies, that offer virtual makeovers (from new hairstyles to surgery), that identify flaws, and that rate attractiveness.[25]
In our private and virtual lives, we must be camera ready so we can
present our best self(ie).

Taken together then, the pressure to meet the beauty ideal falls
on all of us to greater or lesser extents. That this is the case is both
positive and negative. It is positive in that it is a democratization of
beauty. Beauty and its attendant practices are no longer the preserve of the rich, but are practices in which we all engage, or could
imagine engaging. We can all be beautiful, or so we are told, if we
engage in the right practices and procedures. This is, of course, limited by resources: as Blum points out, we have to be able to afford
the surgery.[26] But, while resources do limit, the possibility remains,
and in some contexts, such as Brazil, where the right to surgery and
to be beautiful, is regarded as belonging to all, this is particularly
true.[27] As Edmonds states, "Plástica responds to, and incites, this
view of beauty as an egalitarian form of social capital, one that depends less on birth, education, and connections to cultivate."[28] Of
course the extent to which we can change our appearance is less

than the ideal promises. Moreover, there are significant harms, which I will explore over the next few chapters; harms of increased demandingness, harms of normalization, and justice harms of exploitation and discrimination. Perhaps most obvious is the unprecedented rise in body image worries and body dissatisfaction.

The Rise of Body Anxiety and the Harms of Body Dissatisfaction

The democratization of beauty not only makes engagement possible, it also makes it expected. As a result, as discussed in the last chapter, most of us are dissatisfied with our bodies and want to be thinner. While the focus of many studies is on the young, increasingly it is recognized that body dissatisfaction remains into middle age and late-life.[29] So chronic and extensive is body dissatisfaction that some have called for it to be recognized as a public health problem.[30] Body dissatisfaction is widespread, and myriad devastating consequences attach to it; including lower self-esteem, diminished well-being, disordered eating, lower activity, risky behavior, mental and physical health issues.[31] Further, we also know that the overfocus on appearance is not likely to lead to flourishing. On the contrary, well-being is derived from valuing, and placing value in, a range of capacities and capabilities. Nichola Rumsey suggests we imagine a healthy sense of self as a "pie" with different pie pieces contributing to overall wellbeing.[32] If too much of your pie is made up from appearance pieces, then failure in this area will be destructive in a way that it would not were it just one component in self-esteem. As the next section will show, the younger you are the more pervasive and dominant the beauty ideal is, but all are increasingly under pressure to be thin, firm, and young—and dissatisfied when they are not. This is an epidemic of anxiety, worry, and feelings of failure, in addition to other harmful consequences.

The rise in visual and virtual culture extends the dominance of the ideal as there are more "peers" against whom we can judge our bodies and find them wanting.[33] "Upwards comparisons," where we perceive the comparator as better, lead to more unfavorable self-

evaluations, and predict body dissatisfaction.[34] If some form of social comparison theory is correct, then global virtual culture offers
many more possibilities for comparison. Historically social comparisons would be with relevant peers, for example, those in your own
village or social group. In an age of globalization, the pool with which
we are comparing is much larger, and potentially includes everyone and anyone. With the advent of social media, the perfect bodies
of celebrities no longer seem so out of reach, making comparison of
celeb bodies to our own flawed bodies less of a stretch. In one study
sixteen-year-old girls frequently referred to women in the images
they saw as "just looking perfect."[35] These young women were no
dupes or dopes and clearly understood that the images they were
seeing were illusorily, manipulated and unrealistic, but despite this
they recognized that the images did shape their perceptions of
normal: "They look perfect, and you just want to look like that."[36]
Not surprisingly, studies show a positive correlation between Facebook use and body dissatisfaction.[37] To use just one example, Marika
Tiggemann and Amy Slater found that "as predicted, Internet exposure was associated with internalization of the thin ideal, body
surveillance, and drive for thinness."[38] In selfie culture, not only are
young women valuing appearance more than other attributes, but
they are also judging themselves against images drawn from across
global virtual culture.[39]

Being thin enough is primary in being perfect, and psychologists
speak about the internalization of the thin ideal (or thin with curves;
for example, Harrison speaks of the "curvaceously thin woman").[40]
So we judge ourselves not only against images, but also against our
internalized picture of thinness, again leading to body dissatisfaction. The extent to which the increasing dominance of the thin ideal
is a product of image-ridden visual culture, or of other influences
is fraught with controversy. Psychologists and social scientists dispute the origins and mechanisms of increased body dissatisfaction;
for instance, they dispute whether parents, peer-groups, media, or
social media are most significant. Some argue that the media are primary, some focus on parents and family influence, and some focus
on peer-group influence, and so on.[41] To give just a few examples

from the vast psychological literature, Harrison's body of work suggests that exposure to thin characters in television programs leads to a higher drive for thinness among females and the endorsing of such a drive among males.[42] Similarly, Kelly Kubric shows that exposure to TV makeover shows is related to lower self-esteem, higher perfectionism, and body dissatisfaction.[43] And Jasmine Fardouly and colleagues, suggest that the edited and enhanced selfies on Facebook are also images that are used for comparison, and that Facebook use leads to negative moods.[44] By contrast, Christopher Ferguson and colleagues argue that *only* peer comparison is important.[45] Moreover they suggest that claims regarding the thin ideal are problematic, as exposure to thin images only affects a subgroup of women with pre-existing body concerns.[46] What should we make of these competing and contradictory empirical accounts? I suggest that we are agnostic about what matters most, and conclude that no influence is decisive and that all influences are negotiated. Accordingly, some individuals are less susceptible to internalizing the thin ideal, to increasing body dissatisfaction, and to the harms of self-objectification than others. Thus, even in a toxic environment the pressure of the beauty ideal can be mitigated. Yet, despite such disagreement about the importance of different influences, there is a general agreement that body dissatisfaction is rising as appearance matters more, and that there are significant psychological harms that result from overly attaching identity to appearance.

The unprecedented rise in body dissatisfaction and body image anxiety, with its attendant harms, speaks to the increasing pressure across the board to comply to the beauty ideal and to the increasing dominance of the ideal. In the next chapter, I will argue that the drive to thinness—and its resulting dissatisfaction—is global. For now, I simply wish to note that the scope of the beauty ideal is extending to more types of women, perhaps to all women, and in more contexts. We need to be camera ready in our daily lives and be our virtual best self. In the rest of this chapter, I will turn to other evidence to show that the beauty ideal is extending, in that it begins young, continues old, and applies in areas of life that were previously exempt.

Perfect Younger

That beauty is required earlier has been an area of popular debate and of public concern. In particular, there is concern about the sexualization of young girls.[47] The debate about the sexiness of Disney's *Frozen* princess Elsa is illustrative. Despite worries about the sexiness of the character, the Elsa dress (made with sheer fabric as the three- to eight-year-olds do not have the necessary breasts to hold up a strapless dress) was one of the most popular items of 2014: with dresses reselling on eBay for upwards of $1000.[48] So much panic has there been that in the UK the government commissioned an independent review on the impact of sexualization of young people.[49] The report concludes that young women are under pressure to post pictures of themselves in underwear, to be "hot" and "sexy," and that they are subject to body pressures that previous generations were not. This leads to body dissatisfaction, poor self-esteem, and a host of undesirable consequences. This report, which suggests that the pressure on young people is unprecedented, is no outlier. Report after report tells us that appearance matters and that body dissatisfaction and concerns about body image are growing. For example, the recent YMCA report, "The Challenge of Being Young in Modern Britain," placed body image issues as the third-biggest and most harmful challenge facing young people (after lack of employment opportunities and failing to succeed within the education system).[50]

"The Girl's Attitude" survey, by Girlguiding, is annual, and year on year it has drawn attention to the problem of body image. The 2016 survey addresses body confidence first and states that girls "tell us they have to confront intense and unobtainable appearance pressures to be perfect and many say they feel they're not good enough."[51] Just to take a few statistics from this report: 47 percent of girls aged 11–21 say the way they look holds them back; the youngest girls consulted say they feel embarrassed and ashamed of how they look; 38 percent of girls between 7 and 10 think they are not pretty enough sometimes or most of the time, and this rises to 91 percent of girls between 17 and 21; 40 percent of girls between 7 and 10 think they should lose weight sometimes or most of the time and this rises to 80 percent of girls between 17 and 21; 53 percent of girls between 7 and 10 think they need to be perfect sometimes or most of the time, and this rises to 84 percent of girls between 17 and 21. These statistics speak for themselves.

The beauty ideal exerts its influence on those as young as three; and the earliness of the emergence of beauty concerns should ring alarm bells for those who claim that beauty is just a matter of individual choice, something which I'll return to. Study after study shows that the very young are concerned with some aspect of the beauty ideal; with their size (especially with being fat) or hair color, or some other aspect of how they look. For example, like other studies Hayley Dohnt and Marika Tiggeman found that girls between five and eight want to be thin and know that the thin ideal can be attained by dieting.[52] In another study, by Jennifer Harriger, preschool girls between three and five exhibited strong preferences for thinness.[53] In this study, not only did the girls have preferences for thinness but they attached adjectives to different-sized silhouettes, including those of "nice," "mean," "smart," "stupid," "has friends," "sloppy," "ugly" "quiet," and "loud."[54] Therefore, as young as three, girls are attaching positive qualities, character-traits, to thin body types.[55] By five girls have internalized the notion that thin is good, and ethically good as well as aesthetically desirable.[56] Stereotypes about body size develop before school age, and the desire for thinness grows with age.[57]

If doubt remains that beauty is an important issue, consider the devastating and debilitating knock-on effects of body image concerns. There are a whole host of things that girls report they do not do because of their low body confidence: from wearing clothes they like, to having their pictures taken, to taking part in sport, and to speaking up in class.[58] If we add this to the evidence the harms of body dissatisfaction, then unquestionably worries about appearance severely limit what girls can be and do. The extent of the dominance is unprecedented: in the 2013 Girlguiding survey 87 percent of eleven- to twenty-one-year-old-girls said that women are judged more on their appearance than on ability.[59] This is nearly 90 percent of girls and young women who believe how they look matters more than what they do and say. While we may still want to tell our daughters that "it's what's on the inside that counts," they would not believe us, and, given the evidence, we would not be telling the truth.

Perfect Older

As well as starting earlier the pressure of the ideal also continues into what would previously been considered old age: "thirty is the new twenty"; "forty is the new thirty"; and at sixty you should be reclaiming the joys of your youth, after all you're child-free again! The rise of the "cougars" is illustrative of this extension of the beauty ideal to those who are older, into, what Jones calls "Stretched Middle Age."[60] It used to be the case that beauty expectations decreased with age, but now at fifty a bikini body is still possible—just look at Helen Mirren at seventy-two! And it's not just celebrities who are expected to conform. We all are. To quote Bordo, "my fifty-six-year-old forehead will now be judged against my neighbour's, not just Goldie's, Cher's and Faye's."[61] Studies support this: for instance, a recent study summarizing results of studies between 2010 and 2014 found that "eating disorders and related issues of body-image dissatisfaction are surprisingly common in middle aged and older women."[62] In Bordo's words, "'aging beautifully' used to mean wearing one's years with style, confidence and vitality. Today it means not appearing to age at all. And—like breasts that defy gravity—it's becoming the new bodily norm."[63] Jones has a similar, but less critical take, arguing that beauty as we age, "is less about reclaiming or reinventing youthfulness and more about attempting to create a look of indeterminate age or 'agelessness.'"[64] Yet, whether the aim is to mimic youth or to look good in an age-appropriate way, the features that are aspired to are the same: thin, firm, and smooth.

There are positive aspects of extending beauty requirements and possibilities into old age. Indeed, the mere fact that older women are judged on their beauty past the fresh flush of youth might be positive in itself; and women are certainly embracing the possibilities that body work offers as they age. Yet, older women are suffering from a "crisis of body-image," if not quite as dramatically as the young. For instance in one U.S. online survey of 1,789 women aged over fifty only 12.2 percent reported being satisfied with their body size.[65] Of these most were in the normal weight range (over 80 percent). But staying at this weight is time consuming, and the authors describe the "maintenance of thinness" as "a fairly active endeavour for many women."[66] The authors described this as "novel," although it will come as no surprise to anyone who has tried to maintain weight. In addition, as we age, there is pressure to be "age appropriate"; you must aspire to look young, or good for your, age, but this should not be "overdone"; you should not be "mutton dressed as lamb" (or whatever the appropriate metaphor is when it comes to body reshaping).[67] Here technology is crucial—and analogies with repro-tech are pertinent—pressures that used to end or at least relax at the menopause now continue. Just as you can *choose* to delay childbearing (and your employer might even pay to freeze your eggs to give you this *choice*), so you can choose to maintain your youth and looks—and you might even have a duty to do so.[68] As the pressure grows, and possibilities become requirements and duties, so the positive aspects become outweighed by the harms.

Perfect in Extremes

As well as applying younger and older, the beauty ideal is also expanding into circumstances where previously the pressures of beauty did not apply; those of pregnancy and illness.

Pregnancy used to be a time at which women were not—or at least less—subject to the demands of beauty. However, as Imogen Tyler argues, "pregnant women are no longer released, however briefly, from either the relentless pursuit of beauty or the pressure to perform sexual availability."[69] Tyler argues that this shift occurred in the 1990s, driven by celebrity photographs, with Demi Moore's cover of *Vanity Fair* in 1991 being the iconic image.[70] Now many of us are embracing pregnant beauty: as a quick google of studios offering maternity photography confirms.[71] Pregnancy has become—

at least in the West—a time when bodies are visible and expected to be beautiful, rather than covered and hidden (maternity dresses are no longer tents). Of course, this trend can be viewed—as so much of beauty can—both positively and negatively. Positively, the trend is a celebration of women's pregnant bodies. As Iris Marion Young notes, pregnant bodies can be beautiful bodies that are creative and powerful.[72] However while it is great that not all pregnant bodies are regarded as shameful or to be hidden away (indeed they can even be sexy, and Tyler reports that porn depicting pregnant women, once marginal, is now mainstream),[73] negatively, such bodies have to conform. This is how Tyler reads pregnant beauty, describing it as a "neoliberal project of self-realization, a 'body project' to be directed and managed, another site of feminine performance anxiety and thus ironically a new kind of confinement for women."[74] For it is not all pregnant bodies that are celebrated, which would indeed be positive, but only some. The acceptable pregnant body conforms to the beauty ideal. It is firm and smooth, and, with the addition of a neat bump, slim.[75] Not only are there expectations of the pregnant body, but "quickly slender, even bikini-ready, postpartum bodies are also the new norm."[76] Lynn O'Brian Hallstein argues that this focus on maternal body is significant.[77] Body work and the perfect body replace other indicators of good mothering and as proof of success and happiness. It is how we look in the role, rather than perform in the role, that signals our competence. This is another example of a shift from previous ideals as how we look now defines our success and failure as a mother.

Illness is a further time when beauty ideals increasingly apply, as Breana Monique Musella highlights in her work on the Look Good Feel Better charity.[78] This charity provides "free services for women and teenagers suffering from the visible side effects from cancer treatment" and is "dedicated to improving the wellbeing and self-confidence of people undergoing treatment for any type of cancer."[79] Key to the work of this charity is a focus on appearance shown clearly in their primary and striking advertising campaign "#warpaint4life."[80] One campaign is a series of four images of four made-up, confident and beautiful women—Suzanne, Kreena, Maria, and Ellie—who are accompanied by the statement "you use it to face the day, we use it to face cancer." The message here is one of empowerment, of not being defined by the cancer, and three of the four women emphasize the importance of feeling "normal" (and the one who does not use this word does mention "blending in," suggesting being normal is important to her too).[81] One of the four, Suzanne, emphasizes that make-up allows her to be herself, stating that "make-up is my war-paint, it sets me up for the day and allows me to be Suzanne."[82] However, while beauty processes might indeed make these women feel more normal and confident (as do wigs provided as a standard part of cancer treatment, and in the UK, NHS-funded), it also extends the demands of the beauty ideal into periods of illness. Again an extension of the dominance of the beauty ideal and with it an extension of demands.

Conclusion

In this chapter, I have argued that the beauty ideal is more dominant in terms of the types of women to whom it applies, it begins younger, continues older, and applies in almost every circumstance. This extension is accompanied by an unprecedented rise in body image worries, increased anxiety about appearance, and body dissatisfaction, all of which are potentially debilitating and devastating. The reasons for the increased dominance of appearance are multifaceted and complex. A number of features stand out: the rise of virtual and visual culture, which makes appearance more important; the technological imperative (the increase in what *can* be done adds to the pressure of what *should* be done);[83] the rise of consumerism globally as a way of creating identity and signaling character and status, and the commercial imperatives should not be underestimated. The more people who can be induced to engage, the more markets are created for products and processes to be sold. In addition to these well recognized pressures, the ethical nature of the ideal goes some way to explaining the sometimes all-consuming commitment we have to the beauty ideal. Value frameworks—which reward, praise, and blame, and against which we judge ourselves and others and structure our daily practices—cannot be shrugged off. They are defining. Moreover, as I will argue in chapter 4, a dominant ethical ideal is a greedy and growing ideal. This chapter has claimed that the beauty ideal is increasingly dominant. In the next chapter, I will argue its dominance is extending to the global.

3

A New (Miss) World Order?

In the last chapter, I argued that the beauty ideal applies in the public and private spheres, and that the line between these spheres is blurring, and that it applies to more types of women, for longer, and, at times, when it previously had not. In the previous two chapters, I argued that the beauty ideal is different to past beauty ideals because it is increasingly functioning as an ethical ideal and because of its extended (and extending) scope. In this chapter, I will suggest that the extension of scope is potentially global—the second main argument of the book.[1] Recall from chapter 1 that this claim is not that there is one single acceptable blue print for beautiful, a single determining model that every individual has to fit, but rather that local beauty ideals are converging, resulting in an increasingly narrow *range* of what is considered beautiful, or just good enough.[2] Further, I argued that the scope of the emerging beauty ideal is transformative of the ideal because as the ideal expands there are fewer competitor and alternative ideals from which to challenge the dominant beauty ideal and to provide resources for alternative ideals.

In this chapter, I seek to support the claim that what is now emerging is a global ideal; that trends are converging towards a global mean. Establishing such a claim is difficult, given the lack of equivalent and comparative data. I do not wish to underplay the difficulties of using statistics and empirical evidence in this type of philosophical project, but the empirical evidence is, broadly, going in the same direction and telling a similar story. Not to say there are not places where the ideal does not apply, alternative norms and pockets of resistance, there are. But, while there is not yet a single, homogenizing, global beauty ideal, it is the case that beauty ideals are converging and not only is a shared global beauty ideal imaginable, but it is already discernible.

Globally Dominant?

The scope and the ethical nature of the ideal are mutually reinforcing. As the beauty ideal becomes more dominant, it becomes more accepted, unquestioned, and unquestionable. The more it is unquestioned, the more it is established as a value framework, and the more such moral values are normalized and appear natural. In turn, as the ethical function increases, it becomes harder to resist and reject the beauty ideal, without regarding yourself and others as morally failing, which in turn serves to make the ideal more dominant. These features act in tandem to strengthen the power of the ideal and to make the ideal different from previous beauty ideals. The scope makes it possible for beauty to function as an ethical ideal (enough individuals must conform for the ideal to become embedded and assumed such that it can provide shared standards for ethical judgment). In turn, the ethical nature of the ideal, which promises success and condemns failure as moral failure, encourages increasing investment in the beauty ideal as an important, and perhaps primary, value framework. The ultimate extension of scope is to a global beauty ideal.

Suggesting that there is a global beauty ideal emerging is controversial, because while trends are converging differences remain, and no matter how global the ideal becomes differences will continue as, at communal and individual levels, the ideal is interpreted, negotiated, and embedded. As such interpretations and negotiations happen, differences will always be created, as the ideal must be accommodated by local traditions and meanings, and so will always change. As discussed in the previous chapter, the argument from difference has been presented as if it were a knock-down rejection of the claim that beauty ideals can ever be dominant ideals. In the last chapter, I suggested that this argument becomes weaker as global ideals converge. If trends are broadly moving in the same direction, then the continued existence of difference does not prove that convergence is not happening. I am not claiming that the global ideal is monolithic, imposed from above, or that it manifests in the same way in all contexts. Rather I am suggesting it embodies a narrowing range of acceptable features: broadly, thinness, firmness, smoothness, and youth. Some of these features are more important in some contexts than others, and some are interchangeable—having some may lessen or negate the need to have others—and some matter more in some contexts and less in others. For example, in some contexts so much value is placed on skin tone that the failure to meet other features is negated: "fair skin makes up for other bodily flaws."[3] In other contexts, the opposite is true. For instance, skin color may be irrelevant as long as other features—for example thinness—are met. For example, Imani Perry suggests that message of global pageants is that "You can fit into a silhouette of beauty that possesses the shape and form of the physical ideal even if you are 'other.'"[4] Old colonial hierarchies of racial groups remain, but the message is that irrespective of skin color the beauty ideal is possible.[5] That some features matter less in some contexts does not shake the dominance of the ideal as some of the key features are always required, in some or other combination. For example, it is possible to be bigger, if you are also firm, smooth, and young. It is less likely you will be considered beautiful, or just good enough, if you are bigger *and* hairy *and* have cellulite *and* jowls. The emerging global beauty ideal promotes thinness, firmness, smoothness, and youth—collectively or in combination. Taken together the range of what is acceptable to be perfect, or just good enough, is narrower and narrowing. Furthermore, as beauty ideals converge less divergence is possible.

Given the controversial nature of this claim it is important that I be clear about the arguments that I am not making. First, I am not asserting that there is a single universal beauty ideal, nor an objective account of beauty. Some features of the ideal do seem universal, and could be argued for on evolutionary accounts: for example youth, and perhaps smoothness and firmness as proxies of youth. This said, such accounts fail when it comes to our current preoccupation with flawless skin at the forensic level. Likewise, thinness is notoriously hard to account for using an evolutionary model and is as least as well accounted for by social construction.[6] That said, if it turned out that evolutionary accounts were true, it would not greatly impact my argument as my focus is not on the cause of the emerging norm but on its current features and function as a dominant and ethical ideal. For my argument, the process by which the features come to be valued is less important than that they are valued and the extent to which they make demands on those who fall under the ideal. Thus, what matters is that the beauty ideal, as we currently experience it, is more dominant than past ideals—and I argue likely to become more so unless we act—and that it is functioning as an ethical ideal. Accordingly, my agnosticism about causal accounts should not prevent anyone from accepting my claims about the emerging global norm.

Second, and following, I am not arguing that beauty ideals cannot change. Undoubtedly they can and have (another reason I struggle with an evolutionary account). Indeed, in arguing that there is an emerging global ideal—which, for most women, requires technical help to attain—I am presuming that beauty ideals *can* and *are* changing. Third, I am not arguing that beauty ideals have fully converged and there are no different, local or alternative beauty ideals. There are, and in some instances these are strikingly different. But what I am arguing is that where there are differences these are less than they used to be and often there is evidence that they are moving in the direction of the global mean, weakening claims that there are significant and available alternative beauty ideals. Further, it is important not to confuse the vast differences in some aspects of appearance—such as various and changing global clothing fashions and hair styles—for the features of the beauty ideal: those of thinness, firmness, smoothness, and youth. It is these features that I focus on and that I argue are increasingly globally dominant. These features largely apply irrespective of lifestyle preferences, and variety in other aspects of beauty may serve to obscure the increasing demandingness of the core features. Fourth, I am not arguing that the emerging global norm is merely the imposition of a Western ideal (an argument I will return to at the end of the chapter).

Global Convergence

The claim that the beauty ideal is gradually converging into a global ideal is, in part, an empirical claim. I seek merely to establish that there is sufficient evidence to hypothesize an emerging norm. My aim is not to provide a comprehensive or definitive account, and there may be some instances where I have misinterpreted details in the evidence, misunderstood the methodologies and results of disciplines that are not my own, or failed to take proper account of counter-evidence or have missed significant evidence (although I trust the last two are rare). Such failures on my part are obviously regrettable, but, while they show the weakness of my scholarship, they only pose a challenge to the argument if there is substantial evidence of broad trends running counter to my claims, and in no case does this seem likely. I have sought to draw on data about which there is some consensus (and, where there is not, to note this lack of consensus). In addition, because I am attempting to map general trends, it will be the case that there are anomalies and outliers that may point to alternative trends and that merit further study by scientists and social scientists. Further, if it turns out that I am wholly wrong and all trends flow against the direction of travel I map, then no one could be more delighted than me. So while social scientists may despair at my methodology, and perhaps (I hope) seek to provide better analysis, this brief consideration of empirical data, taken from across the sciences and social sciences, does provide some empirical support for my philosophical argument.

In the first chapter, I argued that beauty is functioning as an ethical ideal in that individuals judge themselves and others in accordance with it, that it provides meaning, identity, and structure, and that it promises the goods of the good life. That this is the case is not limited to the West.[7] Across the globe, women report that appearance matters for employability, marriageability, and relationships.[8] Further the extent to which beauty is an ethical matter also extends beyond the West. For example, Korean women's negative experiences of dieting reveal similar feelings of failure in a culturally appropriate manner:

> When they failed to lose weight, they experienced deep frustration, anger and self-hatred that resulted in low self-esteem and low confidence in their self-control. One intriguing point is that culture seemed to establish the major reasons for those uncomfortable feelings; Koreans' painful emotions were often based on concerns or anxiety related to others' critical judgment for not being thin and attractive as expected.[9]

In addition, concerns about beauty, expressed in terms of body dissatisfaction and self-esteem, are global. For example, Meng Zhang writes that "body image issues are of global relevance and importance because abundant evidence has shown that women suffer from body image dissatisfaction in numerous countries and regions around the world."[10] She notes that "female adolescents across China have reported weight concerns, dieting behaviors, body weight dissatisfaction and eating disorders";[11] and in her own, small study the women felt that "body image dissatisfaction was nothing but 'normal' "[12] That body dissatisfaction and body image concerns are global is now established and not controversial.[13] However, that beauty matters, and appearance is becoming more important is not the same as claiming that there is an emerging global ideal. Beauty could matter—perhaps more than before in more urban and visual cultures—but with very different beauty norms being dominant in different places. To repeat, I am not claiming that there are no cultural differences; there are, and perhaps most obviously with regard to the discourses, motivations, and languages that surround the engagement in beauty practices. For example, Kim argues that while Korean and American women both engage in dieting behavior and wish to be, and feel required to be, thin, the reasons are culturally grounded.[14] However, it may be that while different reasons are given in different contexts each narrative may be the culturally acceptable narrative, which always functions to permit and justify engagement and compliance. I will return to this in chapter 5, when I consider the very different narratives that surround engagement in beauty practices in different cultural contexts.

In this section, I seek to show that while there are significant local differences, and pockets where truly alternative ideals prevail, taken together, the trends and tendencies are moving in the same direction, making it likely that ideals are converging. To make the claim that the ideal is potentially global, I will, first, consider the extent to which the key features of the ideal are global; second, consider evidence for convergence and the emergence of a global mean, focusing first on surgery trends, and second, on skin-color; third, problematize my claim for a global mean by highlighting the uncomfortable erosion (or concealing) of power hierarchies, which a global mean implies; and finally, argue that while recognizing that power hierarchies remain, from poor to rich, black to white, as well as in terms of class and caste, current trends cannot be accounted for simply by positing the expansion of a Western beauty ideal. Thus, I conclude, the global ideal is a convergence, a global mean, and not a mere export of a Western ideal.

Global Drives to Thinness, Firmness, Smoothness, and Youth

Of the key features I set out in the chapter 1, the claim that there is a global trend to thinness is by far the easiest global feature to establish. It is much harder to find direct evidence to establish firmness, smoothness, and youth; and smoothness is particularly problematic because skin tone and skin color cannot be separated. It could be that there is far more evidence for thinness because much of the research is concerned with psychological and physical health—whether the research is on body dissatisfaction, eating disorders, or obesity.[15] For obvious reasons, there are myriad drivers for, and funders of, health research, and far fewer for appearance research, although as the problems of body dissatisfaction become better known this may change. However, the fact that the trend to thinness can be shown to be global is important in itself, because if thinness is desired other key features of the ideal are likely to follow: it is unlikely that the drive to a thin body would not also be a drive for a firm body, and thinner bodies are nearly always younger-looking bodies. Further, youth might be universally valued already as thus assumed to be globally valuable, even if it is not researched as such. That value is placed on youth can be gleaned, in part, from the value placed on particular facial features and skin textures. In this section and in the next section, I will suggest that the key features of the beauty ideal can be regarded as global. I will focus on thinness, which can be evidenced, argue that firmness and smoothness can be inferred, and suggest the desire for youth is globally ubiquitous.

For thinness (perhaps with curves) to be a feature of a global beauty ideal I need to show not that the same level of thinness is desired everywhere, but that the general trend is away from fatter figures and towards some version of thinness. As already noted, the evidence that there are places where fatness not thinness is or has been desired is often presented as if it were a trumping argument to deny the existence or emergence of global beauty ideals. That thinness is globally desirable is evidenced by all kinds of empirical studies, from sociological interviews, to psychological qualitative and quantitative studies of attractiveness and body dissatisfaction, to medical studies that document the global rise in eating disorders. Body dissatisfaction—with its knock-on effects of undermining self-confidence, lowering self-esteem, and negatively affecting many aspects of life is global.[16] Evidence that thinner figures are regarded as ideal is available from China,[17] Korea,[18] India,[19] South Africa,[20] and Pakistan.[21] Evidence of growing eating disorders emerging almost everywhere is overwhelming. For example, a review of eating disorders in Asia documents the rise across the continent, including Japan, Singapore, Hong Kong, Korea, Taiwan, Philippines, Malaysia, Indonesia, Thailand, Pakistan, and India.[22]

That the drive to thinness is global challenges popular, but inaccurate, assertions, that fat is valued in some places. Historically, there is truth to this claim, and Viren Swami and Adrian Furnham suggest that "traditional" cultures "prefer plump, and sometimes overweight, women."[23] That fatness is preferred in some cultures is the most common version of the argument from difference. Swami and Furnham, like others, cite African fattening camps, which fatten girls before marriage, as examples to show that thin is not universally desired.[24] Undoubtedly, it is the case that there are still places where fatness is preferred and women seek to gain rather than lose weight. Furthermore, Swami and Furnham cite a host of studies to show that there is increased tolerance of obesity in Africa, and among the African diaspora and other ethnic minorities (Mexican Americans and Puerto Rican Americans).[25] Accordingly, some racial and ethnic groups are commonly identified as finding thinness less desirable: "it appears that African American men are more willing to idealise a women of a heavier body size, with more curves, than do their Caucasian counterparts."[26] In addition many studies support the view that black women have been less dissatisfied with their weight than white women.[27]

I do not deny that fuller figures have been regarded as ideal in some times and places, nor that there are pockets where they are still regarded as preferable to thinner figures. Nor am I denying that some groups idealize figures that are fuller compared to those idealized by other groups. What I am claiming is that nearly everywhere the movement is in the same direction, and gradually the preference is for figures that are thinner than those that were previously idealized. So even though it may be case that what is ideal in much of Africa may be fuller than what is ideal in the United States, if it is the case that the African ideal is becoming thinner than it was previously, then the direction of travel is nevertheless towards thinness. Recall, my claim is not that the ideal is already established, but that we are gradually moving towards a global mean. For my argument to work, what is required is evidence that the trajectory of trends is moving in the same direction; that if trends continue, we will end up with a global ideal of thinness, and while there will be a range of thin types that are acceptable—thin with curves, model-thin, strong and buff (and thin in the right places)—thin, in one form or another, will be required everywhere to be perfect, or just good enough. The latest evidence suggests that there is a move towards idealizing thinness, even in contexts which have traditionally valued fatness. For example, a 2012 study led by Vinet Coetzee explored appearance preferences in South Africa and concluded that men desired "younger, thinner women with a lighter, yellower skin colour and a more homogenous skin tone."[28] Furthermore, they found, contrary to supposedly traditional African preferences for fatness, that underweight women were preferred to average or overweight women; a finding that surprised them, not only because of traditional African preferences, but also because thinness is an indicator of illness and HIV.[29] This is echoed in other studies and for other places where larger women have previously been preferred.[30]

In addition the claim that membership of nonwhite racial groups protects women from a drive to thinness is being challenged. For example, a 2006, meta-analysis suggests that the divergence between body dissatisfaction between black and white women is reducing.[31] Likewise, a 2014 study concluded that "the present study's findings continue to debunk the myth or stereotype that Black young women are immune to feelings of body dissatisfaction."[32] This is repeated in detailed interviews: for example, Clara Rice reports that "weight restriction became a way of life for a majority of women I interviewed—Black, Asian, South Asian, and white."[33] While the reasons for this are complex and contested, preference for thinness is becoming more widespread and dominant.[34] Differences remain, and slightly fuller figures may be idealized in some contexts, and there may well be some cultures where fatter figures are preferred. Even in the thin-idealizing West there are enclaves of individuals who idealize fat, for example, "FA's," fat admirers, seek out fat women.[35]

Further evidence that thinness is increasingly the ideal, even among groups and cultures where fatness has traditionally been valued, comes from the statistics connected to the rise in eating disorders. While only a small percentage of any population develops an eating disorder, eating disorders signal the valuing of thinness in society, and while still less common than in the West, nonwestern cultures are documenting steady rises in eating disorders.[36] As Bordo puts it, "the starving white girls were just the forward guard, the miners' canaries warning of how poisonous the air was becoming for everyone."[37] As such, while it is not yet the case that globally all prefer thinness, it is likely that most do, or will come to do, if current trends continue. This does not mean that all will value the same thin ideals, but that thinness over fatness is preferred, even in places where previously thinness was not desired.[38] The emergence of a preference for thinness, even in groups and cultures that previously did not value it, is enough to posit a global trend towards thinness and to establish thinness as a key feature of the global ideal.

The other features of the ideal are harder to evidence from currently available studies, and more research is needed. However, simply because direct evidence is harder to find, it is not the case that nothing can be said about these features. That there is substantial evidence for an increased preference for thinness suggests that a particular type of body matters, and it would be unlikely that only thinness mattered and other features did not. Perhaps we can infer that firmness matters as similar images of bodies are globally promoted. For instance, in a study of the global content of four magazines (*Vogue, Elle, Glamour,* and *Cosmopolitan*) "the most salient topics (i.e., fashion and beauty) were homogeneous across cultures, as represented in magazines published worldwide."[39] Indeed, as Michelle Lazer argues, the picture of the globally empowered women we are sold is remarkably uniform: "She may be racially varied to some extent, but otherwise is typically curvaceously slender, of moderate height, and with symmetrically proportioned facial features. She is able-bodied and heterosexual(ized)."[40] That youth is valued throughout is harder to find evidence for, but perhaps less is needed. A proxy might simply be the growth of age-defying cosmetic products as a sphere of global trade. The global market in cosmetic products is largely recession-proof, and while growth has dipped at times, the market continues to grow. Thirty-five percent of the cosmetic market is skin-care products, which speaks to both firmness and youth, as skin care is the section that antiaging and firming products fall into.[41]

Smoothness is easier to evidence, although it is hugely complicated by racial and cultural hierarchies, definitions, and meanings that cannot be separated from debates about skin tone and texture. Later in the chapter, I will return to skin color, but while there are different focuses in different places, clearly texture matters; shown in part by the large sector of the cosmetics market dedicated to skin care. In addition, skin lightening and tanning promise not just skin of a certain color but improved texture. For example, African magazines promote "teint clair" (clear skin),[42] and Asian ads emphasize that " *'good skin'* should be smooth, young, pore-less, line-free, bright, transparent, white, full and fine. *'Bad skin'* is referenced in the ads as skin with fine lines, winkles, aging marks, pores, or yellow spots, and skin that is dark, scratchy, dry and dull, loose, or rough."[43] Accordingly, the emphasis on smooth skin is evident across cultures.

A further element of smoothness, which I will return to in the next chapter, is hairlessness, for which again it is hard to find robust evidence, but which does appear to be a global practice that crosses racial groups, cultures, and classes. The removal of leg and arm hair is normal in the West to the extent that a failure to remove it is abnormal.[44] But, by no means is this practice limited to the West, although racial groups with more hair may emphasize practices of body hair removal more. For instance, there is less focus on hair removal amongst the relatively hairless African, Chinese, and Japanese and more by white women and those of the Indian diaspora. However, while there may be less emphasis on hair removal, this does not mean hairless smooth skin is not valued. For example, Wei Luo notes ads that urge "Chinese women to apply moisturizing lotion to protect their smooth and hairless skin, another aspect of the supposed Chinese femininity, which Western women particularly admire." [45] Certainly hair removal spans ethnicity, and nonwhite celebrities, such as Naomi Campbell and Vanessa Williams, are reported as extolling the Brazilian wax.[46] Further, in a study of pubic hair grooming among low-income Hispanic, non-Hispanic black, and non-Hispanic white women, it was concluded that "demographically diverse women are engaging in various grooming behaviours."[47] Taken together it seems that hair removal transcends "ethnic, racial and regional boundaries."[48] This said, even though visible body hair removal is a global practice, techniques differ, and practices may have different meanings: for instance, threading is largely an Indian hair removal technique, although it is spreading,[49] and in Muslim countries and cultures, female body hair is often removed before marriage and ritually.[50]

In sum, while the evidence is stronger for some features of the ideal than others, there is some evidence for all features. However, and crucially, there is evidence that thinness—the once supposedly knock-down argument against a global beauty ideal—is now globally preferred.

Globally Converging Bodies

In the last section, I argued that some key features of the beauty ideal, as set out in chapter 1, can be regarded as global. Particularly important is the drive to thinness, as this trend marks a rejection of previous cultural preferences for fatter women. In this section, I want to introduce surgery trends to further support the claim that the key features of the beauty ideal are global and to develop the claim that there is a global mean emerging. I will first consider the face and then the body.

The most popular facial surgeries globally are blepharoplasty and rhinoplasty. According to the International Society of Aesthetic Plastic Surgeons (ISAPS) in 2015 there were 1,264,702 operations on the eyelid and 730,287 on the nose.[51] Even given the problems in attaining accurate data (providing data is voluntarily, and there is only data for countries where sufficient numbers of surgeons respond), these figures are dramatic and amount to 20 percent of all reported operations. These data do not include data on Iran or Lebanon, both of which have high numbers of rhinoplasties. Recall that both Beirut and Iran have been termed world capitals of cosmetic surgery, and some figures suggest that as many as 200,000 Iranians undergo rhinoplasty every year.[52] Rhinoplasty operations shape noses in similar ways; they make noses, neat, straightish, and with augmented nose tips. Blepharoplasty puts a crease in the eyelid, which approximately half of East and Southeast Asian women do not have.[53] It makes eyes round and open. This surgery is so common that some regard it as hardly surgery at all.[54] Given that blepharoplasty is the most popular facial cosmetic procedure across people of Chinese descent, and because ISAPS statistics do not include China itself, it is likely that the number of operations is far higher.[55] Increasingly, double eyelid surgery is accompanied by facial surgery to enhance cheek bones and to make the face less "flat."[56] For some, this is regarded as westernization of features; a criticism that has followed surgery from its early use by Jewish women in the United States to reshape their noses.[57] However, in a real sense the ideal is mixed. The "ideal women," as pictured by Chinese women, has both European and Chinese features:

> She has big eyes with double-eyelids, a straight and tall European nose, a small face preferably in the shape of a watermelon seed with a pointy chin, and a fair skin tone. In addition she is also very thin (approximately 20 pounds below average) and tall (3 to 5 inches above average).[58]

To be Western, the flow would all have to be one way, but when it comes to surgery trends this is not the case. While noses and eyes are arguably moving towards a more Western look, other facial features are not. Most obviously, the growth in the popularity of large lips requires changing the features of white women more than those of any other racial groups. The American Society of Plastic Surgeons reports an increase in lip augmentations and states that "lip procedures were part of nearly 9.2 million injection procedures in 2015, a combined increase of more than 1000 percent since 2000."[59] Injectables are now a routine part of many women's beauty routines: fears of the "trout pout" remain in some quarters, but preferences for exceptionally large lips have rendered such fears somewhat outdated. Bigger is increasingly better when it comes to lips. It is not uncommon to read articles giving advice on how to get them, and presenting them as part of standard beauty expectations.[60] The trend to large lips is clear in celebrity culture—again the Kardashians are illustrative—and they are increasingly popular and routine for ordinary women.[61] Even bearing in mind the problems with statistics and the likely under-reporting of such procedures, the number of women engaging in lip enlargement is rising—dramatically. Anecdotally, that bigger lips are now desirable is evident in a number of contexts.[62] The increased popularity of large lips is an example of an intervention used by white women to attain the global mean; blepharoplasty is an intervention used by Asian women; and rhinoplasty is used by women of all racial groups.

In trends for faces then, a global mean can be begun to be discerned: Large round eyes, cheek bones, smallish-straightish noses, and plump lips. Everywhere the removal of wrinkles dominates; and Botox remains the most popular procedure according to ISAPS, at 38.4 percent of nonsurgical procedures; and hyaluronic acid to smooth wrinkles, is second, at 23.8 percent.[63] Together, this is a total of 7,492,838 procedures. Given that these statistics include only procedures carried out by surgeons, and that Botox can be bought over the internet and injected by almost anyone, the likelihood is that the actual figures are far higher. Taken together, this rise in antiwrinkle, youth-mimicking procedures suggests that firmness, smoothness, and youth are globally desirable. With the exception of the very few, treatments never aim to make us look droopy, haggard, blemished, bumpier, or older.[64] In addition, studies show that there is "significant agreement among people of different races and different cultures about which faces they consider beautiful."[65] As Kathy Davis puts it, "the Benetton ideal reigns supreme."[66]

If we turn to the body, again convergence can be seen. The most popular surgeries globally are breast implants and liposuction: breast augmentations account for over 15 percent of cosmetic procedures, and in 2015 there were estimated to be 1,488,992 operations (if you add breast lifts to this figure, the operations to produce round firm breasts rise to over 2,000,000).[67] The four most popular surgeries on the body are on breasts and to reduce fat (liposuction and abdominoplasty), and together they account for 43.1 percent of all cosmetic surgery.[68] The popularity of these operations speaks to the dominance of the thinness-with-curves ideal and to the importance of firmness. Only the young have firm and pert breasts, and to maintain pert round breasts over time surgery is required, especially if you give birth and breastfeed. The demand for round pert breasts is global (the top countries for which we have figures for breast augmentation are the United States, Brazil, Mexico, Germany, South Korea, Columbia, France, India, Italy); similarly with buttock augmentations and lifts. While procedures on buttocks make up a small percentage of global surgical procedures (only 3 percent), the growth in their popularity might be the first indicator of an increasing need to meet the thinness-with-curves ideal.[69] In 2014 in the United States, 11,505 buttock augmentations with fat-grafting operations were performed and 1, 863 buttock implants; these were so rare in 2000 that there are no comparator statistics.[70] In 2015 14,705 operations were reported, a 28 percent rise from 2014.[71] In 2000 there were only 1,356 buttock-lifts, 3,505 in 2014 and 4,767 in 2015. That is a rise of 36 percent in a year, and since 2000 a rise of 252 percent. Therefore, while only a very small percentage of people are currently having operations to create round and lifted buttocks, the increasing popularity does suggest the type of ideal body that is desired. It is likely that far more are seeking to attain round pert buttocks by exercise and body-contorting clothing than are engaging in surgery. Thus, although small, the surgery trends do point to a converging ideal. An ideal that requires large firm pert bottoms and large pert breasts requires extensive body work, usually surgery, irrespective of racial group.[72]

Surgery trends offer some support to the claim that thinness, firmness, smoothness, and youth, are globally desirable, and they provide further evidence for convergence in both faces and bodies. Again, this does not mean there are no differences: for example, some cultures place more emphasis on the body than the face.[73] Further, the ideal women comes in a variety of forms, she can be cute, girly, athletic, powerful, sexy, dominant, subservient, sweet, caring, and so on, and different forms are preferred in different places.[74] But irrespective of type she is always thin, young, and firm, with smooth, glowing, luminous, and hairless skin. These features are converging. Indeed, the practice of surgery itself might enhance such conversion, as there is a "surgical look" that emerges in those who have had cosmetic surgery. As Jones notes, "no matter what the intentions of its recipients the end effect is often that they share a similar look."[75]

Global Golden Skin

A further instance in which trends towards a global mean can arguably be detected are in the general preference for golden or bronze-glowing skin. Making arguments about skin tone, as if all that is going on is beauty or appearance related, is highly problematic, but nonetheless there are emerging preferences for skin tone, which again suggest convergence. Many, by no means all, seek a mid-range skin tone and engage in all kinds of risky and harmful practices in an attempt to attain this global mean.

Darker skin is attained either by tanning or by the application of chemicals and cosmetics. That tanning is harmful and directly leads to cancer is now well documented, and many who have sought to attain the sun-kissed skin of the beach babe or the bronzed goddess have paid the ultimate price.[76] Indoor tanning using sun beds and sunlamps is even more risky, and those who use sun beds, or have ever used sun beds, are at increased and significant risk of developing skin cancer (with the risk of melanoma doubling when a sun bed is first used before age thirty-five).[77] While fake tanning products do not seem to be risky in themselves, it may be that they are used in addition to other forms of tanning rather than instead.[78] As such, even fake tanning may add to the preference for darker, tanned skin and so contribute to the popularity of such practices. Thus, at least amongst those with white skin, whiteness is not usually a desired skin color, but rather a tanned glowing, golden, bronze, or brown is what is sought.[79] The desire of white women (and men) for golden, bronzed or brown skin, is not everywhere same. For instance, following an extensive health campaign—"slip, slop, slap"—Australia has succeeded in making tanned skin less desirable.[80] This said, taken globally, the wish to look golden continues—and the popularly of fake tan, which is an exceptionally involved process for a only few days of color—attests to this.[81]

Skin lightening is perhaps "one of most common forms of potentially harmful body modification practices in the world."[82] Indeed so risky is skin lightening that the WHO regards it as a growing public health risk in parts of Africa, Asia, and Latin America.[83] The use of skin-lightening creams is rising dramatically: projected to reach $19.8 billion dollars by 2018.[84] It is a global phenomenon, and extensive; skin-lightening creams are the best-selling products in the Asian beauty market.[85] The preference for paleness is often given as evidence of a Western ideal; however, paler skin tones have a history of being valued in many places, including, India, Hong Kong, Japan, and Korea, and at least some of this prefigures European imperialism. I suggest that while paler is generally regarded as better, in some contexts, if the trends as a whole are taken together, it is a midtone, a global mean, that is aspired to.

The empirical evidence here is mixed, but there are some instances where skin-lighting cream is used not to look white, nor as pale as possible, but to look brown. For instance, Shirley Tate speaks of the "browning," with a heritage in Jamaican dancehall, but now prominent in the UK; " 'browning' is ultimate fashion accessory in terms of skin or arm candy."[86] The aim is not whiteness, but the brown of Halle Berry and Beyoncé Knowles, and Tate wonders whether it is the mixed aspects that make brown so attractive: "perhaps brown is as positively viewed in the USA, UK and the Caribbean because it is a skin shade that can be achieved by either lightening or tanning."[87] Similar attitudes to skin tone are evident in Brazil, and Edmonds states that in Brazil "unlike in many parts of the world where lightness of skin tone is fetishized, in Brazil *brown* is beautiful."[88] Indeed more than this, white, in at least some form is undesirable, and he cites a study of beach life by Patricía Farias who claims that "bronzed (*bronzeado*) occupies the top position in a hierarchy of skin tones. It contrasts favorably with 'black' and 'white' or 'red as shrimp' ('the punishment of whites who try to become brown'). The capacity to become brown marks Brazilian-ness, health and beauty."[89] However, as Edmonds's nuanced and thoughtful work shows, this preference for brownness and valoriz-ing of "the mixed" takes place in a postcolonial context where racial hierarchies remain: brownness may be preferred, but black is still stigmatized and "good appearance" in job ads means lightness.[90] In part due to a complicated and discriminatory race history, Bra-zilians tend to think in colors or types rather than racial groups—although Edmonds documents some emergence of black identity politics—meaning that a term such as *Moreno* can mean either brown skin or brunette.

However, while there is some evidence for a golden, bronzed or brown skin tone, there are other cultures where it is still the case that lighter is always better. For instance, this would seem to be the case in India, China, and Japan. Again empirical evidence is useful but limited. For, while it is the case that pale skin is desirable in these contexts (consider models and actresses), when considered in the global context, these skin tones are not as light as white skin, and in fact fall in the midrange of the global spectrum. This is, of course, not a conclusive argument, since it could be that lightening products can achieve only so much and that if further whiteness could be achieved it would be. Moreover, even if it is the case that the skin tone that is desired is golden or brown, this does not, as we will return to in the next section, remove the racial, gendered, and classed hierarchies that shadow preferences for skin tone. Indeed, we must be wary when focusing on the global ideal not to obscure the hierarchies of privilege. Meeta Rani Jha puts this well when she discusses Miss Davuluri, a relatively dark-skinned Indian American, becoming Miss America in 2014.[91] This was hailed by some as proof of inclusion and the widening of beauty norms; yet Jha argues that "America seemingly values multiculturalism, diversity and individ-ualism, while the social reality of discrimination and institutional-ized oppression remain untouched."[92] Globally, it is white women who dominate the acting and beauty industries and, with the exception of Grace Jones, the black women who do succeed are rarely very dark—think of Tyra Banks, Naomi Campell, Selpa Shetti, and Aishwayray Raiand. Thus, the inclusion of a small number of women of color can be token and illusory,[93] or othering and titillating, invoking exotic beauty.[94] Moreover, it can serve to confirm and reinforce racist and sexist stereotypes.[95]

In sum, with regard to skin color the evidence is mixed. It may be, as is already the case in Brazil, that traditional racial hierarchies—in which white is right—exist alongside preferences for a more mixed racial ideal in terms of skin tone, and the valuing of a brown, bronze, or golden ideal. The valuing of brown in at least some cultures where skin-lightening is present, coupled with the rejection of white skin amongst Western and white-skinned cultures, is enough to question the simple hierarchy where paler is always better, and palest is best. The evidence is enough to raise the question whether other factors are in play. Yet, while uncomfortable issues of race need to be addressed and preferences should not be taken at face value, global convergence in preferences for a midrange skin color is further evidence of an emerging global ideal.

Global Race and Class Hierarchies

Beauty is saturated with issues of race, class, and ethnicity, and nowhere more prominently than when it comes to skin tone. As already discussed, race is primary in the literature surrounding body shape and weight, and some account for different shape and weight preferences on grounds of class and socioeconomic status.[96] Separating out the influence and interaction of race, class, and gender in this context is impossible, and would fail to take account of the interaction and deep intersection of such features. Thus, while I wish to suggest that it may be that a global mean is emerging, I do not wish to play down the politics of skin tone, or pretend this is all about individual preference; indeed as I will argue later, very little in beauty is about individual choice.

The continuing preference for lighter skin in contexts of darker skin—and the parallel exclusion and discrimination against those with darker skins—has to be understood in a context of historical colonialism, neocolonialism, imperialism, and slavery.[97] There is no simple way to analyze these currents of power. Some argue that seeking to lighten skin is a rejection of racial group membership and even use the language of self-hatred.[98] Without a doubt, the connection of whiteness and paleness with beauty and goodness continues to perpetuate racist constructions of black women (and men).[99] Yet using the language of self-hate, for those who skin lighten or hair straighten can serve to alienate and blame. In addition, it can exclude those who do not have the required features of "authentic blackness."[100] The upshot of such discourse is likely to end in women-blaming; that is, blaming women for lightening their skin (or straightening their hair) as a betrayal of racial identity. Women are pulled in both ways. As a recent study from Tanzania documents, women are not unreflectively engaging, they both "acknowledge the need to internalize Black beauty" and are responding to the "the national and international pressures to look White."[101] The asymmetry is clear: while white women may get criticized for tanning on health grounds, they do not get criticized on race grounds for seeking to become darker.

As well as issues of racial hierarchy, there are also issues of class and caste, which operate across the very varied contexts where skin lightening is a common practice, where lighter skin indicates higher wealth and status and is believed to improve job and marriage prospects.[102] Lighter skin is more likely to deliver the goods of the good life, such that Margaret Hunter has termed whiteness as "form of racial capital."[103] And indeed the marketing of lightening creams plays on this with the "Fair & Lovely" website describing their mission in the following way:

> Fair & Lovely has reflected a Women's Dreams for the past 40 years. This is a brand, which has championed the deepest ambitions and desires of women. Throughout its history, Fair & Lovely has inspired women to go for their dreams, even if they were at odds with what society expected them to do. In the 80's, when society expected women to marry mostly via arranged mar-

riages, Fair & Lovely gave them hope that women could marry by choice. In the 90s, when women desired not just marriage but also an equal partnership, Fair & Lovely inspired them to believe that this was possible. In the 2000s, when society believed that a woman's place was at home, Fair & Lovely encouraged her to choose her own career. And today, when despite much progress, women still don't get equal opportunities and society continues to impose barriers for women, Fair & Lovely will give women the confidence to overcome their own hesitations & fears to achieve their true potential.[104]

However, while there is no question that there is a long history of skin lightening, which is deeply entwined with racial and class discrimination, it is important to be wary of oversimplifying the meanings of color hierarchies.[105] My aim is not to ignore this history, but rather to suggest that, in the current global context, such racial histories are playing out in interesting ways. In terms of skin tone and surgery, what is going on, as I will argue in the next section, is not just westernization and (neo-)imperialism—although some of this remains—but the development of a global mean. All racial groups are inadequate and require change and intervention to attain the ideal. If this is correct, in the move towards a global ideal, we must not miss the patterns of change, and succumb (as so much beauty rhetoric suggests we should) to the notion that this is all about individual choice. Power hierarchies remain, but they are complex and intersect, and are not simply about Western dominance. In addition, as I will argue later, we should avoid blaming individuals for what they do and do not do. We cannot address structural injustices and communal norms by calling on individual women to simply resist.

Global or Western?

The extent of skin lighting across cultures and ethnicities where dark skin is prevalent is a primary reason why so many argue that there is a global beauty ideal emerging that is Western;[106] these include many of the studies that I have drawn on.[107] Similar arguments are made about the drive to thinness, with some suggesting that the spread of eating disorders amongst African college students "might indicate a shift to a new African body ideal closely aligned to Western ideals."[108] In the final section of this chapter, I will argue that while I agree with the claims that a global beauty ideal is emerging, I do not think it is a simple imposition or adoption of a Western ideal. By contrast I suggest that the emerging global ideal is a mixed ideal, which promotes a mix of racial and classed features, along with the ubiquitous promotion of youthfulness. It applies to all women and promises equal opportunity success for all who attain the ideal, and it pretends that structural injustices—of gender, class, and race—are things of the past. While whiteness is desired by those who use skin-lightening creams, it is not mere whiteness that is desired, but a certain type of skin tone. Skin texture is at least as important as color, and the color that is desirable is not white but golden or bronzed.

In addition to skin tone, surgery trends have been cited as evidence of the emergence of a Western ideal. For example, the Asian trends in facial surgery are given as examples of the westernization of global beauty. Big eyes with eyelid creases are standard features of Caucasian faces, and some of the features that Asian women regard as beautiful are not obviously Asian. However, some reject the westernization claim and look to local influences. For instance, Hwang suggests that "the impetus to pursue cosmetic eyelid surgery for Chinese patients may be the desire to look more spirited and energetic—not necessarily to look more 'Westernized.' "[109] Indeed, as Jones points out, if around half of women of Chinese descent are born with double eyelids, then this is a local, as well as, Western feature.[110] Likewise, Wei Luo reports that Chinese heritage places importance on the eyes and the aim of surgery is a distinctive Chinese femininity.[111] Ruth Holliday and colleagues similarly argue that this is not a Western look but a distinctively "Korean look."[112] The look emerged in the local context as surgeons adapted their American-learned techniques to be more appropriate for the faces they found themselves working on. Thus Holliday and colleagues suggest:

> There is evidence that surgical fashions are popularised via (*Hallyu*) and K-pop, which, combined with Japanese Manga, have popularised a particular facial shape for women and men in many countries in East Asia. Narrow jawlines, wide eyes and augmented nose tips create a "Korean look" whose procedures Korean surgeons have developed into an international recognised specialism, and for which aspirant youths from neighbouring China as well as those from the Korean diaspora are more than willing to travel.[113]

Without a doubt, local context is crucial in determining what is popular, what is preferred, and what is regarded as normal. This is more than simply the negotiating of Western norms; as they enculturate, local norms are challenging, shaping, and contributing to the emerging global ideal. However, rejecting the claim that global beauty is westernizing, with "all flows pointing in one direction,"[114] which both Holliday and colleagues and I do, does not necessarily entail the rejection of all globalizing claims.[115] While I reject the Western claim, I argue that beauty ideals are converging, the range of what is acceptable is narrowing, and a global ideal is emerging.[116]

In sum then, the global ideal is mixed, all racial groups require help to attain it, and convergence is happening: thin and slim, with breasts and butt curves, smooth, luminous and glowing skin, and large eyes and lips. This ideal is one that no racial group can embody without some "help." White women are just as unable to attain the beauty ideal without intervention as Asian and black woman are. Plump lips are not "natural" for most white women and require fillers, and large breasts (often) and large buttocks (nearly always) require intervention for white women. Asian women require intervention in faces (eyes, lips, and face shape), and (nearly always) for pert bums and breasts. Black women (stereotypically) have the bums required, but (often) require surgery for large breasts and certainly require skin lightening. And nearly everyone requires work to be (or to stay) thin, firm, and young. This is not to say that the demands fall to the same extent on all racial groups: "while a blue-eyed blond with cellulite and a large nose may require a great amount of effort to become a standard beauty it is not nearly comparable to that required of a voluptuous black woman."[117] Likewise the expectation of racial beauty carries its own demands, and failing to meet the stereotypical standards of racialized beauty, let alone global beauty, can be a source of shame in itself.[118] As such, it would be wrong to suggest that it is equally demanding of all. It is not. All kinds of hierarchies and power networks remain—most obviously, but not exclusively, those of race and class. Nonetheless, a mixed ideal is emerging. As Tate says, a "new beauty category" is in the ascendency, a "Black/white "mixed race"/racially ambiguous"[119] ideal, "adhering to white feminine slenderness allied with Black voluptuousness."[120] This is not westernization, but convergence.

Conclusion

In this chapter I have argued that dominance of the beauty ideal may extend as far as the global. I have argued that, while not yet fully established, trends are converging and there is evidence of a global mean. Finally, I have argued that this is not simply a Western or imperialist ideal. While I have sympathy with such arguments, particularly the way they highlight race, class, and other hierarchies of power, they are not enough to explain what is happening in the current global context. In contrast, I have argued that the emerging global beauty ideal is effectively a mixed ideal, a global mean, towards which beauty trends are converging. In this brave new world, no racial group, and perhaps no individual, is good enough without help. Only time will tell whether, and the extent to which, this is correct, but already when we look across Hollywood, Bollywood, and Nollywood, the images are the same.[121] Even in Tamil movies, where more curvaceous actresses were once preferred, very thin actresses now star.[122] Likewise magazine images are global, and thin models are globally prominent; with local differences expressed less in body type and more in clothes and presentation, for instance with more or less sexy images.[123] While there are all kinds of reasons to suggest that these overtly centralized and globalized instances of culture are not representative, they might still be indicative of trends. For example, in a study of two beauty contests in Nigeria, one national, and one international, little difference was found in terms of the desired weight and shape.[124] Rather local differences were asserted in the focus on local and more modest dress and in the inclusion of cooking skills. As Bordo points out, young Nigerian women, like nearly all women, are dieting and exercising to become *lepa*, thin.[125]

4

Routine, Special, and Extreme

While the last two chapters considered the dominance of the emerging beauty ideal, this chapter will consider its demandingness. How demanding the beauty ideal is matters with regard to whether, and to what extent, it is morally troubling. A globally dominant ideal that functions as an ethical ideal but is relatively undemanding might not be morally problematic. Whether such an ideal could be an ethical one is questionable, but in any case an ethical ideal that is also dominant and demanding is morally troubling, as these features are mutually reinforcing. Together they produce a greedy ideal that expands both its scope and its hold: as you begin to engage in practices so you begin commit to the ideal and believe it will deliver, leading you to engage in more practices, and so to value beauty more, and so on. Yet, despite the vast amount of discussion about beauty—in media, social media, and in daily conversations—the increasing demands of beauty are little commented on. Incrementally, almost stealthily, the demands of beauty rise, and practices that were previously rare, occasional treats, or exceptional measures gradually become regarded as routine. Only when engagement is mapped and what practices entail is considered in some detail does the increase in terms of what is demanded, as well as who it is demanded of, emerge. Increased demandingness, coupled with increased dominance and scope, results in a more exacting and punishing beauty ideal.

In this chapter I focus largely on Western practices, primarily because this is where most evidence is found, although—as argued in the last chapter—there is some evidence to show that trends are global. Moreover, that many, globally, are not able to engage sufficiently to meet the rising demands is an issue of affordability and availability, not aspiration. For example, the Indian school girl who seeks to emulate her favorite Bollywood star in ways she can afford (for example, dieting and using skin-lightening cream) might well engage in further procedures if she could afford to. The evidence suggests that when procedures are available and affordable they are taken up. For instance, the rise in lip injectables in young women is one example from the United States and UK. Poverty is no barrier to aspiring to engage, and that there is a wish to engage is evidenced by affordable engagement (even if this is simply maintaining thinness and purchasing skin-lightening cream). Thus even though only some are able to maximally engage, demands can be shown to be rising based on the evidence of engagement to the extent that is possible for individuals in their particular contexts.

I argue that what is required to meet minimal standards has increased and is likely to continue to increase. Moreover what is regarded as routine—practices that are often not minimal in their demands—is also rising, and if trends continue, what is routine will expand dramatically. Demands increase both in terms of what is required to meet minimal standards, and in terms of pressure to go beyond minimal standards. Gradually, women find themselves doing more, and wanting to do even more, and perhaps watching their daughters want to do even more than this, without realizing that the demands are rising or consciously choosing to expand their routine beauty practices. It should be clear by now that my claim is not that the demands everywhere are the same but rather that demands everywhere are increasing and, as beauty ideals converge, demands become more similar and some demands, in some version or other, are likely to apply everywhere. What is normal in some cultures may not be, or not yet be, normal in others. For example, in both Brazil and Korea cosmetic surgery (of different body parts) is now effectively normal and routine, and while it is becoming normalized in other places, it is not yet routine in the way that weight management and the application of lotions and potions generally is. Furthermore, local variations, as the last chapter emphasized, mean that what features are prioritized will differ; for example, pale skin over thinness or vice versa, or different preferences for breast size and shape, and perhaps with regard to how natural or how surgical breasts look (with some demographics preferring a surgical look). In addition, there are individual constraints in terms of what is affordable and accessible in a particular context. Thus, the claim is not that all must do the same in all contexts—demands manifest differently, and different features of the ideal are prioritized—but over time and across cultures the demands are rising. Furthermore, as argued in the last chapter, the demands are, when taken collectively as general trends, moving broadly in the same direction.

In this chapter, I will track the demandingness of the beauty ideal. I will begin by setting out what, at first glance, might be thought of as different types of practices, distinguishing between routine practices, occasional practices, and extreme practices. I then consider five possible criteria by which to define routine practices: first, necessary for minimum standards; second, frequency; third, requires third-party assistance; fourth, time commitment; and fifth, risk. I suggest that on investigation none of these criteria do in fact demarcate routine practices from other types of beauty practices. Indeed the only one that holds is "necessary for minimal standards," but as minimal standards are movable, this criterion is not useful for demarcating one type of practice from another. Accordingly, routine, occasional, and extreme practices are not distinct, and the language of routine serves not to demarcate but to hide the extent to which practices are demanding. The fact that the rising demands are obscured matters, as it helps to account for why increasingly punishing regimes are not only tolerated but embraced with little critique. Using the example of body hair removal, and to a lesser extent other routine practices, I argue that what is minimally required is rising, making the contemporary beauty ideal increasingly demanding. I then suggest that the lack of clear distinctions between routine and other practices, in part, accounts for the gradual increase in demands. Further, the collapsing of routine into minimal is convenient, even pernicious, as it makes it much easier for the demands of beauty to surreptitiously increase. I argue that the demandingness, and likely future demandingness, of the ideal is particularly morally troubling in light of the growing dominance of the ideal and its increasingly ethical nature. In the final section of the chapter, I return to thinness and slimness, and explore what it means for an ideal to be increasingly demanding if such demands are rarely met.

Categorizing Routine and Extreme

The practices required by the beauty ideal to meet minimal standards, to be good enough, are extensive; and even minimal engagement may not be possible for those who lack funds or access to procedures. To explore what practices are minimally necessary, let me being with the practices of "routine maintenance"; I will argue that while considered routine there is little minimal about many of these practices. Routine practices include the daily application of lotions and potions. These have to be purchased and then used in the correct layered order; in itself a costly and time-consuming business, which has to be learned. For example, a standard beauty routine might be to maintain skin health using lotions, which may include the use of products in turn: cleanser, toner, serum, moisturizer, eye cream, BB/CC cream, and primer. Having prepared and protected the skin, you are then ready to apply make-up. The daily application of make-up is done by very many women, and again, requires the application of products in the correct way. Putting on "your face" usually requires the use of some or all of these products—foundation, powder, blusher, eye shadow, eye liner, mascara, lipstick—sometimes less, sometimes more, and perhaps most for the contoured "natural look."[1] In the UK in 2006 apparently the average women's make up routine was eight steps compared to

27 in 2016.[2] Other daily practices are hair care and styling; hair-removal (from the body and the face); and the oiling, creaming, de-odorizing, and re-odorizing, of the body. And then there is the complex daily issue of what to wear. You must buy and wear the right clothes for the season, your profession, and special occasions (with new clothes largely bought for style reasons rather than for necessity). You must also "accessorize" these clothes correctly, with the appropriate jewelry, shoes, bags, and coats. The list goes on. And while clothes and make-up fashions differ, the need to conform to the fashion of the day does not. Very prescribed standards need to be met; for example, in some contexts you can wear black lipstick to "make a statement," but you are not likely to paint your forehead sky blue pink with yellow stripes and purple dots.[3]

Every step of this process must be learned, and successfully mastering these practices requires the development of a not insignificant skill set. You need to learn to buy the right products: an increasingly demanding and individualized process as you buy for your skin type (oily, t-zone, dry, or sensitive); for your lifestyle (high maintenance and glamorous, fun and flirty, outdoorsy, grungy, and so on); and for your budget (while more expensive products are presented as superior, made with more costly ingredients or developed by more skilled and dedicated scientists (and here the lines between beauty products and medical products blur), alternatives are available for those on a budget). Similarly, there is a skill set to be mastered when it comes to dress: you need to learn your body shape, your colors, your style. Do you follow fashion and change your wardrobe with the changing collections of the season? Or is your style "classic" and your "capsule wardrobe" made up of investment pieces that will always be in style?

Anyone familiar with teen and women's magazines, makeover programs, or simply who engages in conversations with women in the staff room, at the water cooler, over coffee or a drink is likely to find at least some of this familiar. Beauty language has to be gradually learnt by women (and increasingly men), and the fact that it is so familiar is in itself testament to just how embedded in daily life and conversations the jargon of beauty practices is. Mastering the language and the skill sets for engagement in such routine beauty practices requires a significant amount of work. It begins young, with young girls already worrying about hair color, and which colors suit them and what type of girls they are ("I'm not a girly girl," says my nine-year-old, when choosing to wear skinny jeans to a party).

The ability to consume is defining, and there is significant pressure to engage to the extent you can afford across demographics. No matter what your resources, the message is that you too can, and the implication is should, engage in the daily and routine tasks of beauty. Those without resources, it is suggested, can still devote significant time deciding which products they can afford—either alone or sharing them with other women. For example, Angela McCraken considers beauty in Mexico and reports how cosmetic products and knowledge are shared by women, particularly, though not exclusively, at the time of coming of age.[4] Purchasing beauty products (saving for them and deciding on them) are key activities, and the sector is growing with direct sales being the most important mechanism for the sale of beauty products in Mexico.[5] Beauty practices are aspirational, reinforcing the message that engagement is desirable and pleasurable and that these products and practices are worth hard-earned cash.[6] It is worth repeating that aspiration is as important as actual engagement when it comes to the power of the beauty ideal.

Going beyond routine daily practices of grooming and beautifying are occasional practices. These are not regarded as required to meet minimal standards but are optional and often desirable. For some, these practices are fairly routine (in that they are done frequently and are regarded as required). However, for many they are not, they are not done on a daily basis, and they usually require a third party to administer them: a hairdresser; beautician; manicurist and so on. The types of practices that are included in this category are facials or spa treatments, manicures and pedicures, semipermanent make-up, spray tans, hair or body treatments. Other practices that require third parties, and that fall between routine and exceptional, are nonsurgical (sometimes termed noninvasive) practices, such as, the injection of Botox, dermal fillers, laser treatments, and peels. Others which are perhaps slightly more invasive, and to some extreme, include the vampire face- and breast-lifts, and threadlifts.[7]

Moving beyond occasional treats are extreme practices; these are usually done rarely and are exceptional. The most obvious beauty practices that fall into this class are cosmetic surgery. They are exceptional in that even for repeat users surgery is not routine, but deliberated over, seen as significant, and formally consented to.[8] Even when the risks of surgery are minimized, undergoing such procedures is not routine or required in the way that practices of make-up and hair care are, although in some places, such as South Korea and Brazil, surgery might effectively be required if it can be afforded or accessed. Undergoing surgery is a significant commitment: there are physical costs, pain and risk, costs of time, choosing a surgeon, scheduling surgery (which includes re-organizing private and public commitments), and recovery time, and financial costs. Engaging in surgery is a statement that appearance matters. Even those who keep surgery secret usually tell close friends and relatives, and increasingly people are open about having surgery. For example, in Iran nose bandages are worn openly and with pride.[9]

Some surgeries are more extreme than others. For example, blepharoplasty takes an hour for the top eyelid, patients go home the same day, and the patient can usually return to work in a week (although full recovery takes longer).[10] By contrast liposuction takes up to three hours, requires an overnight stay, followed by the wearing of support corsets and compression garments, and it might take six months for the area "to settle."[11] To take a further example, breast surgery, the most common surgery, is less risky than the less common buttock-lift:

> in breast augmentation the surgical planes are more easily defined which makes it easier to make a pocket for the implant and this has been established practice for nearly 50 years. The scars are generally under the breast and not under any tension so they tend to heal very well and not stretch as the weight of the breast

pushes the margins of the wound together unlike the buttocks. The breasts are generally supported much of the time in a brassiere and not routinely subject to the significant pressure resulting from being sat upon. The dissection for a buttock implant has been in evolution and it is only over the last 10 years or so that a consistent subfascial approach has been developed. There is also much less margin for error regarding the dissection of the pocket and size, shape and type of implant if a satisfactory result is to be achieved. The patients have to be careful sitting for several weeks and their bottom is numb for about 4 months which can lead to inadvertent injury. Finally there is the risk of infection as the lower end of the incisions are within 4cm of the anal margin and the site of surgery is difficult to clean completely.[12]

All surgery with implants carries risks that nonimplant surgery does not, and there have been long discussions about the risks of implant seepage and rupture.[13] Yet breast surgery is routine in medical parlance in ways that buttock implants are not.

Defining Routine and Extreme

At first the five criteria—first, necessary to meet minimum standards; second, frequency; third, third-party assistance; fourth, time; and fifth, risk—seem useful for distinguishing between types of procedure and for defining practices. Many routine practices tend to be done by ourselves and frequently, often daily, and are not risky or time consuming. Occasional practices, are less frequent than most routine practices and none are daily; they always require third-party assistance; they often require significant amounts of time, and perhaps "time out" (whether "time out" to engage in the practice or recovery time), and finally, at least some of them are risky. If we turn to extreme or exceptional procedures: first, in most contexts, they are not regarded as necessary to meet minimum presentation standards, though in some contexts some are; second, frequency, exceptional practices are not done daily, and while they may be done periodically, this cannot be said to be frequent; third, third parties are always required; fourth, time and time out are essential; and, fifth, risk, these are risky practices.

Yet, further investigation, suggests that differentiating and defining practices using these criteria are problematic. For example, are occasional practices always less risky than extreme practices? The Royal College of Surgeons categorizes nonsurgical practices, as less risky (a level of risk compared to surgery that is level 1a and 1b); such practices are defined as "usually non-permanent/reversible, day case, local anaesthetic, (if any). These include Botox, dermal Fillers and chemical peels."[14] Yet in the Keogh review, which will be returned to in chapter 6, it was complications from nonsurgical procedures that surgeons reported seeing most frequently, and nearly two-thirds of these complications were irreversible.[15] If reversibility is instrumental in defining risk, then such practices are risky, and the line between nonsurgical and surgical procedures is less distinct than supposed. Thus while all surgery is risky, some surgeries are less risky than others, and nonsurgical procedures may, according to some criteria, be more risky than some surgery. Furthermore, some very routine practices, such as skin lightening and tanning, might be the most risky of all practices. So extreme practices might in general carry more risks, but the extent of the risks varies. For instance, some breast enhancements might be more extreme, in the sense of carrying more risk in terms of side effects and long-term risks of morbidity and even mortality, than others. In some cases, depending on size and type, they might also be regarded as more extreme aesthetically, an attempt to be abnormal rather than normal.[16] Although, as discussed, breast operations in general may be less risky than buttock operations.

Given this and despite the assumptions, especially by policy makers, that beauty practices are of very different types, drawing a clear line between what are routine, occasional, and exceptional practices is more difficult than it first appears. For some, the routine practices set out in the first section of the chapter will already seem extreme. There are some women who engage in very few beauty practices, seeing them as superfluous, time-wasting, and self-indulgent. For the woman who washes with soap and only uses moisturizer when her dry skin is sore, using cleanser or dedicated eye cream is extreme: an unnecessary measure, beyond that which is required for minimal grooming and presentation. Likewise, a woman who has never dyed her hair may be bewildered by the apparent compulsion that many women feel to maintain hair color and touch up roots every six weeks. Conversely, for the woman who has Botox every six months, a nip or tuck once in a while, visits her dermatologist once a month, and religiously follows a skin-care regime, all of the procedures (including those that for many are exceptional) are routine, in the sense of required for minimal beauty standards; simply to be normal. On further investigation, the five criteria fail to distinguish between practices clearly or definitively. Some routine practices require third-party intervention and time out, and some occasional practices carry significant risk, and all practices (or none) can be regarded as necessary to meet minimal standards. If we interrogate these criteria further, none of them are decisive in distinguishing between what is routine and what goes beyond this.

Let us consider hair cutting and dyeing (and for some women styling). First, it is a routine practice in that it is regarded as necessary and required to meet minimum standards. It is not regarded as an occasional treat, though it may be enjoyable, and certainly it is not an exceptional practice. Second, it is not frequent, if this means daily, but it is done periodically and relatively frequently. Third, third-party assistance is often required, perhaps usually required; hair may be done at home, though usually with help from friends or family. But more often, and if affordable, hair cutting and dying are done by experts in the salon. Fourth, time out is required, and this is often a significant amount of time; and the demands of hair styling for some groups are particularly high. Fifth, hair dying and styling is not generally risky, but there are well documented reactions to chemicals as well as instances of injuries, such as burns from hair-styling and hair loss from weaves or overprocessing. Hair dying and styling then are regarded as routine in some very obvious ways, but they are not demarcated by the criteria that are associated with routine. Hair cutting and styling are done frequently but not daily, they always require third-party assistance and time out, and yet are the epitome of routine.

That the criteria fail to effectively sort practices into those that are routine and those that are exceptional repeats across practices. Some practices that are extreme according to some definitions (in that they happen occasionally or require third parties to perform them) are nevertheless done routinely (in that they are regarded as minimal and required). For instance, consider cosmetic dentistry. It is not frequent (it is a single process that results in permanent fixing of the teeth): it always requires expert third-party assistance; it takes considerable time and time out; and it is risky, painful, and often surgical. Cosmetic dentistry, particularly teeth straightening then, is regarded as routine only because it is required to meet minimal standards; on every other criterion it is not routine, but extreme. Some would argue that cosmetic dentistry is not cosmetic at all, but done for health reasons, or correction reasons; however, perfectly straight teeth are not necessary for health.[17] Therefore, while regarded as routine on one axis, and sufficiently so that it is done routinely on children, in most ways it is not.

Considered across the wide range of beauty practices and procedures, "routine" and "extreme" do not denote clearly distinct types of practices. So while this terminology might be demarcating something, it is not clearly differentiating types of practices. Routine does not mean, as it often implies, daily and relatively undemanding grooming practices, done to ourselves at home. All the practices discussed go beyond what is necessary for health, grooming, and presentation. Given this, the terminology of routine—with its implications of relatively trivial, undemanding, frequent, and required—merits attention. The only definition of routine that holds throughout is as a place holder for what is minimal (although which of the practices actually fall into this category differ from context to context and from woman to woman). If this is correct, then routine in fact refers to the practices that are required for minimal standards, just to be normal or good enough.

In practice, routine is used in this way, and working on this topic has led me to the rather unscientific conclusion that where the line is drawn is simply what we do, or would like to do, ourselves. What is regarded as extreme is what we do not currently do, would not consider doing, or could not imagine wanting to do. Furthermore, the practices that fall into these categories change over time and fairly quickly, but, and importantly, nearly always in the same direction. Practices that were once extreme or occasional become regarded as routine, normal, and required. While the line of what is necessary to meet minimal requirements is blurred—it depends on context (race, class, age, profession, relationship status and friendship groups all impact upon what is considered minimal and routine)—as the beauty ideal expands, what is minimally demanded becomes greater than what was previously demanded.

The Demandingness of Routine

While the terminology of routine does not demarcate types of practices, it does make it easier to accept the increasing demands of beauty without recognizing the extent of these demands. It encourages us to disregard the increasing costs of time, money, and effort; effort includes intellectual effort to learn the language and the skills and emotional effort to commit to attaining a normal, better, or more perfect me. To explore the rise in demands, I will consider body hair removal. I will argue that while such a practice is regarded as minimal and, depending on definition, routine (shaving for instance is frequent, done at home by ourselves, and does not require time out), what is necessary to meet this minimal standard is demanding, and increasingly so. The claim that minimal standards are more demanding is a general one. It should not be read as claiming that all individuals everywhere feel compelled to meet these standards. The claim is about general trends and patterns; that in very many places what is required to meet minimal standards of beauty is expanding. In highlighting the trend towards more demanding minimal standards of beauty, I invite us to imagine what the future will look like if trends continue, especially in the context of a globally dominant beauty ideal. The changes to norms of body hair are dramatic and have happened over a relatively short period of time. Given this, these norms are particularly useful when it comes to showing the rise of minimum standards and the way a practice can very quickly become required. Once this happens then, non-engagement becomes "not an option," noncompliance is policed, and failure to comply is regarded as moral failure, which evokes judgment from others and shame and disgust in and with the self.[18]

Body hair includes hair on legs, arms, underarms, and face, and pubic hair. Sometimes visible body hair refers to all pubic hair (as this hair is seen by sexual partners), and sometimes it refers only to the hair that can be seen when wearing a swimming costume or underwear. While, as always, there are some differences in norms of hairlessness, it is now the case that leg hair and underarm hair are regarded as unacceptable in nearly all contexts. This is a very clear change over a short period of time. Only a generation ago, it was far more acceptable to leave visible leg and underarm hair; indeed underarm hair in some contexts was regarded as a sign of sexual liberation and sexiness.[19] Younger women are increasingly removing at least some pubic hair, and nearly complete removal is becoming more common and associated with cleanliness and respect for sexual partners.[20]

The changes in practices of body hair removal illustrate not only the rise in minimum beauty standards, but also the ethical nature of ideal. This is clearly illustrated in a study by Breanne Fahs regarding body hair, which shows that the discourse surrounding body hair presents as one of choice, but further investigation suggests not only that body hair removal is required, but that shame and disgust attach to failure.[21] This study focused on two groups of women: one group was diverse, and women were interviewed about beauty practices generally, including attitudes to body hair; the other group consisted of gender studies students who grew body hair and documented their lived-experience. Most women in both groups initially regarded it as a choice to remove body hair, and one that was relatively trivial. However, while the first group stated that not re-moving visible body hair was a choice open to them, it was not a choice that these women actually made, and their language "often conveyed judgements and negativity toward women who did not shave combined with statements about their acceptance of all bod-ies."[22] This is revealing, as to openly express negative judgments shows how strongly these views are held. The choice paradigm and rhetoric, which we will consider in chapter 9, requires that choice trumps. The interviewees understand this and emphasize that they respect all women's choices, but at the same time, and in contradic-tion to claims to respect choice, "disgust toward other women ap-peared frequently, particularly as women constructed body hair as 'dirty' and 'unclean.'"[23] For example, one interviewee stated that visible body hair is "not very attractive on women, but I don't think I make judgements on it. I might just stand ten feet away from them."[24] The judgment happens in the same breath as the endorse-ment of personal choice and a nonjudgmental attitude towards the choices of others. The ethical dimension is clearly evident: "hairy legs and hairy armpits look gross. I think it's gross. It signifies a woman being lazy and not taking care of herself."[25] Failure to re-move body hair is constructed as a moral failing, a moral vice.

Those in the second group (who were gender studies students and therefore presumably at least familiar with feminist critiques of beauty practices and body discipline), found (and often against their better judgment) that growing visible body hair was hard, and many of them "struggled with feeling disgusting, dirty, and sexually unattractive, even when others did not provide that direct feed-back."[26] For example one of the students said:

My legs looked ugly and fat with their hair on. I constantly thought about my gross hair, especially at the gym. Every time I was taking a shower, every time I changed my clothes, it was always on my mind. I couldn't believe how much time I spent thinking about my hair. It was insane![27]

Further, many received negative comments from friends, fam-ily, and lovers. They found noncompliance exceptionally difficult, and they found it uncomfortable to realize this. Moreover, the feelings that attached to noncompliance were intense and of the type we normally associate with moral failure—shame and disgust. Reflection on just how little choice was involved in the growing of body hair was a revelation for these students and particularly useful in highlighting the dominance, demandingness, and ethical nature of the beauty ideal.

The tension between the required nature of body hair removal and the chosen nature of the practice is repeated in other studies. In a particularly revealing passage, Gail Dines reports:

> the female students talked extensively about how much they preferred to have a completely waxed pubic area as it made them feel "clean," "hot," and "well groomed." As they excitedly insisted that they themselves chose to have a Brazilian wax, one student let slip that her boyfriend had complained when she decided to give up on waxing.[28]

As discussion continued, the women talked about a "trick" they use to avoid sex. Because saying "no" is difficult, to avoid sex, they "purposely don't shave or wax as they are getting ready to go out that night so they will feel too embarrassed to participate in hookup sex."[29] The embarrassment attached to having pubic hair or stubble reveals the strength of the current requirement. Thus while the extent to which women remove body hair removal differs (with younger generations typically removing more), the demand to remove significant amounts of visible body hair (at least underarm and lower leg hair) is increasing. It is now the norm to be relatively hairless. In public—at the beach, or the pool, or on a night out—defluffing is regarded as routine, like washing or teeth-cleaning. Moreover not to remove visible body hair is shameful and embarrassing, and those who grow body hair are outside the norm and even considered brave. Indeed, visible body hair is so unusual it has become effectively a political statement; hence campaigns such as "Armpits 4 August."[30]

While the extent of requirements may not be, as yet, extreme, tracking the direction of trends is important. The current requirement could be met in some contexts by routine shaving of legs and underarms, which is relatively undemanding. Alternatively, it could be much more demanding if, say, full arm and pubic hair were also removed, especially by waxing (which requires both third-party assistance and time out). In addition, while not a particularly risky practice, there are some risks of hair removal, and there are no health benefits (making the practice significantly different from hygiene practices like teeth cleaning).[31] Currently, laser and light hair removal are regarded as relatively risk free, although extensive studies have not been undertaken; and it is to be hoped that these are not another miracle cure for hairiness which will turn out to be deadly (as was previous generations' use of X-rays to remove facial hair).[32] But while there are differences with regard to just how much hair is removed—differences that track to race, culture, age, and class—across the board the trend is to more hair removal, and more hair removal is always more demanding than less hair removal.

Other practices that are becoming more demanding over time and that require more to meet minimum standards are the application of make-up, hair dye, and manicured nails. Putting on "your face" is something that many women—though by no means all—do every day (or every working day). (And some who currently do not would if make-up were affordable and appropriate to their lifestyles: recall the Mexican girls and women sharing and saving to buy beauty products.) In many contexts not to put on make-up is not an option: for work, for special occasions, and perhaps just to feel normal. And studies report that in many walks of life make-up increases perceptions of professionalism.[33] Historically make-up was not permitted for respectable women, only for painted ladies (who advertised their trade using "rouge and kohl").[34] Indeed the reason for so much check pinching and lip biting in nineteenth-century novels is to make the flesh pink without artifice.[35] Gradually make-up became normal and wearing make-up, especially lipstick, was "probably the most significant issue marking the generation gap between mothers and daughters in the 1920s."[36] In the UK by the 1940s, wearing make-up was not only normal but patriotic, so much so that lipstick was not rationed during the war and it was imported across blockades with other necessary supplies.[37] Similar trends happened elsewhere, and "by 1948, 80 to 90 percent of adult American women used lipstick, about two-thirds used rouge, and one in four wore eye makeup."[38] The requirement for make-up, once established, remained, and most women who can afford to regard make-up as part of their daily routine. The dominance of make-up has been fairly steady, arguably with a blip in the 1960s and early 1970s with the rise of hippy culture and second-wave feminism; although it is contested whether the counter-culture norms reached beyond a relatively small, predominantly white and middle class, elite.

Make-up is an example of a practice that, over time, changed from an exceptional practice to something routine and often required to meet minimal standards. That this is the case is demonstrated by social media campaigns such as the 2015 "bare-faced" selfie campaign; which raised £8,000,000 in six days for cancer research.[39] Bare-faced selfies are good for fundraising precisely because it is no longer normal to see most women without make-up in most spheres of life. More than this, women feel uncomfortable— and perhaps even embarrassed and ashamed—to be seen without their "war paint." Of course, there are some areas where women do not usually wear make-up, but these are rarer than they were. Make-up is not just an example of how practices gradually become acceptable, and then routine, required to meet minimal standards, make-up also represents the beginning of a change in beauty ideals. The requirement to make up the face is a precursor of the current dominant, ethical beauty ideal, as make-up became regarded as a way of (re-)constructing the self and asserting identity:

> In the 1920s and 1930s, cosmetics producers, advertisers, and beauty experts shifted the burden of female identity from an interior self to a personality made manifest by marking and colouring the face: Makeup was a true expression of feminine identity, not its false mask, and the makeover was a means of individual self-development.[40]

Make-up is now a routine practice for many women in many contexts. In addition, to being minimally required, it is done daily, or frequently, at home and does not usually take time beyond the daily routine, and it is not risky. Yet even here some aspects are beginning to change—both as the demands of make-up embed and as technical fixes increase, making more alternative procedures available and accessible. For instance, semipermanent make-up (for example, permed and dyed eyelashes, high-definition brows, and tattooed lips) offers alternative ways to meet the routine, and minimal, requirements of make-up. Such practices are similar to occasional practices: they take time, and third-party assistance is required. Thus while the end point is the same—a made-up face—the practices are different. In addition, the use of such technical fixes further embeds the requirement of make-up, as bare faces become less common. For instance, some nurses and doctors have embraced semipermanent make-up because standard make-up is prohibited in sterile environments.[41] If this becomes more common non-made-up faces will be even rarer and make-up more ubiquitous. On the other hand, meeting such standards might be less demanding; tattooed lips do not need constant attention.

A further practice where requirements are changing is with regard to manicures and pedicures. For a long time painted nails, like painted lips, were not something that respectable women displayed. But, and again parallel to lipstick, painted nails have gradually become acceptable and are increasingly regarded as a standard part of being groomed. Unlike make-up and body hair removal, the wearing of nail polish, and the sporting of semipermanent manicures and artificial nails is not routine and is not required to meet minimal standards in most groups. However, I have included it in this section as third-party manicures have become normalized and may be on the threshold of crossing from occasional treats to being required to meet minimal standards.

That third-party manicures are becoming routine was highlighted in the summer of 2015 following an exposé in the *New York Times*, which revealed significant harms to practitioners (something I will return to in chapter 6).[42] For this chapter, what is significant from this expose was that it brought to light the exponential growth in nail bars, the sheer number of which suggest these procedures have become—or are becoming—routine. Similarly Louise Rondel counts thirty-seven places that offer manicures in the two kilometers between Camberwell and the Elephant and Castle in southeast London.[43] Third-party manicures are increasingly common and may be becoming similar to hair cutting and hair dying; whether applying traditional polish or the new longer-lasting gel polishes.[44] In some circles, a professional manicure is regarded as required to meet minimum standards, and even in groups where they are not required they are fairly normal, especially for events such as weddings or holidays. Again, like so many beauty practices, this is not limited to the West or the rich world.[45]

The example of third-party manicures shows how a practice moves from being occasional to being required. While third-party manicures and pedicures may not yet be required to attain minimal requirements of beauty, they are increasingly prevalent in some groups, and if trends continue, it is possible that they may become required in the near future. It is already the case that some practices that require third-party assistance are regarded as required for very many women (and not only in the Western world): most obviously, hair cutting, styling, and dyeing. It is increasingly rare, though by no means abnormal, as it arguably is for body hair removal, for women not to dye their hair over a certain age.[46] Indeed, that we all know what a "bad hair day" is in itself revealing.

These examples show the increasing demands of minimum standards of beauty. That more is required to meet the basic requirements is troubling, even for those who do not wish to engage beyond the minimal, as more becomes necessary just to be "good enough," to be "normal."

Blurring of Routine and Extreme

In this section I return to the categories of routine, occasional, and exceptional and argue that not only is there no clear line between these categories, but that some practices that are generally assumed to be routine might in fact be more demanding than some so-called exceptional practices. For instance, as discussed in the last section, continual body-hair removal is demanding in terms of time, money, and in the case of waxing, pain. Given this, is it really the case that daily (routine) shaving or monthly (routine) waxing, is less extreme or exceptional than laser hair removal? While laser hair removal may carry risks which are not yet fully documented, the risks of shaving and waxing are documented. Shaving carries little physical risk, although some studies document chafing and hypersensitivity of skin (especially when shaving pubic hair), but it has to be re-peated frequently, often daily, if hairless and smooth skin is to be maintained.[47] Waxing includes risks of abscesses as a result of in-grown hairs and risks of infection (with particular worries docu-mented about immune-suppressed women), and waxing is always painful.[48] When compared to the relatively pain-free, and over time less labor-intensive procedure of laser hair removal, the exceptional option might be less demanding and preferable to so-called rou-tine practices (at least for the light-skinned, dark-haired women for whom such treatments are most effective).[49]

Similarly, the continual purchasing and daily application of skin-care products in order to maintain a youthful appearance might not be as routine as we assume. If we consider the cost and time over a lifetime, it might be that a peel or laser treatment every now and then is in fact less demanding. For instance, the purchasing of anti-aging lotions and potions is costly. Premium brands such as Crème de la Mer retail at over £100 for 30ml; and standard up-market main street brands sell antiaging and resurfacing creams at prices of around £40 to £90.[50] Cheaper main street versions are available at a slightly lower cost of around £20 to £40.[51] And there are budget brands and supermarket brands, as well as brands that can be bought on the internet or from door-to-door salesmen; recall the importance of direct sales in Mexico. Likewise, in terms of time, while daily application of lotions and potions might not seem sig-nificant, even if we only spend 2 minutes a day on face cream appli-cation, this is approximately 12 hours a year. If we do this every day between 15 and 75 then this most basic grooming totals of 720 hours or 30 days: nearly a month over a lifetime. Botox costs around £175 to £300 for a single treatment of a single area. It takes less than half an hour, but needs repeating every three to six months (less often over time). So if we compare very roughly: Botox over a lifetime would take only 60 hours between the ages of 15 and 75, compared to the 720 hours of cream application.[52] It would cost £24,000 which is a third less than the £36,000 it would cost for three mid-priced products (say, serum, day cream, and night cream replaced four times a year).[53] Similarly, face-lifts cost between £4000 and £9000 (and much less if you are prepared to travel).[54] So while face-lifts and Botox are regarded as extreme, it might be less demanding to have a face-lift twice a lifetime, or to have Botox regularly, than to continue with the supposedly routine practices of daily cream application.

Such figures are grossly approximate, quick, and simple calculations, drawing on no empirical evidence about what actual women do or have done. Further, such comparisons focus on the costs of money and time, and not on other, at least as important, considerations, such as risk. In addition, it is likely that a women who is willing to have a face-lift would continue to use her lotions and potions, resulting in a higher overall demands. But for at least some practices this would not be the case. For instance, if hair lazering delivers its promise of permanent hair removal, then there is no need to routinely shave, pluck, and wax.[55] Likewise, a woman with permed and tinted eyelashes no longer needs to apply mascara daily. However flawed, what such calculations show is that what is supposedly routine could be considered extreme on at least some measures, and what is extreme might be considered routine (if routine means meeting minimal standards rather the other possible definitions).

This discussion highlights the extent to which assumptions about routine are based on what we happen to do and not on objective criteria. Whatever else they do, the terms "routine" and "extreme" do not track the demandingness of the practices and process that fall under them. Practices done frequently are not necessarily less demanding, and sometimes those done occasionally that take time out and are done by third parties may be less demanding, when the costs over time are considered, than some daily practices. To assess the rising demands of beauty, we need to focus on what is required to meet minimal standards, irrespective of the practices and procedures that are used. What matters is not whether practices are considered exceptional, but rather what the overall demands amount to. Calling practices routine hides and obscures the increasingly punishing requirements of beauty. This in itself is harmful, costly, and risky, but it is far more so if failure to comply is ethical; women who don't comply are seen, and see themselves, as failures.

Routine Failure

Troubling as the rising demands of beauty are, the demands discussed in this chapter are demands we can meet with time, money, and effort. In this final section of the chapter, I wish to return to body shape, and ask how is it that thinness can be a global minimum standard of beauty if it is one that is, so often, not met. While the drive to and desire for thinness is a global phenomenon and we may collectively aspire to thinness, we cannot meet this standard simply by doing more (as we can, for example, when it comes to hairlessness). Becoming thin, or maintaining thinness, requires body work in some form; whether constant dieting and exercise or intervention, for example, gastric surgery (which when effective usually requires further surgery to remove excess skin), or liposuction. In addition, there are a whole host of slimming pills, extreme diets, and new miracle procedures constantly promising weight loss.[56] Trying to be thin, or feeling guilty that we are not thin enough (or just slimmer), is a dominant and familiar feature of many women's daily experience. It is something that collectively and quietly (and sometimes less quietly) we are obsessive about: put a few women together and often common ground will be quickly found in giving complements about body size and shape and/or discussing diet and exercise and in expressing satisfaction or more often dissatisfaction with our bodies. While this talk may serve other purposes, such as female bonding (something I will return to in chapter 6) and some women may reject it and feel uncomfortable with it, for many women body-talk is ubiquitous and arguably equivalent to sports-talk among men. Yet, as our collective obsession with our bodies increases, and key to achieving the ideal is thinness or slimness, fewer of us are able to attain the ideal.

The body shapes we consider ideal have gradually become less attainable. Over time, what we consider thin enough has become thinner. Likewise, while thinness with curves might promise some relief from the pressures to be thin, it is thinness with dramatic and pronounced curves, and not just curves, that is required. If one compares the 1950s ideal of Jane Russell and Marilyn Monroe (admittedly the plumpest ideal of the century) to current ideals of Kate Moss, Jennifer Lawrence, Angelina Jolie, or Kim Kardashian, the earlier figures look decidedly average and nonideal. That the ideal is more demanding is further evidenced by the change in the figures of models: according to the U.S. National Eating Disorders Association in 2002 the average U.S. model was 5 ft. 11 and weighed 117 lb., compared to the average American women who was 5 ft. 4 and weighed 140 lb.[57] In body shape too then, and while recognizing the variations of context, minimum standards are rising, and in this context what is desired cannot be attained easily by adding practices to our routines.

But, while we often do not meet (and may never meet), the ideal standards to which we aspire when it comes to body shape, this does not mean we stop aspiring to them. Almost irrespective of where we are on the weight spectrum, we want to lose weight (we tend to believe that we would be happier if we were lighter).[58] Wolf speaks of the "one stone solution,"[59] the 10 to 15 pounds women believe they should lose, and from 16–60 we aspire to the "tall, slim cultural ideal."[60] Likewise when we lose weight—irrespective of what our starting weight was—we feel a sense of achievement, and we are proud of ourselves.[61] Conversely as we expand—and collectively we are expanding (obesity is rising fast)[62]—we feel disappointed in ourselves and ashamed, and nowhere is "letting yourself go" so damning as when it comes to body weight. Thus, when it comes to body shape, we have to interpret minimum standards as the need to constantly be striving to be better; just as we can interpret aspiration to engage as commitment to the ideal. While there are subcultures, such as the increasingly prominent body-positive movements, which seek to challenge the dominance of thinness, as yet, thinness remains a key feature of the beauty ideal, one that is becoming more rather than less dominant. Recall the global trends to thinness.

That lack of attainment does little to arrest the rise of demands, and body shape may be less dissimilar to other requirements than it first appears. For example, while hairlessness can be met, it is demanding, and there are times, at least when one is waxing, when you will have stubble (remember the young women deliberately leaving stubble to avoid sex). Not only is stubble unavoidable at times, but rashes, blemishes, and imperfections will also be revealed and caused by hair removal. However much we might aspire to perfectly smooth skin, whether on the face or the body, perfect skin is rarely possible; especially as the gaze becomes forensic. Thus, attaining what are presented as minimal standards is hard, perhaps impossible, whether the demand is perfect smoothness or thinness. What is true across practices is that as demands rise, and despite our increased efforts, failure will be increasingly common resulting in more feelings of inadequacy, shame, and disgust. That increasing engagement is likely to result in increasing failure is important for understanding the likely increasing harms that come with the beauty ideal as an ethical ideal.

Conclusion

In this chapter, I have explored the increasing demands of beauty. I have primarily used the example of body hair removal to show the gradual and incremental rise of minimal beauty standards. A dominant and more demanding beauty ideal is ethically concerning, particularly as demands are likely to rise further in the future. In arguing that minimal standards are becoming more demanding across the board, I am emphasizing the breadth of such minimal standards. For some features (such as hairlessness) it is already the case that adherence is required of most women, and while there may be some women, or groups of women, who do not conform, nonconformity is increasingly unusual and costly. In this chapter, I have interrogated assumptions about routine beauty practices and argued that the only definition of routine that holds across practices is what is necessary to attain minimal beauty standards, to be "good enough." But minimal is rarely what it seems; many of these practices are demanding, not minimal at all, and what counts as minimal is widely divergent.

In sum, the minimal standards of beauty that apply to all, or most, women are rising. While there have been more demanding beauty standards in some times and places—foot-binding was far more demanding than hairlessness—there have not been broadly adhered to and normalized minimum standards that result in ethical sanction if they are not met. The global scope, and near-complete dominance, of these minimum beauty standards are such that they gradually become invisible; not regarded as beauty norms, but as minimal grooming practices necessary for health and natural. Body hair, for example, is now regarded as abnormal and unnatural. While these demands are not evident in all places, trends to more demanding practices are clear. This said, there may be some practices where demands are lessening and there is more variety: clothing and fashion are arguably more varied and variable (especially globally), and, as discussed in the last chapter, in at least some places diversity of skin tone (when all other standards are met) is accepted. But across the board the expectation is that we should attain, or continually strive to attain, thinner, firmer, and sometimes curvier bodies, smooth and hairless skin, and young bodies and faces. Moreover, these requirements will embed, as more extreme practices normalize and become routine.

5

Perfectly Normal

In the chapters so far, I have argued that the increased dominance, coupled with the ethical nature of the ideal, is transformative and distinguishes it from previous beauty ideals. Furthermore, I suggested that the gradual increase in minimum standards in the context of a dominant and ethical beauty ideal is significant in that what is required to be normal is increasingly demanding. Yet, because such practices are effectively required of all, they become regarded as normal and even natural, necessary to be "good enough"; as such, the increasing demands are largely unquestioned. In this chapter, I will build on the claims of the last chapter and explore the normalization of beauty practices and the rising bar of normal. In exploring the narrowing of normal, I will consider two contributing factors: first, the extent to which technology both drives and responds to demands and the impact of technology on the gradual normalizing of once extreme procedures; second, the way that it is easy to progress from one practice to the next. I will argue that, just as the escalation of demands occurs incrementally, almost stealthily, so too the move from one type of practice to another is incremental. In the final section, I will argue that there is nothing neutral about normal. "Normal" is always value-laden; it is used to convey judgment, to legitimize or to defend. Moreover, in some contexts the language of "to be normal" does not refer to what is and what is not normal. Rather it is the correct language, the code, that is recognized and accepted to access procedures. I will suggest that ethically this language is not different from claims "to be better" or "to be perfect." In different contexts, all serve as the acceptable language for engagement in beauty procedures.

The Rising Bar of Normal

In the last chapter, I considered a number of supposedly routine beauty practices that are already required to meet minimal standards. Whether the aim is to attain minimal standards, or to work towards them (as in the case of thinness), attempting, and continuing to attempt, to meet such standards (despite previous failures) is compulsory. Engaging in routine practices is demanding. Further, the trend is to be ever more demanding. As more women engage in newly available practices, such as Botox, laser treatments, fillers, and peals, these practices, like third-party manicures, become regarded as normal and necessary to attain minimum standards of beauty. It is this normalization of practices, practices that were once regarded as extreme and absolutely not required, that I will interrogate in this chapter. For while it is not yet the case—for most of us—that we are required to have Botox or "go under the knife," such practices are no longer regarded as extreme. If trends continue, and there is no reason to doubt current trajectories, then it is not hard to imagine that at least some youth-mimicking procedures will become standard, and eventually required, in the not-too-distant future. For example, recall the growth in Botox and fillers. It is not unlikely that the increasing use of such products will tip into a requirement. As seen in the last chapter stepping outside the norm and rejecting minimal practices is not easy and requires conscious, almost political, action. If such normalization occurs, then wrinkles will be as shameful and shaming as visible body hair. Wolf wonders whether it will become the case that "no self-respecting woman will venture outdoors with a surgically unaltered face,"[1] Jones suggests something similar:

> Increasingly in makeover culture the choice is not to have cosmetic surgery rather than to have it. Just as a contemporary woman attending an important public event will probably feel the need to wear make-up, the middle aged women of the mid twenty-first century may well live in an environment where cosmetic surgery is the absolute norm. For middle- and upper-class women the decision not to have cosmetic surgery will be a political (or aesthetically perverse) one, a resolution that says certain things about the bearer of wrinkles or the carrier of jowls. In other words, a face unmarked by cosmetic surgery—or rather a face that retains the marks of age—will be a face that makes a statement.[2]

There are a number of factors that feed the escalation of practices that are required to be normal, including the technological imperative, the democratization of beauty practices, and the rise of consumer models of identity. Together this results in beauty practices becoming normalized; as more of us engage, practices become regarded first as acceptable, rather than extreme, and then gradually they become regarded as commonplace, and eventually required to meet minimal standards. In this way, gradually and incrementally, what is considered normal narrows. What was once normal becomes abnormal, and what was once enough to attain minimal standards of beauty becomes insufficient. There is a gradual escalation of minimal standards along with increased pressure to engage beyond what is minimal and towards what is maximal. Under the beauty ideal as an ethical ideal, engagement becomes regarded as good, as "making the best of yourself," rather than narcissistic and self-indulgent.

Technological Drivers of Normalization

As possibilities for improving or perfecting ourselves—technical, surgical, and chemical—increase so too does the pressure that women feel and the expectations put upon them. Technological advancement both responds to and drives demands. For example, thinness with curves might be a long-standing desire, but only with the development of technology that makes breast implants and, increasingly, buttock-lifts a real option, can these dreams be realized. Likewise, before the easy surgical fix of blepharoplasty the upper eye crease could only be approximated through make-up. There are of course other practical reasons, connected to affordability, accessibility, visual culture, and consumer individualism, and no single reason is decisive. Some argue the changing of technological possibilities is the most important factor in seeking to explain the changing and increasing demands of beauty. For example, Jones argues that "the 'origins' of beauty have changed because of cosmetic surgery: people now have cosmetic surgery in order to look like other people who have had cosmetic surgery."[3] In this framework, technology does not respond to long-standing demands, which now become easier to fulfill, but it begins to define and shape the beauty ideal itself: "Beauty becomes surgical, defined by cosmetic surgery: wide-open eyes, exalted breasts, fattened lips, small noses, prominent cheekbones, all atop a superslim body."[4] While Jones's vision might prove to be the case at present, whether the beauty ideal is a long-standing ideal that technology allows us to realize, or a new ideal, not only shaped by what is technically possible but created by and dependant on what is technically possible, remains to be seen. Yet in either case thinness, firmness, smoothness, and youth, are required, and the sheer amount of youth-enhancing and mimicking procedures is overwhelming. Included in the vast array of products and processes are creams and masks to be applied at home; scientifically proven and patented and full of high-tech ingredients promising to rejuvenate, resurface, erase, plump, firm, smooth, minimize wrinkles and pores, lighten and brighten. There are more invasive treatments, of peels, lasers, vampire face-lifts, resurfacing processes—all of which require some time out and the assistance of a third party. For longer-lasting and more permanent youth maintenance or mimicking (depending on how successful the treatments are) there are semipermanent procedures of fillers, Botox, and mini-face-lifts which can be done in a lunch hour. The most dramatic interventions are surgical, and some of these are permanent (although usually additional treatments will be required periodically, and gradually these may be less effective and even counterproductive). The array of surgery options is vast. Whole faces can be lifted, or problem areas fixed (such as eye bags removed, ageing eyelids lifted, eyes widened, cheek pads replaced, jowls smoothed, and so on). Indeed all surgery arguably aims to improve youthfulness, particularly the most popular procedures of breast augmentation and liposuction.[5]

In offering us new and more effective and sometimes faster (quick) fixes for long desired beauty ideals, technology is responding to demand (helping us achieve our desire to look younger) as well as creating demand for specific procedures and perhaps for whole "looks." While we might desire to look younger in general, we can only desire a face-lift or dermal-fillers once these technologies are available, affordable, and perhaps most importantly, acceptable. That technology is driving demand, as well as responding to long-standing demands, is evident when key features of the contemporary beauty ideal are considered. As argued in chapter 3, the emerging global ideal of beauty is one that is impossible for women of any racial group to meet without technological intervention. Whether a long-standing desire or a new aspiration, technology offers a whole host of new practices and procedures—from creams, through Botox, to face-lifts—to mimic and retain a more youthful appearance. There was little, historically, that women could do as they aged to maintain a youthful appearance. Essentially, the only option was to seek to disguise the signs of aging, for example, by wearing high neck lines to disguise aging jowls and by the application of make-up.[6] Contrast such limited measures to the current availability of antiaging products, processes, and procedures. Technology makes what was previously unattainable, attainable, and, as procedures are increasingly utilized, maybe, eventually, normal.

The increasing requirement of curves as well as thinness illustrates the importance of technology in driving demand. Thinness with curves could not be a beauty ideal, at least not one women could be expected, or expect themselves, to attain or realistically aspire to, in an era without available and accessible technological interventions. Without technological intervention you can have curves (Marilyn and Jane, though their curves are less pronounced than contemporary curves), or you can have thinness (Twiggy and Kate), but you cannot have both. As discussed in an earlier chapter, large, pert breasts over visible ribs and a skinny waist are not possible without technological intervention. Indeed, large breasts that are also pert and round (without the assistance of a bra) are rare and for anyone but the very young, impossible. Likewise for buttocks, what is desired is not large saggy buttocks over thunder thighs and cankles, but large pert, round and shapely buttocks over shapely and firm thighs and slim ankles. For most of us this requires technological help.[7]

In addition, technology drives demand by creating problems that previously we were unaware of and that we now require technological help to fix. For instance, arguably cellulite is created in order to sell anticellulite creams of dubious efficacy, fat-freezing, liposuction, and the list continues. The forensic gaze invites you to examine the flaws in your skin minutely as if under a microscope. This way of looking at the skin is only possible with technology—it is a not a human gaze but a technological gaze—and from this perspective we can be convinced that skin is blemished, marked, or damaged, or that our pores are too large. Once we recognize the flaws in ourselves, we can then fix them by buying the right products or undergoing the correct procedures.

The technological imperative should not be underestimated as a driver in the race towards perfection (at the top end of the scale) and as influential in the raising of minimal standards and in the narrowing of normal (at the bottom end). Separating out the extent of this influence is complex and likely impossible, and it is too simplistic to simply blame the industry, although clearly the needs of big business are influential here. But we can only be convinced that our faces are flawed by large pores or wrinkles or age marks, and flawed enough to spend significant time and money repairing such flaws, if we have already committed to valuing smooth, luminous, and glowing skin (skin that naturally belongs only to the very young). Technology is not the bogyman of the story, though it is one piece of the puzzle without which the dominant beauty ideal could not be emerging as it is. Technology has exponentially extended the possibilities of what we can do in seeking to be normal, better, or perfect.

The Normalizing of Exceptional Procedures

As the possibilities of technology increase—in terms of both invasive and noninvasive procedures—the range of what is acceptable both narrows and rises. More is required to attain normal, raising the lower threshold and so narrowing what is acceptable, while also raising the bar of what is considered acceptable at the top end of normal. In this way, previously extreme procedures become regarded as normal and perhaps even routine. Already, in some circles Botox and fillers fall into this category and it is the untreated and aging face that is abnormal.[8] As discussed, some cosmetic surgery, for example the double eyelid surgery in South Korea, is now so standard amongst at least younger age groups that it is abnormal *not* to have surgery, and the surgery is viewed as necessary for employment. As Blum notes, in some Jewish communities in the United States it is the nose that has not been altered that is abnormal.[9] Likewise in many contexts, and increasingly outside industries that have traditionally been connected to beauty, breast implants are regarded as normal. The stigma that once attached to surgery—shame of vanity or narcissism—has in some contexts disappeared, and patterns suggest that such stigma lessens over time, making it likely that overall it will gradually recede.[10] Breast implants are given as graduation presents or eighteenth birthday presents, to wives and girlfriends and even as prizes.[11] Moreover, surgery can apparently be fun: part of mother and daughter packages, or combined with a trip to the sun. In the UK the Royal College of Surgeons states that "surgeons should refrain from the use of financial inducements that may influence the patient's decision such as discounts, time-limited or two-for-one offers.[12] That this is included suggests that doctors were engaging in such practices. This is not to say that the stigma that once attached to cosmetic surgery has wholly or uniformly eroded, but it is reducing. Moreover, there is significant sanction when surgery goes wrong, and a fascination with botched surgery and "horror stories"; as Jones highlights there is a special place in cosmetic surgery for "monsters."[13] Although there is increasing interest in the botched surgery of "normal" people, and here horror is tempered with sympathy (which may itself be a sign of normalization and reduced stigma).

As cosmetic procedures become less exceptional, and there is less stigma attached, they are normalized. If this trend continues, and there is every reason to think that it will, then what is required to attain minimum standards, to be normal, will increase. Indeed, we may reach the point where engaging in body reshaping practices is no longer a matter requiring significant deliberation, but routine, little different from hair cutting or dying. This process is gradual and incremental. Botox was once regarded as a crazy practice—"why inject poison?"—done by the rich and famous. Now Botox is regarded as normal—something that is completely acceptable for those who can afford to do it—and in some circles it is required. The gradual acceptance of previously unacceptable practices, to the point where they become something that many, perhaps most, women in any given context do, can be tracked for a number of practices. In the previous chapter, I tracked the gradual rising of minimal standards with regard to body hair removal and other routine practices. Similar processes of normalization are evident when considering other practices. For example, women who dyed their hair were once regarded with some suspicion, even derision—"she's a bottle blond"—a prejudice that has largely disappeared.[14] Likewise, with make-up, nail polish, and the removal of pubic hair. I see no reason why a parallel process will not occur for very many other beauty practices, why practices that are currently regarded as extreme or exceptional will not, over time, become regarded as routine and even required. This may already be happening with Botox and fillers, to the extent where Dana Berkowitz suggests that Botox injections are "fast becoming regular body upkeep, just like teeth cleaning and haircuts."[15] In time there is no reason to expect that a similar change in attitude will not happen with cosmetic surgery.

That it is increasingly accepted is already demonstrably the case, and this is the first stage in the normalization process. Already 48 percent of young women in the UK, aged sixteen to twenty-one, would consider cosmetic surgery.[16] And, as discussed in chapter 3, globally the number of surgical and nonsurgical procedures performed rises year on year.

The Normality of the Extreme

Gradually, then, extreme practices, engaged in by unusual types of women, become procedures that some, gradually most, women would consider for themselves and certainly would not judge others harshly for undergoing. There are a number of factors that contribute to the ease with which once exceptional procedures are normalized. In this section I would like to highlight just one, a mundane and practical reason; namely that it is easy to progress from one practice to another relatively seamlessly.

I suggest that the ease of progression from engaging in minimal practices—such as using moisturizer—to more maximal practices, like Botox, is significant in understanding the speed and extent of normalization. Quite simply it matters that in the beauty context there is no clear line between what is routine and minimal and what is not. Indeed, more extreme practices might be a "quick fix" to reach the minimal standard. As discussed in the last chapter, fillers or Botox or even a face-lift, might be a way to attain younger skin more effectively and at a similar or lower price than the application of expensive antiaging creams. The practices are not engaged in for themselves but to attain a goal, to better comply with one feature or another of the beauty ideal. Putting aside for a moment that some practices are more risky and harmful than others, if a different method will give you the results that you desire, and better and more efficiently, then why wouldn't you want this quick fix? There are some areas where quick fixes carry negative connotations. For instance, weight loss surgery, can be seen by some as "cheating," the implication being that weight loss is hard and requires effort, and thinness should be worked for rather than quickly delivered.[17]

But while this view remains, increasingly those who opt for surgery are regarded well, as being active and taking control of their own bodies and lives.[18] Accordingly, differences between antiaging cream, Botox and face-lifts erode.

That there is no clear line between minimal and extreme practices makes it far easier, gradually, and with little reflection, to engage in more beauty practices, and practices that might have previously been regarded as extreme. The first port of call is often the hairdresser—a place we routinely visit—and increasingly other products and treatments are available in these spaces. For instance, why not get gel nails if you can have these done while you wait for your hair dye to take? Or why not move from shaving to waxing, again done at the hairdresser? Once you start waxing regularly, then going to the beauty salon or spa isn't too much of a stretch. And then the process repeats. Once you are used to the beauty salon, why not have some permanent make-up or perhaps Botox? And once you consider Botox, then isn't it only sensible to find a reputable medical practitioner to administer it? At this point, you leave the beauty parlor and enter the clinic, making the step from Botox to cosmetic procedures less of a leap and more of a small shuffle. While surgery might seem extreme to the woman who engages in few beauty practices, it is easy to imagine a gradual embrace of more beauty procedures as a normal and seemingly natural progression. Only gradually do individuals find themselves engaging in practices that previously they would not have imagined doing. For instance, the woman who decides to have a manicure while getting her hair done and then proceeds along the trajectory to cosmetic surgery does not, at the time she decides on a manicure, imagine that she will ultimately end up undergoing cosmetic surgery. As I will argue later, part of the reason that consent does not function well in regulating beauty practices is that from the perspective of the user beauty practices may be more similar than policy makers assume.

The policy maker regards cosmetic surgery as vastly different from hair dye, but in the lived experience of women the practices may not be experienced as such. Incrementally, and without particular attention or intention, exceptional practices gradually become normal. That they do this for some women then impacts on other women. When some women engage in beauty practices, it becomes easier for others, particularly for friends and family, to do so as well. At some juncture, in any particular group, there comes a point when engagement becomes open and commonplace. At the point where most engage, then those who do not suddenly find that they are abnormal, and feel that they are falling below minimal standards. This is the point at which what is normal narrows, minimal standards increase, and what was once normal becomes abnormal and no longer good enough.

This is true within groups, but also collectively and between groups. Recall the earlier discussion that those who resist the beauty ideal are likely to become more visible and under greater pressure to conform. Nonconformity becomes increasingly hard to maintain, unless the group holds strong competing ideologies that serve to protect those who resist the mainstream norm. As the gap between those who resist and those who conform grows, those who do not engage will be regarded as increasingly abnormal, and find it more difficult to function outside their particular group. As a result, many currently resistant groups may conform, especially those who do not regard non-engagement as particularly significant.

Nothing Neutral about Normal

In this final section of the chapter, I wish to problematize the discourse around normal and suggest that claims to be normal serve a number of purposes and should not be taken at face value. The word "normal" is used to justify and medicalize by both surgeons and patients. In some contexts, it is used to demarcate necessary surgery (whether necessary to relieve suffering or to return to normal) from frivolous non-necessary surgery. Yet, while used in this way in some contexts, I want to suggest that ethically there is little difference between the narratives of "to be normal," "to be better," and " to be perfect." Indeed they serve the same purpose. They are the correct languages by which to access desired surgery in a particular context.

Kathy Davis's early study of the narratives of those who access cosmetic surgery emphasized suffering.[19] She reports that "all of the applicants were highly convincing in the accounts of the suffering they endured due to some part of their appearance."[20] Yet even though these patients reported suffering, and wanted nothing more than "to be normal," with one exception Davis could not guess the reason the person had sought surgery. There are a number of ways that normal is functioning in this context and why.

Normal presents in this discourse as a way to distance cosmetic surgery for medical need from cosmetic surgery for aesthetic vanity. In the context of Davis's study, in the Netherlands, patients had to establish that they were "outside the realm of the normal" if funding was to be ascertained.[21] Not surprisingly then the respondents did so. This is not to suggest that there was deliberate manipulation, but rather that we construct narratives around practices in response to institutional structures and the wider social context. The use of such language tracks nothing objective; as Davis states she could not identify the supposed abnormality, rather it shows the correct attitude, which both allows and justifies the use of cosmetic procedures. Accordingly, in different contexts different narratives are available and acceptable. Gimlin shows this when she compares accounts of women who have undergone cosmetic surgery in the UK and the United States.[22] Gimlin argues that what are regarded as "legitimate arguments" may have some overlaps, but "can also be expected to vary cross-nationally because they are informed by the evaluative repertoires of a given society."[23] Gimlin argues that institutions and structures shape experiences and narratives:

> Consumers' narratives also point to a particular kind of boundary-making. They tell us where a given culture draws the line between legitimate and illegitimate aesthetic surgery, when such procedures are seen as more or less a reflection of "vanity," "self-indulgence" or "internalised oppression" and, ultimately, which

consumers can be excused (or not) for engaging in a practice that is not yet fully accepted as "normal."[24]

Given this, it is not surprising that in Davis's study, as Gimlin also notes, the health care system encouraged narratives that emphasized suffering and the need to be normal. Gimlin found that British and American women's narratives were different in ways that fitted with the institutional structures and wider social mores. For instance, British women, in a public health care system, emphasized need and "drew on evidence of physical and/or emotional pain associated with the pre-surgical body."[25] By contrast the American women focused on the importance of maintaining competiveness at work, and emphasized that they had worked hard to be able to afford surgery. These are very different narratives, one of need and one of improvement, and yet both narratives enable the women to gain access to the surgery they wish, and provide them with context-appropriate arguments to defend and justify surgery. Both groups wish to prove that they are undergoing surgery for the right reasons—and what are considered the right reasons cash out differently in the United States and United Kingdom. The British woman takes care to emphasize that she has not spent hard-earned cash, Gimlin argues, to detach the process from the marketplace and to show she has not neglected her family. By contrast the American woman defends surgery by emphasizing the sacrifices she has made, the hard work, and personal effort that makes her deserving.[26]

Other narratives exist elsewhere. For example, in Brazil there is no coyness about the aim of surgery to improve and perfect. Edmonds suggests that the aim of *plástica* "is not a one-time passage into normality but an active and competitive pursuit of the elusive notion of a 'more perfect' body."[27] The competitive rhetoric of wanting to improve is accompanied by a view of cosmetic surgery as being connected to self-improvement in general. For instance, Ivo Pitanguy, a Brazilian plastic surgeon who has celebrity status in his own right, argues that "what you are doing is reconstructing or recuperating her self-esteem, which is not superficial: it's deeper than the skin."[28] So for Pitanguy the "real therapeutic object of plastic surgery is not the body, but the mind," [29] and it is this that has, in part, made cosmetic surgery available on the public health system in Brazil.[30] Improvement and perfection are nothing to be ashamed of in this context; perfecting the body is perfecting the self. Again, what is important is not what is in the narrative but what it enables; the accessing and justifying of procedures.

That these narratives are about what is culturally appropriate is also shown by the changes to them over time. As well as comparing American and British narratives Gimlin maps the changes in American narratives between her 2007 cohort and her original cohort in the mid-1990s. In the 1990s there were far more psychological elements to surgery narratives, such as surgery "as a means aligning the outer body with an 'authentic' inner self."[31] These accounts are now far less prevalent in the United States, and surgery is "less a method for reaching the finite goal of 'authenticity' than a means of participating in a larger, potentially un-ending process of self-improvement."[32] In addition, she notes that there are some wholly new accounts: for instance, narratives that focus on surgical beauty. Rather than just to improve, the intention is to look as if work has been done; showing financial resources and self-care. However, this is still fairly rare, and "with the occasional exception of breast augmentation, cosmetic surgery is generally deemed 'best' when it produces an improved (e.g., younger, slimmer, more ideally feminine) appearance, but not one that has been obviously surgically altered."[33]

That there is an acceptable account, or legitimate defense, is not just true of cosmetic surgery but of other beauty practices that are potentially stigmatized. Recall the academic woman who rejects beauty practices, but nonetheless religiously sticks to a punishing diet; or consider the Indian woman who strives to be thin, but does not describe her practice as dieting because of cultural associations with starving;[34] or perhaps the South African woman, who rejects the language of diet, but who regularly purges, as a culturally acceptable practice.[35] In all cases what is sought is a language that socially permits the engagement; that allows individuals to justify their seeking of skinny and their engagement in cosmetic surgery.

If this is right, then ethically there is little difference between claims "to be normal," "to be better," and "to be perfect." All are learned narratives used to access surgery and by which surgery and beauty practices more generally can be defended. The British woman knows she cannot claim to deserve cosmetic surgery because she's worked hard (without being cast as selfish or vain), just as the American woman knows that she must show she has earned surgery. Likewise the Indian women knows the language of diet is unacceptable, as she seeks to be thin while negotiating cultural norms. I suspect that Brazil and the United States are ahead of the curve in narrative terms, although Brazil is somewhat complicated by the need to fit a public health context as well as to be better. As stigma reduces and cosmetic procedures normalize more of us will be adopting the narratives "to be better" and "to improve." "To be normal" is a more prominent reason in contexts where cosmetic surgery has more stigma attached, particular in need-based health care contexts, as recipients fear being deemed shallow and self-centered. Yet, as beauty as an ethical ideal embeds increasingly improvement and aspirations to perfection will not be regarded as vain and narcissistic, but as ways of working on the self, of being morally good and virtuous. If this is correct, we might expect the language of "to be normal" to be gradually replaced by language of "to be better." Thus, while the language of "to be normal" presents as very different from the language of "to be better," it is not, and, as such, it is normalizing in itself.

A final word on normal is that in both women's discourse and surgical discourse normal is often treated as if it were an objective criterion. Its use implies that there is a consensus with regard to what normal is. Indeed surgeons use normal, as they did in the Netherlands, to justify whether surgery is medically necessary or not. Yet normal is anything but objective. Normal does not mean "functioning normally," but looking normal, and in very few instances are there explicit criteria for normal. What does a normal breast refer to? It is not a population-wide average breast, as given the wide range of breast shapes and sizes, it is unlikely anyone could justify surgery on such grounds. So what normal must refer to is the desirable breast, or perhaps the breast we normally see. Given the standard images of breasts, if our understanding of normal derives from what we normally see, we are likely to think that the normal breast is the enhanced breast. We do not see a wide variety of breast types or naked bodies and aging and old bodies are hardly ever seen. This is not a good vantage point to measure normal breasts, and our own breasts will inevitably appear unfavorably in comparison with our imaginings. Given this, is it surprising that breast surgery is the most common type of cosmetic surgery? There is nothing normal about these judgments, they are value-laden judgments about what is desirable.

Conclusion

In this chapter, I have considered normal and normalization. I have argued that what is considered normal is becoming narrower and harder to attain. Some who are normal now may not be normal in the future, and what was once normal will become the outlier and, eventually, abnormal. Moreover, it might become regarded as unethical *not* to use a process or procedure to attain normal (irrespective of health or other goods). I have highlighted the technological imperative and the mundane lived experience of gradually engaging in more beauty practices as key factors in normalizing, and eventually requiring, ever more beauty practices. I have argued that the language of "to be normal" is normalizing in itself. Further it is ethically similar to the language of "to be better" or "to be perfect." Its purpose is the same: to access beauty practices and surgery and to provide justification and defense of such engagement in a context-appropriate way.

The normalizing of practices and the rising bar of normal compounds the increasing dominance of the ideal and its demandingness. Normalization is anything but normal and hides the rise in requirements and thus the gradual extension of the demands of beauty. As demands rise, so too the ideal requires more—simply to meet minimal standards; this, as I will argue further in the next chapter, is harmful in that it is demanding of those who engage in practices that are costly and risky and take time from other pursuits, harmful to those who do not engage, as non-engagement is increasingly costly and abnormal, and potentially harmful to all as the beauty ideal becomes more unrealistic and beauty regimes more punishing.

6

Hidden Costs and Guilty Pleasures

In the last chapter, I explored normalization. I argued that the use of the term "normal" is not neutral, and taken together the effects of normalization, while manifesting differently in different places, contribute to the raising of minimal standards of beauty and a narrowing of what is considered normal. Normalization is perhaps the greatest cost or harm of the current beauty ideal, as the gradual escalation, or "ratcheting up" of the demands of beauty impacts on all of us.[1] The effect on others is real, as it is real individuals, you and me, who have to conform to the "new normal." Thus, with regard to engagement in at least minimal practices—and, if trends continue, currently maximal practices—what is necessary to be normal rises. Over time, the choices of some to engage eventually means that we all will have less choice not to engage. This is harm indeed.

In this chapter, I map some of the further pleasures and pains of beauty. I provide an overview of the individual harms for those who engage and then move to the communal harms, beyond those of normalization. I introduce the standard justice harms of costs to vulnerable others, costs of resource allocation and opportunity costs, and the harms of discrimination and the creation of a toxic environment. In the final section of the chapter, I turn to the communal pleasures of beauty. This chapter does not seek to be comprehensive, and notes rather than explores these costs and pleasures; in so doing it seeks to set the debate about dominance and demandingness in the wider context. Recognizing the social and communal costs and benefits is crucial as focusing only, or even primarily, on individual harms leads to policy and practice interventions that are, at best, partial and ineffective, and, at worst, counterproductive.

Recognizing Communal Pleasures and Pains

When the beauty ideal is considered in its entirety, rather than each practice separately, it is the social and cultural harms that are the most significant. Yet while communal harms matter most, as they change the context and so what it is possible for individuals to be and do, too often they are ignored, especially in policy making.[2] This is in part because policy makers import inappropriate frameworks from different contexts, without attention to the extent to which the contexts differ. I will return to this argument in chapter 9, when I suggest that informed consent functions differently in the beauty context than it does in the health context. A further reason is that it is simply much easier to monitor and collect data on individual harms and benefits, whereas moving from the individual to the communal is fraught with difficultly. It is a relatively simple matter to map and track individual harm (physical or psychological), at least when compared to communal harm.[3] Recognizing the creeping communal harms, such as normalization and the gradually increasing demands of the beauty ideal, is much more difficult and tends to rely on making suppositions and drawing conclusions from correlations and social trends. When it comes to documenting and providing data for communal harms, we are reduced to mapping patterns. There are no clear causal links, and indeed the causes, for example, of body dissatisfaction are myriad: some focus on the media as a primary cause, others on the rise of visual and virtual culture, and still others on the influence of family, friends, and peer groups.[4] None of these explanations are causal, and individuals will respond differently to different types of stimuli, and some individuals will be unaffected. Moreover, each individual will negotiate her position in a way that is unique to her. The impossibility of finding direct causal links does not mean that we can say nothing about communal harms and benefits, but rather that we have to be satisfied with telling more complex and nuanced stories.

While complex, these stories are important. When population data tell us that there is an unprecedented rise in body dissatisfaction and body image worries (as discussed in chapter 2), we learn *something*. Not necessarily about direct causes, but about *something*, for instance about the increasing importance of the body as a site of identity and selfhood, and about the willingness to change the body as a way of acting on the self. Similarly, when media analysis suggests that the images that are globally promoted are converging, this does not mean that consumers unreflectively and passively accept such images. They do not. But again it tells us *something*, for instance, about the resources that individuals are working with and using in their own imaginings. Likewise, analysis of social media use and the narratives of those who use such platforms, tell us *something* about changing representations of the self. Furthermore, medical data about body concerns and trends in the types of cosmetic procedures that are popular, tell us *something* about the body ideals emerging, and so on. Taken together, data from across disciplines and spheres of life enables us to create narratives of emerging trends, and together this evidence can be used to tell stories about how collectively our views of ideal bodies and attitudes to our own bodies and selves are changing. As such, they can point to emerging preoccupations, and from these the possible, potential, and likely shared harms can be inferred. None of these are directly causal, nor on their own are they explanatory. It is simply not possible to make direct connections from individual behavior to social and cultural trends, to social and communal harm, and from there back to the harms that fall on individuals as a result of the communal harms. Yet, the difficulty in creating causal links to evidence communal harm should not stop us from seeking to identify and address communal harms and benefits. Nor should we accept that because these harms are more complex and of a different type to individual harm, they are any less important. It is communal attitudes that shape the context in which harms and benefits accrue to individuals.

This is not a book about the ethics of individual beauty practices, nor is it a book about the ethics of cosmetic surgery, but about the beauty ideal. How the question is framed, and which ethical frameworks are in play, determine both what is understood as harm and how such harms are regarded.[5] To adopt an ethic of practices is to adopt an individual framework that is not neutral but rather determines which harms will be recognized—harms to engaging individuals—and which harms will not—communal harms and harms to other and future individuals. This type of argument is familiar, but deeply flawed. If it is the case that individuals are increasingly under pressure to engage in practices, the fact that they do so tells us little about individual choices and much about changing communal norms. This is an issue we will return to in chapter 9. For now, I simply want to emphasize that ethical frameworks are not neutral, but profoundly shape the ethical harms and risks that are visible and the weight given to them.

Harms to Engaging Individuals

The harms of cosmetic surgery to engaging individuals are not well documented, and there is no systematic recording of procedures, of outcomes, of complications and side-effects (either immediate or long term). Yet, this said, we know that all surgery is risky. Standard risks of surgery—cosmetic or otherwise—include adverse reactions to anesthesia, bleeding, scarring, risks of infection and complications. Unlike other surgery, cosmetic surgery is not required for health reasons, and therefore the balance is not between physical health risks and physical health benefits.[6] Rather, what must be balanced are the risks to physical health, the physical costs of the surgery, with nonphysical health benefits (such as psychological health or wholly nonhealth benefits, for example beauty or lifestyle benefits). This is a very different calculation. Even if surgery is done well and there are no complications, the physical risks of surgery are not insignificant, and while often minimized in makeover culture, the risks remain. The risks of surgery should not be overplayed (much cosmetic surgery is routine in medical parlance), but neither should they be underplayed. There are, and remain, significant physical health risks of surgery, and in cosmetic surgery there is no physical health gain.

Further, if surgery does not go according to plan there may be consequences for physical health. The risks of botched surgery are well publicized in popular media, although again the lack of robust data complicates this picture. Botched surgery functions as a modern-day freak show, but it tells us little about the frequency and extent of such harms. If data with regard to surgery outcomes in general is hard to attain, data with regard to complications is even less robust.[7] Indeed it is telling that so little evidence was available to the "Keogh Review"—the Department of Health's "Review of the Regulation of Cosmetic Interventions" chaired by Bruce Keogh[8]— that they had to commission a survey of GPs, nurses, and surgeons in order to have data to work from.[9] GPs and nurses reported that most complications followed nonsurgical procedures; although significant complications were also reported from liposuction and fat transfers.[10] Lack of robust data notwithstanding, some procedures are more risky than others. For instance, as discussed earlier, breast augmentation is relatively routine with a fairly high satisfaction rate whereas buttock-lifts are less routine and more risky. Further, some surgery while routine, in that is it fairly frequently carried out, has startlingly high complication rates.[11] Likewise we know that there are particular risks attached to the use of some products. For instance there are long-standing worries about the risks of breast implants, and these are periodically brought to public attention, usually, following a scandal; such as the Poly Implant Prosthese (PIP) scandal, of 2010.[12] In this case, potentially toxic implants made from silicon intended for industrial rather than medical purposes were fraudulently sold. However, in general, complications from these routine procedures are relatively low.[13]

Nonsurgical, sometimes called noninvasive, procedures also have physical risks.[14] Physical complications of fillers listed by Keogh include infection, lumpiness, ulcers, blood vessel blockages, tissue death, allergic reactions, prolonged swelling and bruising, and, in some cases, blindness.[15] If getting accurate data on cosmetic surgery is hard, then accurate data for nonsurgical procedures are even more difficult to find. Again the survey commissioned by the Keogh Review is one of the few sources of data that is not anecdotal or from very small studies. Those who responded to Keogh reported that they saw complications most commonly from Botox, laser treatment, and dermal fillers.[16] Another study, by BAPPS in 2012, reported that 69 percent of its members had seen patients following temporary fillers, and 49 percent following semipermanent or permanent fillers.[17] To this, we can add anecdotal evidence from GPs, surgeons, and accident and emergency staff, all of whom report addressing injuries from beauty practices. Moreover, these go beyond nonsurgical practices, and medics report burns and abscesses from routine practices such as waxing as well as the well documented harmful consequences of practices such as tanning or skin lightening, for example. The most dramatic of such injuries are a constant source of interest in women's magazines and the press, which routinely document failures.[18] Thus there is evidence of physical harm to individuals, although it is patchy, partial, and exceedingly limited.

In terms of physical benefit, cosmetic surgery does not result in direct physical benefit if this is understood as improving physical health or health functioning, although there may be some knock-on physical benefits. For instance, the woman who, after liposuction, feels confident enough to wear gym clothes and exercise regularly for the first time may experience physical benefits. But, for the most part, nonphysical benefits are weighted against physical benefits, and it is primarily psychological benefits that are focused upon.

The evidence with regard to psychological harms and benefits of cosmetic surgery is not robust. Much of the available evidence comes from small studies on how satisfied individuals report being not long after surgery. Hence, generalization is problematic. This said, studies do report that patients gain psychological benefits from surgery, for instance in terms of improvements in body image, and that they are mostly happy with surgery.[19] Further, studies of those who have had reconstructive surgery after mastectomy and breast cancer treatment report some psychological benefit in terms of better body image and improved sense of control.[20] Conversely, other studies report psychological harm: with a particularly dramatic statistic being that there is some correlation between breast implants and suicide.[21] Given the small size and small number of these studies, any attempt to make claims about the psychological harms and benefits of surgery on the individuals who engage should be treated with some caution. But undoubtedly some individuals do benefit, and most report satisfaction.

This said, the more you endorse the beauty ideal, the more likely you are to engage in cosmetic procedures, and thus place value in them, making reports of psychological benefit likely for two reasons. First, simply engaging in body work evokes feelings of satisfaction, as this is active work on the self and, irrespective of outcome, is virtuous. Second, those who undergo such procedures have invested significant time and effort and commitment, and therefore are likely to report that the engagement is worth it, as the alternative is to suggest that they made a mistake. Because the language of choice (and consent) places the whole responsibility on the individual, those who "chose" to have surgery either have to claim that they feel better, happier, for it, or they have to recognize that they made a bad choice. Just as there is an acceptable narrative for choosing surgery ("to be normal" in some contexts and "to be better" in others), there may also be acceptable narratives about how we feel after surgery. In addition, there seems to be some evidence that accepting the outcome, even if there are unforeseen consequences, is regarded as part of the process. In the words of Betty, one of Davis's interviewees: "You have to stand behind the decision."[22]

While the psychological benefit of cosmetic surgery is not clear, the psychological literature is clear that there are significant harms attached to increased body dissatisfaction. In addition to those I detailed in chapter 2, there are psychological harms of self-objectification. I will return to philosophical accounts of objectification in the next chapter; for now, I wish to note that psychologists regard self-objectification as ubiquitous and harmful.[23] For example, Marika Tiggemann and Elyse Williams describe self-objectification as a predictor of mental health issues in young women, particularly those of disordered eating.[24] While I am wary of causal claims, it seems incontestable that increased attention to the body and over-locating identity in appearance does result in severe psychological harms; recall Nichola Rumsey's description of identity as a pie and the need to ensure that appearance is only a piece of the pie.[25] Moreover, there is some evidence to suggest that while surgery might be sought as a solution to body shame and feelings of inadequacy, it may "actually intensify self-objectification for women living in a sexually objectifying cultural milieu, leading to a vicious cycle of psychological distress and surgical alterations to appearance."[26]

Thus there are individual physical harms from engaging in beauty practices, particularly surgery. These may be balanced by psychological benefits of improved self-esteem and well-being. But such reports of increased well-being should be set in the context of what we know about the general rise in body dissatisfaction, low self-esteem and self-objectification, and the psychological harms that we know result from attaching too much weight to appearance. Thus while surgery, or other engagement in beauty practices, may produce improved well-being, and individuals may be satisfied, they may suffer lower self-esteem and overworry about appearance in a way they might not have done had surgery not been an option, or had they not fallen under the sway of the beauty ideal.

It is in this area, of harms to engaging individuals, where action is likely, and there are calls from many quarters for further standardization, information, and monitoring of surgical and nonsurgical cosmetic procedures, and for the collection of data.[27] The Keogh Review recommended changes in three areas: first, in provision, in calls for safe products and skilled and responsible providers; second, in care, to ensure an informed and protected public; and third, in redress.[28] These calls have been responded to in a number of quarters. For instance, in 2016 the General Medical Council introduced "Guidance for Doctors who Offer Cosmetic Interventions," which sought to address many of Keogh's worries.[29] Amongst other requirements it focused on the need for adequate training and experience, the importance of ensuring patients have realistic expectations, the importance of considering psychological need, the importance of doctors attaining consent directly, and the need to ensure responsible marketing. The Royal College of Surgeons, published "Professional Standards for Cosmetic Surgery," to supplement the GMC guidance with more detailed instructions of what is required to meet professional standards.[30]

Some of the recommendations suggest that practice in this sector may not have been all that it should. For instance, the instructions by the GMC that doctors must physically examine patients and "must not therefore prescribe these medicines by telephone, video link, online or at the request of others for patients you have not examined" suggests that some doctors have not been meeting best practice standards.[31] Accordingly there is much to be done if good practice and appropriate governance mechanisms are to be embedded; especially when it comes to nonsurgical procedures. Nonsurgical procedures are scandalously under-regulated, and the Keogh report states:

> Dermal fillers are a particular cause for concern as anyone can set themselves up as a practitioner, with no requirement for knowledge, training or previous experience. Nor are there sufficient checks in place with regard to product quality—most dermal fillers have no more controls than a bottle of floor cleaner.[32]

Yet, even though there are many legitimate concerns about such practices and action is needed, there is a collective recognition that there are significant gaps in data collection, safety of products and procedures, provider training and experience, consumer information and consent practices, and redress mechanisms.[33] But the most significant harms and benefits of the increasingly demanding and dominant beauty ideal are not to those who engage, but to all as demands increase. The creation of the social and cultural context within which agency of all individuals is exercised and the choices of all are shaped is far more important than the current choices of a few.

Injustice and Communal Harms

In this section, I wish to highlight—sadly in brief—as each merits a book of its own, three communal harms, in addition to the significant harm of normalization: first, the exploitation of vulnerable workers (as opposed to consumers); second, the connected harms of opportunity cost and resource allocation; third, discrimination and the creation of a toxic environment for those who fall outside the ever narrower normal range.

The first justice harm I wish to highlight is the direct harms and costs to others from beauty practices. These are classic issues of exploitation and inequality in the service industries, not beauty-specific concerns. I only mention them in passing in order to note their significance and to suggest that, irrespective of other concerns about the beauty ideal, there are justice reasons for considering beauty practices. Policy makers tend to focus primarily on the safety and choices of consumers, but there are also harms to providers who tend to come from poorer and more vulnerable demographics. Too often these harms to relatively powerless and voiceless women (and it is usually women) are left out of the calculation. One timely example is the recent revelations about the toxicity of the products necessary for the application of acrylic nails and gel polish. The potentially extremely harmful effects to the beauty practitioners who provide manicures to New York's well-groomed were exposed by the *New York Times* in 2015.[34]

The harms include miscarriage, cancers, skin irritations, respiratory problems, children born with health issues and learning difficulties. While this is anecdotal, so well-known are such harms within the sector that "older manicurists warn women of child-bearing age away from the business, with its potent brew of polishes, solvents, hardeners and glues."[35] Moreover, undoubtedly "some of the chemicals in nail products are known to cause cancer; others have elevated rates of death from Hodgkin's disease, of low birth-weight babies and of multiple myeloma."[36] Beauty work then can be risky work, and given that it is often performed by those lower down the race and class hierarchies there are clear justice concerns. Indeed, exploitation of vulnerable workers, especially along hierarchies of race and sex, is a standard justice concern with parallels to the maid trade and reproductive labor.[37] Beauty then, no less than other global industries, and perhaps more than some, given its feminized nature, raises issues of economic injustice and exploitation.[38]

The second justice harms, and again not beauty-specific, are the standard global justice concerns of opportunity cost and resource allocation. The opportunities that are lost by diverting so much time, money, and effort to beauty is a matter of justice, especially when considered globally. While citing the familiar caveat regarding my wariness of statistical evidence, from any perspective the beauty industry is big business. For example, in 2001 the global market for cosmetic, toiletry and fragrance products was $175 billion, and re-garded as recession proof.[39] In 2014, the global cosmetic industry was estimated at €181 billion.[40] In 2011, the hair removal market was estimated as $ 2.1 billion in the United States with the UK not far behind.[41] Over 10 million surgical and nonsurgical cosmetic proce-dures were performed in the United States in 2014, costing over $12 billion, an increase of over 400 percent since 1997.[42] In the UK in 2010 cosmetic interventions were estimated to be worth £2.3 bil-lion, and estimated to be £3.6 billion by 2015, with 75 percent of market value on nonsurgical procedures.[43] Parallel arguments can be made about the time and expertise. Recall the discussion in chap-ter 4 about the cost in time, when just two minutes a day adds up to a month over a lifetime. The amount of time the average woman spends beautifying a day seems to be between around 20 to 30 min-utes.[44] If it were 20 minutes a day between 15 and 75 this adds up to 7300 hours, which is 304 days 24 hours a day, over a lifetime.

If it were possible to put together all of the statistics from the vast industries associated with the body beautiful, including the diet and exercise industries, the toiletry and cosmetic industries, the beauty and surgery industries, then it is likely that the total figure would be spectacular and rival other large global industries. We usually worry about large-scale global industries, which cross national borders and rival the GDP of states, for justice reasons. Distributive justice arguments about how goods and expertise should be justly distributed are no less prevalent when it comes to the global beauty industry. For instance, in addition to the vast amounts of time and money spent on beauty products and procedures, significant scientific and medical expertise and resources are devoted to the development of beauty products. Money and expertise that could be devoted, for instance, to addressing life-threatening disease rather than say, hair loss. Standard global justice arguments about resource allocation and opportunity cost apply to beauty, just as they do to any sector of international trade.

The third justice harm is that of discrimination. A consequence of the rise in minimal standards of beauty is discrimination of those who fall outside the normal range. Appearance discrimination—lookism—has been compared to the more familiar sexism and racism.[45] Indeed some argue these biases are pervasive and hard wired.[46] In response, either we seek to outlaw or change societies' discriminatory responses, or we seek to make those who are currently discriminated against more "normal," so they come nearer to the acceptable range, or compensate them in some other way. However addressing discrimination by fixing abnormal bodies—as some health systems already do—is not without problems. First, it assumes that lookism is a proper, and natural, response, rather than a flawed and discriminatorily response. The history of race and sex discrimination alone should lead us to be suspicious of accounts that regard discrimination by visible group traits as natural. We do not accept biases, even unconscious and implicit bias, simply because they exist. Second, it assumes that such discrimination can either be fixed or compensated; yet in practice increased attention to appearance, even if the aim is to address discrimination, further embeds the dominance of appearance and so creates a toxic environment that encourages worries about appearance and appearance discrimination, and so the cycle continues.

To illustrate, those who fall outside the normal range fall into two broad groups. The first are those who are disfigured by disability or accident or have physical features that are dramatically outside the normal range. No matter what those in these groups do they will never be able to attain normal. The second group are those who fall only a little outside the normal range, who could bring themselves within the normal range using products or procedures. For the first group there is no possibility of attaining normal, and therefore as appearance matters more, it is likely that discrimination against this group will increase. In addition, those who fail to measure up to appearance standards will become rarer, as appearance issues become regarded as disabilities. For instance, as individuals choose to select against hare-lips, and hare-lips become rarer, so those with hare-lips (or the tell-tale features of an operation to remove a hare-lip) fall further outside the normal range. Such selection is likely to extend: for example, a recent study found that were the technology available 11 percent of couples would abort a fetus predisposed to obesity.[47] Moreover this type of discrimination intersects with other forms of discrimination; an appearance-focused society that endorses a narrow range of normal will increase its capacity for discrimination.

For the second group, it is possible for them to attain standards of normal, for instance by having surgery or other interventions. However, as more of us have technical fixes to fall within the normal range, the normal range narrows. Accordingly, while such individual responses might help to address individual discrimination— the individual will be normal—collectively it contributes to a more discriminative culture as what is normal narrows. For example, as we increasingly fix appearance abnormalities, for instance, pin back ears that stick out, or remove birth marks, so there are fewer visible birth marks, and the range of normal ears is narrower. While fixing individuals reduces prejudice directed towards particular individuals, it increases prejudice in general. It becomes less possible, for individuals and parents, to resist pressures to change appearance toward the norm, and it makes those with flaws that cannot be fixed more visible and more abnormal. If the normalization thesis of the last chapter is correct, then more people will fall outside normal as normal narrows. Increasingly features such as wrinkles and jowls will be abnormal, as yellow teeth or sticky out ears already are. Thus such interventions contribute to a toxic environment.

In addition, such an individual response places the onus for removing discrimination on the individual who is marked out, rather than on society. Here the social model of disability is illuminating. According to the social model of disability, the extent to which a person is disabled is not a product of the physical impairment but rather of the social context which either imposes or removes obstacles to independent living.[48] While the parallels are not exact, it is likely that an argument could be made that being abnormal is caused by a social context in which appearance overly matters and normal is narrowly defined. Thus, while seeking to address the effects of lookism an individual response may increase rather than decrease discrimination.

Much more could be written about beauty discrimination, lookism, and how to address it. For instance there are arguments about discrimination on equality grounds. If beauty is a good, similar to education or health, or indeed potentially more valuable than these if my claims about the ethical nature of the beauty ideal are correct, then those who cannot attain normal suffer injustice. If beauty opens doors, then a lack of beauty, or a lack of access to beauty, might be regarded as unfairly discriminatory. None of these communal harms figure in much of the debate about the ethics of surgery and yet the extent of the possible injustices and harms that attach to them is vast.

Communal and Collective Pleasures

In the final section of the chapter, I turn to the communal pleasures of beauty. That this section is smaller than the harms is not an indication that the pleasures of beauty are too small to mention; I will return to individual pleasures in the next two chapters. Too often books critical of beauty practices deny the very real pleasures of engagement and success when it comes to beauty. Claiming that there are no pleasures involved in beauty is every bit as disingenuous as claiming that there are no harms of beauty. As we have seen, the harms are significant and extensive, but there are pleasures too. Some are of the obvious self-care and pampering kind, as many of the practices themselves are intrinsically enjoyable. Some pleasures are less obvious, such as the pleasure that is derived from feeling virtuous and proud of body work. That pleasure can be found in inherently nonpleasurable practices is, I will go on to argue, a function of the ethical nature of the beauty ideal and crucial to understanding its ongoing dominance and pervasiveness. In this section, I will focus only on the social and communal pleasures of beauty practices. While some beauty practices are individual, very many are social and communal, and the importance of these shared practices needs to be appreciated in any adequate account of beauty. I will highlight just two, that of the loving touch and female bonding.

Beauty practices are one of the few acceptable places in which nonsexual caressing is acceptable and widely available. For example, the only tender and prolonged, nonmedical, human touch an elderly person may receive is the hour a week she spends having her hair and nails done. In many beauty practices—performed by professionals, friends, and family—touch is central. Think of the hours mothers and friends spend braiding hair, painting nails, painting henna, and so on. At least some of the reason we spend time on such practices is to touch and caress.

The importance of touch for human beings is hard to overestimate. Most human beings have a desperate need to touch and be touched if they are to flourish. Increasingly, this need is downplayed in a visual and virtual culture. In a world where touch is often sexual, or between parent and child, the beauty touch is a permitted and acceptable form of touch, and one where prolonged adult-to-adult touch, is allowed. This is true of all kinds of beauty practices, and happens in nail bars, hairdressers, beauty parlors, and the home. The loving touch is not, of course, necessarily tied to beauty. There could be all kinds of ways in which loving touch could be integrated into social practices. For example, the head massage (which often accompanies hair washing in hairdressers) is not beauty related as such, and could be reproduced in a nonbeauty context. However, while possible, this would require the introduction of a touch-orientated cultural sector, which we do not currently have. Nearly all women go to the hairdresser, a much smaller percentage currently have nonbeauty treatments like massage (and often even massage is presented as being for beauty reasons). Moreover, even where such alternative sources of loving touch are available, they would need to be legitimized and sanctioned. The loving touch in beauty is a by-product of practices that are already regarded as legitimate. To see the loving touch as a legitimate practice in its own right would be a significant change. In a context in which the beauty touch is legitimated by the importance of body work, it is the loving touch, not the beauty touch, that seems unusual, self-indulgent, and narcissistic.

The social benefits of the loving touch connect to the second communal benefit, or pleasure, of beauty, that of beauty as a form of social bonding; particularly, but by no means exclusively, female bonding. Bonding can happen in organized ways in that beauty practices often take place in settings that are safe female spaces. But, it can also happen more generally, beauty-talk as friendship-talk, admiration-talk and connection-talk, as a symbol for, and instance of, affection and admiration. This is what Young is alluding to when she states:

> Girls often establish relations of intimacy by exchanging clothes; sisters and roommates raid each other's closets, sometimes unpermitted; daughters' feet clomp around in their mothers shoes. I love my sweater, and in letting you wear it you wear an aspect of me.[49]

The wearing of, and shopping for and giving of, clothes and beauty products is in some ways an extension of the loving touch, a sign of attention and caress: a recognition of and a valuing of the other as an embodied and loved being. In addition to being a means of demonstrating, and even a manifestation of, affection, beauty-talk is also a way to signal openness to intimacy. In this way, it functions as a shared language that signals good intent and establishes connection. Again to quote Young, "women often establish rapport with one another by remarking on their clothes, and doing so often introduces a touch of intimacy or lightness into serious or impersonal situations."[50]

The bonding and female friendly nature of beauty-talk and communal engagement in beauty practices is often missed, particularly as the dangers of fat-talk are emphasized. There are dangers and harms in beauty-talk: for instance, Rachel Calogero and colleagues, have found that compliments about weight and shape, even when they are positive, can be particularly detrimental.[51] This work is important, as it shows that irrespective of the content, any comment on weight and shape, no matter how positive, or well-intended, can be destructive. Calogero and colleagues, suggest that all comments about looks "remind women that they are being evaluated and valued based on their appearance, in particular with regard to how closely they approximate the thin ideal."[52] This is true even when women are not overfocused on appearance and even when they feel good about receiving compliments about their weight; thus they conclude, "to say something nice may be worse than saying nothing at all when the content of the comments is about the appearance of women's weight or shape."[53] The negative impact of fat-talk provides a cautionary tale that should lead us to be suspicious of the lauding of "female pleasures."

Yet while we should be skeptical, we should not dismiss the social function of beauty-talk and practices to provide women with ways to connect with each other in safe and affirming spaces. For instance, in her study of aerobics, Gimlin found that as well as feeling virtuous for engaging in body work women also valued the connections and networks they built by participating. She found that "they use aerobics to build or deepen female relationships, share accomplishments, and take pleasure in compliments received from women outside the class."[54] Attending diet groups (such as Weight Watchers or Slimming World) or attending exercise classes provide opportunities to be with others, sometimes but by no means always, in predominantly female groups. Such bonding is socially acceptable and even virtuous, in contrast to other forms of socializing. For many women, it is harder to justify leaving family and work commitments to socialize, than to engage with friends in diet and exercise; activities, which are regarded as necessary and virtuous. Again to cite Gimlin's work, "many women report that their favorite aspect of body work is interacting with other women in a predominantly female arena."[55] Ann Cahill makes a similar argument in her account of her and her sisters preparing for her brother's wedding. She recounts a shared, enjoyable, and communal experience of getting ready together; each woman has a different approach, and all worry to some extent about beautifying. But in the process there is care and communication, and even "a paradigmatically feminist model of intersubjectivity, wherein the bodies actions and possibilities of these two persons are deeply entwined with each other's."[56] Moreover, she notes that the getting "dressed up" may be the best part of the event; an experience of getting ready together that many women and girls recognize.

This is not to claim that female spaces and bonding are always wholly positive. For instance, while beauty salons and clothes shopping can provide female spaces for women to bond and share and support each other, they can also be spaces that are used to criticize and intimidate. While some women love engaging in such practices, and find going to the hairdresser a time of great pleasure and relaxation (almost irrespective of how their hair turns out), others find such places daunting and uncomfortable. Moreover, the fact that bonding occurs is not necessarily a reason to continue the practice; while it might be a pleasure, it might still be harmful. As Chambers reminds us, "some pleasure-endowed internalised norms are better than others."[57] Some would regard claims to bonding over what they regard as harmful pleasures ludicrous; for instance, Sheila Jeffreys argues that "bonding to swap survival tips under domination, though it may be necessary, constitutes accommodation to oppression rather than an example of women's agency and creativity that is worth celebrating."[58] Nonetheless, for some women there is joy to be found in looking at, and touching, wearing and shopping for clothes, whether alone or with others—to the extent, as Young says, that "some of our clothes we love for their own sake, because their fabric and cut and colour charm us and relate to our bodies in specific ways—because, I almost want to say, they love us back"⁵⁹—for others clothes are alien objects, and the language of joy and bonding that many women report is alien and exclusionary. Across the board, many women undoubtedly find pleasure in beauty-orientated shared practices.

Such communal benefits are perhaps even harder to measure and qualify than communal harms, but nonetheless they should be part of the picture. In addition, they serve a social function, touched on in chapter 3, of crossing, and perhaps breaking down, class and race barriers. In the next chapter, when I move to focusing on the self, the communal context needs to be borne in mind.

Conclusion

In this chapter, I have sought to track some of the pains and pleasures of beauty. I have focused on the communal pains and pleasures. I have argued that while there are harms to engaging individuals in the beauty context, to focus only on these harms not only misses the most pressing and far-reaching harms, but it skews the discussion. It fails to recognize harms to current and future others. In a small attempt to redress this lack, I have highlighted the justice harms of discrimination: opportunity cost and the allocation of scare resources and the risks of exploitation of vulnerable providers. I have not dwelled on these justice harms, not least because as standard justice harms they are not beauty specific. In addition, it may be that even these harms are overshadowed by the communal harm of normalization, discussed in the last chapter. In addition to recognizing the justice harms, I have also sought to recognize that these are not the whole story and there are important social and communal pleasures of beauty that are life and community enhancing and that need to be taken account of in a consideration of the beauty ideal as a whole.

7

My Body, Myself

That beauty practices are pleasurable *and* harmful and sometimes both simultaneously helps to explain the dominance of the beauty ideal. In this chapter, I wish to explore further why the beauty ideal continues to be embraced despite its increasingly stringent and punishing demands. One reason for why we continue to strive for the ideal, even as we age, wrinkle, and sag, is because giving up on the ideal is costly. It requires giving up on the possibility of attaining the goods that the ideal promises and on giving up on the better, perfect self we are striving for. Heyes echoes this describing the experience of giving up dieting "as much as grieving as liberation"[1] and Wolf speaks of weight control as the equivalent of a religious cult.[2] Some dismiss the pleasures of beauty: in Sandra Bartky's words, "the satisfactions of narcissism are real enough, but they are *repressive* satisfactions";[3] although the nature of the pleasures was something she continued to question.[4] To think that nothing is lost but subordinate pleasures if beauty practices cease is to miss the ethical nature of the ideal, it fails to recognize that we can succeed on a day-to-day basis—and that this matters to us—even if ultimately the ideal is unattainable. Moreover, as the ethical ideal embeds and beauty matters more, such practices are less often regarded as vain and narcissistic, but rather, as Jones argues, as acts of "courage, bravery and self-determination."[5] Crucial here is how we conceptualize the self. What is it to give up on ourselves? In this chapter, I will explore this. I will argue that to understand beauty as an ethical ideal requires understanding of how the self is constructed under the beauty ideal. I will argue that at the heart of the beauty ideal is the imagined self, and the journey towards the imagined self. The argument for the imagined self is the third main argument of the book, and my claim is that only by understanding the power of the imagined self, and its dominance, can we understand the dual nature of the beauty ideal and why, despite the harms and the costs, simply telling individuals to reject it is unfair and unrealistic.

In this chapter, I first describe the self under the beauty ideal, in particular the imagined self, the end point of the ideal. Second, I argue that the first stage in locating the self, in part, in the imagined self is locating the self in the body. To make this argument, I introduce accounts of sexual objectification and self-objectification. I then develop my account by denying that objectification is always sexual. I argue for an account of beauty objectification that does not imply sexual threat and is distanced from sexual desire. Let me be clear. I am not arguing that there are not gendered and gendering elements to the beauty ideal or that worries that the increasing sexualization, even pornification, of beauty is damaging to women and perhaps to all are not correct. At least as it manifests in the West, the contemporary beauty ideal is hypersexualizing and binary. However, arguments about the harms of increasing sexualization track differently and perhaps diametrically, to the arguments made in this chapter about beauty objectification and in the later chapter on gender exploitation. Those arguments suggest that sexualized and binary norms are more dominant and suggest gender difference and inequality may be growing. This may or may not be true, but it is not the argument of this book. Here I argue that—as an ideal to be aspired to and as practices engaged in—beauty is not necessarily sexual. Recall from the introduction that originally I had intended to include arguments about looking sexy in contrast to feeling sexy, but was forced to put these concerns aside to pursue the core beauty arguments of *Perfect Me*; I will return to these questions in future work.

The Imagined Self

The self that is constructed under the beauty ideal is identified with the body; the actual, transforming and imagined body. The imagined self is the self, symbolized by the body, which it is believed, hoped, or imagined will emerge at the end of the beautification process. It is the after-self of makeover culture—the after of surgery, the after of weight loss and exercise regimes, the after of religiously stuck-to beauty regimes—it is even the after we seek to approximate with doctored and enhanced selfies.

The imagined self has a number of features that it is important to understand. First, while the imagined self identifies the self with the body, it identifies not just with the actual body that we have, but with the body we will, or could, have if only we engaged as we should. Second, the imagined self is the self we already identify with—at least in part—and we may even regard this as our best or real self, the self we are seeking to become.[6] Third, imagining attaining this self—and the goods and life that we will have once we succeed—provides a powerful motivator for continuing engagement. This is true even when we know that the perfect, imagined self will never be attained. Actually attaining the imagined self is less important than engaging in practices and habits of beauty and committing to this self. Identifying with the imagined self makes us critical of our real flawed and failing current body, but also positive about how we are a transforming self, actively working to improve. The gap between our current self and the imagined self is less important than we might suspect, as action and movement towards the imagined self, however ultimately unattainable, are positive and feel empowering. Accordingly, commitment to our imagined self can be rewarding even though it is never attained. Recognizing that the self is located in the body—the actual, the transforming, and the imagined body—is crucial to understanding how the beauty ideal is functioning as a successful ethical ideal. In short, we project pictures of ourselves, which range from critical judgments of our actual bodies, to successful pictures of our transforming bodies (the-ten-pound lighter self, the toned self, the golden-skinned self, the improved self), finally to pictures of the imagined self we'd like to be, our best self, the perfect me. These pictures, constructions, and imaginings of ourselves and our bodies—actual, becoming, and imagined—are the self we identify with. Of course, all of these bodies are pictures and imagined in a sense, as there is no real or natural body, our actual body, as much as our ideal body, is constructed and imagined.[7]

This is not a psychological claim about the location of the self— although there are psychological parallels in social comparison and self-objectification theories—but a philosophical and ethical claim about identity, meaning and value.[8] The claim is that we experience and value ourselves as bodies and across a spectrum: sometimes as failing—fat, frumpy, and having a bad hair day—other times as succeeding, active, and powerful and fulfilling some aspect of our ideal self. Always the ideal, the perfect me, or even just the good enough, imagined self, remains unattainable, to be strived for, providing both an impossible standard and holding out possibilities and promises of the better, perfect, life that will be awarded to that better, perfect, self. In the next chapter, I will return to the dual nature of the beauty ideal and to how the imagined self is crucial for explaining how a demanding and often punishing beauty ideal is not only adhered to but embraced and elevated. For now, and in brief, my claim is that identifying with the imagined self reduces the negative responses we might otherwise have to being regarded as, and regarding ourselves as, flawed, failing, and ugly (especially as experience shows that improvement is hard). The promise of the after self, the better self, keeps us active and positive, despite the setbacks. The imagined self helps transform the critical gaze we apply to our actual bodies into an optimistic and desiring gaze as we focus forward to what might be and to the goods that we imagine will follow as we approach our improved, better, and best self.

Locating the Self in the Actual, Becoming, and Imagined Body

Before moving to my claims for the imagined self and how it helps to understand the dual nature of the beauty ideal, I first want to make an argument for how we have come to identify ourselves with the imagined self. I argue that identifying the self with the imagined self first requires an identification of the self with the body, and more than this, as a body that can be evaluated: the body as an object, as something "to be looked at" and judged. As the body is judged so we are judged. To make this claim, I turn first to feminist work that has critiqued the objectification of women and the reduction of women to objects. I begin with such accounts, but distinguish my account from these by arguing that beauty objectification is not necessarily sexual if it does not carry an implied sexual threat and can be distanced from sexual desire. Essentially, I use objectification theory to establish the "to be looked at" nature of the self and the identification of the self with the body. Having established this, I go on to argue that the imagined self that emerges under the current beauty ideal—the "to be looked at," objectified, self—is not wholly negative, as it manifests in the transforming, transformable, and imagined self.

The Self as Body and Object

The equation of the female with and in the body is a core feminist critique of patriarchy. A classic text is Simone de Beauvoir's *The Second Sex*; where man is subject and women is other.[9] The apparent essentialism of this view has been critiqued and for good reason, but the core notion of the gendered nature of socialization of those who present as women as other, objects and bodies is useful: the extent of the essentialism of de Beauvoir is contested.[10] The location of the self in the body is systematized in philosophical accounts of objectification and self-objectification. The paradigmatic example of objectification comes from Bartky's landmark book, *Femininity and Domination*.[11] Bartky describes the process of objectification as the reduction of women to a mere object. She does this using a now famous example of catcalling:

> It is a fine spring day, and with an utter lack of self-consciousness, I am bouncing down the street. Suddenly I hear men's voices. Catcalls and whistles fill the air. These noises are clearly sexual in intent and they are meant for me; they come from across the street. I freeze. As Sartre would say I have been petrified by the gaze of the Other. My face flushes and my motions become stiff and self-conscious. The body which only a moment before I inhabited with such ease now floods my consciousness. I have been made into an object.[12]

In this account objectification is done by men to women. As Bartky continues, "I must be *made* to know that I am a 'nice piece of ass': I must be made to see myself as they see me."[13] The oppressive and devastating effect of objectification for Bartky is everywhere, a given incontestable and part of the subordination of women: I will return to gendered exploitation is chapter 10. Bartky continues her account of objectification by arguing that the observer and observed can be the same person. Objectification can be internalized becoming self-objectification; not just something done to us by others, but something we do to ourselves. According to Bartky, "a woman can become a sex object for herself, taking towards her own person the attitude of the man. She will then take erotic satisfaction in her physical self, revelling in her body as a beautiful object to be gazed at and decorated."[14] In this way, the male gaze is internalized, and the women is the "seer and seen, appraiser and the thing appraised";[15] that "subject to the evaluating eye of the male connoisseur, women learn to evaluate themselves first and best."[16] The transformation of the male gaze, into our gaze, *the* gaze, is key to what Bartky terms the "fashion-beauty complex."[17] For those who adopt this perspective, the woman is an object, a body, to be worked on: the "female body is revealed as a task, an object in need of transformation."[18]

From Bartky's critique, I wish to take forward the objectification thesis: that women turn themselves into objects, locate their selves in their bodies, and regard themselves as "to be looked at."

Objectification and self-objectification are the mechanisms by which we locate the self in the body, and thus offer a conceptual account of the first stage by which the self is constructed under the beauty ideal. However, while endorsing the "to be looked" aspect of objectification, I will reject some of Bartky's other claims. In this chapter, I will argue, contra Bartky, that objectification is possible in the beauty context without it always or simply being sexual objectification. In the next chapter, I will argue that reduction to the body in a visual culture might not be quite as reductive as has been claimed.

Sexual Objectification

That objectification is always *sexual* is assumed in traditional philosophical accounts of objectification. I will argue that while beauty norms are fundamentally connected with what is sexually desirable, in that what is considered beautiful is highly influenced by what is sexually desirable (and arguably especially in the West as porn mainstreams), in beauty it is possible to offer an account of objectification that is separate, or at least separable, from sexual threat and even sexual desire.[19] In order to do this, I will first offer a fuller philosophical account of sexual objectification, highlighting that in these accounts objectification is always sexual.

Accounts of objectification and self-objectification derive from Kantian thinking about how to treat ourselves and others with respect and as persons. Particularly relevant here is Kant's second formulation of the Categorical Imperative set out in *Groundwork of the Metaphysics of Morals.* The requirement is to "act in such a way that you treat humanity, whether in your own person or in the person of any other, never simply as a means, but always at the same time as an end."[20] Objectifying another person, regarding her as an object, is a failure to treat that person as an end in herself; in Kantian terms as a person at all (and crucial to Kant's concept of personhood is the setting of your own ends as well as the respecting other's ends). The injunction to always treat persons as ends would seem to preclude—from a moral point of view—objectification. As Lina Papakaki describes Kant's view "objectification, then is a necessarily negative phenomenon because it involves seriously harming a person's humanity. In being reduced to a mere thing for use, the objectified individual's humanity is diminished."[21] In his *Lectures on Ethics* Kant considers sexual objectification directly; speaking of sexual love making "objects of appetite." This to Kant denies the personhood of the other, and reduces her to an object: "for as soon as anyone becomes an object of another's appetite, all motives of moral relationship fall away; as object of the other's appetite, that person is in fact a thing, whereby the other's appetite is sated, and can be misused as such a thing by anybody."[22] Sexual objectification then in Kant is wholly reductive—it reduces a person to an object—and this makes her vulnerable to the harms of being used as such.[23] For Kant, once an object always an object.[24]

This account of sexual objectification has been built on by feminist theorists, with the most influential accounts coming from Andrea Dworkin and Catharine MacKinnon. Dworkin and MacKinnon take a broadly Kantian view about the problems of objectification and develop their views in response to patriarchy. Similar to Bartky, the dominance of women by men is crucial and accordingly asymmetry and hierarchy are underpinning assumptions. Dworkin, like Kant, thinks that objectification depersonalizes and makes persons into things. An objectified woman becomes an object, a thing, and for Dworkin (and MacKinnon) always a *sexual* object. Moreover, objectification does not happen only when a woman is viewed, or used, as a sexual object, but, and importantly, sexual objectification is pervasive. The fact that women can be, and, usually, are viewed as sexual object effects—and for Dworkin and MacKinnon is harmful to—all women and all of the time. For MacKinnon all women in patriarchal society suffer as a result of the fact that women are sexual objects. Because women *can* be reduced to sexual objects, in a way that they argue men (structurally) cannot, it becomes defining of what *women* means. For Dworkin and MacKinnon women actually become objects; it is not *as if* they are objects, but in patriarchal society they become such.[25]

Further, it is the relation of domination that defines gender, and effectively creates male and female. Thus gender is constructed; it "emerges as the congealed form of the sexualisation of inequality between men and women."[26] Consequently, as Sally Haslanger, discusses, "male" and "female" do not necessarily map to "man" and "woman."[27] What matters here is that objectification is connected to a binary of dominance and submission that is eroticized. Those who are submissive are "*viewed as* and *treated as* an object" and treated functionally "*for* the satisfaction of others."[28] Haslanger formalizes MacKinnon's account of gender as, "x *is woman* iff there is a y such that y sexually objectifies x; x *is a man* iff there is a y such that x sexually objectifies y."[29] So for MacKinnon (and similarly for Dworkin) hierarchy of one group over another is crucial.[30] Haslanger sums this up as "what we share, as women, is that we are perceived and treated as sexually subordinate. Our commonality is in the eye, and the hand, and the power of the beholder."[31] Objectification is fundamentally sexual, always about power, domination, and subordination. These second-wave feminist arguments placed the evils of the subordination and the exploitation of women firmly at the door of men: not as individuals (although of course individuals contribute to this), but as a structural injustice that requires much more than individual men treating individual women better for equality to be attained.

The assumptions and conclusions of these arguments have been challenged in a number of ways, and I will return to accounts of gender hierarchy and exploitation in chapter 10. In addition, such arguments are in tension with contemporary feminist emphasis on women's agency and empowerment and with theories that insist on embodiment and reject objectification critiques on the grounds they assume a flawed individualist, Kantian model of persons.[32] Even thinkers who retain some objectification concerns, such as Gill, question the usefulness of the concept, asking "how useful is the notion of "objectification" in a mediascape in which far from being presented as passive objects women are increasingly depicted as active, desiring sexual subjects?"[33] This issue I will return to in the next chapter. For now let me seek to take forward the account of objectification as "to be looked at," which identifies the self with the body, but which rejects some of the more problematic implications of objectification.

Reclaiming Objectification

For Kant, Bartky, Dworkin, and MacKinnon objectification is always harmful. It is always wrong to objectify, to deny a person subjectivity and autonomy, to treat her as if she were an object that can be used and broken. While we might well agree with this—surely it is wrong to treat a person as an object?—we might not agree with the implications of sexual objectification and self-objectification theory. For instance, we might object, as Gill's critique implies, to the correlation of "object" with "passive" and "victim." Furthermore, we might worry about what has been read, sometimes wrongly, as a prudishness or antisex element of objectification accounts. To be sure, this is evident in Kant who regards all nonmarital sex as objectifying (particularly of women). Kant, undoubtedly was prudish and puritanical—we might say he had issues with sex—but this does not apply to other accounts. For example, Dworkin is in favor of exploring sexuality and sexual norms.[34] However, while criticisms that objectification theory is prudish or antisex are questionable, the picture of positive sexual encounter they present is distinctively nonvisual and perhaps, rather than prudishness, this is what makes them seem outdated. Looking sexy is crucial to being sexy in a visual and virtual culture. This equation of looking sexy with being sexy is part of what Dworkin and MacKinnon wish to critique and disrupt. They wish to endorse being sexual in terms of having fabulous sexual experience (embodied) and reject being sexually evaluated as an attractive body (objectified). As I develop the account of the imagined self, I will reject this dichotomy and argue that the self in the beauty context is object and subject, and that objectification, especially as we do it to ourselves, is not necessarily or wholly reductive. To make this argument, and to argue for an account of objectification and self-objectification in the beauty context which is not always sexual, I will begin by introducing the work of Martha Nussbaum and her claim that not all objectification is harmful. Nussbaum's account, like those before her is of sexual objectification, and therefore it does not advance my account of beauty objectification as such. But, it is a plea for attention to context, and she argues that in some contexts some features of objectification might not always be harmful and reductive. As such, it does not offer a systematic account in which x is always harmful and y is not, but it does suggest that all objectification is not the same, and it is this which I will take forward in making my argument for a distinctive account of objectification in the beauty context.

Nussbaum seeks to distinguish the elements of sexual objectification and argues that in some contexts objectification may be benign, and perhaps "necessary or even wonderful features of sexual life."[35] To make her argument Nussbaum lists seven ways in which objectification, the treatment of people as things or objects, can occur. These are instrumentality, denial of autonomy, inertness, fungability, violability, ownership, and denial of subjectivity.[36] Of most importance for sexual objectification is the denial of autonomy and subjectivity (treating a person as if she lacks self-determination or feelings), which denies personhood, and instrumentality (being treated as a tool for use). For Nussbaum, objectification is a cluster term, which signals a number of possible concerns about the way that people can be thought of and treated, but to determine which feature is in play or whether it is problematic or not, each of these features needs to be considered and in the context of the wider relationship.

Nussbaum considers six examples of sexual relationships taken from literature (from D. H. Lawrence to *Playboy*). Some examples she concludes are objectifying in ways that are familiar from Dworkin and MacKinnon, such as the *Playboy* example. The example describes pictures of Nicollette Sheridan playing tennis, showing her knickers with the caption "Why we love tennis!"[37] This for Nussbaum is a classic example of sexual objectification:

> the *Playboy* caption reduces the young actress, a skilled tennis player, to a body ripe for male use: it says, in effect, she thinks she's displaying herself as a skilled athletic performer, but all the while she is actually displaying herself to *our* gaze as a sexual object.[38]

In this form, objectification denies autonomy and subjectivity, and reduces to a body that is presented as fungible and available to be used for pleasure. This for Nussbaum has all the marks of morally problematic objectification (and is not benign simply because it is supposedly about pleasure). The message is clear:

> what *Playboy* repeatedly says to its reader is Whoever this women is and whatever she has achieved, for you she is all cunt, all her pretensions vanish before your sexual power. For some she is a tennis player—but you, in your mind, can dominate her and turn her into cunt.[39]

Like Kant, Dworkin, and MacKinnon, Nussbaum is not defending sexual objectification in this form, and she is particularly critical of treating persons as tools or instruments.[40] But not all objectification, she argues, is of this type. Nussbaum introduces the example of using her lover's stomach as a pillow as a nonproblematic form of objectification, despite reducing her lover to an object. She argues that "in the matter of objectification, context is everything,"[41] and while she is treating her lover as an object it is not as a mere object. Using Kantian-type reasoning Nussbaum claims that sexual objectification is nonproblematic if it is not total: if the person remains an end as well as a means. This is an advance and a challenge to Kant's puritanical views about the corrupting nature of sex. Admittedly, this does not address the structural claims of Dworkin and MacKinnon: the global, rather than local, effect that marks women as a subordinate class, but it does reclaim some potentially positive, or at least benign, forms of objectification.

Nussbaum then goes further. She claims not only that objectification is nonproblematic as long as it is not total (as long as the other is treated as end as well as means), but also suggests some (moral or sexual) virtue in being objectified in very particular ways in sexual relationships. To make these claims, she focuses on D. H. Lawrence's *Rainbow*, which presents lovers as being absorbed in each other to the point where they are "consumed," even "destroyed."[42] Here there is a denial, perhaps surrender, of subjectivity and autonomy and, Nussbaum suggests, perhaps even fundability and violability. It is this objectification of the person (and, using examples from *Lady Chatterley's Lover,* the objectification of body parts) Nussbaum wishes to defend in the context of a certain type of sexual relationship.[43] This type of sexual objectification she argues is mutual and importantly *equal* and not *instrumentalizing.*

According to Nussbaum then, objectification *can*, in certain contexts not only be not problematic but be wonderful. Moreover, this is the case even when there are features of objectification that would be morally problematic in other contexts. Denial of autonomy and subjectivity she regards as only objectionable if they extend beyond the sexual context and permeate other aspects of the relationship, but in the context of sex they are acceptable. But, and importantly, this is because the subjectivity and autonomy of the person as a whole is respected and only at times is it *mutually* sacrificed. Some argue that the emphasis on context and the overall respect of autonomy and subjectivity mean that these scenarios are not really objectification (and that it would be better not to have a benign category of objectification at all).[44] Effectively in Nussbaum's "wonderful" examples humanity is not denied and instrumentization, if it happens at all, happens within clearly defined limits. What matters is not that a person is objectified, whatever that breaks down into, but that she is not treated as a thing overall and across all aspects of the relationship, nor, and importantly, is she subject to or threatened with use against her will.

Taking the Sex out of Objectification

Nussbaum's attempt to reclaim benign forms of sexual objectification, or at least to argue that in some contexts even extreme objectification that turns not only the person into a thing, but a person into body parts, is rewarding and illuminating not only for its conclusion, but also for its method. In this section, I ask whether objectification, as it is manifested under the beauty ideal, is always sexual objectification. I suggest that a person can be objectified, without at least some of the features of sexual objectification. I do not to deny that sexual objectification is often what is going on in visual and virtual culture, but argue that it is not always or at least not only, sexual objectification.

Let us return to the sexual objectification accounts of Dworkin and MacKinnon, for whom objectification is always sexual. The only function of beauty norms for Dworkin is to serve, embed, and maintain sexual subordination. This is shown clearly in Dworkin's detailed description and analysis of the practice of foot binding.[45] She outlines the process, and the extreme pain, of breaking and deforming functional feet and turning them into the ideal, "golden lotus": a three-inch broken mass of skin and bones, nails, and pus well wrapped in intricately embroidered tiny shoes. As a beauty ideal, foot binding was overtly sexual: the tiny foot was a highly erotic object, and it defined male status; only the rich could afford to disable *their* women. Dworkin reports that "the manipulation of the tiny foot was an indispensable prelude to all sexual experience."[46] The equivalence of beauty objectification and sexual objectification is clear in this passage:

> Beauty was the way feet looked and how they moved. Certain feet were better than other feet, more beautiful. Perfect 3-inch form and utter uselessness were the distinguishing marks of the aristocratic foot. These concepts of beauty and status defined women: as ornaments, as sexual playthings, as sexual constructs. The perfect construct, even in China was naturally the prostitute.[47]

Dworkin moves without pause from beauty to sex (and from sex to prostitution). She argues that this nexus (what she calls the "romantic ethos"), continues to be passed from mother to daughter in twentieth-century America and Europe. The technologies of beauty are performed to make women "women" and are always about man-pleasing. They are, as foot binding was, painful.[48] The pain, she argues, is not accidental, but "teaches an important lesson: no price is too great, no process too repulsive, no operation too painful for the women who would be beautiful."[49] Those who are defined as women are sexual objects for those defined as men. This asymmetrical structure is clear in Bartky's catcalling example. Catcalling is always and overtly sexual: done by men to women and with *sexual* intent. For Bartky, objectification is not just the making of women into an object, but into a *sexual* object: Remember, "I must be made to know that I am a 'nice piece of ass'."[50]

Following Nussbaum's methodology of separating out features of objectification, I wish to ask whether objectification is always *sexual*? If the aim is not to make me know "I am a nice piece of ass," but for some other reason, for instance to judge how normal or perfect some aspect of my appearance is, could I still find myself "petrified by the gaze of the Other"? And would it be the same gaze? For Bartky, there is no question that objectification is an instance of male subordination of women, and by definition sexual (even when we do it to ourselves).[51] However, I am not convinced that such a reading *has* to apply or *always* applies. I wish to argue that there are some aspects of sexual objectification that do not, or not necessarily, feature in objectification as I construct it in beauty.

I wish to distinguish beauty objectification, the status of "to be looked at," from accounts of sexual objectification in two particular ways: First I wish to claim that the accounts of sexual objectification from Bartky, Dworkin, and MacKinnon, include a threat of sexual use (the instrumental feature that Nussbaum identified as particularly harmful); and second that in beauty, even though there is an intimate connection between sexual desirability and beauty norms, sexual desire is not always explicit or dominant. Therefore it is possible to be objectified, "to be looked at," without the invocation of sexual desire. If I am correct, then beauty objectification and sexual objectification can be separated, at least in some contexts and in theory.[52] Given this, the self that is identified with the body need not always, or primarily, be focused on sexual desirability when seeking to be good enough, better, or perfect. Establishing this will allow a space for my further claims that the self-located in the body (actual, transforming, and imagined) is not wholly negative, but has positive features, which in turn helps us understand the continuing power of the beauty ideal.

OBJECTIFICATION WITHOUT SEXUAL THREAT

First, if we return to Bartky's catcalling example, does the harm result from the fact that the woman is objectified, for my purposes turned into "something to be looked at," or from the sexual threat that this example implies? In other words, how much of what is wrong in this cat-calling example relies on our knowledge that bad things—sexual violation and rape—happen to "nice pieces of ass"?

The purpose of being made to feel like a "nice piece of ass" is to induce a state of vulnerability that I might be so used. I am not just an object, "to be looked at" (whether with ridicule or admiration), but an object who can be used in a particular sexual way. The fear of sexual violence and the possibility of rape is prominent. To me, it is this threat that makes the catcalling example so chilling. The implied sexual violence—the use to which an object can be put—is important for the kinds of claims that Dworkin and MacKinnon want to make about the status and definition of women, prostitution, and pornography. They emphasize that once made into an object women (all women) are violable and open to instrumental use. What is going on is not simply the objectification of a woman, but the subordination of all women. This is very different from other forms of being an object, "to be looked at," whether as an image (for example, on Instagram), or in person, with regard to the extent to which I come up to scratch in beauty terms. Such evaluation may be harsh and potentially harmful, but it is perfectly possible for it have no element of sexual threat, nor to be overtly gendered. Indeed this is often overtly what beauty objectification entails. For example when we evaluate—in persons or in images—whether a friend or colleague or actress looks good or not—objectification is happening. We are turning the women into an object (or evaluating an image, already an object). Questions about whether she looks her best, young, radiant and as if she's "made an effort" or old, tired and "badly put together," are all questions that are answered by evaluating the object. As too are body-part evaluations—"her arms look good, she must have been working out," "her skin looks great, she must have had work done," or "she looks older, maybe she should have work done," "dress looks great, has she lost weight"—and so on. In these contexts the evaluation is of the body as an object, but this is done, and done routinely, without any threat of sexual use.

Too much work in the catcalling example is done by the sexual threat, and it is possible to reframe at least some elements of the catcalling example to get a more accurate account of objectification in beauty. For objectification in beauty, there is no need to imply violation or instrumental sexual use. This does not mean that in being turned into an object other forms of instrumentalization will not occur but the threat of rape or other forms of sexual use and misuse is removed. To understand objectification as it functions in the contemporary beauty ideal, we need to take the "to be looked at" element of objectification, and recognize that objectification without sexual threat is not only possible but is often what is going on. Accordingly, I can become an object, regarded by myself and others as "to be looked at," without the implication that I can be used and abused as a sexual object. This would be denied by Bartky and Dworkin, beautification is woman-making, as is sexual objectification, and women-making subordinates and establishes a gender hierarchy. I will return to this in chapter 10, and will suggest that while certainly beautification encourages traditional gendering it is harder to make arguments about the subordination and exploitation of women work as the beauty ideal expands and dominates and men are increasingly subject to it.

OBJECTIFICATION WITHOUT, OR WITH LESS, SEXUAL DESIRE

In the last section, I argued that it is possible to be objectified, to identify the self with the body, without becoming overtly a sexual object in the sense of being open to violation and use. In this section, I want to argue that not only is it possible to be objectified without being sexually objectified in the sense of being vulnerable to sexual use, but also that sexual desire and desirability, while intimately connected to beauty, are not always primary or explicit in beauty objectification.

At first glance, a likely response is: "But of course beauty objectification is sexual. Beauty is all about being sexually desirable!" On
this view, beauty is always sexual in that beauty norms are regarded
as codified versions of what is sexual attractive. This view can be
endorsed whether or not you regard beauty as evolutionary (youth
is attractive because it symbols reproductive capability), or socially
constructed (youth in women is attractive because it signals pliabil-
ity and enhances male status).[53] However, while recognizing that
undoubtedly beauty norms are intricately connected to sexual desire and what is desirable is often what is beautiful, this is not a binary or uncomplicated relationship. On the one hand, sexual desire
is wider and more diverse than dominant beauty norms, and the
narrower and more sanitized beauty norms become the more actual
sexual desire will fall outside these.[54] On the other hand, and this is
what is important for my claims, even if beauty norms are shaped
by standard (or standardly gendered) notions of what is sexually
desirable, this does not automatically mean that sexual attraction
or desire is actually in play when we objectify in beauty. In the previous section, I argued it is possible to be objectified in beauty—to
be regarded as an object and to be evaluated as such—without any
threat of sexual violation. In this section, I want to go further and
argue that not only does objectification in beauty not carry the threat
of sexual violation, but the "to be looked at" status can be invoked
without invoking sexual desire and desirability as key features.

It is not hard to imagine being regarded as an object without
being overtly a sexual object (vulnerable to sexual use or an object
of sexual desire). Indeed much of beauty falls into this class. If we
turn to some key instances of objectification in beauty from catwalk
modeling, to dressing up, the aim is to be objectified, in the sense
of deliberately aiming "to be looked at," and to be judged according
to the beauty ideal, but not necessarily to be sexually desired. Likewise, as the examples of the last section show, when we judge a
woman on how she is looking this can be without sexual desire. The
idealized bodies of models, actresses, celebs, peers, and Facebook
friends looked at as images in traditional or social media or as
bodies in person, might well evoke sexually desire in someone, but

evoking sexual desire is not necessarily the aim, and nor does evaluation have to be about desirability. The intention is "to be looked at," to be evaluated according to the extent to which the beauty ideal is met. In some of these examples, such as images in a magazine, it is literally objects we are evaluating, but objectification happens, not because the images are objects, but because we look at, and use them, in a particular way. Effectively we use them to compare ourselves, or to take features for our own imagined self, or as inspiration—or thinspiration.[55] We ask are they good enough, better than us, nearly there, ideal, and we rework and build these images into our own ideal.

This type of objectification does not need a male gaze, or internalized male gaze, indeed in many contexts this is a largely women's domain—scrutinizing women's magazines, devouring celeb twitter feeds, and posting and monitoring our image in retouched selfies. While sexual desire shadows beauty (beauty norms are in part instances of what is sexually desirable), it is not always a part of objectification.[56] Sexual desire *might* be a part of beauty objectification: you might be attracted to the model or, more likely, focus on what will make you more sexually attractive, and to be sure this is sexual self-objectification, although without the sexual threat therefore potentially less harmful. But, just as easily you might focus on the image, the object, and want to be it not overtly for sexual desirability but because this would be an improved, better version of you. The fact that we connect sexual rewards with beauty success (particularly with regard to finding and keeping a partner) does not mean that sexual desire is always involved in objectification. We can be objectified and objectify in nonsexual ways.

To illustrate, it is perfectly possible to imagine being objectified in the beauty context in a parallel way to Nussbaum's account of problematic sexual objectification. In the *Playboy* example, Nussbaum described how women are reduced to objects in a way that is very similar to the claims of Dworkin and MacKinnon. All the subjectivity is on the male side of the equation with women on the other side as interchangeable objects. Recall that Nussbaum goes as far as to say that here women are like cars or suits, so they are not just objects but commodities to be bought and sold. In a parallel, but nonsexual way, just as Nicollette Sheridan was turned into a sexual object, we can be turned into beauty objects. The young actress thinks she's displaying herself as a skilled artist or performer at a film premier, but she's actually displaying herself as an example of achieving (or failing to achieve) the beauty ideal. Likewise, the female politician or sportswoman thinks she's displaying herself as a professional or expert in one field or another, but all the while she's actually displaying herself as an example of achieving (or failing to achieve) the beauty ideal. Indeed, given the increasing prevalence of beauty objectification, the actress and politician might be well aware she is presenting in part as a beauty object. The common practice of seeking to identify flaws and beauty failures exemplifies this gaze. For instance, Gill refers to the "red circles," which are used in magazines or online to draw attention to the flaws in the bodies of those they depict.[57] The type of flaws that might be highlighted include unshaved armpits, cellulite, wrinkles or too much Botox. In such instances, the person is being reduced to a body, or body parts, but not in a sexual way. This is objectification without— or with very little sexual—element. Sexual objectification only potentially enters the picture insofar as sexual attractiveness is related to beauty norms. In this sense then objectification, the denial of autonomy and subjectivity, as well as instrumentalization is present in beauty, but without sexual connotations. Similarly, the self can be reduced to an object, judged as such, but not straightforwardly as a sexual object.

To repeat, the claim that objectification can be sexless is not intended to wholly disconnect beauty from sexual attractiveness. It is the case that beauty norms are shaped by sexual desire and assumptions about sexual desirability—and sexual desirability of a very narrow type. Further, as discussed in chapter 1, the beauty ideal promises to deliver the goods of the good life—and top of the list is the belief that the beautiful will be loved; and therefore by implication being beautiful is connected to being sexually attractive. However, the beauty ideal is not always or necessarily concerned with sexual attractiveness, or at least not overtly and not all the time. So for instance, while it might be the case that beauty norms are derived from what is sexually attractive—high heels being a good example—you can wear high heels, because you wish to be beautiful, better, more perfect and with little (or not much) sexual concern. However, you cannot, as an individual, change the fact that heels are sexualizing and carry a sexual message: they make women "throw back their shoulders and arch their backs, making their breast look bigger, their stomachs flatter, and their buttocks more rounded and thrust out."[58] Here the line between beauty objectification and sexual objectification is difficult to draw and to some extent arbitrary. In a sense it is irrelevant how the woman might feel; she *will* be judged sexually if she wears sexually provocative clothes, and in this sense sexual objectification is alive and well. But, at the same time, as the beauty ideal becomes more dominant and shapes the lives of individuals, conforming to the ideal and evaluating women in light of the ideal—objectifying them—may be done by themselves and others without sexual objectification, as beauty objectification becomes a shared and dominant gaze. Of course, because an individual does not aim to use heels to invoke sexual desire does not mean it is not invoked. Chambers illustrates this point particularly clearly arguing that it is not knee implants, but breast implants that are chosen by women:

> Choosing to have breast implants regardless of the desires of actual men is not the same as choosing to have them immune from patriarchal norms.... Practices are cultural: they do not submit to the meanings that an individual wants them to have, either for herself or others. We can see this by considering the extreme oddity of a woman who did want to have breast implants in a society in which large breasts carried no meaning, one in which women were not objectified and sexualised in a way in which large breasts were not considered more attractive by society as a whole. Why on earth would anyone want to have surgery to insert heavy and dangerous alien objects into her body if there were not social meaning to, or social payoff from the practice? A woman who did want to have breast implants in such a society would be like someone who wanted to have cosmetic knee implants.[59]

Chambers' example of knee implants is particularly important, as it points clearly to limits of attempts to separate beauty from sexual objectification. Norms are communal, individuals cannot change their meaning, and high heels and breast implants do conform to sexualized stereotypes. But, while beauty norms are shaped in conditions of patriarchy this does not mean that beauty norms are mere responses to sexual desire, or that other alternative meanings cannot be emerging as alternative or parallel norms.

Collectively, meanings change, and high heels can signal to the women wearing them, to other women, and to men, beauty (and perhaps other things such as power) in addition, or sometimes instead of, sexual desirability. We do not create meaning individually but only collectively, and that gendered sexual desire shapes beauty norms is undeniable. However, it is the case that, in the beauty context, sexual desire and attractiveness are not always in play, and if we wish to address what is happening under the beauty ideal, this needs to be recognized. For example, to understand the young girl who wears sexually provocative clothes, we need to recognize that while she might be playing with sexual attractiveness, she is also likely (perhaps more likely) to be seeking to approximate beauty ideals. She aims to succeed in attaining some aspect of the beauty ideal and very likely hopes to be judged as such by her friends. It is attaining this that is primary, and the fact that this is understood differently by (some) of those who behold her, does not deny that to herself, and to some of those who behold her, she is a beauty object, to be visually assessed, not a sexual object to be sexually violated or desired. Of course, this separation is precarious, not least as "hot" and "beautiful" are often equated in the West, and those who do read through the lens of sexual objectification will miss other lenses and deem the women or young girl to be "asking for it." Even though she is engaging in a quite different practice, she cannot choose the lens that is applied to her. While beauty objectification might be becoming more common, sexual objectification continues; which makes conforming to the beauty ideal a risky business. Moreover, sexual and beauty objectification can happen concurrently—particularly in cases where what is beautiful is hypersexualized. But it is crucial to understand that, under the beauty ideal, the objectified self is not quite, the reduced and diminished self that theories of sexual objectification suggest.

To claim that beauty objectification does not have to be sexual objectification is to reject the asymmetrical and hierarchical aspect of traditional accounts of objectification and self-objectification. However, while I argue that it is possible to have a nonsexual beauty account of objectification, I do not wish to deny the gendered nature of beauty norms; indeed, the current beauty norm further embeds ever narrower gender norms. Nor do I wish to deny that in some instances, perhaps many, beauty objectification is sexual and aims to dominate and subordinate along gendered lines. There are many instances where the traditional accounts still have much to tell us about the nature of gendered power dynamics, and more importantly there are a number of spheres where only by recognizing gendered domination and sexual exploitation can the abuse of power be recognized. For instance it is hard to account for the prominence of gonzo porn without thinking that sexual objectification is alive and well, and as porn mainstreams beauty norms will reflect such images.[60] However, I claim an alternative, nonsexual, objectifying gaze is possible and increasingly prevalent. If I am correct then, accounts of sexual objectification remain important, but they are not sufficient to account for what is happening under the contemporary beauty ideal, where women objectify each other and themselves and not as (or not wholly and perhaps not primarily as) sexual objects, but in comparison with each other, and with their own imagined self, and as instances of the beauty ideal. Accordingly, it is possible under the beauty ideal to objectify without sexual threat or sexual desire.

Conclusion

In sum then, objectification theory is important to understanding what is going on in the contemporary beauty ideal, because it gives us a framework to understand the self as something "to be looked at." So while objectification is problematic, in that it has unhelpful associations, it is a concept that it is important to retain, as it gives a compelling and useful account of how the self is located in and identified with the body. The "to be looked" at element of objectification and self-objectification is crucial in identifying the self with the body. Therefore, despite the perception of objectification as an old-fashioned and potentially moralizing concept, objectification is particularly useful for understanding how we can come to see ourselves and others as objects.

Beauty objectification and self-objectification are part of the dominant way in which we view ourselves and others in an increasingly visual culture, and particularly for those who identify with the beauty ideal. To make this argument, I developed arguments for beauty objectification and self-objectification by arguing that objectification does not need to be sexual. Not that sex, most obviously in the form of sexual attractiveness, is not connected to objectification in beauty, but that beauty objectification can be separated from sexual objectification at least as sexual objectification is traditionally understood. This allowed a number of moves in understanding the objectified self; it allowed some recognition that objectification in this sense might not be threatening and perhaps in some instances might not be wholly objectionable, a discussion I will continue in the next chapter. In the next chapter, I will build on this account. I will argue that the objectified self that equates the self and the body is only the first step in understanding the self; we also need to recognize the transforming and improving self and the imagined self: the self that will, or could, emerge at the end of the beautification process, my best self, the perfect me.

8

I Will Be Worth It!

In the last chapter, I argued that the first step in understanding the self as it is constructed under the beauty ideal is to locate the self in the body. To do this, I introduced objectification and self-objectification theory. I developed the traditional account of sexual objectification into an account of beauty objectification without sexual threat and distanced from sexual desire. A woman (or man) can be objectified and self-objectified, made an "object to be looked at," in whole or in part, and judged according to the beauty ideal without the primary consideration being sexual desirability. Skin can be judged for its flawlessness and luminosity (or for wrinkles, spots, and blemishes), legs for their length and lack of cellulite (or for their chunkiness and bumpiness), or the whole as a beautiful, ideal and perfect, (or ugly, flawed, and downright imperfect). In this chapter, I wish to develop this argument further, and argue that identifying the self with the body is only the first stage of a conception of the self under the beauty ideal. I will return to the imagined self, set out at the beginning of the last chapter. I will suggest that in beauty objectification, the self is the body, but not just the actual body. It is also the transforming and imagined body. I will argue this conception of the self helps to explain the power of the beauty ideal, in particular, its dual nature. In so doing, it provides some explanation for the continued embracing of it, despite its increasingly extreme requirements and harmful consequences. Taken together, this chapter and the last provide an account of the location of the self in the body, of objectification under the beauty ideal, and of the dual aspect of both the self (negative and critical of the current self, and positive, full of promise and possibility with regard to the future self) and of the ideal (demanding and rewarding).

In this chapter, I will argue that objectification and self-objectification do not preclude subjectivity and that under the beauty ideal we are both subject and object. Further, I argue that in the beauty context all objectification might not be harmful, or at least not harmful in a parallel way to sexual objectification. In particular, I claim that in beauty objectification we are not reduced to a *mere* body, as the body we are identified with is not just our actual flawed and vulnerable body, but also our transforming and imagined body. Further, because our actual body is already, in part, our transforming body—and contains the promise of the imagined body—the actual body has positive features.

Bodies as Objects and Subjects

Before I turn directly to the dual nature of the beauty ideal, I will first return to sexual objectification to address the claim that objectification always results in a denial of subjectivity. I suggest that the location of the self in the actual and possible and imagined body accords with claims that the self is simultaneously subject and object. To make this argument, I will return to a criticism of objectification theory that I left unaddressed in the last chapter: that objectification theory presents women as objects and so denies their subjectivity and agency, making women passive and inert and vulnerable to being used, and so ultimately victims. In contemporary discourse, to deny agency is unacceptable: Women are, and should be, presented as empowered subjects exercising real agency. In the next chapter, we will return to issues of agency and choice in more detail. For now I wish to focus on the claim that objectification creates inert objects lacking subjectivity. Contrary to this, I argue that being objectified in the beauty context does not preclude subjectivity, rather under the beauty ideal we are both object and subject.[1]

To make this argument, I will return to the work of Gill, and her question about the usefulness of (sexual) objectification theory when women are not presented (to themselves or others) as passive, but as "active, desiring sexual subjects."[2] Gill argues that a key shift in the portrayal of women is from inert stereotypes, say of the happy housewife or the sexual object, to women as sexually assertive agents. Gill argues that this move from sexual objectification to sexual-subjectification—from sex object to desiring subject—is primary to understanding media shifts in how women are portrayed (and in the images of women that we embrace and endorse).

In contemporary media portrayals women are presented as sexual subjects—who are desiring and "up for it" (seemingly all the time)—but, and crucially for my claims, they are no less "to be looked at" than the passive sexual objects of previous eras. Gill illustrates this claim using a 2004 ad for a motor show.[3] In this ad, three women, dressed in shiny black bikinis and thigh length boots, tower over cars. These women are not passive, draped objects, but confident and active. But they are—notwithstanding their implied subjectivity and agency—still wholly to be looked at. As Gill notes, "in the shift from passive to active, from smile to pout, from submissive to empowered, the link between cars and sexy women is not severed but merely given a gloss for the twenty-first century. Sexy 'babes' are still selling cars."[4] Often such portrayals of women as "hot" and "wanting" are linked to the mainstreaming of pornography, as "women's magazines, fashion ads, TV, music videos, and box office movies bombard women with images that would have, a decade or so ago, been defined as soft-core porn."[5] Undoubtedly what was once considered pornographic imagery is increasingly normal in mainstream fashion and is behavior modeling for ordinary girls and women. There are worries here about the messages that sexualized beauty norms give out: for instance, the "up for it" subject is the subject of gonzo porn, of women who are "always ready for sex and are enthusiastic to do whatever men want, irrespective of how painful, humiliating, or harmful the act is."[6] The move to "hotness" is concerning for a number of reasons; however, that is not the topic of this book. For the purposes of my argument, the point is not about the sexiness, but the agency that is implied.[7] In addition, as I have discussed in beauty objectification as opposed to sexual objectification, even sexy items of clothing (for example high heels) can be worn purely, or at least mostly, with the intention of attaining the beauty ideal. Part of attaining beauty in some contexts is *looking* sexually confident and empowered, but key here is the looking; the aim might be simply to look a certain way and the look might be evaluated as such. Yet, while such ideals as beauty ideals are "for women" or "for all," they are simultaneously offered "for men" to sexually enjoy. Thus sexual objectification continues, but what is objectified are "up for it" and sexually demanding sexual objects, rather than passive and inert ones. None of this active portrayal lessens the identification of women with their bodies as objects "to be looked at." But it is presented as a mere accident and happy coincidence that such sexually desiring images of women are also attractive to men. Women are presented as pleasing themselves, pleasing men is just a by-product; that these are norms we insist we choose I will return to in the next chapter.

Gill argues that this way of presenting women as choosing and identifying with sexual-subjectivity, allows objectification to continue, but makes it harder to criticize. The fact that women are still to be looked at—by themselves, by other women, by men, by everyone—is supposedly nonproblematic as there is nothing passive about these voracious and confident and empowered women. Gill persuasively argues when commenting on this portrayal of women in ads:

> The fact that the models speak a language of empowerment in no way detracts from the impact of this shift—indeed it serves merely to defend against critique. Subjectification, it might be argued is just how we "do" objectification today. But women are still located in their bodies indeed *as* bodies, albeit voraciously heterosexually desiring ones, as in conventional pornography.[8]

Arguably then, presenting women as subjects does not reduce the sexual objectification and self-objectification of women. Indeed, as Gill argues, it may intensify it, but it does make it more difficult to criticize. As Gill concludes her book, *Gender and the Media*:

> A shift in the way that power operates: a shift from an external, male judging gaze to a self-policing narcissistic gaze. I would argue that it represents a deeper form of exploitation than objectification—one in which the objectifying male gaze is internalized to form a new disciplinary regime. In this regime power is not imposed from above or from the outside, but constructs our very subjectivity. We are invited to become a particular kind of self, and endowed with agency on condition that it is used to construct oneself as a subject closely resembling the heterosexual male fantasy that is found in pornography.[9]

Gill's worry that sexism and misogyny, and its harms to women, remain, despite the rhetoric of choice and empowerment and the relentless positing of women as the choosing subject is an increasingly important critique. Angela McRobbie's work has been pivotal in this move. She argues, similarly to Gill, that the displacement or undoing of feminism, by such apparent assertions of agency, is a function of postfeminism. She points to Eva Herzigová's Wonderbra —"Hello Boys"—ad, and Claudia Schiffer's striptease ad as examples of such undoing: ads that invoke the feminist critique and then undo it with the agential subject.[10] This feminine/feminist knowingness is reproduced across ads, programs, and social media. The postfeminist rationale insists on the choosing, consuming, individual (a model of the self we will return to), but "the new female subject is, despite her freedom, called upon to be silent, to withhold critique in order to count as a modern sophisticated girl."[11] I will return to gender hierarchies, but for now I simply want to recognize that including subjectivity in sexual objectification does not remove the objectification.

I endorse much of this reading but again seek to develop it in line with my previous suggestion that removing the threat of sexual objectification can allow beauty objectification in which we judge ourselves and others as objects, but not just as inert objects but also as becoming, promising, and potential objects. In addition, like Gill, I recognize that sexual objectification still occurs, although I suggest this is alongside beauty objectification, which is not primarily about sexual desirability. Accordingly I wish to argue that recognizing subjectivity does not deny objectification, and in turn, regarding ourselves as objects does not remove our subjectivity. We can—and do—simultaneously regard ourselves as subjects and objects. We identify ourselves with our bodies, which we regard as "to be looked at," but not as mere bodies. Under the beauty ideal, as I argued in chapter 1, we expect aspects of our subjectivity—or, in more ethical language, character—to be read directly from our bodies. Our bodies then are objects, but in the context of beauty as a value framework, a body is never just a body—a *mere* object—but a carrier of meaning and identity. The body has resonance in the context of the ideal and holds the promise of delivering the goods of the good life. Under the beauty ideal, we hold in tension our dissatisfaction with our current body (which needs work) and our anticipation for our future body (which we imagine attaining) and move between these always with our eye on the promise and possibility of improving, progressing and becoming better.

Importantly, as we move from sexual objectification to beauty objectification, the subjectivities that we read from our bodies are not simply sexual subjectivities (although this may be part of our picture of our self), but the ideal also promises other goods; such as being in control, loved, powerful, and happy. We do not picture ourselves as inert objects (sexual or otherwise), but we project subjectivity into the body as an object. The imagined self is tied to the material self, as the actual body is; and of course the actual body is also imagined. Furthermore, the imagined self is an acting subject with desires. Even though the imagined self is just that—imagined—and so by definition not limited by material concerns, it remains rooted in and bound to the body. But the body under the beauty ideal is not material, mundane, and inert; it is in transition, a carrier of meaning and identity, it symbolizes success and promises reward if you make the grade. So the imagined self is not a perfect, but inert, body, but rather a doing body that embodies the successful, perfect, person who is actively reaping the rewards of the beauty ideal.

Accordingly, the transforming and imagined self is located in the body, but it is not a mere thing or object. The improved self—twenty pounds lighter and wrinkle-free—might be imagined as sexually alluring and desiring, on holiday or in the bedroom. But she might also be in a work context, looking fabulous and in control, in a neat suit with designer glasses (eye wear), or in a family context, at an upcoming wedding or party, or simply taking a child to school or visiting a friend, looking fabulous and feeling happy. The ideal body symbolizes the happy and successful life, and the happy and successful self. Indeed imagining looking the part is now a very real step on the way to being the part: for instance, in the words on one sixteen-year-old girl: "If you want to be a successful business women, you view yourself as this really attractive, skinny person."[12] This is a significant change in how we think about the self and the successful self. No longer is mastering skills and talents key to preparing for or attaining some good. In contrast, preparation is imagining ourselves in the role and what we would look like if we were in the role. The subjectivity with which we imbue images, especially when we consider objectification without the sexual threat (and at least sometimes objectification without sexual desire or desirability), suggests that the identification of the self with the body is not a denial of subjectivity, but rather a reconstruction of subjectivity located in, and symbolized by, the body. Thus, theories of objectification and self-objectification are steps on the way to theorizing the imagined self. The imagined self is not material in fact, and furthermore it is exceptionally unlikely that the imagined self could ever be real (we have notoriously high expectations about what the end point of our transformation will be) but it is an object or pseudo-object.[13] The ideal self is imagined as an object, symbolizing the subject, who has attained the goods of the good life that the beauty ideal promises. As such, under the beauty ideal objectification includes subjectivity making those who fall under it both subject and object.

Reduced to a Body

Traditional accounts of sexual objectification regard objectification as always harmful—either because being an object is always a denial of key aspects of personhood, or because of wider structural claims, such as sexual subordination, by which all of a group are turned into things for use. For example, in Bartky's account the reductionist nature of becoming an object is assumed. Bartky claims that a "person is sexually objectified when her sexual parts or sexual functions are separated out from the rest of her personality and reduced to the status of mere instruments or else regarded as if they were capable of representing her."[14] In the last chapter, we considered Nussbaum's argument that there are times when sexual objectification is not only benign, but positive. Nussbaum's account is important as she shows that all objectification is not the same and that the context and relationships in play are key. The harms of objectification do not depend on whether parts of the body are objectified, as in the pillow example, or whether it is done for pleasure, as in the *Playboy* example, but on the quality of the relationship and whether there is mutuality, or to use Kantian language, whether you are an end as well as a means.

It is this argument I wish to return to in the beauty context. Given the dominance of visual culture, the prevalence of images—of the ugly and the beautiful and everything and everyone in between—and the extent to which we use these images to create ourselves, to suggest that it is *always* harmful to see a person as an object is difficult to sustain. If turning a person into an object via becoming an image (whether real or imagined) is harmful, this kind of harm is so prevalent that it is almost meaningless, and impossible and pointless to object to. Moreover, not only is this form of objectification routine, but it is part of how we construct ourselves, present ourselves and communicate with others. Accordingly, a requirement not to do this would undoubtedly be harmful; for many it would be a denial of themselves and a dismissal of their selves. To claim that objectification in this sense is always harmful runs contrary to our experience of ourselves as bodies under the beauty ideal. Underpinning beauty as an ethical ideal, I argued in chapter 1, is a commitment to body work and to the body as something to be worked on. The body then must be an object. Likewise images of persons are objects. The images in magazines, on websites, on Facebook profiles, or staff pages are objects. Our pictures of ourselves, whether the image we see in the mirror, or the image we imagine of our transforming and imagined self, are not objects in the same way as actual pictures, but they are in the sense that they are imaginings, *pictures*, of the self that we appraise and judge for their approximation to the beauty ideal. In this sense, they are pseudo-objects and not wholly dissimilar to magazine pictures. As my argument for beauty objectification sought to show, it is these images of others and ourselves that we evaluate for conformity with the beauty ideal, and while there are harms attached to such objectification—whether shame and disgust, body dissatisfaction, or just costs in increasing time and effort—there are also pleasures. On traditional accounts of sexual objectification, to identify the self with the body is always harmful. It is a *reduction*, it *reduces* the person to a body, makes a person into a thing, and importantly a thing to be used. I have already argued that beauty objectification does not carry the threats that such reduction implies in the sexual context. In the next section, I want to argue that, in a visual culture and under the beauty ideal, there might be further reasons to question the extent of the harms of objectification.

In beauty objectification, unlike sexual objectification, we are not just reduced to our actual flawed and vulnerable body, but the self is also located in transforming body and the ideal and imagined body. Both of these bodies have positive aspects that complicate and disrupt the negative features of objectification. I wish to spend the rest of this chapter considering ways in which beauty objectification is not a reduction to a mere actual and flawed body.

Crucially, the actual body (however fat and failing, or energized and successful) can always be improved. As such, the body, as discussed in chapter 1, is always a task and project to be worked at, and while this can be experienced as demanding and punishing, it can also be experienced as creative and positive; a site of almost limitless possibilities given what we believe under the beauty ideal, the body can deliver. This is a very different model of the self to that of previous times.[15] The imagined self, the best self, the perfect me, holds promises not only about the possibilities of what our bodies can be, but promises a lifestyle and the goods of the good life. The imagined self, who *looks* a certain way, is also imagined *being* a certain way. The imagined self is a self who has achieved the goods of relationships, friendships, career, and success. While we might be reduced to our current body, and in all likelihood dissatisfied with it, the promise that the body can deliver remains. We see *through* our current body to our possible body. This is not experienced negatively as vulnerability, but positively, inculcating a hopeful and forward-looking attitude.

The future-orientated nature of this identification does a number of things.[16] First it potentially protects from some of the harms of objectification, as the body we are reduced to is no inert object waiting to be looked at (and used). We may be reduced to a body, but the body is full of potential, and we are not trapped in or stuck with our current bodies, but experience them as the very sites that have the potential for change and promise a transformed self. Second, we imagine improvement, and so we focus not on the costs and demands of beauty, but on the future rewards. Practices such as continual dieting, body-hair removal, and the application of lotions and potions are experienced as less demanding because we imagine our transforming and ideal selves. We believe that it will be worth it in the end. Doing these practices shows commitment to the transformation and is, or can be, experienced as positive and empowering, an investment in the self, making the actual self into the better self. That action is possible is important for the experience of empowerment; even if the action is harmful, risky, and dangerous (such as using skin-lightening cream or cosmetic surgery), it is experienced as positive not just because it is good to do—it is virtuous—but because it will help us achieve our better, more perfect selves. It is a means to a very desirable end. Third, in undergoing transformative procedures the transforming self begins to exhibit and capture elements of the lifestyle we associate with the imagined self. So undergoing surgery—any surgery—can feel glamorous and rewarding and can be an affirmation, almost irrespective of the outcome. To have surgery at all is to be "living the life." As discussed earlier, more of us feel we should be working on ourselves (our bodies) and that beauty ideals apply to all, not only, as past ideals did, to the elite. Accordingly, we increasingly engage in potentially transforming practices, and as we do so we picture, imagine our improved self and are reassured that we are succeeding. Thus, the ideal does not need to be attained for the experience of the transforming self to be positive: a manicure or new pair of shoes can feel like a step along the way. Indeed, that this is positive is known by the beauty industry: as Heyes points out, dieting companies not only exploit "the desire to produce an appropriate body (with all the symbolism that adheres to it), but also the active, creative sense of self-development, mastery, expertise, and skill that dieting can offer."[17]

The Self as an Image-Object

The self under the beauty ideal then is always in progress, and the ideal self remains beyond. The sense of constant movement—you are working on improving or you are letting yourself go—further explains the ease with which we embrace more practices without reflection and with little recognition that the practices are different. The movement and need to show improvement in the self may also help to explain the increasing work that is involved in the posting of selfies and the management of our virtual selves.[18] Often the posting of a selfie requires significant time in dressing and making up, as well as in digitally retouching as apps become accessible and easy to use. The status of such images is illuminating; they stand between the actual self and the imagined self, steps upon the way, just as our images of our improved selves stand between our actual self and the imagined self. Such images, like the engagement in beauty practices, can serve to prove that the self is improving and that we are doing what we should. They serve to reassure and to display our potential, offering a glimpse of what we can, and hope we will, be.

In this way the concept of the self under the beauty ideal helps to account for some of the beauty aspects of visual culture. Selfies are not, in this context, trivial, which goes some way to explain why advice simply "not to post pictures" (whether sexually explicit or face shots) is unlikely to be successful. These images hint at the imagined, perfect self, and the self (actual, transforming, and possible) is manifested in these images. Thus, when they are posted and evaluated, there is a real sense in which it is the self that is being evaluated. As Heyes puts it, "pictures of the self—reinforced through language, imagery, embodied practices and mental habits—hold us captive in ways we are not even aware of."[19] If this is correct, then the amount of time and effort that goes into creating selfies, and the elation or disappointment that results from how the image is received (how many likes it gets), is explained.

A Body Nonetheless

In the discussion of the self as constructed under the beauty ideal, the ideal again reveals itself to be dual. Both positive and negative. This is true of the self as constructed under the beauty ideal no less than the ideal itself. Unlike sexual objectification, the reduction is not to a *mere* object. The transforming and imagined self provides some resistance to such reduction and may provide some resources for self-protection and resilience: self-esteem can be raised by actions that contribute to the body-project. Focusing on actions that can be taken can be empowering, so too can imagining the improving and improved self I am working towards. Such positive and promising elements serve to alleviate some of the feelings of failure when faced with the flaws I perceive in my actual body.

However, this is not the whole story. While the transformative and imagined body may be empowering and creative, it is always the body that is the focus. While we do not have to attain the ideal body, the commitment to the transforming body is, as discussed earlier, demanding. The more committed to the beauty ideal we are the more demanding it is. Likewise, the more our sense of self is determined by appearance (actual and possible), the more we judge ourselves and others by appearance, and the more we invest our identity and meaning in appearance and less in other capabilities. So while it might be positive in the short term, making practices that would otherwise be unbearable—like surgery for no health benefit or continual, daily firming, smoothing, and buffing—bearable, and even enjoyable, in the longer term it is illusory. The imagined, perfect, self can never be attained and, as we age, the myth of the transforming self is harder to maintain. However, the more we embrace the self under the beauty ideal the harder it will be to resist, reject, and modify our commitment to beauty ideal. Reducing engagement becomes harder: not only will I be letting myself go, I will also be relinquishing the possibility of the improved future self; a self I have invested with meaning and identity and that holds the promise of a better life. So while the self of beauty objectification is more positive than the self of sexual objectification, it may more firmly locate the self in the body, and so condemn us to punishing and ultimately harmful regimes.

Catcalling and sexual objectification make us feel bad, vulnerable, like a nice piece of ass, and motivate us to reject such diminution. Beauty objectification does not make us feel bad; or at least only sometimes. At others we feel active, creative, and empowered, and it promises success and happiness. It is seductive, promising everything, if only we commit and engage, and increasingly at the expense of other activities. The time given to beauty, as discussed in chapter 6 in justice terms of opportunity cost, is also true in personal terms: the time we spend devoted to beauty is time we do not spend on other activities and other aspects of our selves. This has a number of potentially harmful consequences. The first is that quite simply there are others things that we could do that we do not do. The worry about this is twofold; first, that we are simply missing out on engaging in other activities and developing other personal projects; and second, that it is destructive to pay too much attention to beauty at the cost of attention to other skills, capacities, and capabilities. It is likely to be self-defeating; recall Nichola Rumsey's image of a pie, and the need to give attention to diverse aspects of ourselves.

The second, is that the types of activities that beauty encourages might not be as rewarding as other types of activity. This is a hierarchy of pleasure claim, and one that I am wary of: recall my response to the dismissal of beauty pleasures as subordinate. Yet it is the case that beauty pleasures may encourage certain perspectives. For instance, as Michelle Lazar points out, the "the kind of freedom that is enacted is personal and individual, rather than social and collective."[20] While, as argued in chapter 6, there are communal beauty pleasures, the individual nature of beauty endeavor and success is primary, at least in the current way we "do" beauty. Beauty then might make us focus on the individual rather than on the social and communal.

Third, not all beauty gazes are the same, and a particularly worrying trend is the "surveillant gaze," identified by Gill and Elisa.[21] This is a technological gaze, like the surgical gaze, or what Bernadette Wegenstien calls the cosmetic gaze; this is not a human gaze.[22] It is inhuman, unforgiving, critical, clinical, and cold. If this gaze becomes predominant and overwhelms the positive aspects of the self and the possibilities for the self, we will be destroyed by it. We will become, in the language of Estella Tincknell, abject, "a collection of disparate body parts to be endlessly worked on or even replaced as part of the plenitude of consumer choice."[23] Under this gaze, beautification will rarely be fun, and even the best advertising will struggle to convince us that it is: Gill argues that current advertising hides the discipline and high expectations by presenting beauty as playful and a pleasurable hobby.[24] If this gaze becomes dominant, the dual nature of the self under the beauty ideal, and the dual nature of the ideal itself, will collapse. It will no longer be dual. This gaze will destroy, highlighting our failures and offering standards we can never even begin to attain. At this point, the burdens of beauty will no longer be compensated by pleasures, and I would expect that eventually women will reject such norms. However, for the time being we have to live with and under an increasingly technical and inhuman gaze, which while more demanding and punishing is not yet intolerable.

Thus, ultimately and collectively, beauty objectification might be more harmful than sexual objectification. Because we buy, and embrace, beauty objectification, we are more subject to it, it is more difficult to resist, it is, as I have argued throughout, more dominant, more demanding and defining of ourselves (in a way sexual objectification is not). Accordingly, some harms might be mitigated and the ideal made bearable, but the overall harms of a demanding and dominant beauty ideal functioning as an ethical ideal remain and increase. For now, what is important to recognize and respect is that there are positive aspects of the self as an object/subject (actual, transforming and imagined), which need to be understood if the continued dominance of the beauty ideal is to be explained.

Conclusion

In this chapter, I continued the argument of the last chapter that under the beauty ideal the self is equated with the body, but not only with the actual body, also with the transforming and imagined body. To make this claim, I began with theories of sexual objectification to offer an account of how the self can be identified with the body. I then argued that in the beauty context objectification is not always sexual. This, I suggested, allows for an account of beauty objectification in which being reduced to a body or object might not be as reductive as it seems.

This account, at the very least, captures some of what it means to always be judged according to beauty standards and helps us understand the constant and routine evaluation by appearance that increasingly all women (and some men) across the lifespan and across spheres of activity are subject to. Understanding the pull of the transforming and imagined self explains, at least in part, the dual nature of the beauty ideal: that we continue to strive for at least minimal standards of the ideal, and often more maximal standards, despite knowing that they are unattainable, that we will ultimately, and often continually, fall short; that, we continue to find pleasure

Beauty at many (perhaps most) levels has both positive and negative aspects. To illustrate, recall a few of the ways in which it is both positive and negative: First, practices are costly and time-consuming (and sometimes painful and risky) *and*, at the same time, pleasurable and regarded as investments in, and care of, ourselves; second, beauty invokes negative, critical and self-destructive experiences of failing to measure up *and* empowering and self-enhancing experiences of taking control and acting to become better as we work to shape our bodies (and selves); third, engagement is divisive as we compare ourselves to others and to images (near and far) *and* inclusive as it crosses race and class barriers and provides a shared language and culture that can be loving, supportive, and empathetic.[1] In this chapter, I wish to interrogate a fourth consideration, the chosen *and* required nature of the beauty ideal.

If engagement in the beauty ideal is both required and chosen, and can be experienced as either or both, then to endorse a choice framework is flawed. As we saw in the removal of body hair example, the choice rhetoric is dominant, but this does not mean that non-engagement is (freely) chosen (and the ability not to engage without suffering significant cost is part of what "free choice" implies). The costs of non-engagement, in external sanction (being judged as dirty or ugly) and internal sanction (feeling ashamed and disgusted) are high, making non-engagement not a live option. Given this, claims that engagement is voluntary and that these practices are freely chosen cannot be accepted at face value. To explore the chosen and required nature of the beauty ideal, I will first consider why choice is regarded as important in liberal frameworks. Second, I will argue that even in a liberal model choice alone is insufficient in the beauty context as consent is undermined. Having argued that even on its own terms the liberal choice model is insufficient, I will then consider coercion and whether beauty choices are desperate choices, false consciousness, or adaptive preferences. I will argue that although these accounts are useful in illuminating what is—and perhaps more importantly what is not—going on under the beauty ideal all are partial and flawed. However, even though these accounts are not sufficient, relying on the liberal model of individual choice alone is at least as unsatisfactory. I finish the chapter by mapping three devastating consequences of adopting a liberal model of individual choice: first, that it artificially polarizes actors into empowered agents or passive victims; second, that it silences debate; and third, that, despite claims to respect autonomy and empower the agent, it is ultimately victim-blaming.

Choice Matters!

That choice matters is a foundational (and largely unquestioned) assumption of two dominant models of persons, that of the informed consumer, and of the liberal self-directed agent; models that underpin most of our shared ethical frameworks and moral intuitions in a liberal society. The liberal model aims to facilitate the opportunity for all to engage in the life they choose, and particularly to consume.[2] It overtly rejects attempts to promote a version of the good life and is (or claims to be) silent about thick and substantive values. The only exception to this is autonomy, often reduced to choice, which is valued over and above other values, and thus it effectively becomes a thick value in the liberal model.

The liberal model values procedural not substantive values, and aims to put in place a framework within which individuals are able to choose the way of life they wish to follow and make choices in accord with the ends of their chosen way of life. The only limit on such choices is the harm principle; the choices of one person should not harm another. Of course this is not strictly speaking how things play out, and there are many examples in which the choices of individuals are curtailed in liberal societies directly—and not just because they harm others but also because of harm to the self. For instance, smoking policy is concerned with harm to others (for example, though passive smoking or though accumulating costs to health and social services), but it also aims to reduce harms to the self, by making it harder to continue to smoke and through public health policies that encourage individuals to quit. Indeed reducing and preventing harm to the self is increasingly an acceptable part of public, and particularly health, policy, and this is demonstrated in the increasing emphasis on "nudging" as legitimate intervention. Nudging requires that we believe that some practices, or ways of life, are better or worse than others, as nudging is premised on the view that pushing individuals towards better practices, or ways of life, or at least away from worse practices and ways of life, is justified. The aim is not to forbid or prohibit practices, but to change the choice architecture without banning options.[3] While rejected by libertarians, nudging is rarely regarded as unjustified intervention in individual's freedom. However, much of the rhetoric (academic, policy, and popular) surrounding choice continues to assume that choice alone is primary.

In much ethical theory and policy making, liberal assumptions about choice are the background conditions that underlie and frame discussions not only about choice in the beauty context but about all choices. Two key assumptions are, first, that autonomy, which is usually reduced to "having choice," is a good in itself; and, second, that choice is so important that it is the primary ethical consideration, which trumps other considerations. That choice is a good in itself is such a dominant feature of liberal models and is so embedded that, in at least some contexts, it can feel odd to question it. Choice becomes a placeholder for all kinds of valuable features: autonomy, agency, empowerment. Indeed elsewhere I have argued that the liberal model effectively, and falsely, reduces all of ethics to whether something is genuinely chosen and so minimizes, and even renders invisible, other injustices.[4] *The* ethical question in this model is "did she or he genuinely consent or choose for herself?" and "was this choice free, without coercion?" In short, what matters is whether people knew what they were getting into. This focus on choice can be counterproductive, as it undermines the core liberal values of equality and freedom. Indeed, Chambers, argues that these liberal values can be used to reform liberalism and challenge the current situation in which "many liberal policies that aim to maximise freedom and equality actually perpetuate systematic inequality."[5] She argues that liberals have failed to recognize the constraints of social construction and aims to show that while "each form of liberalism goes some way toward securing universal freedom and equality in the face of social construction, no one approach goes far enough."[6] She argues that the power of culture is such that ultimately "it is unreasonable for liberals to expect individuals to take sole responsibility for altering conditions that disadvantage them,"[7] and she advocates state action, when either the "disadvantage factor" or the "influence factor" are evident.[8] Thus she uses liberal principles to critique the reliance on choice.

It is this recognition that contexts constrain choice that is so fundamental, but too often ignored. In the liberal framework, it doesn't matter *what* is chosen, but *that* it is chosen. Accordingly, the liberal subject is the choosing subject: choosing what way of life to value and then living according to these values. In this model then, choice is doing the ethical work. In Chambers's words, it is functioning as if it were a "normative transformer"—transforming an unjust situation into a just one—or as I have argued, using more colloquial language, choice is functioning as if it were "fairy dust."[9] Both Chambers and I argue that choice cannot do this. I have argued, in some detail, that choice cannot make an unjust or exploitative practice or act somehow, magically, just or non-exploitative.[10] Choice, despite liberal assumptions, is not fairy dust. To know if a practice is ethical—and whether it should be permitted or not—we need to look at the nature of the practice, its risks and harms, and the extent to which it subordinates or discriminates. My concern in this book is not to ask, practice by practice, whether each practice is harmful or risky but to consider the beauty ideal in its totality. Therefore, at this point all I wish to note is that the primary assumption of the liberal framework that choice (or consent) alone determines what is ethical is false. I will go on to argue that the communal nature of this ideal and its power, as an increasingly globally dominant ethical ideal, further undermines the liberal reliance on individual choice.

It's for Me!

Given the assumptions of the liberal framework, it is not surprising that the reason for engaging in beauty practices, or other practices, is, and *has* to be, because they were chosen. To remove body hair, to purchase breast implants, to wear high heels has to be "for me!" To claim that it is "for me!" in the liberal context, is the correct and acceptable narrative. Like the "to be normal" narrative, "I chose it, I'm doing it for me!" is the only acceptable reason for action. As discussed in chapter 5, the language of "to be normal," is something of a learnt language; one which women learn in order to access the surgery that they want, or to avoid criticisms of the narcissism variety. By contrast, the language of the liberal individual, making self-directed choices, is more ingrained and feels less learned. It is *the* acceptable language, and is used unconsciously and less deliberately than the "to be normal" narrative. Because it is ubiquitous and ingrained, it is almost invisible, making it particularly difficult to challenge. The dominance of the "pleasing yourself" narrative—and the somewhat parallel language of being "true to yourself"—is evident throughout discussions of beauty practices.

Recognizing that "I chose this, for me" is the only acceptable language goes some way to accounting for why we continue to insist these practices are chosen, and for ourselves, even when we know they are required. In a liberal society, choosing is regarded as the very heart of autonomy, agency and self-expression. That we are choosing-selves, picking our own goals and allegiances is primary. Any suggestion that we are limited, not free to choose (except by the very real restraint of how much money we have) is resisted and rejected. Recognizing constraint, in a nonmonetary form, is regarded as unacceptably limiting. Indeed, to suggest that we are limited and constrained, and influenced, for instance, by patriarchal norms, is anathema, and in some quarters, almost offensive. It is as if suggesting that in fact our choices are not as free as we might wish, and that we are constrained and influenced in all kinds of ways, is threatening and reductive: as if suggesting this makes us lesser selves. Considered critically, this kneejerk rejection is a strange response, as the reality is—of course and always—that we are constrained and choice is always in context and limited by myriad and complex factors. But, and this is crucial to understanding what is going on, the myth of being a free chooser, making our own choices, should not be underestimated. It is this myth that makes critique of beauty practices so difficult, an all-or-nothing affair, as any suggestion that choices are constrained, socially constructed, and influenced is dismissed, as if to say this is tantamount to claiming that individuals are not making choices at all. Individuals *are* making choices, and real choices, between the options that they have available, they are negotiating, using the information they have, in the situations they find themselves, and, as we will return to, they are not passive dupes or dopes. But, and importantly, this does not mean that such choices are wholly free and unconstrained, or that action is enough to indicate agency.[11] To make this argument, I will consider informed consent, the procedural version of choice in medical (and other) contexts, and argue that consent is undermined when it comes to making decisions about engaging in many beauty practices.

Information Is (Not) Enough

Even in the liberal model of informed consent, it is not any or all choices that must be respected. Choices that should be respected must have a number of elements. The most important of these—especially when we move from respecting choice to formal consent—is that first, individuals must have the full information and be able to understand it; second, they must have the capacity to consent—and here issues like age, maturity, and cognitive ability are key; and third, they must be free from coercion and inducement.[12] I will consider these in turn and argue that the dominance of the ideal coupled with the power of the imagined self make it unlikely that beauty choices can be fully informed.

First then, for a choice to be a valid ethical choice in the liberal model it must be informed. This means that the individual who engages must not only have information, but must understand and be able to assess the risk and benefits. In a formal sense, when it comes to cosmetic procedures that explicitly require consent, the "full information" condition of consent is met in that usually patients presenting for cosmetic surgery are given the full information: if they are not, then bad practice has occurred. This is also largely true for beauty practices administered by third parties: for example, hair-dressers do strand tests and inform clients of the risks of hair-dye, and beauticians warn of pain and other side effects of hair removal; although much more could be done to improve information and consenting procedures in this area.[13] The full information criteria is more difficult to apply when it comes to what we do to ourselves. Consent arguments do not neatly extend to all choices—very few of us check chemicals in creams and potions—though very broadly we know some things are risky (like sun beds and skin-lightening cream). Despite the problems with extending the consent model to all choices, in some broad sense those engaged in beauty practices are (mostly) informed: they have access to information and know that some practices are risky and may be harmful.[14] Moreover, if they are not, then the conditions of the liberal model have not been met. Therefore, let us assume for the sake of argument that the liberal model is functioning optimally and that individuals are relatively well informed of risks and benefits.

Being informed does not simply mean that individuals have information; it also requires that they *understand* the risks and benefits. What is meant by understanding here is key, as there is evidence that, in the beauty context, risks are systematically underestimated. If risks are underestimated, then there is a real question with regard to whether or not they are understood. I suggest that the power of the ideal, its very dominance and demandingness, makes claims of *understanding* problematic. In short, the beauty ideal creates such strong expectations that procedures and practices will have transformative results that the risks of procedures and practices are minimized. Moreover, while there are constant reminders that surgery can be "botched" or fillers done badly—recall the red circles—the primary message is that these processes are good to do, you are valuing yourself when you undergo them, and, assuming you go about it the right way, you will get the results you want. This, of course, is not the case. There is always a risk with operations; even by the best surgeons in the best premises with the best products. And bad reactions to skin peals, laser treatments, hair dye, or nail treatments—and horror stories are not hard to find—are not always predictable or preventable.

Those who engage in risky beauty practices may well *know* the risks, in that they have the information, and indeed may even know the risks in great detail. However, the question is whether this is the same as *understanding*. Individuals do not expect the side-effects of botched surgery to happen to them. Likewise, studies show that those who have had cosmetic surgery commonly report that they would not have changed their mind, no matter what information had been given to them at the point of consent; implying that at this point had they been alerted to additional risks they would still have gone ahead. For example, Davis's interviewees reported that more information would not have altered their decision. This suggests that the point of consent is not a point at which people seeking cosmetic surgery are likely to change their mind and consider alternatives (if this is the case, effective intervention needs to be earlier in the decision-making process).[15]

Failure to recognize risks might be thought of as continuous with other practices in that human beings are notoriously bad at assessing risk. However, in the beauty context the power of the ideal and the value placed on the promise of success are such that accurately estimating the risks and harms is particularly difficult. In addition to the power of the ideal, the construction of the self under the beauty ideal is crucial to understanding the extent to which the risks of engagement are minimized. Because we already identify with, and have invested in, the imagined self, the potential damage to our actual body is obscured by our focus on the transforming and transformed body. The end point is primary (either dramatically in the case of surgery or routinely as you maintain your youthful un-winkled face by applying potions and lotions). This does not mean we are not aware that there will be pain and risk—we are— and the watching of reality TV has made the pain more visible than it once was (it is no longer hidden by before and after photos).[16] When we seek, choose, beauty practices, we regard the pain as worth it, as, under the ideal, working on the self requires effort and is hard (no pain no gain). Further, we perceive the pain as transitory, a stage on the way; we do not regard the pain or harm as the end point or potentially permanent. And finally we value engagement for its own sake. By engaging in the practice (whether dieting or surgery), we are demonstrating our commitment to the ideal and to ourselves. Given this heady mix of a dominant and demanding beauty ideal, an increasingly visual culture, and the fantastical promises of the transforming and imagined self, it is hard to imagine how we could possibly understand the risks accurately. The whole point is the context. The rewards of beauty are not nothing, and for those who fall under the ideal and who are focused on the imagined self, they could indeed be everything. Moreover, the promise of the beauty ideal is that if you've committed properly, planned properly, and sacrificed, it will go right. After all, you're worth it, and you deserve it too.

Accordingly my claim is not that individuals are not given full information, but that even when they are, they do not hear the information in the way they would in a different context, in a context where they had less invested in the end point of the procedure and were more focused on process and less on outcome.[17] Being informed (or knowing) is not the same as *understanding* or properly taking account of the risks and benefits. This is not to deny cognitive ability or to suggest that individuals are somehow not capable of assessing risks, but rather to recognize that the power of the ideal and the construction of the self make the risks look different in this context.

To illustrate, we can consider the narratives surrounding cosmetic surgery. Cosmetic surgery, carries significant risk, yet the discourse and culture that surround it makes it hard to do justice to the risks. If we take just one example, that of breast implants, implants involve significant surgery and usually require repeated surgery every ten to fifteen years, depending on implant type and its acceptance into the particular woman's body. Yet breast implants are bought by women as gifts to themselves, gifts from parents and partners, and seen as investments, to increase life chances; something that is increasingly true, not just for those who wish to enter the beauty or glamour industries, but more generally. The positive messages that attach to surgery are ubiquitous; to take just one example, the clinic chain MYA stands for "make yourself amazing," and its website is upbeat and positive and full of testimonials.[18] The overriding message from clinics, advertisers, magazines, and everywhere, is that surgery will make you feel better, more confident, and perhaps more "yourself." This context could not be more different from the contexts in which other surgery decisions are made. Compare the woman researching breast augmentation by reading testimonials and comparing clinics and participating in on-line forums of others considering and undergoing cosmetic surgery to the woman who is facing breast reconstruction following cancer treatment. Isn't it likely that the women seeking cosmetic surgery is less able to weigh the risks against an imagined end point she has not experienced compared to the women who seeks to be cancer free and returned, as near as possible, to her pretreatment self?[19] This does not mean that those who seek cosmetic surgery are taken in; they know full well that testimonials are really ads and recognize and dismiss the ploys of clinics.[20] However, while respecting this and recognizing that consumers are savvy, it is still the case that the situations are different in ways that make it easier to dismiss risk. This is a recognized phenomenon and the Keogh Review noted:

> People considering cosmetic surgical procedures have a natural tendency to focus on outcome and unless guided may not pay enough attention to limitations and risks. This differs significantly from most surgery where patients may have no knowledge of the procedure but are acutely aware of, and alert to, the risks. Those actively seeking an aesthetic procedure may have a tendency to underplay the risk, in contrast to the apprehensive patient required to undergo a significant medical procedure.[21]

When you have surgery in a health context, you focus on the risks of allowing some illness to continue unchecked compared to the risks of undergoing and recovering from surgery. The benefit is returning to health, a state you have been in and therefore have an ability to weigh against the risks of surgery. In the cosmetic context, it is more difficult, as the end point is imagined. You are weighing an imagined state that you have not yet experienced, against the risks of surgery. In such a scenario, might it not be the case, at least for some, that any risks are worth it? Given this, it is likely that the risks of cosmetic surgery are not regarded in the same way as they would be in another context. Recall the worries, for instance, regarding buttock implants, from chapter 4, and the high risk of complications. Is it likely that such risks in another sphere of life would be deemed "worth it"? Of course, most cosmetic surgery does not result in serious harm, but some does, and for some procedures, such as buttock-lifts, the risks are high. However savvy the consumer, the power of the ideal and the pull of the imagined self cannot simply be dismissed; the context of the beauty ideal and everything that comes with it is paramount. Furthermore, that consent may be taken in a health setting not dissimilar to other health decisions does little to alter the claim that these are different types of assessment: indeed given the easy progression from beauty salons to clinic, discussed in chapter 5, the contexts may be less similar than a first glance suggests. Taking together these features—first, the focus on end point rather than the process, second, that by the point of consent the decision has been made, and third, the different contexts and processes of cosmetic surgery decisions—it is not unreasonable (or dismissive of the real attempts of individuals to seek out and weigh information) to suggest that informed consent in the beauty context may be undermined.

The second criteria of informed consent I wish to consider is vulnerability which poses a particular challenge in the beauty context. In traditional consent arguments, capacity must not be undermined by vulnerability, and in many instances those in vulnerable groups will be deemed not to have the capacity to consent. Those who normally fall within the category of vulnerable groups include children and the cognitively impaired; although increasingly a more case-by-case approach is regarded as best practice. Some standard vulnerable groups might apply in the beauty context, such as not considering some types of surgery for those below a certain age. For example, it might seem unproblematic to declare young women seeking labiaplasty before they become sexually active, as vulnerable.[22] But vulnerable groups in standard health care arguments, do not map directly to the beauty context. Just as the above discussion argues that the power of the imagined self, coupled with the dominance of the beauty ideal, threatens to undermine the weighing of the risks and benefits, so more of us may be vulnerable when it comes to beauty. For instance, surgeons are cautioned against operating on certain women; those with unrealistic expectations, or who have been made vulnerable by a traumatic event.[23] Such reasons feature in beauty in ways that are not paralleled in other consent practices. Concerns about body image are often tied up with, and triggered by, stress factors and life changes (such as divorce, unemployment, or bereavement). As the self is increasingly located in appearance and as visual culture becomes more dominant, life traumas will increasingly be enacted on the body. As Blum argues, those who have already adopted what she terms the surgical gaze will use changes to the body to "fix" the self.[24] Given the discussion in the last chapters in this context, it is unsurprising that we write our*selves*—and our insecurities—on our bodies, for our bodies, actual, transforming, and imagined, are ourselves. The rise in eating disorders in demographics not generally considered to be vulnerable is telling. Those suffering from eating disorders are increasingly not just adolescents, but those in their thirties and forties.[25] This is not a group we usually consider vulnerable; but arguably very many of us are vulnerable when it comes to the beauty ideal and its power. Considering beauty as a whole, who is vulnerable may extend far beyond the norms of consenting to procedures in the health context. Further vulnerability is not limited to procedures that fall under medical practice and require consent but applies to all beauty practices (including to practices of buying beauty products, diet and exercise, beauty treatments, and nonsurgical procedures).

On the grounds of weighing risk and benefit and of vulnerability, informed consent is at least potentially undermined and in need of supplementing. Whether or not, and the extent to which it is actually undermined, may depend on a number of factors. The first is the extent to which someone falls under the beauty ideal and is invested in the imagined self. Those who fall less under the beauty ideal are more likely to weigh risks as they would with other, similar procedures; but then, as Blum points out, only those who have already identified with the beauty self—for her the surgical self, for me the transforming and imagined self—will use such procedures. Further, as more of us fall under the beauty ideal, or as more of us accord it greater importance, more of us will reason in this way.

Measuring Up to Shared Standards

If beauty choices cannot be regarded as free choices, in the way informed consent requires, are they coerced choices? Coercion in the beauty context is a difficult claim to establish, given the chosen nature of beauty practices. However, if we cannot reveal body hair without getting funny looks, or thinking of ourselves as dirty or abnormal, then asking whether we are coerced is an obvious question. There are lots of similar examples of ways in which women feel that they *must* conform: have paler skin, bigger breasts, wider eyes, or less wrinkles to look normal or good enough. And some women report conforming, even though they wish they did not have to.[26] Given this, it is worth exploring whether individuals are coerced in some sense.

It is abundantly clear—and has become clearer with every chapter—that as individuals we do not choose our beauty ideals. Beauty ideals are always and undoubtedly shared. For example, in a foot-binding culture large feet are ugly, shameful, and disgusting, just as monobrows, or unibrows, have at times been regarded as beautiful.[27] That norms are cultural and communal does not mean there is no space for individual choice. But what it does mean is that the scope of choice is more limited than the individual choice narrative suggests. I can choose the extent to which I comply with and endorse the beauty ideal. For instance, exposure to second-wave feminist critiques such as Bartky's might lead me to reject the whole beauty project as illusory pleasures, which serve to subordinate women (though fewer women have done this than once might have been imagined). Or I might find a way to resist by adopting a sub-culture norm that promotes a different ideal of beauty (for instance, body modification or body-building).[28] I might even find a counter-culture where appearance matters less and even where attention to appearance is regarded as a vice. Recall the discussion of possible resistant cultures and communities, such as religious cultures and even academia.[29] However, while I can choose these options, as I have argued throughout, to choose not to conform is harder as the ethical beauty ideal embeds and extends. Resistance is more costly—both internally in terms of self-esteem, shame, and disgust, and externally in terms of failing to attain the goods of beauty. But even if I, despite the cost, do reject the beauty ideal and refuse to dye my hair, remove my body hair, and generally to "make the most of myself," I can do nothing—as an individual—to alter the beauty ideal.

As an individual I cannot—whatever I personally feel—make it suddenly beautiful to be big-waisted, with bingo or bat wings, cankles, and cellulite. I can of course still feel beautiful if I have all these features, for instance, if I have high self-esteem, perhaps from a great relationship, in which I feel attractive and desired or from valuing my body for what it can do rather than how it looks. I might even resist appearance norms altogether and value other measures of esteem over appearance, such as being a good mum or a good philosopher, making me relatively resistant to pressures to conform. However, as I argued, this becomes harder as appearance becomes more prominent, as culture becomes increasingly visual and virtual, and as technological fixes become accessible and affordable and as the beauty ideal functions as an ethical ideal. Thus while some might continue to resist the ideal, in the current context, resistance is harder, becomes political and is increasingly regarded as abnormal.

If we recall some of the statistics from earlier chapters about the dominance of the beauty ideal—for instance that three-to-five-year-olds are making character judgments based on silhouette size and 90 percent of young women and girls believe that how they look is more important than anything they will do or say—then the fact that beauty norms are not individually chosen is abundantly clear. The conformity of views, and the trends towards a narrow ideal, show that within the ideal the opportunity for choice is limited. Despite all the pleasures of beauty, and the positive aspects of the self under the beauty ideal, ultimately what we are actually choosing is highly prescribed.

It is the collective nature of the beauty ideal that narratives of informed consent cannot accommodate. Because informed consent is *only* and *always* concerned with individual choices, a one-off act of consent, it cannot begin to recognize, let alone address, the structural issues.[30] If we only focus on consent and fail to account for the pressure from the communal norms, we will be effectively blind to structural and social injustices and harms. If we shift our focus from whether or not the individual made a choice and instead look at the wider practice and the pattern of individual choices, then communal concerns, concerns that are literally invisible on an individual-choice model, come into view. For instance, on a case-by-case basis each instance of breast augmentation, or vaginal surgery, or even pubic hair removal, might appear to be wholly a matter of individual choice. Concerns about harms are reduced to mere questions of whether she wants the individual benefits or not, or indeed whether she wants them enough to risk being harmed. In this framework, standard concerns are about physical and psychological risk; for instance, whether individuals know the risks and are realistic about the likely outcome. At this level individual claims are the focus, for instance in the familiar statements of "I chose breast enhancement because my breasts have always been too small and I'd be more confident if they were more normal"; "I need vaginal surgery because bike-riding is uncomfortable, and I've become increasingly ashamed of my long labia"; and "I remove all my pubic hair, because I like to feel clean and smooth." On a case-by-case basis every reason is valid, and engaging in each of these practices may be successful in that the individual may be happier after engagement. Yet, when individuals continually choose practices that are always conforming to the beauty ideal, something else is going on. These are not just instances of individual choice—though they are that too—but they also indicate social and communal pressure. To seek to understand the pressure to conform I will consider whether beauty choices are desperate choices, a version of coercion, instances of false consciousness, or adaptive preferences.

It's Not an Option

One way of understanding coercion by social or cultural pressures is to use a version of a desperate choice argument. A paradigmatic example of a desperate choice or a coercive choice is the case of the poor Indian women who "chooses" surrogacy. In such instances, where poor women are paid far less than surrogates elsewhere, "it can be argued that the gestating woman's consent is invalid, insofar as there are limited alternative ways for them to meet their basic needs for food, shelter and so on."[31] "Desperate choices" then are choices when it feels as if they are not really choices—"I had no choice"—when the choice is the "least worst option" from a range of undesirable options.[32] Strictly speaking, choice remains as other options are available, but as no options are desirable they should not be considered as "freely chosen" (or equivalent to other choices). All choices are not the same, and more choices do not equate to more autonomy.[33] Choices differ qualitatively, some choices matter—they affect our life projects in some way or our sense of self—and some do not (they are trivial, and different choices would not have resulted in significantly different outcomes).[34] Counting the number of choices a person has tells you very little about her autonomy or agency. Nothing hangs on the number of choices a person has as such, but everything on the quality and content of the choices. Indeed, arguably, if you have only one hugely desirable option, you have more agency than if you have very many options to choose from but which you do not really want. Elsewhere I have argued that some practices are so harmful and only chosen in desperate choice scenarios that individuals should be prevented from (protected against) such choices.[35] This is not to say that consent is irrelevant in desperate choice scenarios (it might lessen exploitation as well as ensure that there is not deception or inadequate information or some other unethical practice). But what consent does not preclude is coercion. On this model, we can choose to engage in some practice or another and still be coerced by force of circumstance: a desperate choice.

But while there is clearly economic and cultural pressure to conform to the beauty ideal, the desperate choice model does not obviously apply. Neither of the two conditions of desperate choice are met: beauty choices are not "the least worse" option (one undesirable choice among others), nor are they the only way to achieve the end. It is possible to imagine something not wholly dissimilar to a desperate choice scenario: For instance, the woman who buys skin-lightening cream before food or medicine, or the women who saves money, forgoing other goods, for an operation she believes is *necessary* (such as the double eye lift in South Korea or breast implants in the glamour industry).[36] However, even in such instances, only some women could be regarded as being in desperate choice scenarios. Given this, the desperate choice model seems particularly unsuited to beauty choices. Moreover, those who are most likely to maximally engage, or to strive for more than minimal standards of beauty, are those who do not suffer economic pressure. Those who have the money to engage are likely to feel under pressure to "make the most of themselves," and feel a *duty* to engage more. Those who lack economic resources may feel less pressure as they lack the money that makes such options possible (although they may, as those who argue for a right to beauty do, consider the inability to access beauty products and processes a further injustice compounding economic injustice).[37] Indeed, as discussed in earlier chapters, engaging in beauty practices is aspirational and desirable. We are not (usually) coerced into having surgery, into removing our body hair, or into continual dieting. Very often we want to buy the product, engage in the practice or undergo the procedure. Saving money and forgoing other goods in order to engage in beauty practices suggests that these are goods that are desperately desired not desperately chosen. Given this, even though these are effectively required practices, and hugely conditioned by context, they are not desperate choices or coerced. But, nonetheless if it is "not an option" to reveal body hair, then nonconformity is costly and often not a viable response.

Deluded or Adaptive Beauty Choices?

If not coerced, another possible explanation is to suggest that women are duped or tricked into engaging in beauty practices that do not in fact advance or improve their situations. Women are simply wrong about the benefits, and they would not make these choices if they had not been misled. If this is correct, then women are suffering from false consciousness.[38]

False consciousness is a concept with Marxist heritage that is broadly used to describe the experience of class subordination. The subordinate class experience their situation of domination and subordination wrongly; they do not recognize the reality of the situation. Theories of false consciousness come in different forms and have developed over time.[39] In debates about beauty it is later versions of the concept which are invoked, for instance those of the Frankfurt School, who employed "false consciousness to refer not only to cognition but also to a distorted sense of being, of feeling and emotion, that gripped an individual in his/her false beliefs."[40] The argument goes that in a class-based society where some dominate others, distortions, illusions, and delusions must be created and sustained in the minds of the subordinate in order to keep them blind to the truth of their subordinated position. It is the inability to recognize the truth of their position, their false consciousness, which keeps the subordinate class in its place. In essence, then, false consciousness is the holding of false beliefs, beliefs that you are deluded into holding, that are against your interest, and that keep you disadvantaged. Were you able to recognize these false beliefs for the lies they are, you would (as an individual or a group) cease to engage in the behavior that these beliefs promote and support and reject your (class) domination and inferiority.

The use of false consciousness as a way to explain why women have been so passive with regard to their status as a dominated and subordinate class has been used by both feminist theorists and feminist activists, particularly in second-wave feminism. Adopting false consciousness as an explanatory framework accounts for why "consciousness raising" was employed as a tactic by the women's liberation movement. The assumption is that if women have their consciousness raised they will come to recognize the truth of their subordinated status and reject feminine roles and practices. Dworkin's argument falls into this framework, and she is up front about her intent of consciousness-raising, which she thinks works particularly well for women freeing themselves from patriarchy. Her overt aim in *Woman Hating* is revolutionary: "This book is an action where revolution is the goal."[41] She describes how consciousness raising leads to liberation: "we recognized all of our social behaviour as learned behavior that functioned for survival in a sexist world: we painted ourselves, smiled, exposed legs and ass, had children, kept house, as our accommodations to the reality of power politics."[42] Bartky's work also sits in this framework, and she looks to theories of class oppression to understand gender oppression, and her aim, stated at the beginning of *Femininity and Domination*, is "to understand how the values of a system that oppress us are able to take up residence inside our minds."[43] She overtly aims to open women's eyes to the injustice of women's status to change women's experience and behavior: "I am trying to give women permission to feel the anger that I believe is already there."[44] In this false consciousness model, women engage in beauty practices because they are deluded, tricked, or duped. The expectation is that once women recognize the falsity of their beliefs and develop properly feminist consciousness, then the false consciousness will be rejected and the behaviors that flow from it will stop. This will not be easy or without pain, indeed Bartky's description of attaining feminist consciousness is anything but comfortable, but as a result of recognizing the true state of our subordination we will stop engaging in practices that make us subordinated and subordinatable.[45]

Along with others, I reject claims of false consciousness (and also the somewhat similar concept of adaptive preference, which

I will return to). The false consciousness claim has been roundly challenged in many discourses for presenting women as if they are dupes or dopes, as passive adopters of the messages of patriarchy, unable to assess and negotiate. I will return to this topic before the end of this chapter. Before I do, there are other reasons for rejecting the false consciousness argument.

First, false consciousness is just not true. Women are not deluded about at least some of the rewards of beauty. As set out in the first chapter, there are some real external benefits attached to conforming to the beauty ideal. These may not be as significant or as important as other goods, and certainly less so than advertisers and women's magazines would have us believe, but there are some external benefits and pay-offs. Furthermore, as the last few chapters have shown beauty practices are (sometimes) pleasurable, and there are other benefits, in terms of a positive sense of self, a moral pay-off as the beauty ideal becomes an ethical ideal, and many practices have social goods attached to them. These are not simply narcissistic pleasures, or the false pleasures of man-pleasing, but are real wins. Plus the external and internal costs, as we fall further under the beauty ideal, are extremely high and will likely become higher. While collectively we would all be better off with a less demanding beauty ideal, in the world we find ourselves in it makes sense to invest in beauty. This is true even if the processes are demanding, painful, and harmful (although the more painful and harmful, the less sense engagement makes). As Chambers states, this is not false consciousness, "people might autonomously choose to follow harmful norms because they believe they cannot access the desired benefit without complying with the norm."[46] Likewise, Heyes argues that "ideological captivity in the form of false consciousness cannot explain all of the power of weight-loss dieting as a cultural practice."[47] It is rational and sensible to engage at least to minimal levels to avoid abnormality and increasingly beyond what is minimal. Moreover, as the beauty ideal becomes a more dominant and ethical ideal, it makes sense to prioritize beauty; something that, as discussed in chapter 2, young women already seem to believe. In sum, engaging in beauty practices is not all harmful; although some of it is, and it is likely that it will become more harmful—both individually and communally—as compliance becomes more demanding and the ethical aspect of the ideal strengthens. The beauty ideal is mixed, and the pleasurable aspects are not just the sugar on the bitter pill; they are real and experienced. We are not simply deluded or tricked because we buy in.

The second reason for rejecting false consciousness is that, as a response to overly demanding beauty norms, the feminist project of consciousness raising simply has not worked. When Dworkin and Bartky were making arguments for consciousness raising as a means of rejecting beauty practices, this approach may have had some chance of success. Such critique may have tapped into the anger, which Bartky refers to regarding women's general subordination, and provided a swell of resistance and movement for change. But the time was different in terms of women's relative status, the status of the beauty ideal, and the wider context: for instance, it was largely a previrtual culture. The aim was culture change, and these calls were within a broader project to make women less dependent on men and less subordinate. In some areas, in many places, at least some of the feminist agenda has been attained—for instance in education and employment—but not when it comes to beauty. As Kathy Peiss notes in her history of beauty, feminist "critique has increased women's scepticism toward the beauty industry, but it has hardly stopped them from buying cosmetics, reading fashion magazines, trying out new looks, and sharing makeup tips with friends."[48] The anger that Bartky infers has dissolved as other feminist goals have been attained and beauty practices have further embedded. Beauty no longer seems, even after exposure to consciousness raising, to be "for him" or be simply explained by accounts of sexist oppression.

Women look at such claims and think "are you crazy?"—not because they are deluded, but because they know beauty is not completely pointless or harmful. This should not simply be dismissed as false consciousness and to claim it is to deny the lived experience and knowledge women have. Rather, women recognize the extreme costs of rejecting all beauty norms. Why on earth would someone chose to do that (especially when at least some of the practice is enjoyable and self-enhancing)? As Holliday and Sanchez Taylor point out, "feminist discourses of victimization or internalized oppression are likely to alienate a generation of young women for whom sexual self-determination, expressed through the glamourous body, is a central component of identity, associated with pleasure and success."[49] This does not mean we should not be critical of what are homogenizing, and as will be argued in the next chapter, hypergendered norms, but it does mean that simple rejection will not work.

Moreover not only are calls to resistance ineffective, they are counterproductive. There is nothing natural about the natural body, and "natural beauty" is often the preserve of the elite. Appeals to natural beauty, or the "true" body, are every bit as worrying as demands to act on the malleable body. All bodies are fundamentally socially constructed; there is no natural body, and claims to such either essentialize bodies or they promote some form of raced and classed beauty that is used to dominate others. As Holliday and Sanchez Taylor state, "access to a system that equates beauty with value has been central for both black and working-class women, women whom feminism, in adopting and anti-beauty position therefore excludes."[50] You have to be particularly privileged, as I argued in chapter 2, to resist beauty norms, and usually protected by a distinct community with counternorms. If we take seriously the evidence of women and adopt an intersectional approach, then any suggestion that individuals should simply resist is not only unrealistic, but unfair. It falls more heavily on those who are not privileged in terms of class, education, and race and less on those who are protected by their privileged communities and who have alternative ways to access the goods of the good life. It asks women as individuals, individuals who increasingly fall under the beauty ideal, to resist despite the cost to them externally and internally. This divides women, and makes them guilty; as Heyes puts it, it is a "silencing gambit."[51] Blum makes a similar point when she argues that "we need to transcend feminist criticisms of body practices that can wind up being as shaming as the physical imperfections that drove us to beautify in the first place—as though some of us are superior to the cultural machinery while others desperately fling ourselves across the tracks of cultural desires."[52] I will return to this in the final chapter of the book, but for now it is enough to note that accounts that make women guilty and shameful cannot be worthwhile theories to promote. Accusations of false consciousness divide "virtuous" feminists (who do not engage) from women who are wrongly engaging and who need to be educated to behave as true feminists. Such feminist politics is antiwomen and can only fail.

At this point in time we know that consciousness raising in the traditional form does not work; if there was a window when it could have done, that is now past. In the current context, rather than showing feminist solidarity such critiques serve to criticize individual women for what they do and what they do not do. Further, they raise uncomfortable questions about the role of privilege and power. Finally, it makes change harder, because it dismisses the middle ground. At the outset, it denies that activism to find better beauty norms—such as the body positive campaigns—are valuable. Bartky is clear on this: she argues that any feminist who thinks that femininity and female body display can be preserved, is simply "incoherent."[53] This, I think, is not true. Following Heyes, we are not "captive" if we do not wholly dismiss beauty norms. To present the situation as one in which all femininity makes women "unfree" is both damaging and inaccurate, and fails to recognize the range of options for change that women, particularly together, do have.[54] I will argue in the final chapter, there are at least some measures that women (and all of us) can take together to challenge the rise of narrower and more demanding beauty norms, without suggesting that we should not engage in beauty practices at all. To believe that change is possible, we must recognize that women do have choice and agency, even if constrained, and reject narratives of false consciousness.

If we turn from false consciousness to adaptive preferences, similar concerns arise. Adaptive preference is a concept that comes from the capabilities approach and the work of Amartya Sen and Nussbaum. It is a means to account for the way in which the preferences of deprived people can perpetuate their deprivation and poverty.[55] In *Women and Human Development*, Nussbaum presents the case of Vasanti, a poor Indian woman who accepts her situation because she believes it is part of women's lot to suffer.[56] This account of adaptive preference has been read by a number of scholars as essentially false consciousness and critiqued along such lines.[57] Alison Jaggar's critique of adaptive preference is rightly regarded as decisive, and only significantly revised accounts of adaptive preference survive it.[58] Most worrying in the adaptive preference account is that "raising questions about adaptive preferences and false consciousness only when confronted by views that oppose their own encourages dismissing those views without considering them seriously."[59] As such, adaptive preference critiques tend to privilege liberal views and effectively blame local cultures (and people within them) for global injustice.[60] While local cultures may well be complicit, Jaggar is keen to foreground the impact of the global economic order and the role we all have in sustaining it. In light of such criticism, to use adaptive preferences as a way of accounting for the preferences of other, supposedly very different women, in illiberal cultures is not tenable.

Yet when it comes to beauty these are not issues that are primarily or only concerned with poor (other) women, and while accounts of adaptive preference tend to focus on poverty and deprivation, attempts have been made to expand the focus to other practices. Beauty practices have most often been invoked when seeking to apply adaptive preferences in situations without economic deprivation. Illustrative is Natalie Stoljar's essay, which treats engaging in beauty practices as a paradigmatic example of adaptive preference and deformed desires.[61] Her example of an adaptive preference, taken from Benson, is of an excellent student who nonetheless and misguidedly spends time on her appearance.[62] In this formulation, adaptive preferences look like false consciousness almost unmodified, and thus this approach is subject to the same criticisms I gave above.[63] However, the false consciousness objections are not sufficient to dismiss Serene Khader's revised, and women-friendly and women-empowering, account of adaptive preference. Khader suggests that adaptive preferences extend beyond poor and deprived women, and she discusses Chambers's example of a fifteen-year-old girl who wants breast implants.[64]

Khader's reworking of adaptive preference seeks to respect women and their choices, while not taking at face value such choices or assuming, as the liberal model so often does, that such choices are in themselves statements about what women want and value. Like Jaggar, she worries about what the account says about poor women and states that "to act as though having one's preferences shaped by social conditions is particular to deprived people is to put forward a conception of deprived people as less likely to make choices and reflect on their lives than people in positions of privilege."[65] Instead she puts forward an account of adaptive preferences that does not entail that adaptive preferences "need to be experienced as self-esteem deficits at all."[66] Accordingly, she denies that women engage in such practices because they do not believe themselves to be equivalently or sufficiently worthy. Likewise, she does not "understand adaptive preferences as undermining people's capacities for autonomy."[67] Rather, she argues that a "preference is adaptive only if it is likely that a person will change it and endorse her change of it under better conditions."[68]

At first pass, this approach seems more promising for understanding beauty preferences. Women who engage in beauty practices need not think that they are either inferior or unworthy; they may, but they are at least equally likely to think that they are worthy and deserving and entitled. Likewise, as I've argued throughout, women are certainly making choices, and while these choices are significantly constrained by the dominance and demandingness of the ideal, they are choices that make sense in the contexts in which women find themselves.

However, on closer reading the critique seems less suitable. In Khader's account, deprivation, and the limits it places on the range of desirable options that are actually available to women, is doing a lot of work. For example, she states that when we give an adaptive preference account we are not "merely saying that that person lives according to a conception of the good with which we disagree.

Rather, we are saying that a person's preferences are preferences that we cannot imagine many people really wanting to have."[69] This is overtly not the case when it comes to beauty norms: very many of us wish to engage in beauty practices, and surely even those who do not can imagine—on some level—why women would wish to. Khader recognizes this, as she continues that "identifying adaptive preferences as any preferences complicit in perpetuating bad social norms makes an implausibly large number of preferences adaptive."[70] Given this, I struggle to define beauty ideals as adaptive on Khader's account. This reading seems consistent with her claim a few pages later that:

> Both deprived and nondeprived people make choices based on social values that are internalized. Both deprived and nondeprived people have preferences that are chosen and causally related to social conditions (i.e. that would change under different social conditions). I think that what our foregoing analysis suggests is that APs are not simply imposed preferences; they are imposed *by deprivation*.[71]

So while I embrace much of Khader's approach I do not think it easily translates to situations that are not characterized by deprivation. Given that the original intention in extending adaptive preference accounts was to make them applicable in contexts where deprivation isn't a background condition, and the best account of adaptive preferences we have returns us to deprivation, it would seem that this extension, while promising, ultimately fails. Whatever else characterizes living under the beauty ideal, those who engage most extensively are not those who are economically deprived or lacking in significant options.

Beyond the Individual

So while beauty norms are communal and the pressure is real and we are conforming to an ever more demanding beauty ideal, we are not being coerced. Nor, I have argued, is this false consciousness or adaptive preference. Essentially these are choices that make sense in the current context, given the already dominant and likely increasingly dominant ideal. However, while not coerced, these choices are not free in the way that the liberal model suggests. Simply having information, especially as late in the decision-making process as the point of consent, is not enough to make a free choice, given the extent of the pressure of the ideal and the power of the imagined self. Given the current polarization of the debate, this is a difficult case to make. The image of individuals as the authors of their own lives is an incredibly powerful one. It legitimizes all kinds of practices on the grounds that they are "chosen," and in many contexts it has become the only ethical requirement (good examples where consent is frequently regarded as all that matters are decision making in medical and sexual contexts). I have argued in many contexts—from organ sale to prostitution—against the dominance of choice and consent, on the grounds that the choice model of ethics is flawed.[72] I have made a series of arguments about why to focus on choice is to fail to recognize substantive ethical issues, as to focus exclusively on choice obscures injustices, blames individuals for structural problems, and wrongly equates what is ethical with what is chosen. Some of these arguments are particularly pertinent to the beauty debate, and I will finish by highlighting three undesirable consequences of not challenging the choice model (while recognizing that choices, within limits, are being made): First, the polarized nature of the debate falsely presents women as either empowered choosers *or* passive victims, (dupes and dopes *or* creative interpreters and savvy consumers); second, this polarization then serves to silence critiques by labeling them as paternalistic or moralistic (a tactic that is familiar from the objectification debate); and finally, that to focus on choice privatizes ethics and, despite the rhetoric of empowerment, blames the individual.

EMPOWERED CHOOSERS OR PASSIVE VICTIMS

Underlying the rhetoric of "being true to oneself" and making active choices is the assumption that anything that is not a "free choice" and actively chosen is inauthentic, an instance of failing to take control and direct your own life. Such assumptions result in a polarized picture of moral agents: you are either an empowered chooser, taking control of your own life and authentically making decisions for yourself *or* you are a passive victim to whom things are done (elsewhere I have argued that at times the language of empowerment can be alienating rather than empowering).[73] Given that the polarity is set up in this way, it is not surprising that we want to present ourselves as empowered agents, not passive victims. Indeed part of the reason why the objectification debate appears at first glance out of date is that objects are passive and inert, while the self in the liberal, particularly neoliberal model, is active, choosing, and consuming. But, as discussed in the previous chapter, we experience ourselves as both subjects and objects. We actively choose to engage but simultaneously recognize that nonconformity is not a possible choice, and so we act and are acted upon.

In the liberal myth, the agent is the master of his or her own destiny; all that this empowered chooser needs is information about the options available. But no choices are actually like this. In the real world, when we reject the myth of the free liberal chooser, all choices are in context. There are no unconstrained fully free choices; we are all embedded in particular cultures and come from a particular racial group or class, and with particular sets of familial and social relationships and commitments. As McRobbie argues, the emphasis on the consuming individual is disingenuous. It presents a picture of a confident, discerning, consumer who is—or should be—empowered to make her own choices. This not only places the emphasis on the individual, but prevents protest and action; thus "women are currently being disempowered through the very discourses of empowerment they are being offered as substitutes for feminism."[74] The free, choosing self of the liberal model quite simply does not exist.[75]

Despite the arguments on both sides, in practice we are not empowered choosers or passive victims, dupes or critics, subjects or objects. We are both, we choose in a narrow and influenced context, we critique the images we see but recognize their impact on us, and we objectify ourselves and others at the same times as we (re)create identity and subjectivity. We live in the mix, negotiating as best we can in the situation in which we find ourselves. But articulating this middle ground is notoriously difficult. In the liberal and neoliberal choice paradigm, where autonomy, often reduced to choice, is the primary ethical value, then what matters is that we have chosen, and this alone is supposedly proof that this choice was most desirable.[76] There is little space for recognizing choices regrettably taken, or taken while wishing there were alternative options. Similarly, finding middle ground in the cultural literature is equally hard, and those who have criticized beauty trends and practices have been accused of treating women as dupes or dopes, and of failing to recognize that images are always interpreted and that individuals are well able to discern critique and re-interpret the images and messages they receive. But, while I may interpret and renegotiate all kinds of images, this does not make me immune. We all live in a culture and are shaped by the images and expectations of it. Just as we are not agents or victims, subjects or objects, we are not dupes or critics, dopes or savvy consumers. We are constrained choosers and influenced critics making choices in context.

We need to find a way to inhabit the middle ground and to find ways to articulate the ways that the demands of the beauty ideal actually function: We are constrained, but we are not coerced, and we make agential and active choices in contexts that are extremely limited and highly prescribed. To suggest that individual's choices are highly prescribed is not, as the liberal and neoliberal model sometimes suggests, similar to saying that women have no agency, that they are victims, dupes or dopes. There is nothing contradictory about recognizing these as agential, but extremely limited, choices.

DON'T TELL ME WHAT TO DO!

As well as falsely regarding agents as either fully free and empowered or passive victims and dopes, a further consequence of the choice rhetoric is the implication that it is inappropriate to criticize any practice that has been chosen. This leads to the silencing of debate and criticism. To elaborate, the polarization of the debate into victims *or* agents, passive dupes *or* savvy consumers, has led to a further claim that whatever is chosen is always the best choice and by extension not to be criticized. What is chosen then becomes equated with what is acceptable and, in the liberal model, with what is ethical: remember the fairy dust. Because this is the case it becomes problematic to criticize, debate, or ask questions about the rightness of chosen practices. In this context, it becomes almost impossible to critique any practice if someone—anyone—has chosen it—as to do this is said to criticize the women who made the choice. So to criticize, for example, the increasing use of buttock-lifts or breast implants (say, on the grounds that they are unnecessary or carry health risks, or simply that time could be better spent elsewhere), is regarded as a patronizing, paternalistic, and moralizing critique. It is a denial of individual's choices; a position that is anathema in the liberal choice framework. That practices can be criticized without criticizing women—or telling them what to do—is not recognized on the liberal model. This, I have argued, happens elsewhere, but it is a particularly prominent tactic in the beauty debate. The silencing feature of the choice rhetoric is important for understanding the dominance of the choice model and why it is so difficult to recognize the limits of choice. Those who would raise questions about emerging trends and the increasing use of some practices or about the overall increasing dominance of the beauty ideal feel unable to do so if this is to be understood as dismissing the women who undergo such practices. Effectively then, debate is silenced.

This silencing occurs in part because the logic of the choice rhetoric suggests that criticism, or debate, about any practice that has been chosen is paternalistic. The fear of being accused of paternalism is a real one (especially for ethicists), as "paternalism is considered to be prima facie unethical."[77] As Graeme Laurie puts it, "paternalism has come to be seen as the very antithesis of autonomy and self-determination because implicit in its operation is a disregard for the wishes of the subject towards whom the paternalism is directed."[78]After all no one, especially a feminist, wants to be deemed antichoice, paternalistic, moralizing, or prudish. Not surprisingly many scholars and activists have given up on wider critiques and simply sought to ensure that choice is informed and that practices are as safe as possible. Hence emphasis on trying to give women who want surgery as much information as possible to allow them to make a "free choice." Broader questions about the value of the beauty ideal as an ethical ideal and questions about whether we should—collectively—be choosing these practices at all have become almost unable to be articulated. To be critical in this context then—no matter what the critique is—is a costly and risky business.

Whatever else silence on this topic is something that we cannot allow: beauty matters, and it matters for all of us. It is not the case that to criticize and debate whether it is good that we are increasingly hairless, struggling to be thin with curves, or increasingly tempted by Botox, fillers, and cosmetic surgery is to criticize individual women who engage in these practices. Nor is it the case that engagement signals that you are not concerned about the practices.[79] To pretend that choice is all that matters ethically or that engagement alone somehow proves that these practices are good to do is just as disingenuous as arguing that women do not know what they are doing when they engage. Silencing is not respectful of women's choices; on the contrary, it isolates women and leads to victim blaming, it also makes it impossible to raise collective concerns about beauty as a social norm or ethical ideal.

IT'S YOUR FAULT! YOU CHOSE IT!

The final destructive consequence of the choice model is that ultimately, and despite the rhetoric of individual empowerment, it is victim blaming. Rather than making us collectively responsible it *privatizes* ethics, by making whether to do something or not wholly a matter of individual choice. If everything hangs on whether or not the individual chose a course of action, then if something goes wrong, that too is on the individual: "You chose it, you have no one to blame but yourself." This is particularly important in the beauty debate. Given the rising demands of beauty and the significant pressure to engage—in response to the power of the ideal and the pull of the imagined self—it is unfair to place blame solely on the individual when things go wrong. But the individual choice model does just that. This type of reasoning was clearly in play with the treatment of women following the PiP scandal (as discussed in chapter 6).[80] You are free to choose whatever you wish, all choices are equivalent, and it is nobody's responsibility but your own; and accordingly you should to live with the consequences. However, while this works in the mythical world where individuals freely choose, in the real world where choices always take place in context it is wholly unethical to assume that just because someone chose something that there are no further ethical concerns.

Contrary to the myth of the individual choice model, all choices are not the same, and if we want to respect individuals, then we have to pay attention to what they can actually be and do. We choose whether to have a breast augmentation or liposuction, or to live with our sagging bodies. But we do not, and cannot, individually choose our beauty ideal, and just as we can no longer choose to show visible body hair, we may not, if trends continue be able to choose not to have breast augmentation or liposuction in the future. Just as cosmetic dentistry is now routine for those who can afford or who have public health care systems, so too may breast augmentation be routine and required for the next generation. Recognizing communal pressure also allows us to recognize communal responsibility and thus take some care for each other as we engage in beauty practices.

Conclusion

In this chapter, I have argued that choice is much more complex than the rhetoric suggests. I have argued that wholly free choice is a myth, that we are neither empowered choosers nor passive victims. We have agency and can choose but always in context and only between certain options. Most importantly, I have emphasized that we cannot—as individuals—choose our beauty ideals. We have some choice over the extent to which we conform, but, as trends continue towards an ever narrower, more dominant and demanding global beauty ideal, such choices become more limited. This looks like more choice, in that we can choose which of the ever increasing menu of beauty products and procedures we wish to spend our time and money engaged in, but it is increasingly hard to step outside the ideal. To seek to explain the paradox, that engagement in beauty practices is often required and yet chosen, I explored the extent to which these are free choices, using the model of informed consent. Having shown informed consent, even for those who endorse a liberal model, is undermined in beauty, I then sought to explore the pressure to conform. I found that, though significant, the pressure does not amount to coercion. Further I argued that women under the beauty ideal are not exhibiting false consciousness or adaptive preference. I finished the chapter by arguing that three problematic consequences of the choice rhetoric are the false polarization of empowered agents and passive victims, the silencing effect, and blaming individuals. Taken together understanding beauty as being about individual choices does little to help us address the increasing demands of beauty, the normalization of harmful and risky practices, and the growing dominance of the beauty ideal as an ethical ideal. The next chapter will address the outstanding topic remaining from the objectification debate: whether the beauty ideal is an instance of gendered exploitation.

10

More Pain, Who Gains?

The last chapter focused on how we can make sense of the choice rhetoric that surrounds beauty practices and the tension between insisting that we choose beauty practices while recognizing that they are required. In particular, the "I'm doing it for myself" narrative was discussed as the dominant and correct discourse for engaging in beauty practices (and many other practices). That this narrative fits well with the liberal picture of the individual as an empowered chooser was discussed, and it was concluded that although a powerful image it bears little resemblance to reality. For while we are agents and we do choose—we are not passive victims, dopes, dupes, or inert objects—our choices are hugely constrained, limited, and prescribed. However, while I rejected the liberal account, I also rejected theories of coercion, false consciousness, and adaptive preference as simplistic and unproductive. By denying the pleasurable and rewarding aspects of beauty, such accounts fail to resonate with women's lived experience. Women are not wrong to believe that they will benefit from conforming to the beauty ideal, and the practices of beauty can be pleasurable and rewarding. This does not mean that we should simply accept the increasing demands and dominance of the beauty ideal, and in the next chapter I will make some tentative suggestions for ways in which we might seek to transform the beauty ideal into one that is kinder and more forgiving, but it does mean that to say we should not care about beauty and appearance is unrealistic.

In chapter 1, I introduced a Foucauldian account of power to explain that the pressure and demands of beauty cannot be placed at the door of a particular individual or group, but rather that the nexus of power is everywhere and nowhere. This account allows us to recognize that there are many drivers for the increasing demands of beauty—including globalization, individualism, the rise of visual and virtual culture, the technological imperative, and, I have argued, of particular importance is the ethical nature of the ideal— but there is no power source who is imposing demands. To make this claim is to deny traditional accounts that the demands of beauty are imposed on women by men; or at least to deny that this is all that is going on. It is this argument that I will address in this chapter. I will argue that the claim that men exploit women in beauty is not sufficient to account for what is going on in the contemporary context.

Exploitation of Women by Men

A traditional feminist argument against beauty practices is that beauty norms exploit women for the benefit of men. Men benefit, first, from women making themselves sexually desirable, and apparently sexual available. High heels and breast implants, as discussed in chapter 7, are classic examples of beauty sexualizing for male pleasure. I argued that this might not always or only be what is going on. Second, beauty regimes serve to constrict and control women's bodies, to reduce what women can actually do. They physically limit—controlling and shaping garments include high heels, bras, corsets, burkas, kimonos, spanx (and corsets becoming fashionable again in some circles),[1] and psychologically limit as women become self-conscious and self-police.[2] In short, women must not let it all hang out; they must control their unruly lumps and bumps, and, as a consequence, move, sit, and stand in a certain way, and be ashamed if they transgress.

In this argument, the hierarchical and asymmetrical elements are paramount. Women must engage in restrictive beauty norms to succeed as women; and there are no parallel requirements placed on men. But, and here is the rub, while required, success in beauty is trivialized and belittled. Beautifying is dismissed as mere "women's pleasures." As discussed in chapter 4, the languages and skill set involved in beauty practices are not insignificant. Describing such practices as routine or minimal not only hides the extent of the demands but also minimizes and reduces the extent of the knowledge-base, language and skill set that is involved. As the demands increase, so too do the things that need to be learned and mastered for successful engagement. In the traditional account, this trivializing is wholly accounted for by gender exploitation; it is a way of first making women women and second making women subordinate and inferior (recall the arguments of MacKinnon and Dworkin from chapter 7). Men exploit and dominate women by requiring women to master skills that they themselves are not required to master, and, in a kind of double-whammy, they then belittle and trivialize such pursuits. Women are condemned as "sentimental, superficial, duplicitous, because we attend to and sometimes learn to love the glamourous arts."[3] This passage from Jeffreys captures the key elements of the traditional account:

> Beauty practices can reasonably be understood to be for the benefit of men. Though women in the west sometimes say that they choose to engage in beauty practices for their own sake, or for other women and not for men, men benefit in several ways. They gain the advantage of having their superior sex class status marked out, and the satisfaction of being reminded of their superior status every time they look at a women. They also gain the advantage of being sexually stimulated by "beautiful" women. These advantages can be summed up in the understanding that women are expected to both "complement" and "compliment" men.[4]

Bartky makes similar claims in, *Femininity and Domination*, stating that the "'art of make-up' is the art of disguise ... [which] presupposes that a women's face, unpainted is defective. Soap and water, a shave and routine attention to hygiene may be enough for *him*; for *her* they are not."[5] And likewise, that "in spite of the unrelenting pressure to 'make the most of what they have,' women are ridiculed and dismissed for the triviality of their interest in such 'trivial' things ... [as] clothes and make-up."[6] In this account of exploitation, a number of claims are made; men benefit from female engagement in beauty practices; first, because they attain pleasure from being titillated by beautified women; second, because beauty provides a means to assert superiority and inferiority; third, because beauty helps to constrain and limit women, both physically and psychologically. All of these elements assume that these demands fall only on women—indeed they make women women—and that such practices are not required of men. If men too are subject to the demands of beauty, then the exploitation claim which, like the arguments of MacKinnon and Dworkin in chapter 7, is premised on asymmetry and hierarchy between men and women, is undermined.

Failures of Gender Exploitation Accounts

While I have strong sympathies with many of the gender-based arguments, particularly when it comes to the role of beauty practices in gendering, they are not sufficient to account for the current demands, and changing demands, of beauty. No longer do the claims of male benefit convince. Men too are beautifying and becoming "to be looked" at, and increasingly falling under the beauty ideal. If men too fall under the beauty ideal, then the trivializing and subordinating claims are harder to sustain. First, if the demands of beauty fall on both men and women, then the demands of beauty fall on all and not only on one group. Once all are engaging (or at least many), then the claim that one group uses the engagement to subordinate the other is not sustainable. This is true of any practice: practices are used to assert status and determine hierarchy, but such demarcation relies on the maintaining of different practices, and the shunning of the subordinate practice by the dominant group. In a very real sense, the fact that men are increasingly worrying about their appearance and engaging in more beauty practices upsets the traditional claim. It is no longer true that women have to spend time and money and effort on this sector of life, while men do not. Men may have largely skipped the "second shift," of childcare and housework, but they increasingly do body work; the "third shift."[7]

Second, to claim that beauty is trivial is not true in the context of a dominant global ideal, which is functioning as an ethical ideal. The importance of this change should not be underestimated. Being beautiful, and engaging in beauty practices, is no longer (in most contexts) a guilty secret, but rather is regarded as good to do, self-enhancing, and even a moral duty. The more we fall under the ideal, the more that this is the case, and, as appearance matters more and as the ethical nature of the ideal embeds, beauty can no longer be dismissed as trivial. It has become central. Recall, that to engage in body work is virtuous and valued; primary rather than peripheral. In a world in which we are engaging in beauty for beauty's sake—as I argued in the account of beauty objectification—at least in some contexts it is just not the case that this is for men or that men benefit. The second argument is addressed by the claims I have made about the nature of the beauty ideal as an ethical dominant, demanding, and potentially global ideal. The transformation of beauty into an important ethical ideal by definition challenges claims to triviality. To explore whether the first argument holds, I will consider the extent to which men are vulnerable to the demands of beauty.

Exploitation arguments are premised on asymmetry and hierarchy, or inequality, to use more familiar language of exploitation debates. While exploitation is defined differently by different scholars, some significant inequality must be present for a group or person to be able to exploit another group or person. In very general terms, exploitation is taking unfair advantage of something like vulnerability or need or powerlessness (with this being required for exploitation to be possible), or abusing power in a way that fails to respect something of value (like personhood or equality).[8] While there are arguments that exploitation should cover more than vulnerability, vulnerability (in economic, cultural, or social power) is a necessary condition for exploitation. Accordingly, in all circumstances, for exploitation to happen there must be some imbalance of power, or some inequality, or some vulnerability that allows the exploiter to take unfair advantage.

In the previous chapter, I argued that vulnerability is an extensive category in beauty; and far more extensive than is generally recognized in practices of informed consent. The fact that women are vulnerable when it comes to beauty is not in question, and vulnerability is a key driver for engagement. Indeed, if vulnerability is understood as insecurity or low self-esteem, then there is a sense in which it is not only being exploited but also created in order to be exploited. We need to be convinced that bingo wings, visible body hair, or protruding labia are problems if we are to buy the right products or engage in correct beauty regimes to address them. Yet while vulnerability is present—and dramatically, remember the extent of the dissatisfaction women feel and the extent to which they feel shame and disgust for not measuring up—if men too suffer from such vulnerability then the inequality between men and women is lessened, and so the asymmetry and hierarchy are challenged. Therefore whether and the extent to which the beauty ideal falls on men and the extent to which it falls in similar ways is key for any account of gender exploitation that rests on inequality.

Men Succumb to the Demands of Beauty

Without a doubt the pressures of visual and virtual culture are impacting upon men, and how men look is becoming more important than it has been in the past.[9] For young men the pressure to conform to some beauty ideal, to be body confident, to look good, and to dress well is growing. Increasingly, men are suffering from body insecurity and low body esteem. Recall the YMCA report discussed in chapter 2, where body image was ranked as the third-most-important issue for young people in the UK. In addition, statistics on eating disorders suggest that as many as a third of young sufferers of eating disorders, perhaps more, are male.[10] Likewise, the "Sexualisation of Young People" report details that boys are under pressure to display their bodies in the virtual world in ways that show muscles and are hypermasculine.[11] Some reports do suggest, however, that the beauty ideal continues to fall more on young girls than on boys: for instance, the Children's Society's 2016 report highlights a gender gap in happiness connected to body image.[12] But even if the ideal continues to fall on women and girls more than on men, it is no longer the case that men are immune.

In addition to the fact that men, particularly young men, are demonstrating body image concerns, the beauty ideals to which men aspire are, like women's ideals, becoming less realistic and more demanding. For instance, among certain groups of men there is pressure to bulk up the chest, shoulders, and arms; and increasingly visible and well defined muscle is required for men to attain what some would consider minimum standards of beauty. The trend to visible and larger muscles requires, at the very least, demanding regimes of diet and exercise and pumping iron. The muscled look shares many of the features of the female ideal. It is firm, smooth, and young. And while not thin, it is not fat; big but not fat.[13] That this look is increasingly prominent is well documented and the "drive to muscularity" is said to be the male version of the "drive to thinness."[14] In her second edition of *Body Image*, published in 2008, Sarah Grogan warned that we should be concerned by the increasing social pressure on men to conform to the muscled look, and she noted the increasing use of steroids and cosmetic surgery by men seeking to attain this look.[15] In her third edition, published in 2016, she notes that the pressure on men to be more muscular and more toned is far more prevalent.[16] This is supported by other studies.[17] In addition, and again parallel to women, the more men buy the muscled ideal, the more likely they are to be dissatisfied with their bodies, leading to harmful consequences, such as disordered eating.[18]

Attaining the muscled ideal, like attaining thinness with curves, is demanding. It requires dedicated adherence to extreme diet and exercise regimes, and, depending on body type and physique these might not be sufficient. For many men "help" is required; either chemical assistance (steroids or hormones) or surgery. While cosmetic surgery is still largely a female activity men are increasingly going under the knife. For example, BAAPS report a rise in operations on men, dubbed "the daddy makeover," including an "epic rise of 20% in male liposuction and a 13% jump in "man boob" reductions."[19] Wolf jokes about the beauty ideal falling on men and invites us to image "penis implants, penis augmentation, foreskin enhancement, testicular silicone injections to correct asymmetry, saline injections with a choice of three sizes, surgery to correct the angle of erection, to lift the scrotum and make it pert."[20] Her purpose is to show how crazy and unimaginable it is that such things could be offered to men, and yet much of this has come to pass. It is still the case that operations on men are around 10 percent of total operations in the UK, but the numbers of operations are growing. If Brazil is at the top of the beauty curve for men as it is for women, then the fact that men are the fastest-growing demographic of cosmetic surgery patients in Brazil might foreshadow a general trend for men to engage in cosmetic surgery.[21]

Just as the trend to firmness is evident in the muscled ideal, so too is the trend, in some groups of men, towards hairlessness. For example, in the United States, "as of 2005, more than 60 percent of men were regularly reducing or removing hair from areas of the body below the neck."[22] Recent studies report similar figures, with a 2011 study reporting that a majority of American and Australian college men and women report removing pubic hair.[23] Such figures are further supported by the growth of hair removal practices, such as the "sack, back, and crack."[24] Among some groups of men, hairlessness is becoming expected, and is regarded as normal and required. However demanding hairlessness is for women, and I argued in chapter 4 that the demands of hairlessness are significant, it is more demanding for men. While much of the research has been done in the United States, Australia, and the UK there are some studies that suggest that this trend is not limited to the West.[25]

Further evidence that the demands of beauty fall increasingly on men can also be found in the dramatic extension of the male market in beauty products.[26] Men are buying more products, and cosmetic lines aimed at men are increasingly comparable to women's lines and the global male grooming market was estimated to be $21.4 billion in 2016.[27] No longer are men "borrowing" women's products but unashamedly buying their own, and the male market in make-up and grooming products is a growth area. Engaging in fashion and beauty is no longer a women's preserve, or something that men do on the quiet. Men spend money on clothes, hair, grooming products in not dissimilar ways to women, and even traditionally female products, such as make-up, are now being aimed at men.[28]

Accordingly, it is the case that men are engaging in beauty practices and are increasingly, at least in some quarters, subject to demanding and unrealistic appearance ideals. This is particularly true in the rise of the muscular form as a dominant male ideal. The rise of this type of male body can be seen dramatically in the changing shapes of male actors and film stars. Compare the changing bodies of James Bond, moving from the suave and sophisticated, and by today's standards slightly flabby and most definitely hairy, Sean Connery, to the chiseled, muscle-bound, and hairless Daniel Craig.

Moreover, men, like women, are increasingly to be looked at and evaluated. For example, Gill highlights a "dramatic trend towards idealized and eroticized presentations of male bodies that have transformed the visual landscape over the past two decades."[29] The Diet Coke ad is perhaps the classic example, where women perform a version of ogling, of sexual objectification, that adopts a traditional account of sexual objectification and reverses the gender roles. The intention is to suggest that men can be sexually objectified, by women, in exactly the same way as women are imagined to be in traditional accounts.[30] Of course, that such sexual objectification could ever be the same is illusory, if I am correct, and key to what is going on in such accounts is sexual threat.[31] Furthermore, the meanings of gender norms are not the same, and acts and practices have different meanings when enacted by those who have different gendered roles. Nonetheless, and despite the differences between objectification of men and women, it is a significant change that men too are to be looked at and evaluated on their looks and as bodies. Wolf's claim that "to live in a culture in which women are routinely naked where men aren't is to learn inequality in little ways all day long."[32] This hierarchy and inequality has eroded as the depiction of naked men has increased. Responses to the objectification of the male body have varied; some have welcomed the increasing objectification of men on gender equality grounds—and in some ways it does indeed seem like progress that men can be ogled too—others have responded with concern.[33] A further change is that the type of men who fall into the "to be looked at" category is expanding. It is no longer just celebs or sportsmen who are to be looked at; and Tate, rightly points out that some male bodies have always been in this category and objectified and reduced, in parallel ways to women.[34] But white, rich, powerful men, are also increasingly judged in this way: for instance, much of the international coverage of the election of Justin Trudeau focused on his good looks.

In sum there is significant evidence to suggest that men are increasingly subject to the demands of beauty. Men are valuing their appearance more and increasingly worrying about body image. Male beauty ideals, like female beauty ideals, are increasingly demanding, and men are increasingly engaging in body work to attain such ideals. In sum, and significantly, men like women, are now "to be looked at."

Less Unequal but Still Gendered

As men become subject to the demands of beauty the inequality between men and women is eroded. A soap and a shave is no longer enough. Men are increasingly engaging in beauty practices, and appearance matters to men too. In addition, men's bodies are increasingly "to be looked at," as women's bodies have long been. The extent to which men fall under the beauty ideal should not be overemphasized: for example, men are still a small proportion of those going under the knife. Yet, it could be that in a visual and virtual culture, in which appearance matters more (and perhaps ultimately most), men may follow women and increasingly value beauty. Alternatively, it might be the case that no matter how demanding male beauty norms become the significant gender differences will mean that inequality remains. In this section, I will highlight three differences that remain; first, there is no emerging global male ideal; second, male norms are broader and less demanding; and third, the male ideal is not (yet) a dominant ideal.

First, and perhaps most important, there is not an emerging global norm of male beauty. When it comes to male beauty there are far more competing norms, both within and between, societies. If we look only at the United States—just to take one example—there are very many norms of male beauty that compete with the muscle-bound pumped up version; the waif, the hipster, the emo, and the ageing powerful older man. Globally divergence is replicated, while in a global culture, there are some trends towards convergence. For instance, the emphasis on firm (often naked) bodies and the increased emphasis on hairlessness might have resonance in many cultures, convergence for men is not yet evident in the way it is for women. Indeed, only tallness is a global feature.[35] Moreover there are many challenging and alternative beauty ideals to provide resources for resistance. For instance, while there are trends to remove face and body hair in some quarters, in others body hair is a feature of male beauty and signals virility, and facial hair is widely regarded as key to male beauty globally: and in the United States, and the West generally, the rise of the hipster has made facial hair fashionable again. To put it simply, the argument from difference is stronger when it comes to male norms than female norms.

Second, as well as there not being a single global norm, male norms are also broader, less demanding, and more forgiving. Consider the classic example of the difference between the expectations of older male and female actors. Undoubtedly, more is required of aging male actors than it once was. Aging leading men need to keep in shape and meet ideals of physical beauty, which previously they did not. But, unlike women, men are still allowed to age, and this is an important difference. While the (naked) bodies of men need to conform to some aspects of youth, and the firmness requirement does invoke youth, older men are still regarded as attractive and are visible leading men. There is no equivalent of "rugged" for women. In part, this is connected to the gendering function of beauty ideals and their meanings, a topic I will return to. However, for now, a difference between the demands of male and female beauty is that what women have to aspire to is narrower. Even when older women

are perceived as attractive, much more youth-mimicking procedures are required.

In general, for men, there is more variation in what are acceptable features. Given this, however dominant male beauty norms
become they are likely (at least in any future we can foresee) to remain less demanding than they are for women.

Third, the beauty ideal is not yet a dominant ethical ideal for
most men. It might be that for some men it does function very
similarly to the way it functions for women; for example, in certain
professions, perhaps models and actors, and celebs in general, and
in certain demographics, such as some parts of the gay community.[36] But while looks increasingly matter, they are rarely the dominant value framework for men. Outside the visual professions, men
are less defined by their bodies, and measuring up to the beauty
ideal is not yet paramount for all men. For instance, beauty may be
a benefit and advantage, but it is not an unbending ideal used to
chastise those who fail to meet it. To illustrate, the good looks of
Justin Trudeau, or JFK, might be an advantage, but a lack of good
looks is not an insurmountable problem. Donald Trump's looks
are commented on, but with nothing approaching the consistency
or vitriol that Hillary Clinton's are.[37] Accordingly even where men
are judged according to their beauty, it is not the defining feature,
but an additional quality seen to further enhance other qualities.
This type of dominance is akin to the dominance some individuals
will have placed on beauty under any beauty ideal, but it does not
imply a dominant ethical ideal, which, by its nature, has to be shared
and communal.

Thus while the demands of beauty are growing, differences of
scope remain. Just as I argued that scope matters in the transformation of the beauty ideal into a dominant ethical ideal, so too the
lack of these features in the male ideal is significant. This could be
wishful thinking or naïveté on my part. If the concerns about body
image that young men are currently evidencing translate into greater
attention to appearance and men, like women before them, seek to
improve their appearance by body work in one form or another,
then such differences may erode. But, as yet, the tipping point from

a competing ideal amongst other ideals to a dominant and increasingly ethical ideal has not been reached. Quite simply most men are not *required* to engage in beauty regimes. Men are not judged on their looks as a primary evaluative assessment of their worth *irrespective* of their other talents and across domains. This does not—of course—mean that looks do not matter for men. They do. But, as yet, the demands of beauty are not equivalent, and the ideal is not dominant. Accordingly despite the current panic regarding the lack of self-esteem and body confidence among boys and young men, most men, especially older men, are not subject to a dominant and demanding beauty ideal as an ethical ideal.[38] Most men do not (yet) feel shame going to the beach or the swimming pool with visible body hair; perhaps with the exception of back hair, which evokes particular disgust.[39] Yet even though the ideals are not the same, it is the case that conforming to beauty ideals (or failing to conform) is mattering more to men, and therefore, here at least, the inequality between men and women is eroding. Beauty is increasingly non-trivial for men, and beauty concerns and practices are no longer solely a women's preserve.

Gender, Gendering, Gendered

However, while the claim that women beautify and men do not is no longer sustainable, the gendered and gendering nature of beauty norms is, if anything, far more prominent under the current beauty ideal. In this section, I will explore this by first noting the extremely gendered and binary nature of the female global ideal and at least some of the emerging male ideals. As discussed in earlier chapters, while we have an unprecedented number of options for altering our bodies, the bodies to which we aspire to fall within an increasingly narrow range; they reduce diversity and are hyper-gendering.

Some argue we will come to use the available technologies to create and celebrate more diversity: for example, Holliday and Sanchez Taylor argue that surgery consumption might produce a "proliferation of difference."[40] Yet the primary example they use is the mixed "ideal body," which they take from *Heat*—"Jlo's bottom,

Halle Berry's breasts, Cindy Crawford's legs and so on"[41]—this is not diversity but the global ideal of thin with curves. This ideal is increasingly required of all, and all need help to attain it. Holliday and Sanchez Taylor do give examples of truly diverse surgery— such as amputations, collarbone implants, and surgery to look like a tiger. Jones similarly claims that:

> alternative and subversive adoptions of cosmetic surgery are possible and are happening, not just with "extreme practitioners" like Orlan and Lolo Ferrari, but also with people who use cosmetic surgery to design, rather than deny age, to call into question traditional intergenerational relationships, and to challenge surgeons' traditional monopoly over provision and acceptable aesthetics of cosmetic surgery.[42]

But surgery that does not conform to the ideal is exceptionally rare, as are women like Orlan, who use surgery to challenge and transgress. Thus, while there is the potential in surgery to create and celebrate diversity, for the most part surgery is embedding rather than challenging hypergendered and restrictive norms. We are using technology not to expand concepts of acceptable appearance but, by processes of normalization, to narrow them. This results in promoting not only a narrower range of acceptable bodies, but increasingly binary and hypergendered stereotypes of masculine and feminine. As Heyes states, "the makeover creates (more) feminine women and (more) masculine men" and "every body appearing on the show must be measured for its deviation from a norm set by heterosexual desirability and youth read through a binary gender system."[43] The makeover program serves as microcosm of the surgery culture as a whole. For example, McRobbie speaks of the hyperfeminine masquerade that returns women to a traditional gender hierarchy.[44] She argues that "it becomes increasingly difficult to function as a female subject without subjecting oneself to those technologies of self that are constitutive of the spectacularly feminine."[45] Thus, while both women and men might be beautifying, the gendered nature of beautifying creates different types of beings.

To caricature, feminine norms make women vulnerable, and masculine norms make men powerful. Tight clothing and high heels, literally make us vulnerable. Unable to stride, stomp, or run away, we totter. Even in the most active and powerful images of female beauty, where women are presented as strong, demanding subjects, for instance, Laura Croft or Tank Girl, women are still firm and thin (possibly with curves) and youthful. By contrast, whether muscle bound or bearded, men are not made vulnerable by gendering; even the waif is not constrained in an equivalent way to gendered female. Therefore while we might now be strong and buff—no longer soft, but powerful and with visible muscles—women's bodies are still constrained in ways that men's are not. Moreover, what seem like similar practices for both genders might have different meanings. Hairlessness for women implies youth and girliness. By contrast, hairlessness in men emphasizes muscles and masculinity and power. The symbolism of pubic hair is debated and is often it is traced to porn. It has been suggested that public hair removal is infantilizing in women, making us girl-like, whereas in men it does the opposite, it emphasizes a man's erection making him more dominant; a bigger man.[46]

In the embedding of stereotypical gender norms of hyperfemininity and masculinity, inequality is alive and well. There are numerous undesirable consequences of strong gender norms; first, they demarcate and subordinate; second, they are unrelentingly sexualizing; and third, they are exclusive, confining, and discriminatory.

First, the traditional claim. A more gendered norm that makes women appear weak and vulnerable and men powerful does appear to be very similar to the original worries about gender exploitation. Indeed Jeffreys argues that beauty practices (from make-up to labiaplasty) should be regarded as "Harmful Traditional Practices": defined by the UN as those "performed for men's benefit, to create stereotyped roles of the sexes and to be justified by tradition."[47] Jeffreys argues that while lipstick wearing and surgery are not the same, both are harmful as they serve to embed gender stereotypes that make women unequal and subordinate.[48] For her it is not the sexualization of women that is the key problem, but the gendering:

as such she argues that the veil serves the same purpose as sexualizing Western practices, as "both sets of appearance rules, however, require that women should be "different/deferent," and both require women to service men's sexual needs, either by providing sexual excitement or by hiding women's bodies lest the men should be so excited."[49] Inequality then continues to exist, as gender norms, carry different meanings for the males and females they create.

Second, the hypersexualization of gender norms, at least in the West—although I have argued that the focus on the body extends to the global—chimes with the traditional claim that men benefit from the sexualization of women. As discussed, current beauty norms require women to be "up for it" and "hot"—but for themselves. McRobbie argues that the only acceptable presentation of women is in the hyperfeminine subject. She suggests that there are a number of versions: the "working girl," for whom feminist battles are over, leaving her to pursue her own desires; the "phallic girl," equal to men, "up for it," and pursuing her desires (like a man); and the "global girl," who all women are supposed to aspire to, as "a kind of global femininity," a women who expresses herself in her "new found freedoms, her wage earning capacity, her enjoyment of and immersion in beauty culture and in popular culture."[50] All of these "girls" (and McRobbie provides a powerful critique of this culture) are committed to attaining beauty ideals and promoting very narrow types of hyperfemininity. Thus while these women are choosing for themselves, in the acceptable liberal language, they are also, as if by accident, choosing what he would like. As Gill states, "women are presented not as seeking men's approval, but as pleasing themselves and, in so doing, they *just happen* to win men's admiration."[51] The claim that hypergendered and hypersexualized norms are not "for men" should arouse suspicion, not least, as Gill points out, because these images of women are similar to the images of soft porn.[52] It is not a "happy accident" that for him and for her look similar, but it is conditioned, as discussed in so many chapters, by shared norms and expectations. As Chambers rightly notes, women's "desires to please themselves and others by conforming to beauty norms is not an isolated, individual decision or preference. It is defined and reg-ulated by the social context that they live in, exemplified by *Sex and the City*, Barbie dolls, and the Disney version of Cinderella."[53] Like Gill, I am suspicious "of claims about choice and empowerment when the thing being celebrated seems to map so perfectly onto what is the required cultural norm."[54]

Third, hypergendered norms are limiting, constraining, and dis-criminatory. They are limiting of both those who identify with such masculine and feminine norms and those who do not. For those who identify with dominant gender norms, certain forms of behav-ior are prohibited. Thus, acceptable behavior and the feelings that underlie certain behaviors are denied. For those who do not iden-tify with such norms, they are exclusionary and discriminatory. Indeed the heteronormativity of the gender norms enacted under the current ideal is unprecedented. This is partly because of tech-nological possibilities: thinness with curves and the bulked-up male silhouette can only be aspired to if the means to attain such ideals (chemical, surgical, and behavioral) are available and afford-able. Yet, for whatever reasons, the result is narrower norms, which exclude those who identify outside binary gender norms, as well as those who fail to measure up. Again, this might not be the whole story; for instance, Holliday and Sanchez Taylor argue that "glam-our is not classed, or 'raced,' or gendered—boyz can be glamourous and then there's lesbian chic—glamour is democratic."[55] If they are correct, then there may be some ways that an increasingly demand-ing beauty ideal will result in inclusion rather than exclusion. How-ever, as argued in chapter 6, I suspect that appearance discrimina-tion is likely to increase as appearance matters more, and that those who fail to meet binary norms might be particularly subject to discrimination.

However while there are problems with gendered norms, par-ticularly those that embed binary, highly stereotypical and hyper-sexualized gender norms, the changes to the demands that fall upon men are significant, and I suggest significant enough to unsettle the simple claim of gendered exploitation—even if some elements of it remain. If we return to the traditional account of gendered exploitation, we can take the supposed benefits that accrue to men in turn. First, men benefit because they attain pleasure from the sexualization of beautiful women. This is true, but, as discussed in this and previous chapters, women also attain pleasure from presenting themselves as active sexual subjects. More important, at times when women are presenting themselves as apparently sexual objects, they might in fact be presenting themselves as beauty objects. As I argued in my account of beauty objectification, it is not the case that all instances of conforming to the ideal are about sexual objectification. Therefore, while we should be suspicious of the choice narrative, we should not regard engagement and conforming as not chosen, as false consciousness or adaptive preference, nor deny that there are pleasurable and rewarding aspects to conforming and that there is more going on that the simple account of "for men" suggests. In addition, women also benefit from the sexualization of men, and regard men to "be looked at" and enjoyed; and while male and female norms carry different meanings, they are both hypersexualized. Thus, while some differences remain, the relevant inequality between women and men is lessened. Both women and men fall into the exploiter and exploited camps when it comes to conforming to beauty ideals.

Second, beauty norms assert male superiority (and women's inferiority). Again this is arguably the case in the resulting hyper-gender norms (for example, in the creation of powerful-looking men), but in the practices of body work men are not superior to women. The necessity to engage in body work is far less gendered than traditional accounts claim, and it is no longer the case that the third shift is required of women but not men. That men increasingly *have* to engage in body work and that appearance is important to male identity is a significant change, and one that upsets the traditional critique.

Third, beauty norms and practices constrain and limit women. To be sure, this feature of beauty norms remains, as we enact and create gender and so determine the shape of bodies and the space they take up. Indeed, it might be the case that as the ideal requires more and irreversible work that women are more constrained and limited than under previous beauty ideals. However in a very real sense the hypergendering falls on men too. Men are required to be a certain shape, and some male ideals are particularly demanding with the regard to the extent that men are expected to bulk up.

Taken together, while differences remain, inequality is reduced. Men are increasingly subject to the demands of beauty and vulnerable in the beauty context, making the claim that beauty practices are tools by which men exploit women difficult to sustain. It is no longer the case that "*she* is under surveillance in ways *he* is not."[56] Further, to support such a claim I would have to deny that women benefit and find pleasure in beauty, a claim I have argued against throughout, while recognizing the extensive harms. Women benefit and suffer from the beauty business at all levels.

Gender Equality Is Not Enough

In this final section, I want to suggest that gendered inequality is no longer the primary concern when it comes to critiquing the beauty ideal in its current form; rather what matters is the dominance of the beauty ideal as an ethical ideal and its increasing demands. Accordingly, while there are concerns about hypergendering beauty ideals, and the consequences of such ideals, which we should recognize and challenge, the main worry is not gendered exploitation. Chambers argues that "the problem with disciplinary appearance norms is not just that they are different for men and women, and not just that they are more exacting and expensive (in both time and money) for women, but that their effect is to cast women as inferior."[57] For Chambers the inequality is the primary harm or wrong: "I do not argue that having breast implants will somehow corrupt or deprave a women, or compromise her moral character; I do argue that it renders her inferior and subjects her to discourses of inequality."[58] It is this point, that inequality is the core moral worry, which I challenge.

I have argued that as men fall under the demands there is less inequality and body work cannot be dismissed and trivialized as "women's work." Men are engaging in body work, and body image matters to men. Accordingly, body work does not obviously fall into the category of practices that Jeffreys identifies as "practices required of one sex class rather than the other" and therefore important to examine "for their political role in maintaining male dominance."[59] Men are "to be looked at" and evaluated, and men too are insecure and engaging in body work to improve themselves. Inequality remains in the hypergendering of beauty ideals and the different meanings of male and female beauty ideals. But if it was possible to fully erode the gender differences so that women and men fell under equally demanding and dominant global beauty ideals, we would still have reason to be concerned. Imagine a scenario where men believed that their appearance mattered more than any other capacity or ability, and where men sought to improve themselves primarily by working on their appearance, and where men were vulnerable to critique and being judged negatively on appearance grounds in a way that is very familiar to women. In this scenario, both men and women would be 'to be looked at' and would be judged, and judge themselves, according to the extent to which they conformed or failed to conform to the beauty ideal. Men too would locate the self in the body, suffer external moral sanction for "letting themselves go," and experience shame, guilt, and disgust for their failing bodies. Women and men would be equal in these regards. All would be equally attempting to improve, minimal standards of normal would continue rise for both genders (or all without gender), and there would be pressure for all to be good enough, and to engage beyond the minimum.

The fact that this is hard to imagine suggests that the differences in the nature of the demands and how the demands fall is significant. But such a situation is, at least partially, imaginable, but while in this context inequality would be at least lessened, if not wholly eroded, the troubling features of a demanding and dominant beauty ideal would remain. A world in which both men and women were equally subject to ever more punishing demands of beauty is not a desirable end point. To be sure, it might be better than the current situation, as there are many reasons to think that gender equality is desirable, regardless of its form. Moreover, this hypothetical scenario might result in far more fluid concepts of gender and gender roles; indeed, we might even begin to do away with such concepts. But it would still be morally problematic. The problems with the increasing demands of beauty are not just that they are demanded more of one gender than another but the nature of the demands.

Conclusion

In this chapter I have (mostly) rejected the claim that conforming to beauty ideals is a form of gendered exploitation, done by men to women, and to create and signal women as a subordinate class. While there are some ways in which the critique still has traction, for the most part, the changes in men's attitudes and behavior mean that gendered exploitation no longer has explanatory force when it comes to accounting for the demands of beauty. I have argued the fact that the beauty ideal increasingly falls on men is significant, and significant enough to undermine traditional arguments of gender exploitation. This is not to claim that no inequality remains. It does, and particularly morally troubling is the inequality that is invoked and implied by hypergendered binary norms. Such norms are discriminatory, and may also signal increased and required sexualization, which raises additional issues of moral concern. However, in beauty terms, inequalities are eroding, and gender exploitation accounts are accordingly limited. Quite simply, as the demands of beauty fall on men as well as women, there is no clear group of exploiters and exploited: individuals fall into both groups, and move between them. If inequality is being eroded, then exploitation accounts cannot stand. Yet the failure of this traditional account, like the failure of accounts of coercion, false consciousness, and adaptive preference, is useful. It unmasks the workings of the beauty ideal, and challenges simple assumptions, and again it is the case that more is going on under the beauty ideal than might appear at first glance. Just as the beauty ideal is rewarding and demanding, and

Conclusion

Beauty without the Beast

In *Perfect Me* I have mapped the changing nature of the beauty ideal. I have argued that the current and emerging beauty ideal is different from previous ideals. It is an ethical ideal, which is dominant and on the way to being globally dominant. The ethical nature of the ideal is new and, together with its dominance, is transformative. Moreover, the beauty ideal is increasingly demanding, and, as normalization of beauty practices and procedures continues apace, the future looks frightening. If the worst of current trends continue, we will find ourselves in a world where we are preoccupied with appearance to the point of obsession, where our effort is channeled primarily into improving our bodies at the expense of the myriad other activities and tasks that we could do, both individually and collectively. Moreover, as we are already beginning to discover, a beauty ideal as an ethical ideal is not as rewarding as its promises suggest. If we invest too much, value appearance too much, we do not flourish, we are not happy, and yet, as beauty matters more, failing to strive for better selves is to fail and morally fail. As technological possibilities increase, the amount that we could, and should, do to better our selves will go on increasing. Those who can afford it will do whatever is possible, and those who cannot will aspire to it; they will save and sacrifice, and such goods will become even more desirable. As this happens, so too the pressure to engage and the risks we are willing to subject ourselves to will also rise. And, if current models of ethics are not replaced and choice remains sovereign, taking extreme risks will be routine. Indeed, as beauty matters more, almost any risks will be "worth it": after all, I *am* worth it.

It is already the case that some of us feel like this. Most of us believe our appearance is crucial to identity, girls as young as three judge character based on body shape, and young women would rather be thin than smart: "I reckon that if I fitted into size 10 jeans I would be happier. I would rather have that than straight A's."[1] Attaining the ideal matters more than almost anything else, and girls prioritize their bodies over their health.[2] This is not an isolated rich white girl's problem, although the extent to which engagement is possible does depend on resources. As the authors of a study of Indian young women put it, "for all the choices the participants may have felt they had, being 'fat' was not one of them."[3] Men too are feeling the pressure, and for all of us bodies matter more, and failure to comply to the beauty ideal is costly and increasingly political. The process of worrying about our bodies, striving, succeeding, failing, and striving again is normal and continual. It is a background condition of our lives, a preoccupation of daily conversation, and increasingly dominating of our thoughts and habits. It is core to the way we structure our lives and our very selves. We are our bodies, and our bodies are ourselves, and no matter how much success we have we ultimately fail. We sag, bulge, wrinkle, and crumple. No matter what we do, thinness, firmness, smoothness, and youth cannot be maintained.

This is a bleak picture indeed. In such a scenario, the pleasures of beauty will recede, and the pressure to engage in ever-more-risky beauty practices will become overwhelming. At this point the harms to our physical and psychological health and to our social structures and relationships will be vast, and yet, having embraced the ideal difficult to forgo. The extent of what will be required to be normal is potentially unending and the pursuit of the body beautiful could supersede all other agendas and achievements. The epidemic of body anxiety could be a foreshadowing of worse to come.

Yet none of the traditional arguments are sufficient to account for what is happening under the current beauty ideal. The old arguments of coercion and desperate choice, adaptive preference, and gender exploitation fail. They do not capture the most pressing moral concerns of the new beauty ideal, nor do they chime with, or respect, women's lived experience under the ideal. This is not because they have nothing to offer. They do. The desperate choice argument fails, but it shows how it is possible that context and force of circumstance can be limiting and leave us with little choice. Likewise, while we might think a world where appearance did not matter would be better, in the world we do have beauty does matter, undermining claims of false consciousness and adaptive preference. And while men benefit from women beautifying, arguments of gendered exploitation do not account for the engagement of women; particularly financially independent and postfeminist women. Such arguments are no longer, if they ever were, explanatory, but they are illuminating. They highlight what is and what is not going on. That choice is profoundly limited matters; that there are gendered differences matters; that over-engagement in beauty practices is not good for us and comes at the expense of everything else matters. But these arguments miss the dual nature of the beauty ideal and the dual nature of the self under the beauty ideal.

The brutal future sketched above of an ever more dominant, demanding, and punishing ethical ideal is not the only possible future. There are elements within the beauty ideal that offer other possibilities. The beauty ideal is not merely an evil taskmaster, but also a beckoning seducer. It promises, it inspires, and it is alluring and empowering, hopeful and positive. Importantly, unlike calls to reject the ideal, it is not shrill. Its iron fist is hidden beneath smooth skin, manicured nails, bejeweled fingers, and silk gloves. Recall the students who grew their body hair and were *surprised* to find it hard to be hairy. The pleasures of beauty are not illusory, beauty offers pleasurable individual and communal practices, and it sanctions other forms of pleasure that are currently only available in a beauty context. Moreover, in a visual and virtual culture where beauty matters more—and maybe eventually most—the inherently unpleasant nature of many beauty practices is off-set by the rewards. Beauty work is rewarded in social and communal ways—beauty success is valued and praised—and beauty work is increasingly moral work. Body work is virtuous. It is good for us and good to do.

Ignoring the pleasures of beauty and focusing only on the harms not only fails to take account of the evidence and ignores women's lived experience, but it fails strategically. It does not work. Women do not stop engaging, worse because some of it does not ring true, so all the critique is dismissed. Women know that they benefit from beauty, and they know they enjoy (some of) the practices of beauty and (some of) the successes and rewards of beauty. Moreover, they know that they will suffer if they do not engage. They will be dismissed, ignored, and criticized. For most women, in most contexts, rejecting beauty expectations is not possible, and it would not be advisable. To understand and respond to the beauty ideal, we need to address it as it is actually functioning. It is not wholly harmful or wholly creative. But, whatever else the beauty ideal is, it is serious, important, and powerful. And it becomes far more powerful as it becomes ethical.

The beauty ideal in its current form is new. It is dual, it is demanding, and rewarding and, as it transforms into a dominant ethical ideal, it profoundly shapes the ways in which we understand and create our very selves. It is this change which I have tried to capture in the concept of beauty objectification, which is far more than sexual objectification. In a virtual culture, beauty objectification is increasingly likely to be dominant. The presentation of the self as an image in the virtual world is always removed from sexual threat and the immediate acting out of sexual desire, even if other harms of evaluation and humiliation are present. Beauty objectification is not wholly harmful. It is also empowering, protective, and promising, as we work to transform ourselves and attain our imagined self, our perfect me.

Let me finish with some thoughts about where we might go from here. I do not want the scenario painted at the beginning of the chapter, to come to be. I do not want to live in an inhuman and hypercritical world, where we all engage to the extent we can afford, and yet all fail, and feel like failures, with little respite or reward. Nor do I want to live in a world, however, where the body is denied, or where a version of "natural" beauty is elevated. Appearance does and should matter, and denying the body has proven, on very many occasions, far more dangerous, destructive and inhuman than over-emphasizing the body is likely to be. Likewise, "natural" beauty does not exist, bodies are always constructed, and "natural" beauty makes beauty the preserve of the blessed few; and usually these blessed few are those who already have economic, social, and cultural power. While beauty hides power, it also erodes it. The extent to which beauty cuts through hierarchies is often exaggerated, and Edmonds speaks of beauty in Brazil as "an essential form of value and all-too-often imaginary vehicle of ascent for those blocked from more formal routes of social mobility."[4] Nonetheless, beauty can shortcut some power hierarchies, and, as beauty matters more, other social goods, such as class and wealth, might matter less in comparison. Furthermore, beauty serves other egalitarian purposes, in that it provides a shared topic that crosses racial groups, class, age, and, if we move to less gendered norms, sexualities. Therefore the question is what can be done to nurture and extend the positive aspects of beauty, those that enhance, respect, connect, and cherish, as opposed to those that criticize, humiliate, and shame. In short, can we have beauty without the beast?

Whether or not we can, we have to try. Indeed what other option is there? If I am right and a globally dominant beauty ideal that functions as an ethical ideal is emerging, then we are in new territory. We have never before been in a situation where appearance and bodies are so central, especially in this particular hypervisual way. Pretending that we can deny appearance ideals and advocating non-engagement is not a good enough response. It abandons young women (and older women and others) to increasingly demanding norms. Throughout, I have rejected the approach of telling women what to do and not do. Such an approach is women-blaming and divisive, and it does not address the beauty ideal. Only collectively can change happen, and if we seek to mitigate the harms and costs of the emerging inhuman and punishing beauty ideal, we should focus collectively. Collectively there are a number of possible sites of interventions. For instance regulation on some issues might begin a culture change. Regulation could be on images, ads, and beauty coverage: for instance, on what you are permitted to say and imply beauty practices can do for you. Recall the advertising of the "make yourself amazing" clinics, or consider the reporting of the Meg Matthews' face-lift (which if not quite an endorsement is hard not to read as encouragement).[5] Regulation could broadly follow the French law and only permit factual statements, or it could require health warnings or statements of risk, and information labels could be placed to alert the consumer to the fact that images are digitally altered.[6] In addition, the regulatory changes suggested by Keogh and others could improve the safety of practices and procedures by improving training and qualifications, information and consent procedures, and redress. These changes however must not focus only on protecting those who engage, but also the providers of processes, and they must be attentive to communal concerns. If they are not, then such regulation will be counterproductive, as it will, whatever its intention, make procedures more normal and mainstream. In addition, perhaps most pressingly, regulation or improved voluntary governance could ensure routine and robust collection of data, so that as we move into the future, we will have an accurate picture of the extent of engagement, risks, and complications: data we quite simply do not currently have.

Such regulation contributes to cultural change, but more than this is required if the beauty ideal is to be challenged and the extensive and significant harms that attach to it reduced. Collectively, we need to focus on creating a less toxic environment. Collective action has to begin with collective discussion, and the first step in such action must be to recognize how important beauty is, and is becoming, and how extensive the demands of beauty are under an increasingly dominant and potentially global ethical ideal. We need to be able to speak about the extensive harms of beauty, the harms of normalization, of the epidemic of anxiety that is increasingly regarded as normal and about the massive physical, psychological, social, and financial costs that accompany the beauty ideal in its current and emerging form. This will only happen if we are not afraid to speak and listen. Collectively, we need to speak to each other without fear of being criticized for the beauty practices we do and do not do. We need to be able to state our worries, without being dismissed as "bad old feminists," kill joys, vain, narcissistic, paternalistic, or moralistic.[7] Particularly devastating in the beauty debate has been the silencing of discussion; a function of the choice myth. Silence isolates and makes us vulnerable, angst-ridden, and afraid.[8] Being heard, sharing experience, and finding you are not alone, empowers. When it comes to beauty, I can guarantee you are not alone, but we need to hear it more, and the depth of the pain as well as the high of joys. It is unlikely there are many who have no empathy or sympathy when it comes to body worries. First, then, we need to open up debate and recognize that what is happening is new, that it is not all about choice and pleasure, and at least in part it is a moral issue.

We can also seek ways to take collective action to challenge the increasing narrowness of the beauty ideal by resisting normalization processes. Key to the normalizing of practices and the narrowing of normal is the visibility of only some types of bodies, ideal bodies. If we all saw more bodies and bodies of different types, perhaps we would feel less inadequate. There are many suggestions about how this can be done and most focus on attempts to increase diversity by requiring a larger range of sizes of models and mannequins, unretouched or labeled digital images, as well as encouraging the beauty industry to promote more varied looks.[9] I am not sure what else can be done, and have joked (or half-joked) about fly-posting images of "normal" breasts on every bus stop and billboard. The images we see are core to the creation of our own images and our expectations of our transforming and imagined selves. In a virtual culture where image sharing is so often cited as a problem, could it not also be a solution? Remember the bare-faced selfies, or twitter trends to post "real" pictures alongside your tinder picture, and so on. It is important to challenge the visual diet that so constantly feeds our image creation.

Finally, while I reject criticizing individuals for their engagement in beauty practices (or lack of engagement), there are things that we can do at the individual level to incrementally contribute to cultural change. While we should not criticize the teenage girl who spends three hours daily on social media, and regularly takes hours to perfect her contouring make-up for her perfect selfie and then hours obsessively monitoring her "likes," we can recognize that this behavior will not make her happy or successful. We need to focus on how to make an enhancing and supporting, rather than a toxic, environment, an environment in which it just will not make sense to spend so much time on the perfect self, or selfie. For while, it might seem to young women that succeeding in a role is about picturing yourself in that future role, how you look is, of course, not what will deliver such success.[10] Being a successful doctor or scientist takes more than being slim and investing in a white coat and great eyewear; being a successful lawyer takes more than being thin, with a sharp haircut and short-skirted suit; and, being a great mum takes more than being slim, youthful, and dressed in great weekend casual wear with a bright white smile. We need to remind ourselves, and our girls (and boys), that the myths are just that, myths. They are not true. While it might be the case that beauty matters more, it matters *as well* and not *instead* of all the other qualifications, skills, and achievements necessary for success. Time invested in beauty really is time away from other life skills and opportunities. Moreover, while some beauty engagement might be fun, too much we know is self-defeating, anxiety-inducing and prevents the development of a rounded character. So perhaps a long make-up session and selfie-taking is fun to do very occasionally and particularly with others; with the process of cocreation and expression of friendship, love, and admiration being at least as important as the outcome. But it would not be good to do every weekend, and it is not good to invest too much of your identity in the number of likes you receive.

It is important to remember that while the reach of the beauty ideal extends it is still the case that only a small number of us succumb to the most excessive demands of beauty. We can work on ways to make others more resilient, and there are many programs under way that focus on schools and include body positivity in the curriculum.[11] In addition, for all the criticisms of body positive campaigns (and many of these I have sympathy with), such campaigns may be the beginning of a more celebratory and women-loving culture. Such campaigns focus on raising resilience, on encouraging young women to be proud of their nonbeauty attributes as well as their appearance and, when it comes to the body, to focus on what the body can do, as well as how it looks.

We can also seek to change how we look at our selves and others. We do not have to endorse the view that "every woman somehow finds herself, without her consent, entered into a beauty contest with every other woman."[12] We can change the way we treat others and collectively see the body and appearance as always to be celebrated. To this end we can reject some wholly harmful practices. For instance, we can collectively shame not failing bodies, but shaming talk. Body shaming should be as unacceptable as other forms of discrimination. If I am right, even a little, about the extent to which our selves are located in our bodies, then criticisms of how we look, whether in the flesh or virtually is likely to be particularly devastating. This is a practical place to start, regulation may help, but we can also collectively make body shaming talk unacceptable. Perhaps "everyday lookism" could be a sister campaign to "everyday sexism"?[13] Let me add, on a personal note, it is possible to change your own attitude to bodies. Since beginning this project I have changed how I look at others. I now look for something beautiful in everyone, and I have never yet failed to find it. This has not only reduced my own anxiety at first meetings and made me kinder to those who I might not have the best relationships with (it's hard to be hostile to someone when you are thinking what great hair texture they have), but it has also made me much less critical of my own aging, and increasingly flawed body. It is a tactic that anyone can adopt.

NOTES

Introduction

1. Many have noted the moral elements of beautifying although they have not conceptualized beauty evaluation and compliance explicitly in terms of an ethical ideal. For instance Sandra Lee Bartky speaks of a "virtual duty," (*Femininity and Domination: Studies in the Phenomenology of Oppression* (New York and London: Routledge, 1990), 29); and Cressida Heyes, argues that "despite the rationality of the age, we seem more than ever to act as if (even though we may not believe that) one's outer form reflects one's virtues," (*Self-Transformations: Foucault, Ethics, and Normalised Bodies* (Oxford and New York: Oxford University Press), 5). Likewise, Bernadette Wegenstien argues that the cosmetic gaze is "one through which the act of looking at our bodies and those of others is informed by the techniques, expectations, and strategies of bodily modification. It is also a moralizing gaze—a way of looking at bodies as awaiting a physical and spiritual improvement that is present in the body's structure as an absence or a need" (*The Cosmetic Gaze: Body Modification and the Construction of Beauty* (Cambridge and London: The MIT Press, 2012), 2).

2. It is often stated that lesbian culture is protective against demanding beauty norms, but most studies have not found significant differences and have concluded that "both lesbians and heterosexual women are under mainstream social pressure to be thin, and that gender may be a better predictor of eating and exercise motives than sexuality in this context." Sarah Grogan, *Body Image: Understanding Body Dissatisfaction in Men, Women and Children*, 2nd ed. (London and New York: Routledge, 2008).

Chapter 1. A Duty to Be Beautiful?

1. See Plato's *Phaedrus*. This position has continued to inspire virtue ethics, such as Iris Murdoch; see Heather Widdows, *The Moral Vision of Iris Murdoch* (Aldershot: Ashgate, 2005).

2. Stepmothers are punished, routinely: in Snow White the wicked queen's crime is to seek to keep her beauty, to remain fairest of the them all; and in *Tangled* (Disney's latest retelling of Rapunzel) the stepmother steals Rapunzel as a

way to steal—or maintain—beauty, and is punished with aging, ugliness, and death.

3. According to Tertullian, early church Father.

4. Similar to what Diana Meyes terms the "facial legibility postulate" (that the inner can be deciphered from the outer); see Diana Tietjens Meyers, *Gender in the Mirror: Cultural Imagery and Women's Agency* (Oxford and New York: Oxford University Press, 2002), 156. Meyers goes on to show the problems with this claim, especially for older women.

5. 1933 Abe Lyman song, "Keep Young and Beautiful."

6. An argument that I will make over the course of the next chapters as the dominance and demandingness of the ideal are described and an argument made for the mutually reinforcing nature of the dominance and ethical nature.

7. Viren Swami, Ulrich S. Tran, Stefan Stieger, and Martin Voracek, "Associations Between Women's Body Image and Happiness: Results of the YouBeauty. com Body Image Survey (YBIS)," *Journal of Happiness Studies* 16, no. 3 (2015): 705–718, 714.

8. There may be some subcultures who offer critique of this: for instance some refer to body-building as an alternative culture focusing on the power of bodies; however, the extent to which such subcultures challenge the ideal or are slightly revised versions of it (as the focus remains the physical and naked body, and body work is defining) requires further study.

9. For instance there are campaigns and social movements emerging that oppose the thin ideal: for instance, fat acceptance and body positive movements and campaigns call for bans on using dangerously thin models. However, while these aim to embrace diversity, they continue to focus on the physical, and are critical of such campaigns, on the grounds that they remain body-focused, and while fatter figures are permitted they continue to meet other aspects of the beauty ideal. This said, as I argue at the end of *Perfect Me!* body positive movements might be the beginnings of a kinder and more forgiving beauty ideal.

10. There are fat loving subcultures, but again, as perhaps with body-building, these may not challenge the ideal, but be a variation, in that the focus is always the body. Moreover, that shame is attached to finding fat attractive complicates the picture. As Debra Gimlin tells the story of NAFTA (National Association to Advance Fat Acceptance) women, even in the context of a group seeking to celebrate and sexualize fat, the understanding of fat as abnormal, stigmatized, and deviant remains, and "fat admirers' leave NAFTA events if they are likely to be captured on camera. Debra L. Gimlin, *Body Work: Beauty and Self-image in American Culture* (Berkeley, Los Angeles and London: University of California Press, 2002), 135.

11. For example, a 2015 article in Marie Claire reports "what we kind of already knew—that women put more value on thinness and men like big boobs." Ali Grey, "Is a woman's idea of the perfect body really that different from a man's", Marie Claire http://www.marieclaire.co.uk/news/celebrity-news/is-a-woman -s-idea-of-the-perfect-body-really-that-much-different-than-a-man-s-81453, accessed November 22, 2016.

12. Rosalind Gill, *Gender and the Media* (Cambridge: Polity Press, 2007), 73.

13. The nearest to scrawny that fashion gets is "heroin chic," but there is an idealized, ethereal aspect to such images that glamorizes and is far from haggard; indeed had they been haggard they would not have caused controversy, as they would not have been aspirational.

14. "Cankles" is a term which emerged over the last ten to fifteen years to describe the "unattractive" merging of the calf and the ankle. Cankles are a flaw to be fixed, and may beset even the thinnest and richest of us, described by the Daily Mail in 2015 a "curse" to be fixed by yoga, surgery, diet. Antonia Hoyle, "The Curse of Cankles (Chunky Ankles): Even Being Beautiful, Thin and Rich Won't Save You from Ankles That Merge into Your Calves, *Daily Mail,* December 2, 2015, http://www.dailymail.co.uk/femail/article-3343461/The-curse-cankles-chunky-ankles-beautiful-rich-won-t-save-ankles-merge-calves.html, accessed February 10, 2016.

15. Even in cultures where bodies are largely covered, naked bodies are still visible, in magazines and on line, although often it is Caucasian bodies used in sexual portrayals (Wei Luo. "Aching for the Altered Body: Beauty Economy and Chinese women's Consumption of Cosmetic Surgery," *Women's Studies International Forum* 38 (2013): 1–10).

16. So-called revenge porn is not always images shared by an angry ex, but also images shared by friends or hacked. Given that between 15 and 40 percent of young people are "sexting" very many will be vulnerable to having their naked or seminaked images shared. In addition, sexting is part of a wider youth culture that it permeates, making suggestions that we should simply teach children not to share pictures unrealistic. NSPCC Report, Children Young People and Sexting. https://www.nspcc.org.uk/globalassets/documents/research-reports/sexting-research-summary.pdf, accessed November 8, 2016.

17. David J. Constable, "Boobs, Botox and the Babes of Beirut," Huffpost United Kingdom, http://www.huffingtonpost.co.uk/david-j-constable/beirut-boobs-botox-and-babes_b_1759183.html, accessed November 1, 2016; Deni Kirkova, "Iran is the nose job capital of the world," Daily Mail, March 4, 2013, http://www.dailymail.co.uk/femail/article-2287961/Iran-named-nose-job-capital-world-SEVEN-times-rhinoplasty-operations-U-S-Iranian-women-strive-western-doll-face.html, accessed November 1, 2016. Iran has seven times more procedures than the United States.

18. The recent development and marketing of BB and CC creams (aimed to improve complexions) and additional products to reduce pore size and improve skin tone and the increasing focus on pigmented and marked skin as a problem of aging skin (rather than just wrinkles) all testify to the trend for smoothness, as well as the more obvious focus on hairlessness.

19. Ana Elisa and Rosalind Gill, "Beauty Surveillance: The Digital Self-Monitoring Cultures of Neoliberalism (SIDigiplay)," *European Journal of Cultural Studies* (forthcoming).

20. The latest L'Oréal campaign fronted by Helen Mirren endorses older women to be visible, http://www.loreal-paris.co.uk/goldenage, accessed October 30, 2016.

21. Slimming world has now changed the spelling of "sin" to "syn."

22. Naomi Wolf, *The Beauty Myth: How Images of Beauty Are Used Against Women* (London: Vintage Books, 1990), 100.

23. Gimlin, *Body Work,* 51.

24. Data on diets suggest that diet and exercise rarely radically alter body size and 95 percent of diets fail.

25. Virginia L. Blum, *Flesh Wounds: The Culture of Cosmetic Surgery* (Berkeley, California and London: University of California Press, 2003), 77.

26. I am grateful to one of my anonymous reviewers for a detailed criticism on this point and the "messy son" example, I hope that this clarifies the difference between these oughts.

27. This is echoed in numerous television programs such as *Body Shockers* and *Botched Up Bodies.*

28. Informal discussion at second Beauty Demands workshop on "Professionals, Practitioners and Beauty Norms," http://www.birmingham.ac.uk/generic/beauty/events/2015/workshop2.aspx, accessed 31 October 2016; blog post by GP Paquita de Zulueta, "Labiaplasty—Female Genital Mutilation Western Style?" http://beautydemands.blogspot.co.uk/2017/06/labiaplasty-female-genital-mutilation_19.html, accessed 12 July 2017.

29. For instance, Angela B. V. McCracken argues that globalization has brought a diversification in clothing and challenged what were previously extremely limited norms of beauty. But this argument is about variety in dress, and the features of youth and thinness remain desired across all groups. Moreover, some of the subcultures McCracken focuses on as alternatives, such as the *vampiras*, are embracing hyperfeminine norms (including wearing corsets. *The Beauty Trade: Youth, Gender, and Fashion Globalization* (New York: Oxford University Press, 2014).

30. Ironically not treating it as personal responsibility, but treating it as beyond the individual's control, for example as a disease, might promote discrimination on such grounds. See Hofmann, Bjørn, "Obesity as a Socially Defined Disease: Philosophical Considerations and Implications for Policy and Care," *Health Care Analysis* 24, no. 1 (2016): 86–100.

31. For instance the 2014 Chief Medical Officer's report highlighted obesity as a national priority, and while recognizing environmental factors, it also emphasized education and personal responsibility. Sally Davies, "Annual Report of the Chief Medical Officer, 2014," https://www.gov.uk/government/uploads/system/uploads/attachment_data/file/484383/cmo-report-2014.pdf, accessed December 14, 2015.

32. Including feminist criticisms, most definitively Susan Orbach's classic, *Fat Is a Feminist Issue* (London: Random House and Penguin, 1978); and critics of the social determinants of health who note that obesity disproportionately affects

those below the poverty line and minorities, see, e.g., Deborah L. Rhode, *The Beauty Bias: The Injustice of Appearance in Law and Life* (Oxford and New York: Oxford University Press, 2010), 43.

33. Clara Rice, *Becoming Women: The Embodied Self in Image Culture* (Toronto, Buffalo, London: University of Toronto Press, 2014), 133.

34. Primarily health goods and ideals are usually prudential not moral—although there is a blurring between ethical and prudential ideals and between health and beauty ideals—particularly in an era of clean-eating where health is increasingly a lifestyle choice and may, for some, become an overarching moral framework. Yet, while health has some features of a moral ideal, it is not yet at least functioning as a fully-fledged ethical ideal. It is possible that it might become this, for instance, with ever more personalized genetics, and duties to have (or not to have) children with certain physical defects or characteristics, and with the blurring of health and beauty (for instance, in the rise of the self-monitoring tech, such as the Fitbit).

35. Such a view is widely held as Grogan reports (*Body Image*). Likewise Heyes notes that "fatness declaims sloth, lack of discipline, greed, and failure to moderate appetite; choosing cosmetic surgery and the look it can achieve is (not always successfully) represented as go-getting, courageous, and self-determining" (*Self-Transformations*, 9). In addition, not only are the fat stereotyped as lazy, sloppy and so on, but this is now extended to those who have lost weight the "wrong" way, using surgery instead of will power. See Jasmine Fardouly and Lenny R. Vartanian, "Changes in Weight Bias Following Weight Loss: The Impact of Weight-Loss Method," *International Journal of Obesity* 36, no. 2 (2012): 314–319.

36. Susie Orbach, "Obesity Isn't the Half of It: Fat or Thin, Our Eating Is Disordered," *The Guardian*, December14, 2015, http://www.theguardian.com/com mentisfree/2015/dec/14/obesity-chief-medical-officer-war-on-fat-troubled-eat ing, accessed 14 December 2015]).

37. Sally C. Davies, "Annual Report of the Chief Medical Officer, 2014," https://www.gov.uk/government/uploads/system/uploads/attachment_data /file/484383/cmo-report-2014.pdf, accessed 14 December 2015.

38. On many occasions academic women have, privately and quietly, "confessed" to their use of (or wish to use) all kinds of beauty products and practices. These encounters have increasingly convinced me that very few women are immune to the demands and the pressure of the ideal, despite their public personas, and those that are often hugely privileged and protected.

39. Here I am speaking particularly of my own discipline of philosophy. I find it deeply suspicious that so many female philosophers reject the beauty ideal, often claiming equality in a discipline that is overwhelmingly male dominated and that perpetuates many sexist norms. Beauty may well be demanding and oppressive of women, but it also delivers and does give women some power. In philosophy, it may be that women are being stripped of the power that they have (supposedly on equality grounds), as they enter an arena where they need to succeed they must become as male as possible.

40. Ruth Holliday and Jacqueline Sanchez Taylor, "Aesthetic Surgery as False Beauty," *Feminist Theory* 7, no. 2 (2006): 179–195.

41. Holliday and Sanchez Taylor, "Aesthetic Surgery as False Beauty."

42. Blum, *Flesh Wounds*, 49.

43. Susan Bordo, *Unbearable Weight: Feminism, Western Culture and the Body* (Berkeley, Los Angeles and London: University of California Press, 1993, 2003), 30.

44. Marika Tiggemann and Amy Slater, "NetGirls: The Internet, Facebook, and Body Image Concern in Adolescent Girls," *International Journal of Eating Disorders* 46, no. 6 (2013): 630–633, 649.

45. Giovanni Busetta and Fabio Fiorillo and Emanuela Visalli, "Searching for a Job Is a Beauty Contest" (2013), https://mpra.ub.uni-muenchen.de/49392/2/, accessed June 2014.

46. Hamermesh presents a case from many studies that there is a beauty premium and an ugly penalty. For men there is 17 percent difference in earnings between good-looking men and bad looking men, and 12 percent between good-looking women and bad looking women. Daniel S. Hamermesh, *Beauty Pays: Why Attractive People Are More Successful* (Princeton and Oxford: Princeton University Press), 46.

47. Using UK Biobank data of 119,669 participants, researchers aimed to study the causal effects of difference on stature and BMI against measures of economic status. It found that short stature and higher BMI were "observationally associated with several measures of lower socioeconomic status." Frayling et al. "Height, Body Mass Index, and Socioeconomic Status: Mendelian Randomisation Study in UK Biobank," BMJ (2016): 1–5 doi: http://dx.doi.org/10.1136/bmj.i582.

48. Nicola Davis "Genetic Study Shows Men's Height and Women's Weight Drive Earning Power," *The Guardian*, March 8, 2016, https://www.theguardian.com/science/2016/mar/08/genetic-study-shows-mens-height-and-womens-weight-drive-earning-power, accessed March 10, 2016.

49. Simply put, evolutionary claims of beauty do not directly map to beauty in the way it is culturally instituted. Further, rightly we see bias against ugly, disfigured, and disabled as discrimination and morally wrong, even if natural. The history of racism and sexism should serve to make us skeptical about claims about the naturalness of difference justifying different treatment of human beings.

50. Although, against popular presumptions that beauty and cleverness are competing qualities, evidence suggests that beauty adds to rather than impedes expectations of intelligence. Tonya K. Frevert and Lisa Slattery Walker, "Physical Attractiveness and Social Status," *Sociology Compass* 8, no. 3 (2014): 313–323.

51. Nancy Etcoff, *Survival of the Prettiest* (New York: Anchor Books, 1999), 25.

52. Diane Barthel, *Putting On Appearances: Gender and Advertising* (Philadelphia: Temple University Press, 1989).

53. Methodologically the heavy reliance on photographs is critiqued as lacking resemblance to actual attractiveness, especially the attractiveness of dynamic faces. Adam J. Rubenstein, "Variation in Perceived Attractiveness Differences

between Dynamic and Static Faces," *Psychological Science* 16, no. 10 (2005): 759–762.

54. For instance, a 1991 meta-analysis confirms that "good looks induce strong inferences about social competence" (124), although the effect is less in some categories and "in none of our categories of evaluative meaning were attractive people perceived less favourably than unattractive people," Alice H. Eagly, Richard D. Ashmore, Mona G. Makhijani, and Laura C. Longo, "What Is Beautiful Is Good, But . . . : A Meta-Analytic Review of Research on the Physical Attractiveness Stereotype," *Psychological Bulletin* 110, no 1 (1991): 109–128, 121.

55. Genevieve L. Lorenzo, Jeremy C. Biesanz, and Lauren J. Human, "What Is Beautiful Is Good and More Accurately Understood: Physical Attractiveness in First Impressions of Personality," *Psychological Science* 21, no. 12 (2010): 1777–1782.

56. Elliott identifies this transience as part of globalization, one of the three drivers of the rise in cosmetic surgery he identifies (along with consumption and celebrity culture): "The fast, short-term, techy culture of globalization is unleashing—I am suggesting—a new paradigm of self-making. In a world of short-term contracts, endless downsizings, just-in-time deliveries and multiple careers, the capacity to change and reinvent ourselves has become fundamental. A faith in flexibility, plasticity and incessant reinvention—all this means we are no longer judged on what we have done and achieved; we're now judged on our flexibility, on our readiness for personal makeover." Anthony Elliott, *Making the Cut: How Cosmetic Surgery is Transforming Our Lives* (London: Reaktion Books, 2008), 122.

57. Elliott, *Making the Cut*, 122.

58. That happiness will be attained if the body is closer to the ideal is popular and ubiquitous. Lukasz D. Kaczmarek, Jolanta Enko, Małgorzata Awdziejczyk, Natalia Hoffmann, Natalia Białobrzeska, Przemysław Mielniczuk, and Stephan U. Dombrowski, "Would You Be Happier If You Looked Better? A Focusing Illusion," *Journal of Happiness Studies* 17, no. 1 (2016): 357–365.

59. Iris Murdoch, *The Sovereignty of Good* (London: Routledge & Kegan Paul, 1970); and Iris Murdoch, *Metaphysics as a Guide to Morals* (London: Chatto and Windus, 1992).

60. Susan Bordo, *Twilight Zones: The Hidden Life of Cultural Images from Plato to O.J.* (Berkeley, Los Angeles, London: University of California Press, 1999), 7.

61. Alexander Edmonds, *Pretty Modern: Beauty, Sex, and Plastic Surgery in Brazil* (Durham, NC, and London: Duke University Press, 2010), 120.

62. Meredith Jones, *Skintight: An Anatomy of Cosmetic Surgery* (Oxford and New York: Berg, 2008); Gimlin, *Body Work*; Gill, *Gender and the Media*; Heyes, *Self-Transformations*; Meyers, *Gender in the Mirror*.

63. If the body were not malleable, we could not believe there were things we should do to it, and the extent to which this is believed may itself be important in predicting appearance worries and the negative effect of the ideal. See Melissa Burkley, Edward Burkley, S. Paul Stermer, Angela Andrade, Angela C. Bell, and

Jessica Curtis, "The Ugly Duckling Effect: Examining Fixed versus Malleable Beliefs about Beauty," *Social Cognition* 32, no. 5 (2014): 466.

64. There is, however, beginning to be significant work in this area, for instance, by Virginia Blum, Alexander Edmonds, Rosalind Gill, Debra Gimlin, Ruth Holliday, Cressida Heyes, Meredith Jones, Shirley Tate, and many other social scientists who do amazing work which I'm just beginning to assimilate and am immensely grateful for.

65. For example, the central claim of Meredith Jones's insightful book is that in makeover culture "becoming" is more important than "being" (*Skintight*).

66. Jones, *Skintight*, 1.

67. Jones, *Skintight*, 12.

68. Stories of death from beauty practices—from slimming pills to surgery gone wrong—are common news stories and a Google search brings up hundreds.

69. Sport England, https://www.sportengland.org/about-us/what-we-do/, accessed 12 June 2016. Other ads mention hot (implying both sexy and warm from sweating).

70. Jane Hunter "Inscribing the Self in the Heart of the Family," quoted in Joan Jacobs Brumberg, *The Body Project: An Intimate History of American Girls* (New York: Vintage Books, 1997), xxi.

71. Meyers, *Gender in the* Mirror, 164.

72. The overt measuring of women's weight and height—for instance as famously happened to air hostesses—is largely a thing of the past. See Victoria Vantoch, *The Jet Set* (Philadelphia: University of Pennsylvania Press, 2013). Yet even in 2016 the BBC reported a women being sent home for refusing to wear heels for a nine-hour shift. "London Reptionist Sent Home for Not Wearing Heels," http://www.bbc.co.uk/news/uk-england-london-36264229, accessed June 12 2016. In addition, in some contexts women are required to, or not to, wear certain clothes for religious reasons.

73. In *Sex, Culture and Justice*, Chambers gives sustained attention to why liberalism is poor in this regard and why it should not be given its commitment to freedom and equality. Chambers argues that liberalism should pay attention to persistent discrepancies between groups, particularly to those derived from disadvantage or undue influence. *Sex, Culture and Justice: The Limits of Choice* (University Park: The Pennsylvania State University Press, 2008).

74. Including many of the scholars whose work I rely on for this work, such as, Sandra Bartky, Susan Bordo, Clare Chambers, Cressida Heyes, and Shirley Tate.

75. Michael Foucault, *Discipline and Punish: The Birth of the Prison* (Harmondsworth: Penguin, 1990).

76. Chambers, *Sex, Culture and Justice*, 28–29.

77. Jeffreys criticizes the term "social pressures," and argues that "it is an underlying problem with liberal feminist thought that relations of power in Western cultures are reframed as simply "pressures" which women have the education to withstand." Sheila Jeffreys, *Beauty and Misogyny: Harmful Cultural Practices in the West* (London and New York: Routledge, 2005), 36. As will become clear, I do

not think women have the education to withstand beauty pressures or that information can ever be enough to "resist" such pressures. However, I continue to use the term as other terms are value-laden and overdetermined and assume coercion or oppression.

78. Chambers, *Sex, Culture and Justice*, 28.

79. Ibid., 23.

Chapter 2. Life Is One Long Catwalk

1. Etcoff, *Survival of the Prettiest*, 66.

2. As discussed in the introduction, research is needed with regard to the extent to which body-building and modification subcultures provide real alternatives or to which they provide variations on a similar theme.

3. Until the 1960s UK models were often drawn from the aristocracy.

4. Jennifer Anette Lueck, "Friend-Zone with Benefits: The Parasocial Advertising of Kim Kardashian," *Journal of Marketing* Communications, 21, no. 2 (2015): L 91–109, DOI:10.1080/13527266.2012.726235.

5. See Kim Kardashian and Kylie Jenner's Twitter pages at https://twitter .com/KimKardashian; https://twitter.com/KylieJenner, accessed November 1, 2016.

6. Every women's magazine carries weight loss and/or gain stories of celebrities, and often of "ordinary" women too. For a few examples, see Miriam Habete-sellaise, "Amazing Celebrity Before and After Weight Loss Pictures!" http:// www.womanmagazine.co.uk/diet-food/amazing-celebrity-weight-loss-pictures -64964, accessed October 4, 2016; "Changing Weight Fluctuations: Stars with Ever-Changing Bodies," http://www.usmagazine.com/celebrity-body/pictures /celebrity-weight-fluctuations-stars-with-ever-changing-bodies-2013177/31674, accessed November 1, 2016; Andrea, "12 Celebrities Who Yo-Yo in Size," http:// stylecaster.com/12-celebrities-who-yo-yo-in-size/, accessed November 1, 2016; "Shocking Celebrity Weight Gains," http://www.fashionstylemag.com/2015/ce lebrity/shocking-celebrity-weight-gains/, accessed November 1, 2016.

7. Even the most famous celebs, known for the their beauty and bodies, can struggle to be taken seriously on other grounds. For example, Marilyn Monroe struggled rather unsuccessfully to be taken seriously as an actor, and in her "New York" phase tried to rectify this. Lois Banner, *Marilyn: The Passion and the Paradox* (London and New York: Bloomsbury, 2012).

8. Diane Ponterotto, "Trivializing the Female Body: A Cross-Cultural Analysis of the Representation of Women In Sports Journalism," *Journal of International Women's Studies* 15, no. 2 (2014): 94.

9. "Jessica Ennis: I don't think I am attractive" *Telegraph*, January 6, 2012.

10. Shirley Tate, *Black Women's Bodies and the Nation: Race, Gender and Culture* (Basingstoke: Palgrave MacMillan, 2015), 108–114.

11. Rhode, *The Beauty Bias*, 64.

12. Tate, *Black Women's Bodies and the Nation*, 99.

13. On February 26, 2016, the BBC reported that "being the best female surfer in Brazil wasn't enough to secure Silvana Lima the sponsorship she needed for her surfing career. In an image-driven market, she wasn't considered pretty enough to get full sponsorship for the first 13 years of her career." "The Surfer Who Wouldn't Take No for an Answer," http://www.bbc.co.uk/news/magazine -35663889, accessed 29 February 2016.

14. Andrew Edgar, "The Athletic Body," *Health Care Analysis* (2016): 1–15 (on-line first).

15. Headlines and cover pictures, as well as content of political discussion, all mentioned shoes. See my discussion of this at http://beautydemands.blogspot .co.uk/search/label/hair, accessed November 1, 2016.

16. Gillian Bowditch and Jason Allardyce, "From Frump to Fabulous: Secrets of the Sturgeon Style Squad," http://www.thesundaytimes.co.uk/sto/news/focus /article1548641.ece, accessed November 1, 2016.

17. Ben Dowell, "Mary Beard Suffers 'Truly Vile' Online Abuse after Question Time," https://www.theguardian.com/media/2013/jan/21/mary-beard-suffers -twitter-abuse, accessed March 10, 2016; John-Paul Ford Rojas, "Mary Beard Hits Back at AA Gill after He Brands Her 'Too Ugly for Television,'" http://www.tele graph.co.uk/news/picturegalleries/celebritynews/9223149/Mary-Beard-hits -back-at-AA-Gill-after-he-brands-her-too-ugly-for-television.html, accessed March 10, 2016.

18. Vantoch, *The Jet Set*.

19. "Web Site to 'Rate Professors,'" https://www.ratemyprofessors.com/cam pusRatings.jsp?sid=1258, accessed November 1, 2016.

20. For example, the web site will post pictures of what you are wearing each day. https://www.todayimwearing.com/, accessed 16 October 2016.

21. This is true of brief contacts over twitter, what's ap, my space, Facebook and so on; with on-line profiles meaning that employers are checking out applicants before interviews; and even the hallowed halls of academia are not immune as academics are increasingly judged on their visual performance (whether recorded lectures, MOOCs, or distance learning teaching).

22. Jasmine Fardouly, Phillippa C. Diedrichs, Lenny R. Vartanian, and Emma Halliwell, "Social Comparisons on Social Media: The Impact of Facebook on Young Women's Body Image Concerns and Mood," *Body Image* 13 (2015): 38–45.

23. Fardouly et al., "Social Comparisons on Social Media," 39.

24. Hamilton, "Greater Access to Cell Phones than Toilets in India: UN," https://unu.edu/media-relations/releases/greater-access-to-cell-phones-than -toilets-in-india.html, accessed November 1, 2016.

25. Elias and Gill, *Beauty Surveillance*.

26. Blum, *Flesh Wounds*, 52.

27. For instance Ivo Pitanguy, the leading cosmetic surgeon in Brazil, has led the move to cosmetic surgery in public hospital, stated that "the poor have a right to be beautiful too," Edmonds, *Pretty Modern,* 14.

28. Edmonds, *Pretty Modern*, 252.

29. Lisa Smith Kilpela, Carolyn Black Becker, Nicole Wesley, and Tiffany Stewart, "Body Image in Adult Women: Moving Beyond the Younger Years," *Advances in Eating Disorders: Theory, Research and Practice* 3, no. 2 (2015): 144–164, 145.

30. Lauren Fiske, Elizabeth A. Fallon, Bryan Blissmer, and Colleen A. Redding, "Prevalence of Body Dissatisfaction among United States Adults: Review and Recommendations for Future Research." *Eating behaviors* 15, no. 3 (2014): 357–365.

31. Dianne Neumark-Sztainer, Susan J. Paxton, Peter J. Hannan, Jess Haines, and Mary Story, "Does Body Satisfaction Matter? Five-Year Longitudinal Associations between Body Satisfaction and Health Behaviors in Adolescent Females and Males," *Journal of Adolescent Health* 39, no. 2 (2006): 244–251.; Kilpela et al., "Body Image in Adult Women."

32. Personal correspondence with Nichola Rumsey, Professor of Appearance Research at University of the West of England and Co-Director of the Centre for Appearance Research.

33. Social comparison theory, devised by L. Festinger, asserts that humans self-evaluate, and where no objective measurement of our attributes is possible, as with appearance, we do so through comparison with others. Festinger, "A Theory of Social Comparison Processes," *Human Relations,* 7 (1954): 117–140.

34. T. A. Myers and J. H. Crowther, "Social Comparison as a Predictor of Body Dissatisfaction: A Meta-Analytic Review," *Journal of Abnormal Psychology*, 118 (2009): 683–698.

35. Marika Tiggemann, Maria Gardiner, and Amy Slater, "I would rather be size 10 than have straight A's": A Focus Group Study of Adolescent Girls' Wish to Be Thinner," *Journal of Adolescence* 23, no. 6 (2000): 645–659, 649.

36. Tiggemann, Gardiner, and Slater. "I would rather be size 10 than have straight A's," 649.

37. Other studies suggest that social media use is similar rather than different in its effects on body dissatisfaction, but both focus on images and raise body dissatisfaction. Rachel Cohen and Alex Blaszczynski, "Comparative Effects of Facebook and Conventional Media on Body Image Dissatisfaction," *Journal of Eating Disorders* 3, no. 1 (2015): 1.

38. Marika Tiggemann and Amy Slater, "NetGirls: The Internet, Facebook, and Body Image Concern in Adolescent Girls," *International Journal of Eating Disorders* 46, no. 6 (2013): 630–633, 632.

39. Fardouly and Vartanian report that "close friends, distant peers, and celebrities, but not family members, appear to be a source of upward appearance comparisons for female Facebook users." Fardouly et al., "Social Comparisons on Social Media".

40. Kristen Harrison, "Television Viewers' Ideal Body Proportions: The Case of the Curvaceously Thin Woman," *Sex Roles* 48, no. 5–6 (2003): 255–264. Lisa Smith Kipela and colleagues argue that the "thin-young-ideal," which directly

associates "youth with beauty, acceptability, fame, and value in the media and advertisements," continues to be dominant as we age and we have countless images to upwardly compare with." Kilpela et al., "Body Image in Adult Women," 148.

41. Some focus on the media, arguing that the link between idealized thinness in the media and body images issues is now demonstrated in many studies. Jannath Ghaznavi and Laramie D. Taylor, "Bones, Body Parts, and Sex Appeal: An Analysis of #thinspiration Images on Popular Social Media," *Body Image* 14 (2015): 54–61. Some reject the claim that media are primary in internalizing the thin ideal. For example, Eric Stice et al. argue that the effects of internalizing the thin ideal are a result of the experimental structure and are not long lasting except in those who are already vulnerable. They emphasize family and friends rather than media. Eric Stice, Diane Spangler, and W. Stewart Agras, "Exposure to Media-Portrayed Thin-Ideal Images Adversely Affects Vulnerable Girls: A Longitudinal Experiment," *Journal of Social and Clinical Psychology* 20, no. 3 (2001): 270–288. Michelle Abraczinskas et al. argue that parental influence is key, even after media and peer influences are controlled for, and that it is direct parental influence and modeling of parental behavior that is associated with disordered eating and the drive for thinness. Michelle Abraczinskas Brian Fisak, and Rachel D. Barnes, "The Relation between Parental Influence, Body Image, and Eating Behaviors in a Nonclinical Female Sample," *Body Image* 9, no. 1 (2012): 93–100.

42. Harrison, "Television Viewers' Ideal Body Proportions," 255–264.

43. The statistical difference was not huge, and accordingly the authors claim that this should not be regarded as causal. Kelly N. Kubic and Rebecca M. Chory, "Exposure to Television Makeover Programs and Perceptions of Self," *Communication Research Reports* 24, no. 4 (2007): 283–291.

44. Fardouly et al., "Social Comparisons on Social Media."

45. Christopher J. Ferguson, Mónica E. Muñoz, Adolfo Garza, and Mariza Galindo, "Concurrent and Prospective Analyses of Peer, Television and Social Media Influences On Body Dissatisfaction, Eating Disorder Symptoms and Life Satisfaction in Adolescent Girls," *Journal of youth and adolescence* 43, no. 1 (2014): 1–14.

46. Ferguson et al., "Concurrent and Prospective Analyses of Peer, Television and Social Media Influences on Body Dissatisfaction, Eating Disorder Symptoms and Life Satisfaction in Adolescent Girls.

47. For example, see mum's net campaign, "Let Girls Be Girls Campaign," http://www.mumsnet.com/campaigns/let-girls-be-girls, accessed November 23, 2016.

48. Annable Fenwick Elliot, "$1,000 for a KIDS COSTUME? Disney's sold out elsa dress from Smash Hit Frozen Sells for Astronomical Prices on eBay," http://www.dailymail.co.uk/femail/article-2605253/1-000-KIDS-COSTUME -Disneys-sold-Elsa-dress-smash-hit-Frozen-sells-astronomical-prices-eBay.html, accessed November 23, 2016.

49. Linda Papadopoulous, "Sexualisation of Young People: Review," http:// webarchive.nationalarchives.gov.uk/; http://www.homeoffice.gov.uk/documents /sexualisation-of-young-people.pdf, accessed February 24, 2016.

50. YMCA, "World of Good Report," http://www.ymca.co.uk/campaigns /world-of-good [accessed 24 February 2016].

51. Girlguiding, "Girls' Attitude Survey, 2016," https://www.girlguiding.org .uk/globalassets/docs-and-resources/research-and-campaigns/girls-attitudes -survey-2016.pdf, accessed October 4, 2017.

52. Hayley K. Dohnt and Marika Tiggemann, "Peer Influences on Body Dissatisfaction and Dieting Awareness in Young Girls," *British Journal of Developmental Psychology* 23, no. 1 (2005): 103–116.

53. Jennifer Harriger, "Age Differences in Body Size Stereotyping in a Sample of Preschool Girls," *Eating Disorders* 23 (2015): 177–190. The study recruited through day-care and preschools in the southwestern United States; the sample size was 102, with each session lasting approximately an hour.

54. The last pairing is disturbing and perhaps helps explain why it takes so much to get girl students to speak and to speak with confidence. I find it particularly troubling that both the researchers and the girls did not question, as far as I can gather from the paper, the assumption that "quiet" is a positive attribute for girls.

55. There were some variances between 3–4 year olds compared to 4–5 year olds, and the differences are interesting; however, for the purposes of this study it is the overall preferences, particularly against the "fat" body type figure that are most important; the age-variance being mostly around attributing of attributes to the average figure.

56. Harriger, "Age Differences in Body Size Stereotyping in a Sample of Preschool Girls," 187.

57. Dohnt and Tiggemann show the impact of school, with reception girls showing little body dissatisfaction, but over 70 percent desiring thinner figures by year two. Dohnt and Tiggemann, "Peer Influences on Body Dissatisfaction and Dieting Awareness in Young Girls."

58. Girlguiding, "Girls' Attitude Survey, 2016," https://www.girlguiding.org. uk/globalassets/docs-and-resources/research-and-campaigns/girls-attitudes -survey-2016.pdf, accessed October 4, 2017.

59. Girlguiding, "Girls' Attitude Survey, 2013," http://www.girlguidinglaser .org.uk/wp-content/uploads/2013/12/2013_Attitudes_EqualityForGirls.pdf, accessed October 4, 2017.

60. Jones, *Skintight*, see chapter 4 titled "Stretched Middle Age," 83–105.

61. Susan Bordo, *Unbearable Weight*, xxv.

62. Barbara Mangweth-Matzek, Hans W. Hoek, and Harrison G. Pope Jr., "Pathological Eating and Body Dissatisfaction in Middle-Aged and Older Women," *Current opinion in psychiatry* 27, no. 6 (2014): 431–435. 434

63. Bordo, *Unbearable Weight*, xxiv.

64. Jones, *Skintight*, 86.

65. Cristin D. Runfola, Ann Von Holle, Christine M. Peat, Danieelle A Gagne, Kimberly A. Brownley, Sara M, Hofmeier and Cythia M. Bulik, "Characteristics of Women with Body Size Satisfaction at Midlife: Results of the Gender and Body Image Study," *Journal of Women and Aging*, 25 (2013): 287–304, 297.

66. Runfola et al., "Characteristics of Women with Body Size Satisfaction at Midlife," 297.

67. Glen S. Jankowski, Phillippa C. Diedrichs, Heidi Williamson, Gary Christopher, and Diana Harcourt, "Looking Age-Appropriate While Growing Old Gracefully: A Qualitative Study of Ageing and Body Image among Older Adults," *Journal of Health Psychology* 21, no. 4 (2016): 550–561.

68. I will develop this argument in future papers.

69. Imogen Tyler, "Pregnant Beauty: Maternal Femininities under Neoliberalism," in *New Femininities: Postfeminism, Neoliberalism and Subjectivity,* eds. Rosalind Gill and Christina Scharff (Basingstoke: Palgrave Macmillan, 2011 2013), 21–36, 27.

70. Arguably among the most controversial magazine covers of all time. WebdesingerDepot Staff "The Most Controversial Magazine Covers of All Time," http://www.webdesignerdepot.com/2009/09/the-most-controversial-magazine-covers-of-all-time/, accessed November 23, 2015.

71. Marianne Power, "Naked Baby Bump Photos Are the Latest Pregnancy Trend. But Are They a Precious Memento or Just Plain Tacky?" http://www.daily mail.co.uk/femail/article-2347006/Naked-baby-bump-photos-latest-pregnancy -trend-But-precious-memento-just-plain-tacky.html#ixzz3eoo4aP9p, accessed June 15, 2014.

72. For example, Iris Marion Young points to this potential positive aspect: "In the experience of the pregnant women, this weight and materiality often produce a sense of power, solidity and validity. Thus, whereas our society often devalues and trivializes women as weak and dainty, the pregnant women can give a certain sense of self-respect." Iris Marion Young, *On Female Body Experience: "Throwing Like a Girl" and Other Essays* (New York: Oxford University Press, 2005), 53.

73. Tyler, "Pregnant Beauty," 25.

74. Ibid., 29.

75. A view that Tyler echoes; also drawing attention to class differences, she states that, "only specific types of pregnant bodies are beautiful and/or sexually desirable—white, tight, youthful bodies with social capital and appropriate aspiration; "lower-class" pregnant celebrities, for instance, are deemed trashy and sluttish if they bear their bumps" (ibid., 27).

76. Lynn O'Brien Hallstein, *Bikini-Ready Moms: Celebrity Profiles, Motherhood, and the Body* (New York: State University of New York Press, 2015).

77. Ibid.

78. Presentation at Beauty Demands workshop 1 on "Changing Understandings of Body Image," http://www.birmingham.ac.uk/generic/beauty/events/2015 /workshop1.aspx, accessed 31 October 2016.

79. LookGoodFeelBetter website, http://www.lookgoodfeelbetter.co.uk/, accessed 3 July 2015.

80. #warpaint4life http://www.lookgoodfeelbetter.co.uk/warpaint4life, accessed 3 July 2015.

81. #warpaint4life http://www.lookgoodfeelbetter.co.uk/warpaint4life, accessed 3 July 2015.

82. #warpaint4life http://www.lookgoodfeelbetter.co.uk/warpaint4life000, accessed 3 July 2015.

83. An argument I will return to in chapter 5.

Chapter 3. A New (Miss)World Order?

1. Others have begun to make similar arguments, for instance Imani Perry suggests that "globalisation creates hybrid beauty norms." Imani Perry, "Buying white beauty," *Cardozo JL & Gender* 12 (2005): 579–608, 591.

2. I will return to the issue of what is required for minimal standards in the next chapter and to the rising bar of normal in Chapter 5.

3. Meng Zhang, "A Chinese Beauty Story: How College Women in China Negotiate Beauty, Body Image, and Mass Media," *Chinese Journal of Communication* 5, no. 4 (2012): 437–454.

4. Perry, "Buying White Beauty," 584.

5. Sarah Proansky argues that "Sasha and Malia Obama function as both evidence that 'all people' can achieve the American Dream—hence as the most model of model minorities—and as post-racial girl role models who maintain a healthy, balanced, and modest lifestyle, regardless of their surroundings or how famous and how powerful their father is." Sarah Projansky, *Spectacular Girls: Media Fascination and Celebrity Culture* (New York: New York University Press, 2014), 69.

6. See Swami and Furnham's account, which makes it clear that there are some traits, like muscularity in men, that are in fact associated with poor health outcomes, while it's possible to find evolutionary ways to explain the preference (maybe they were good hunters) social construction accounts seem to offer at least as strong explanations. Swami and Furnham, rather sensibly, argue that we should seek multidisciplinary accounts as everything is ultimately a mixture of biology and culture, so rather than continue the nature, nurture fight focus on what each discipline can tell us. Viren Swami and Adrian Furnham, *The Psychology of Physical Attraction* (London and New York: Routledge, 2008).

7. Despite problems with "West," for ease I have used this terminology throughout.

8. Chinese women in one study "stressed importance of first impressions and how being attractive could be an advantage in social and personal relationships." Meng Zhang "A Chinese Beauty Story," 447; South Sudanese women state close ties between appearance, education ,and employment. Caroline Faria, "Styling the Nation: Fear and Desire in the South Sudanese Beauty Trade," *Transactions of the Institute of British Geographers* 39, no. 2 (2014): 318–330.

9. Kyung Bo Kim "Narratives about the Media, Diet, and Body Image: A Cross-Cultural Comparison between Young Female Adults in the Midwestern

United States and South Korea," *Journal of Intercultural Communication Research* 43, no. 4 (2014): 283–303. 300.

10. In this paper studies are cited from Belize, Fiji, Korean, and the United States. Zhang, "A Chinese Beauty Story," 438.

11. Ibid., 439.

12. Ibid., 448.

13. Christopher J. Ferguson, "In the Eye of the Beholder: Thin-Ideal Media Affects Some, But Not Most, Viewers in a Meta-Analytic Review of Body Dissatisfaction in Women and Men," *Psychology of Popular Media Culture* 2, no. 1 (2013): 20.

14. Kim argues that the Korean women's reasons are more interdependent and communally orientated; by contrast U.S. women are more independent and focused on their own bodies and weight. Kyung Bo Kim, "Narratives about the Media, Diet, and Body Image: A Cross-Cultural Comparison between Young Female Adults in the Midwestern United States and South Korea," *Journal of Intercultural Communication Research* 43, no. 4 (2014): 283–303.

15. Even when we do have such figures it is not the case that the same phenomena play out in similar ways in different contexts: for instance, body dissatisfaction might be relevant globally, but may not uniformly trigger eating disorders. For instance, familiar and social pressure against such practices, or in favor of different practices might be strong, as Gupta et al. argue is the case in India, and Morris and Szabo in South Africa. M. A. Gupta, S. K. Chaturvedi, P. C. Chandarana, and A. M. Johnson, "Weight-Related Body Image Concerns among 18–24-Year-Old Women in Canada and India: An Empirical Comparative Study," *Journal of Psychosomatic Research* 50, no. 4 (2001): 193–198; P. F. Morris and C. P. Szabo, "Meanings of Thinness and Dysfunctional Eating in Black South African Females: A Qualitative Study," *African Journal of Psychiatry* 16, no. 5 (2013): 338–342.

16. Gordon B. Forbes, Jaehee Jung, Juan Diego Vaamonde, Alicia Omar, Laura Paris, and Nilton Soares Formiga, "Body Dissatisfaction and Disordered Eating in Three Cultures: Argentina, Brazil, and the US," *Sex Roles* 66, no. 9–10 (2012): 677–694.

17. Zhang, "A Chinese Beauty Story."

18. Kim, "Narratives about the Media, Diet, and Body Image."

19. Jaita Talukdar, "Thin but Not Skinny: Women Negotiating the "Never Too Thin" Body Ideal in Urban India," *Women's Studies International Forum* 35, no. 2 (2012): 109–118; Megha Dhillon and Priti Dhawan, "But I Am Fat": The Experiences of Weight Dissatisfaction in Indian Adolescent Girls and Young Women," *Women's Studies International Forum* 34, no. 6 (2011): 539–549.

20. Vinet Coetzee, Stella J. Faerber, Jaco M. Greeff, Carmen E. Lefevre, Daniel E. Re, and David I. Perrett, "African Perceptions of Female Attractiveness," *PloS one* 7, no. 10 (2012): e48116.

21. Kausar Suhail, "Prevalence of Eating Disorders in Pakistan: Relationship with Depression and Body Shape," *Eating and Weight Disorders: Studies on Anorexia, Bulimia and Obesity* 7, no. 2 (2002): 131–138.

22. Kathleen M. Pike and Patricia E. Dunne, "The Rise of Eating Disorders in Asia: A Review," *Journal of Eating Disorders* 3, no. 1 (2015): 1–14.

23. Swamiand Furnham, *The Psychology of Physical Attraction*, 98.

24. Mohamed Rguibi and Rekia Belahsen, "Fattening Practices among Moroccan Saharawi Women," *Eastern Mediterranean Health Journal* 12, no. 5 (2006): 619–624; Mohamed Rguibi and Rekia Belahsen, "Body Size Preferences and Sociocultural Influences on Attitudes towards Obesity among Moroccan Sahraoui Women," *Body Image* 3, no. 4 (2006): 395–400.

25. Swami and Furnham, *The Psychology of Physical Attraction*, 100–101.

26. Ibid., 92.

27. To cite some fairly typical studies, Deborah Schooler argues that black women have more positive body image. Deborah L. Schooler. Monique Ward, Ann Merriwether, and Allison Caruthers, "Who's That Girl: Television's Role in the Body Image Development of Young White and Black Women," *Psychology of Women Quarterly* 28, no. 1 (2004): 38–47. Jane Ogden and Sheriden Russell argue that black identity protects women from focusing on and internalizing the thin ideal. Jane Ogden and Sheriden Russell, "How Black Women Make Sense of "White" and Black" Fashion Magazines: A Qualitative Think Aloud Study," *Journal of health Psychology* 18, no. 12 (2012): 1588–1600.

28. Coetzee et al., "African Perceptions of Female Attractiveness," 5.

29. Coetzee et al., "African Perceptions of Female Attractiveness," 5.

30. For example Roberts et al., in a meta-analysis found a preference for underweight women (compared to normal or overweight women). They too note it is different from previous ideals in Africa and surprising given thinness is an indicator of illness. Alan Roberts, Thomas F. Cash, Alan Feingold, and Blair T. Johnson, "Are Black-White Differences in Females' Body Dissatisfaction Decreasing? A Meta-Analytic Review," *Journal of Consulting and Clinical Psychology* 74, no. 6 (2006): 1121–1131. A study of Arab women also showed the trend to reduce weight, against previous valuing of heavy figures. Abdulrahman O. Musaiger, Nora E. Shahbeek, and Maryama Al-Mannai, "The Role of Social Factors and Weight Status in Ideal Body-Shape Preferences as Perceived by Arab Women," *Journal of Biosocial Science* 36, no. 06 (2004): 699–707.

31. Roberts et al., "Are Black-White Differences in Females' Body Dissatisfaction Decreasing?" 121.

32. Jennifer B. Webb, Phoebe Butler-Ajibade, and Seronda A. Robinson, "Considering an Affect Regulation Framework for Examining the Association between Body Dissatisfaction and Positive Body Image in Black Older Adolescent Females: Does Body Mass Index Matter?" *Body image* 11, no. 4 (2014): 434.

33. Rice, *Becoming Women*, 245.

34. Other studies are suggestive: for instance, that nearly 90 percent of women in rap videos are thin. Yuanyuan Zhang, Travis L. Dixon, and Kate Conrad, "Female Body Image as a Function of Themes in Rap Music Videos: A Content Analysis," *Sex Roles* 62, no. 11–12 (2010): 787–797.

35. Gimlin, *Body Work*.

36. Gemma L. Witcomb, Jon Arcelus, and Jue Chen, "Can Cognitive Dissonance Methods Developed in the West for Combatting the "Thin Ideal" Help Slow the Rapidly Increasing Prevalence of Eating Disorders in Non-Western Cultures?" *Shanghai archives of psychiatry* 25, no. 6 (2013): 332; Maria Makino, Koji Tsuboi, and Lorraine Dennerstein, "Prevalence of Eating Disorders: A Comparison of Western and Non-Western Countries," *Medscape General Medicine* 6, no. 3 (2004).

37. Bordo. *Unbearable Weight,* xx.

38. For example, Jaita Talukar, reports the Indian women she interviewed claimed not to want "ultra-thin" bodies, but at the same time expressed distaste for fat bodies and were trying to lose weight. Talukdar, "Thin but Not Skinny." Likewise others suggest that there might be distinctive thinness ideals in local contexts, for example, a distinctive Indian concern about the upper torso (particularly visible in Indian fashions). Gupta et al., "Weight-Related Body Image Concerns among 18–24-year-Old Women in Canada and India."

39. Yan Yan and Kim Bissell, "The Globalization Of Beauty: How Is Ideal Beauty Influenced by Globally Published Fashion and Beauty Magazines?" *Journal of Intercultural Communication Research* 43, no. 3 (2014): 194–214, 209

40. Michelle M. Lazar, "'Discover the Power Of Femininity!' Analyzing Global 'Power Femininity' in Local Advertising," *Feminist Media Studies* 6, no. 4 (2006): 505–517, 515.

41. Consultancy.UK,"Global Cosmetics Market Worth €181 Billion, L'Oreal Dominates," http://www.consultancy.uk/news/2810/cosmetics-market-worth-181 -billion-loreal-dominates, accessed November 1, 2016.

42. Pascal Del Giudice and Pinier Yves, "The Widespread Use of Skin Lightening Creams in Senegal: A Persistent Public Health Problem in West Africa," *International Journal of Dermatology* 41, no. 2 (2002): 69–72.

43. Eric P. H. Li, Hyun Jeong Min, and Russell W. Belk, "Skin Lightening and Beauty in Four Asian Cultures," *NA-Advances in Consumer Research* 35 (2008): 444–449, 446.

44. For the West, see Tiggemann and Hodgson, "The hairlessness norm extended"; studies suggest that body hair removal is not a simply Western practice and cite other studies to show the practice as occurring in Egypt, Greece and Rome, the Trobriand Islands, Uganda, South America and Turkey. Merran Toerien, Sue Wilkinson, and Precilla YL Choi, "Body Hair Removal: The 'Mundane' Production of Normative Femininity," *Sex Roles* 52, no. 5–6 (2005): 399–406.).

45. Wei Luo, "Selling Cosmetic Surgery and Beauty Ideals: The Female Body in the Web Sites of Chinese Hospitals," *Women's Studies in Communication* 35, no. 1 (2012): 68–95, 88.

46. Megdala Peixoto Labre, "The Brazilian Wax: New Hairlessness Norm for Women?" *Journal of Communication Inquiry* 26, no. 2 (2002): 113–132.

47. Andrea L DeMaria and Abbey B. Berenson, "Prevalence and Correlates of Pubic Hair Grooming among low-Income Hispanic, Black, and White Women," *Body Image* 10, no. 2 (2013): 226–231.

48. In her history of hair removal in the United States, Rebecca Herzig recounts that over 99 percent of women in the U.S. remove hair and most of these daily and across all groups. Rebecca M. Herzig, *Plucked: A History of Hair Removal* (New York and London: New York University Press, 2015).

49. Sandya Hewamanne, "Threading Meaningful Lives: Respectability, Home Businesses and Identity Negotiations among Newly Immigrant South Asian Women," *Identities* 19, no. 3 (2012): 320–338.

50. "On the day before the wedding, the bandandâz (hair remover or cosmetician) uses cotton thread, lime-base depilatory paste, a razor, and wax to skillfully transform the girl's hairy body into a woman's perfectly smooth body." Christian Bromberger, "Hair: From the West to the Middle East through the Mediterranean (the 2007 AFS Mediterranean Studies section address)," *Journal of American Folklore* 121, no. 482 (2008): 379–399, 384.

51. ISAPS, "International Survey on Aesthetic Cosmetic Procedure Performed in 2015, http://www.isaps.org/Media/Default/global-statistics/2016percent20 ISAPSpercent20Results.pdf, accessed November 3, 2016.

52. Deni Kirkova, "Iran Is the Nose Job Capital of the World with SEVEN Times More Procedures than the U.S. – but Rise in Unlicensed Surgeons Poses Huge Risk," http://www.dailymail.co.uk/femail/article-2287961/Iran-named -nose-job-capital-world-SEVEN-times-rhinoplasty-operations-U-S-Iranian -women-strive-western-doll-face.html, accessed 1 November 2017.

53. Harry S. Hwang, and Jeffrey H. Spiegel, "The Effect of 'Single' vs 'Double' Eyelids on the Perceived Attractiveness of Chinese Women," *Aesthetic Surgery Journal* 34, no. 3 (2014): 374–382.

54. Zhang, "A Chinese Beauty Story," 449.

55. Hwang, "The Effect of 'Single' vs 'Double' Eyelids on the Perceived Attractiveness of Chinese Women."

56. "Patricia Max About Face: Why Is South Korea the World's Plastic-Surgery Capital?" *The New Yorker*, March 23, 2015, http://www.newyorker.com /magazine/2015/03/23/about-face, accessed 1 November 2017.

57. Jewish women have routinely had nose surgery (Jeffreys, *Beauty and Misogyny*, 155).

58. Zhang, "A Chinese Beauty Story," 450.

59. American Society of Plastic Surgeons, "In the Age of Selfies, America's Love Affair with Lips Is Leading to a Boom In Cosmetic Procedures," https:// www.plasticsurgery.org/news/press-releases/in-the-age-of-selfies-americas -love-affair-with-lips-is-leading-to-a-boom-in-cosmetic-procedures, accessed 2 November 2016.

60. "Lip Fillers: Everything You Need to Know," *Marie Claire*, http://www .marieclaire.co.uk/beauty/skincare/lip-fillers-everything-you-need-to-know -31500, accessed November 2, 2016.

61. After it became public that Kylie Jenner had used lip fillers enquires for the procedure escalated. Emma Akbareian "Kylie Jenner Lip Filler Confession Leads to 70% Increase in Enquires for the Procedure," http://www.independent

.co.uk/life-style/fashion/news/kylie-jenner-lip-filler-confession-leads-to-70 -rise-in-enquiries-for-the-procedure-10232716.html, accessed 18 October 2016.

62. My local beauty salon tells me they are under increasing pressure from young customers to offer such treatments.

63. ISAPS, "International Survey on Aesthetic/Cosmetic Procedures Performed in 2015," http://www.isaps.org/Media/Default/global-statistics/2016per cent20ISAPSpercent20Results.pdf, accessed October 11, 2016.

64. Some do, such as Orlan, but while diversity is possible, it is rare, and beauty procedures and practices almost always conform to gender norms.

65. Etcoff, *Survival of the Prettiest,* 138.

66. Kathy Davis, *Dubious Equalities and Embodied Differences* (New York and Oxford: Rowman and Littlefield Publishers: 2003), 6.

67. ISAPS, "International Survey on Aesthetic/Cosmetic Procedures Performed in 2015," http://www.isaps.org/Media/Default/global-statistics/2016per cent20ISAPSpercent20Results.pdf, accessed October 11, 2016.

68. ISAPS, "International Survey on Aesthetic/Cosmetic Procedures Performed in 2015," http://www.isaps.org/Media/Default/global-statistics/2016per cent20ISAPSpercent20Results.pdf, accessed October 11, 2016.

69. ISAPS, "International Survey on Aesthetic/Cosmetic Procedures Performed in 2015," http://www.isaps.org/Media/Default/global-statistics/2016per cent20ISAPSpercent20Results.pdf, accessed October 11, 2016.

70. American Society of Plastic Surgeons, "2014 Plastic Surgery Statistics Report," https://www.plasticsurgery.org/documents/News/Statistics/2014/plastic -surgery-statistics-full-report-2014.pdf, accessed October 4, 2017.

71. ISAPS, "International Survey on Aesthetic/Cosmetic Procedures Performed in 2015," http://www.isaps.org/Media/Default/global-statistics/2016per cent20ISAPSpercent20Results.pdf, accessed October 11, 2016.

72. In 2014, 11,505 buttock augmentation with fat grafting operations were performed in the United States and 1863 buttock implants; so rare were these in 2000 there are no comparator stats. In 2014 there were 3505 buttock lifts compared to 1356 in 2000 a rise of 158 percent. "2014 Plastic Surgery Statistics Report," American Society of Plastic Surgeons, http://www.plasticsurgery.org /Documents/news-resources/statistics/2014-statistics/plastic-surgery-statsitics -full-report.pdf, accessed July 20, 2016.

73. For example Frith et al. posit that "In Western societies, women may think it is mainly their bodies that get noticed by men, whereas in Asia, women may think it is their faces which are most important." Katharine Frith, Ping Shaw, and Hong Cheng, "The Construction of Beauty: A Cross-Cultural Analysis of Women's Magazine Advertising," *Journal of Communication* 55, no. 1 (2005): 56–70, 66.

74. For example, "cute" looks being dominant in Asia and "sexy" looks in the West—although there is always crossover, hybridity and some variation. Frith et al., "The Construction of Beauty"; Zhang, "A Chinese Beauty Story"; Chyong-

Ling Lin and Jin-Tsann Yeh, "Comparing Society's Awareness of Women: Media-Portrayed Idealized Images and Physical Attractiveness," *Journal of Business Ethics* 90, no. 1 (2009): 61–79.

75. Jones, *Skintight*, 46.

76. J. Mark Elwood and Janet Jopson, "Melanoma and Sun Exposure: An Overview of Published Studies," *International Journal of Cancer* 73, no. 2 (1997): 198–203.

77. Mathiue Boniol, Philippe Autier, Peter Boyle, Sara Gandini, "Cutaneous Melanoma Attributable to Sunbed Use: Systematic Review and Meta-Analysis," *British Medical Journal* (2005): doi 10.1136/bmj.e4757; Mackenzie R. Wehner, Melissa L. Shive, Mary-Margaret Chren, Jiali Han, Abrar A. Qureshi, and Eleni Linos, "Indoor Tanning and Non-Melanoma Skin Cancer: Systematic Review and Meta-Analysis," *BMJ* 345 (2012): e5909.

78. Katie Brooks, Daniel Brooks, Zeina Dajani, Susan M. Swetter, Erin Powers, Sherry Pagoto, and Alan C. Geller, "Use of Artificial Tanning Products among Young Adults," *Journal of the American Academy of Dermatology* 54, no. 6 (2006): 1060–1066.

79. The "tanning craze" began in the 1920s, and tanned skin has largely remained desirable for those with white skin. Kathy Peiss, *Hope in a Jar: The Making of America's Beauty Culture* (New York: Henry Holt, 1998).

80. Cancer Council Australia, "Slip, Slop, Slap, Seek, Slide," http://www.cancer.org.au/preventing-cancer/sun-protection/campaigns-and-events/slip-slop-slap-seek-slide.html, accessed October 17, 2016.

81. Spray tanning is now the most popular tanning treatment in beauty salons, and its popularity is growing, according to the statistics of the industry. Beautyguild.com, https://www.beautyguild.com/Survey/Results/Tanning-062014.aspx, accessed November 2, 2016. See Louise Rondel's account of the spray tan process, http://beautydemands.blogspot.co.uk/2016/08/i-didnt-even-notice-youd-had-spray-tan.html, accessed October 17, 2016).

82. Kelly M. Lewis, Navit Robkin, Karie Gaska, and Lillian Carol Njoki. "Investigating Motivations for Women's Skin Bleaching in Tanzania," *Psychology of Women Quarterly* 35, no. 1 (2011): 29–37, 29.

83. "Mercury in Skin Lightening Products," WHO, http://www.who.int/ipcs/assessment/public_health/mercury_flyer.pdf, accessed July 20, 2016.

84. Susie Neilson, "Why Are Women Still Dying to Be White," www.iol.co.za/lifestyle/fashion/why-are-women-still-dying-to-be-white/1.1705800#.vsutqfnF-so, accessed November 1, 2016.

85. Eric P. H. Li et al., "Skin Lightening and Beauty in Four Asian Cultures."

86. Shirley Tate, "Black Beauty: Shade, Hair and Anti-Racist Aesthetics," *Ethnic and racial studies* 30, no. 2 (2007): 300–319. 307.

87. Tate, *Black Women's Bodies and the Nation*, 156.

88. Edmonds, *Pretty Modern*, 26.

89. Ibid., 133.

90. Ibid., 26 and 109.

91. It is interesting that Davuluri would not have won Miss India given the dark shade of her skin. Meeta Rani Jha, *The Global Beauty Industry: Colorism, Racism, and the National Body* (London and New York: Routledge, 2016).

92. Jha, *The Global Beauty Industry*), 5.

93. Margaret L. Hunter, *Race Gender and the Politics of Skin Tone* (London and New York: Routledge, 2005).

94. For example, with the sexualizing of black women's bodies and especially their "battys" (bottoms) to be other, and even obscene. Janell Hobson, "The "Batty" Politic: Toward an Aesthetic of the Black Female Body," *Hypatia* 18, no. 4 (2003): 87–105. This sexualizing of black women has a long history and "recurring negative manifestation of African American beauty include the oversexed jezebel, the tragic mulatto, and the mammy figure." Tracey Owens Patton, "Hey Girl, Am I More than My Hair? African American Women and Their Struggles with Beauty, Body Image, and Hair," *NWSA Journal* 18, no. 2 (2006): 24–51, 26.

95. See Meeta Rani Jha's discussion of Beyoncé, *The Global Beauty Industry*, 45–47.

96. For example, that those with a lower-class or lower socioeconomic status prefer heavier women, especially in contexts where food is scarce, as larger frames signal wealth and high status; by contrast in context where fattening food is cheap and readily available it is thinness that signals wealth and high status.

97. Oliver Picton, "The Complexities of Complexion: A Cultural Geography of Skin Colour and Beauty Products," *Geography* 98 (2013): 85.

98. Christopher A. D. Charles, "Skin Bleaching, Self-Hate, and Black Identity in Jamaica," *Journal of Black Studies* 33, no. 6 (2003): 711–728.

99. bell hooks, *Black Looks: Race and Representation* (New York and London: Routledge, 2015).

100. For instance, authentic skin is dark, and authentic hairstyles are afros, cornrows, and so on. Shirley Tate recounts the story of Teresa, a mixed race women who plaited her hair and wore a head wrap to hide its straightness and argues that such standards are also normalizing and exclusionary. Tate, "Black beauty."

101. Lewis et al., "Investigating Motivations for Women's Skin Bleaching in Tanzania," 33.

102. As documented in China, (Zhang, "A Chinese Beauty Story"); India (Picton, "The Complexities of Complexion"); Tanzania (Kelly M. Lewis, Navit Robkin, Karie Gaska, and Lillian Carol Njoki, "Investigating Motivations for Women's Skin Bleaching in Tanzania," *Psychology of Women Quarterly* 35, no. 1 (2011): 29–37)).

103. Margaret L. Hunter, "Buying Racial Capital: Skin-Bleaching and Cosmetic Surgery in a Globalized World," *Journal of Pan African Studies* 4, no. 4 (2011): 142–164.

104. Fair & Lovely, "our story." https://www.fairandlovely.in/our-story, accessed July 30, 2016.

105. Margo Okazawa-Rey, Tracy Robinson, and Janie Victoria Ward, "Black Women and the Politics of Skin Color and Hair," *Women & Therapy* 6, no. 1–2 (1987): 89–102, 101.

106. I use the term "Western" rather than "European" as this is the standard terminology in the literature on this topic.

107. Including Picton, "The Complexities of Complexion"; Lewis et al., "Investigating Motivations for Women's Skin Bleaching in Tanzania"; Patton, "Hey Girl, Am I More than My Hair?"

108. Coetzee et al., "African Perceptions of Female Attractiveness."

109. Hwang, "The Effect of "Single" vs "Double" Eyelids on the Perceived Attractiveness of Chinese Women."

110. Jones cites Browell that double eyelids are natural features of up to 50 percent of the Chinese population (*Skintight*, 41).

111. Wei, "Selling Cosmetic Surgery and Beauty Ideals."

112. Ruth Holliday, David Bell, Olive Cheung, Meredith Jones, and Elspeth Probyn, "Brief Encounters: Assembling Cosmetic Surgery Tourism," *Social Science & Medicine* 124 (2015): 298–304; Ruth Holliday and Joanna Elfving-Hwang, "Gender, Globalization and Aesthetic Surgery in South Korea," *Body & Society* 18, no. 2 (2012): 58–81.

113. Holliday et al., "Brief Encounters," 301.

114. Ibid., 302.

115. Holliday et al. reject "homogenizing" along with "Westernizing"; in this I disagree.

116. I hope separating out the global from the Westernizing meets some of the concern that Holliday et al. and others have about positing a global ideal. For instance, in positing a global ideal in the way that I do I am well able to recognize that "the global and local mix, reworking each other, producing new transnational hybrids" (Holliday et al., "Brief encounters," 302). Likewise, I concur with Edmonds that "it would be hard to see the growth of beauty industries there as simply an effect of Westernization." Edmonds, *Pretty Modern*, 25–26. It may be that this does not go far enough to satisfy all those who are critical of a global beauty ideal. For instance, Angela McCracken, argues that it more diverse ideals are emerging, in part because of globalization, but these do not seem diverse in the context of a global mean, in that while *metaleros, hippies, grunge,* and *vampiras* are challenging traditional beauty norms in Mexico, this is a slightly different point. Such subcultures fall very much within the norms of the emerging global beauty ideal, at least as I have described it. Indeed, given the breath of the beauty ideal I have set out McCracken may even agree. McCracken, *The Beauty Trade*.

117. Perry, "Buying White Beauty," 588.

118. For instance, black women who do not have large buttocks can feel self-conscious and suffer ridicule. Laurel B. Watson, Dawn Robinson, Franco Dispenza, and Negar Nazari, "African American Women's Sexual Objectification Experiences: A Qualitative Study," *Psychology of Women Quarterly* 36, no. 4 (2012): 458–475.

119. Tate, *Black Women's Bodies and the Nation*, 114.

120. Ibid., 93.

121. These trends go beyond these three dominant movie-making sites: for instance, Tamil movies, which traditionally used curvaceous actresses, now use very thin actresses. Premalatha Karupiah, "Have Beauty Ideals Evolved? Reading of Beauty Ideals in Tamil Movies by Malaysian Indian Youths," *Sociological Inquiry* 85, no. 2 (2015): 239–261.

122. Karupiah, "Have Beauty Ideals Evolved?"

123. Yan and Bissell, "The Globalization of Beauty."

124. Oluwakemi M. Balogun, "Cultural and Cosmopolitan Idealized Femininity and Embodied Nationalism in Nigerian Beauty Pageants," *Gender & Society* 26, no. 3 (2012): 357–381.

125. Bordo *Unbearable Weight* xiv; similarly claims are made about Tanzania. Kamryn T. Eddy, Moira Hennessey, and Heather Thompson-Brenner, "Eating Pathology in East African Women: The Role of Media Exposure and Globalization," *Journal of Nervous and Mental Disease* 195, no. 3 (2007): 196–202.

Chapter 4. Routine, Special, and Extreme

1. Kat Hayes, Ju Zhang, and Brook Streatfield, "How to Do a Natural Contor Make-Up Look," The Telegraph, April 21, 2016, http://www.telegraph.co.uk/beauty/tips-tutorials/how-to-do-a-natural-contour-make-up-look/, accessed November 1, 2016.

2. Bianca London, "The Kim Kardashian Effect? Women Today Have 27 STEPS to Their Makeup Routine – Compared to Just Eight a Decade Ago," November 14, 2016," http://www.dailymail.co.uk/femail/article-3919548/The-Kim-Kardashian-effect-Women-today-27-STEPS-makeup-routine-compared-just-eight-decade-ago.html, accessed November 1, 2016.

3. As Bartky notes "making up the face is in fact, a highly stylized activity that gives little rein to self-expression." *Femininity and Domination*, 71; Bianca London "'The menopause left me feeling flat and s***': Former Brit pop star Meg Matthews, 50, looks VERY youthful as she turns back the clock through surgery," *Daily Mail*, November 7, 2016.

4. McCracken, *The Beauty Trade*.

5. McCracken reports 1.9 million Mexicans are direct sellers, and this is the primary way that make-up is sold. *The Beauty Trade*, 120ff.

6. Holliday and Sanchez Taylor point out that beauty is a central value for working class and black women. "Aesthetic Surgery as False Beauty," 184.

7. This article about Meg Matthew's threadlift is effectively an endorsement, and advert. Bianca London, "'The Menopause Left Me Feeling Flat and s***': Former Brit Pop Star Meg Matthews, 50, Looks VERY Youthful as She Turns Back the Clock through Surgery, http://www.dailymail.co.uk/femail/article-3898170/The-menopause-left-feeling-flat-s-Meg-Matthews-looks-youthful-following-2-000-threadlift.html, accessed November 7, 2016.

8. Although in Chapter 9 I will argue that, even when formally consented to, informed consent might not be sufficient in the beauty context.

9. Jones, *Skintight*, 5.

10. NHS (National Health Service), "Eyelid Surgery," http://www.nhs.uk/Conditions/cosmetic-treatments-guide/Pages/eyelid-surgery.aspx, accessed November 3, 2016.

11. NHS (National Health Service), "Liposuction," http://www.nhs.uk/Conditions/cosmetic-treatments-guide/Pages/liposuction.aspx, accessed November 3, 2016.

12. Personal correspondence with Mark Henley, Consultant Plastic, Reconstructive and Aesthetic Surgeon to the Nottingham and Derby NHS Hospitals.

13. The most recent the PIP scandal is touched on in chapter 6.

14. Royal College of Surgeons, "Professional Standards for Cosmetics Surgery," https://www.rcseng.ac.uk/library-and-publications/college-publications/docs/professional-cosmetic-surgery/, accessed November 8, 2016.

15. Department of Health, "Review of the Regulation of Cosmetic Interventions: Final Report (Keogh Review), https://www.gov.uk/government/uploads/system/uploads/attachment_data/file/192028/Review_of_the_Regulation_of_Cosmetic_Interventions.pdf, accessed March 10, 2014 31.

16. Examples include those known primarily for their breasts, such as Jordan and Lolo Farrari (of Eurotrash fame). See Jones, *Skintight,* chapter 6, for a case study on Farrari.

17. For example the NHS only covers treatment necessary for health reasons. NHS (National Health Service) "Which Dental Treatments Are Available on the NHS?" http://www.nhs.uk/chq/Pages/985.aspx?CategoryID=74, accessed 3 November 2015.

18. Some argue that the "hairless" trend (and perhaps labiaplasty) is part of an aesthetic that emphasizes not only youth but extreme youth as a way of infantilizing women so diminishing and dismissing them. G. Zwang, "Vulvar Reconstruction: The Exploitation of Ignorance," *J. Sexol.* 20, no. 2 (2010): 81–87. I will briefly return to this in chapter 10.

19. Herzig argues that "within a single generation, female pubic hair had been rendered superfluous," Herzig, *Plucked,* 137, and that "women often request their first full genital waxes as special 'surprises' for their partners before weddings, anniversaries, or Valentine's Day," Herzig, *Plucked,* 142.

20. One study of Australia College students found that 60 percent removed some public hair with nearly half removing most or all of it. Marika Tiggemann and Suzanna Hodgson, "The Hairlessness Norm Extended: Reasons for and Predictors of Women's Body Hair Removal at Different Body Sites," *Sex Roles* 59, no. 11–12 (2008): 889–897.

21. Breanne Fahs found that "women of colour received particularly harsh judgements from their families when growing body hair." Breanne Fahs, "Perilous Patches and Pitstaches: Imagined Versus Lived Experiences of Women's Body Hair Growth," *Psychology of Women Quarterly* 38, no. 2 (2014): 167–180.

22. Ibid., 171.

23. Ibid., 171.

24. Ibid., 171.

25. Ibid., 171.

26. Ibid., 175.

27. Ibid., 174.

28. Gail Dines, *Pornland How Porn Has Hijacked Our Sexuality* (Boston: Beacon Press, 2010), 99.

29. Ibid., 100.

30. Chloe Marshall, "Armpits4August Is Making Women's Body Hair a Feminist Issue," The Guardian July 18, 2013, https://www.theguardian.com/lifeandstyle/2013/jul/18/armpits-4-august-body-hair-feminist, accessed March 10, 2014.

31. Body hair removal has no proven health benefits, but many (most) forms of hair removal have some risks, which increase when hair is removed from more sensitive body parts. Risks include skin irritation, infection, allergic and irritant dermatitis, and scarring. M. Haedersdal and H. C. Wulf, "Evidence-Based Review of Hair Removal Using Lasers and Light Sources," *Journal of the European Academy of Dermatology and Venereology* 20, no. 1 (2006): 9–20). Risks of pubic hair removal include irritation, razor burn, folliculitis, dermatitis, and a number of infections. Jonathan D. K. Trager, "Pubic Hair Removal: Pearls and Pitfalls," *Journal of Pediatric and Adolescent Gynecology* 19, no. 2 (2006): 117–123. There is also increased risk of infection for some. Mark G. Kirchhof and Sheila Au, "Brazilian Waxing and Human Papillomavirus: A Case of Acquired Epidermodysplasia Verruciformis," *CMAJ* 187, no. 2 (2014): 126–128.

32. In her history of body hair removal, Rebecca Herzig tells of the extremes that women have gone to for hairlessness, including using X-ray machines, which did result in hair removal, but also "scarring, ulceration, cancer and death" (Herzig, *Plucked*, 96).

33. In a study on make-up at work, it was found that "appropriate makeup use is strongly associated with assumptions about health, heterosexuality, and credibility in the workplace" and that these factors limited women's ability to subvert makeup practices. Kirsten Dellinger and Christine L. Williams, "Makeup at Work: Negotiating Appearance Rules in the Workplace," *Gender & Society* 11, no. 22 (1997): 151–177, 151.

34. Peiss, *Hope in a Jar*.

35. In the Victorian era wearing cosmetics was unacceptable. Carol Dyhouse, *Glamour: Women, History and Feminism* (London and New York: Zed Books, 2011), 20.

36. Ibid., 19.

37. Ibid., 82.

38. Peiss, *Hope in a Jar*, 245.

39. Press Association, "No-Makeup Selfies Raise £8m for Cancer Research UK in Six Days," The Guardian March 25, 2014, https://www.theguardian.com/society/2014/mar/25/no-makeup-selfies-cancer-charity, accessed June 12, 2015.

40. Peiss, *Hope in a Jar*, 166.

41. Anecdotal reports from health care professionals and a small number of beauticians, of the use, for example of semi-permanent make-up, such as eyelash perming and tinting.

42. "Similar stories of illness and tragedy abound at nail salons across the country, of children born slow or 'special,' of miscarriages and cancers, of coughs that will not go away, and painful skin afflictions. The stories have become so common that older manicurists warn women of child-bearing age away from the business, with its potent brew of polishes, solvents, hardeners, and glues that nail workers handle daily." "Perfect Nails, Poisoned Workers," http://www.nytimes .com/2015/05/11/nyregion/nail-salon-workers-in-nyc-face-hazardous-chemicals .html? accessed 29 July 2016.

43. Louise Rondel, http://beautydemands.blogspot.co.uk/2016/02/manicur ing-indifference-exceptionality.html, accessed July 29, 2016.

44. Gel polish and Shellac are sealed with UV light and require professional removal.

45. For example development projects train young women to open beauty salons, which suggests that in these contexts there is a demand for such services. For an example see Afghanaid, http://www.afghanaid.org.uk/case_studies.php /7/home_beauty_salons_training_afghan_women, accessed November 3, 2016.

46. Many women over sixty do not, and have never, dyed their hair, but there are far fewer women in their forties and fifties who have not, and routinely, dyed their hair. The reason for this is partly connected to improvement in the technol-ogies and techniques that are available and accessible. Hair dying is now relatively easy and inexpensive, and while it can be done in the salon it can also be done at home. Accordingly, hair dying has become increasingly regarded as normal and necessary to meet minimum standards of beauty.

47. Kirchhof, "Brazilian Waxing and Human Papillomavirus."

48. Cancer is suggested in some recent reports, but there are no systematic studies as yet. Roni Caryn Rabin, "Laser Hair Removal's Risks," http://well.blogs .nytimes.com/2014/01/06/laser-hair-removals-risks/, accessed March 10, 2015.

49. Lazering and IPL treatments target melatonin and therefore are ineffec-tive on pale skin with blonde or grey hair, and on dark skin they cause blistering and pain. But for those for whom they are suited, it is suggested that laser and IPL hair removal practices are preferable to shaving waxing, epilation ,and electroly-sis. Haedersdal and Wulf, "Evidence-Based Review of Hair Removal Using Lasers and Light Sources."

50. For instance, a selection bestselling products in this range are Dior's *Dream Skin* described as "exceptional skincare that pushes the limits of tradi-tional cosmetics. For the 1st time, a skincare treatment is capable of acting simul-taneously on the quality, evenness and youthful beauty of skin," retailing at £79 for 30 ml; Lancôme's *Visionnaire Serum Plus*, which makes the skin appear "more radiant, smoothing uneven texture and tone, enlarged pores and even wrinkles" at £48 for 30 ml; and Estée Lauder's *New Advanced Night Repair Synchronized Recovery Complex II* is "proven in consumer testing: Lines and wrinkles appear

significantly reduced. Skin feels smoother, hydrated, stronger. Looks younger, radiant, more translucent and even toned. Proven effective for all ethnicities," yours for £50 for 30 ml. Prices and descriptions from John Lewis. http://www .johnlewis.com, accessed February 29, 2016.

51. For instance, a selection of bestselling products in this range are Boots own *No 7 Perfect and Protect Intense Advanced Serum*, promises which "younger looking more radiant skin in just 2 weeks" and retails at £24.99 for 30 ml; Olay's *Regenerist Luminous Skin Tone Perfecting Serum* which "regenerates skin's appearance to help recapture healthy-looking, youthful luminosity" at £29.99 for 40ml; and, L'Oréal's *Revitalift Laser Renew Super Serum*, which is "proven in a 6 month study to reduce the appearance of crow's feet wrinkles, boost skin density and improve bounce," selling at £24.99 for 30 ml. Prices and descriptions from Boots. http://www.boots.com, accessed March 1, 2016.

52. These estimates are taken from the NHS website. http://www.nhs.uk /conditions/non-surgical-cosmetic-treatments/pages/introduction.aspx, accessed March 15, 2016.

53. The guestimates are botox every 6 months at £200 (400 × 60 = £24 000) ((50+50+50) × 4 × 60 = £36000).

54. UK Health Center, http://www.healthcentre.org.uk/cosmetic-surgery /facelift-cost.html, accessed March 15, 2016.

55. "Stay continuously hair-free with no re-growth with Philips Lumea." http://www.boots.com, accessed March 11, 2016.

56. From liposuction and fat freezing to the old favorites of the cabbage soup and grapefruit diet. Pills go from the relatively benign herbal pills sold on the high street, to fatal pills. "Lethal' DNP Diet Pills Still on Sale Despite Crackdown, BBC Finds," http://www.bbc.co.uk/news/uk-england-37789191, accessed November 3, 2016.

57. Cited in Grogan, *Body Image*, 108.

58. Grogan reports that most "women interviewed, irrespective of their body size, reported that they would be delighted to lose half a stone (7lb)," (Ibid., 50).

59. Wolf, *The Beauty Myth*, 186.

60. Ibid., 30

61. And anyone who has struggled with their weight—which is most of us—will understand this, as losing weight is hard.

62. According to the World Health Organisation obesity has doubled since 1980 and by 2014 nearly 2 billion adults were obese. WHO, "Obesity and Overweight; Fact Sheet," http://www.who.int/mediacentre/factsheets/fs311/en/, accessed November 3, 2016.

Chapter 5. Perfectly Normal

1. Wolf, *The Beauty Myth*, 269.
2. Jones, *Skintight*, 95.

3. Ibid., 46.

4. Ibid., 46.

5. See chapter 3.

6. Hence the use of ruffs and concealing clothing and make-up from white lead to candle wax to hide pock marks.

7. For description of cankles, see chapter 000 note 17.

8. Karen Kay "Is Cosmetic Surgery the New Acceptable Face of Womanhood," *The Guardian*, June 28, 2015, http://www.theguardian.com/lifeandstyle /2015/jun/28/cosmetic-surgery-normal-acceptable-face-womanhood, accessed July 1, 2016.

9. Blum, *Flesh Wounds*, 125.

10. This is being recognized in policy making circles too: for example, the Keogh Review notes that no longer are people keeping procedures secret, but admitting and perhaps celebrating them. Department of Health, "Review of the Regulation of Cosmetic Interventions: Final Report" (Keogh Review), https://www .gov.uk/government/uploads/system/uploads/attachment_data/file/192028 /Review_of_the_Regulation_of_Cosmetic_Interventions.pdf, accessed March 10, 2014, 9.

11. Edmonds reports that in Brazil "radio shows offer breast implant prizes, and a mayor provided free cosmetic surgeries to public employees" (*Pretty Modern*, 58).

12. Royal College of Surgeons, "Professional Standards for Cosmetics Surgery," https://www.rcseng.ac.uk/library-and-publications/college-publications /docs/professional-cosmetic-surgery/, accessed November 8, 2016.

13. Jones, *Skintight*, 107.

14. For instance, even though dyed blonde became acceptable in the 1950s and 1960s, some stigma remained, for example, airlines would not employ stewardesses with blonde hair (Vantoch, *The Jet Set*, 116).

15. Dana Berkowitz, *Botox Nation: Changing the Face of America* (New York: New York University Press 2017), 45.

16. Girlguiding UK, 2010 Girls Attitude Survey (no longer available on-line); slightly lower figures of 40 percent of teen girls were cited in a survey of 2000 girls in 2015. BBC, "40% of Teens Want Plastic Surgery," http://news.bbc.co.uk /1/hi/health/4147961.stm, accessed July 26, 2017.

17. For example, the classed view that going to the gym is active and good but surgery and beauty is passive and bad. Holliday and Sanchez Taylor, "Aesthetic Surgery as False Beauty," 185

18. Such negative attitudes to fat surgery might be connected to fat shaming in general and may recede as stigma recedes.

19. Kathy Davis, *Reshaping the Female Body: The Dilemma of Cosmetic Surgery* (New York and London: Routledge, 1995).

20. Ibid., 70.

21. Ibid., 6.

22. Debra Gimlin, *Cosmetic Surgery Narratives: A Cross-Cultural Analysis of Women's Accounts* (Basingstoke: Palgrave Macmillan, 2012).

23. Ibid., 8.

24. Ibid., 71–72.

25. Ibid., 92.

26. Ibid.

27. Edmonds, *Pretty Modern*, 223.

28. Ibid., 54.

29. Ibid., 52.

30. Along with a whole host of other reasons, including that Brazil trains many of the world's plastic and cosmetic surgeons in its public hospitals and that this "right to beauty" is in a context where there are few basic rights.

31. Gimlin, *Cosmetic Surgery Narratives,* 126.

32. Ibid., 138.

33. Ibid., 149

34. Talukdar, "Thin but Not Skinny," 113.

35. Morris and Szabo, "Meanings of Thinness and Dysfunctional Eating In Black South African Females."

Chapter 6. Hidden Costs and Guilty Pleasures

1. The term "ratcheting up" is Tom Shakespeare's.

2. Elsewhere I've argued that more attention should be on group goods and group harms because ultimately these harms fall on individuals and harm them significantly as individuals, although they are often ignored because of the dominance of the individual model. Heather Widdows and Peter West Oram, "Revising Global Theories of Justice to Include Public Goods," *Journal of Global Ethics* 9, no. 2 (2013): 227–243; Heather Widdows, "Global Health Justice and the Right to Health," *Health Care Analysis*, 23, no. 4 (2015): 391–400.

3. By saying this I don't want to trivialize how hard psychological harm is to map, but rather to emphasize the extreme difficulty in measuring and evidencing communal and social harm.

4. For fuller evidence and discussion, see chapter 2, note 41.

5. I have argued this in other contexts, regard to antibiotic resistance and climate change. Widdows and West Oram, "Revising Global Theories of Justice to Include Public Goods."

6. This is a somewhat arbitrarily division of cosmetic surgery and reconstructive surgery. However, even when similar surgeries are carried out making the decision in an overwhelmingly health context compared to a beauty context, as I will go on to argue in chapter 9, is significantly different.

7. Often presented as cautionary tales to those who do not research and plan their surgery properly, as expertise is required in getting surgery right—to choose the correct procedure, surgeon, and product—as it is in mastering skills.

8. Department of Health, "Review of the Regulation of Cosmetic Interventions: Final Report (Keogh Review), https://www.gov.uk/government/uploads/system/uploads/attachment_data/file/192028/Review_of_the_Regulation_of_Cosmetic_Interventions.pdf, accessed March 10, 2014.

9. That there is little robust data is a constant theme of debate in this area, and the statement in the Keogh report is representative of frustration in this area: "There is no central collection of data on the complications following cosmetic interventions and hence no information on the type or frequency of complications." Department of Health, "Review of the Regulation of Cosmetic Interventions: Final Report (Keogh Review), https://www.gov.uk/government/publications/review-of-the-regulation-of-cosmetic-interventions, accessed September 10, 2016, 39.

10. Department of Health, "Review of the Regulation of Cosmetic Interventions: Final Report (Keogh Review), 39, https://www.gov.uk/government/publications/review-of-the-regulation-of-cosmetic-interventions, accessed September 10, 2016.

11. For example, as many as a quarter of those who have abdominoplasty (tummy tuck) may require further surgery. K. J. Stewart, D. A. Stewart, B. Coghlan, D. H. Harrison, B. M. Jones, and N. Waterhouse. "Complications of 278 Consecutive Abdominoplasties," *Journal of Plastic, Reconstructive & Aesthetic Surgery* 59, no. 11 (2006): 1152–1155.

12. Bruce Keogh for the Department of Health, "Poly Implant Prothèse (PIP) Breast Implants: Final Report of the Expert Group," https://www.gov.uk/government/uploads/system/uploads/attachment_data/file/214975/dh_134657.pdf.

13. For example, in a BAAPS 2008 review of data on over 25,000 procedures the average rate of infection and hematoma was less than 1.5 percent, and annual re-operation rate was just over 2 percent. http://baaps.org.uk/about-us/press-releases/404-surgeons-reveal-uks-largest-ever-breast-augmentation-survey, accessed September 10, 2016. A Danish study found that between1999 and 2007 16.7 percent of the women had an adverse event and 4.8 percent had required re-operation for a complication. Gitte B. Hvilsom, Lisbet R. Hölmich, Trine F. Henriksen, Loren Lipworth, Joseph K. McLaughlin, and Søren Friis, "Local Complications after Cosmetic Breast Augmentation: Results from the Danish Registry for Plastic Surgery of the Breast," *Plastic and Reconstructive Surgery* 124, no. 3 (2009): 919–925. Given that Denmark has a national registry for implants it is likely that the higher figures are more accurate.

14. In medical and policy circles "nonsurgical" tends to be used (for instance by the NHS, Keogh, and the Nuffield Council on Bioethics in its working party on cosmetic procedures). But, although "nonsurgical" is becoming more common outside these circles, it is still the case that (currently) noninvasive is often commonly used in ordinary language.

15. Department of Health, "Review of the Regulation of Cosmetic Interventions: Final Report (Keogh Review), https://www.gov.uk/government/uploads

/system/uploads/attachment_data/file/192028/Review_of_the_Regulation_of
_Cosmetic_Interventions.pdf, accessed March 10, 2014, 24.

16. Eighty-six GPs, 129 nurses, and 57 plastic surgeons collectively reported 1180 complications, most from nonsurgical treatments. Department of Health, "Review of the Regulation of Cosmetic Interventions: Final Report (Keogh Review), https://www.gov.uk/government/uploads/system/uploads/attachment _data/file/192028/Review_of_the_Regulation_of_Cosmetic_Interventions.pdf, accessed March 10, 2014, 31.

17. British Association of Aesthetic and Plastic Surgeons (BAAPS), "Press Release," http://baaps.org.uk/about-us/press-releases/1500-two-out-of-three -surgeons-seeing-botched-filler-ops, accessed November 22, 2016.

18. Bianca London, "Woman 26 Is Left with Giant Cysts and Acne Covering Her Face after Having a Reaction to a £1200 Chemical Peel to 'Freshen Her Skin," http://www.dailymail.co.uk/femail/article-3422879/Woman-26-left-giant -cysts-acne-covering-face-having-reaction-1-200-chemical-peel-freshen-skin .html#ixzz3yia6Wh00, accessed November 22, 2016; Victoria Finan and Alley Einstein, "Man, 52, Reveals how £5,000 Botched Fillers Left Him 'Ageing by the Day' after the Silicone Hardened to Form Scars and Crevices," http://www.daily mail.co.uk/femail/article-3534034/Male-yoga-teacher-botched-fillers-left-pus -filled-lump-needed-surgery.html, accessed November 23, 2016; https://www .thesun.co.uk/living/1256551/my-lip-exploded-one-student-reveals-the-trauma -of-her-botched-lip-filler-job/, accessed November 23, 2016. Laura Donnelly "More Women Suffer Botched Filler Injections," http://www.telegraph.co.uk /news/health/news/9700361/More-women-suffer-botched-filler-injections .html, accessed November 23, 2016; Kashmira Gander "Botched Dermal fillers which disfigures woman's face left her for blind in one eye" http://www.indepen dent.co.uk/life-style/health-and-families/woman-dermal-fillers-ruin-cosmetic -surgery-gone-wrong-face-ruin-carol-bryan-los-angeles-florida-a7531766.html, accessed October 2, 2017.

19. David B. Sarwer, Alison L. Infield, James L. Baker, Laurie A. Casas, Paul M. Glat, Alan H. Gold, Mark L. Jewell, Don LaRossa, Foad Nahai, and V. Leroy Young, "Two-Year Results of a Prospective, Multi-Site Investigation of Patient Satisfaction and Psychosocial Status Following Cosmetic Surgery," *Aesthetic Surgery Journal* 28, no. 3 (2008): 245–250.

20. R. M. Nicholson, S. Leinster, and E. M. Sassoon, "A Comparison of the Cosmetic and Psychological Outcome of Breast Reconstruction, Breast Conserving Surgery and Mastectomy without Reconstruction," *The Breast* 16, no. 4 (2007): 396–410.

21. Loren Lipworth and Joseph K. McLaughlin, "Excess Suicide Risk and Other External Causes of Death among Women with Cosmetic Breast Implants: A Neglected Research Priority," *Current Psychiatry Reports* 12, no. 3 (2010): 234–238.

22. Davis, *Reshaping the Female Body*, 145.

23. Rachel M. Calogero, Stacey Ed Tantleff-Dunn, and J. Thompson. *Self-Objectification in Women: Causes, Consequences, and Counteractions* (Washington, DC: American Psychological Association, 2011), 39.

24. Marika Tiggemann and Elyse Williams, "The Role of Self-Objectification In Disordered Eating, Depressed Mood, and Sexual Functioning among Women: A Comprehensive Test of Objectification Theory," *Psychology of Women Quarterly* 36, no. 1 (2012): 66–75.

25. See chapter 2, "The Rise of Body Anxiety and the Harms of Body Dissatisfaction."

26. Rachel M. Calogero, Afroditi Pina, and Robbie M. Sutton, "Cutting Words Priming Self-Objectification Increases Women's Intention to Pursue Cosmetic Surgery," *Psychology of Women Quarterly* 38, no. 2 (2014): 197–207.

27. Department of Health, "Review of the Regulation of Cosmetic Interventions: Final Report" (Keogh Review), https://www.gov.uk/government/uploads /system/uploads/attachment_data/file/192028/Review_of_the_Regulation_of _Cosmetic_Interventions.pdf, accessed March 10, 2014; Beauty Demands Briefing Paper, http://www.birmingham.ac.uk/Documents/college-artslaw/beauty demands/beauty-demands-briefing-paper-june-2016.pdf, accessed November 7, 2016.

28. Department of Health, "Review of the Regulation of Cosmetic Interventions: Final Report (Keogh Review), https://www.gov.uk/government/uploads /system/uploads/attachment_data/file/192028/Review_of_the_Regulation_of _Cosmetic_Interventions.pdf, accessed March 10, 2014.

29. General Medical Council (GMC), "Guidance for Doctors Who Offer Cosmetic Interventions," http://www.gmc-uk.org/Guidance_for_doctors_who_offer _cosmetic_interventions_210316.pdf_65254111.pdf, accessed July 20, 2016.

30. Royal College of Surgeons, "Professional Standards for Cosmetics Surgery," https://www.rcseng.ac.uk/library-and-publications/college-publications /docs/professional-cosmetic-surgery/, accessed July 20, 2016.

31. General Medical Council (GMC), "Guidance for Doctors Who Offer Cosmetic Interventions," http://www.gmc-uk.org/Guidance_for_doctors_who_offer _cosmetic_interventions_210316.pdf_65254111.pdf, accessed July 20, 2016.

32. Department of Health, "Review of the Regulation of Cosmetic Interventions: Final Report" (Keogh Review), https://www.gov.uk/government/uploads /system/uploads/attachment_data/file/192028/Review_of_the_Regulation_of _Cosmetic_Interventions.pdf, accessed March 10, 2014, 5.

33. In the AHRC-funded Network on "The Changing Requirements of Beauty," we found broad consensus with regard to what needs to be done as basic regulation. See legal section of Beauty Demands Briefing Paper, http://www .birmingham.ac.uk/Documents/college-artslaw/beautydemands/beauty-de mands-briefing-paper-june-2016.pdf, accessed November 7, 2016.

34. The expose was in two parts: Nir, Sarah Maslin, "The Price of Nice Nails," http://www.nytimes.com/2015/05/10/nyregion/at-nail-salons-in-nyc-manicurists

-are-underpaid-and-unprotected.html, accessed August 3, 2016; "Perfect Nails, Poisoned Workers," http://www.nytimes.com/2015/05/11/nyregion/nail-salon -workers-in-nyc-face-hazardous-chemicals.html?, accessed August 3, 2016.

35. Nir, "Perfect Nails, Poisoned Workers."

36. Ibid.

37. Alison M Jaggar, "Transnational Cycles of Gendered Vulnerability," in *Global Gender Justice,* ed. Alison Jaggar (Cambridge: Polity Press, 2014): 18–40.

38. In addition to harms of other service industries the beauty industry might put additional pressures on its workers, for instance, to "become living advertisements for the beauty salons and for their products and services." Jie Yang, "Nennu and Shunu: Gender, Body Politics, and the Beauty Economy in China," *Signs* 36, no. 2 (2011): 333–357, 348.

39. Sameer Kumar, "Exploratory Analysis of Global Cosmetic Industry: Major Players, Technology and Market Trends," *Technovation* 25, no. 11 (2005): 1263–1272.

40. Consultancy.uk, "Global Cosmetic Market Worth €181 Billion, L'Oreal Dominates," http://www.consultancy.uk/news/2810/cosmetics-market-worth-181 -billion-loreal-dominates, accessed November 7, 2016.

41. Jeremy Laurance, "Physician calls for an end of bikini waxing," *The Independent* (2012), http://www.independent.co.uk/life-style/health-and-families /health-news/physician-calls-for-an-end-to-bikini-waxing-8008628.html, accessed September 26, 2016.

42. 2014 Plastic Surgery Report, American Society of Plastic Surgeons, http:// www.plasticsurgery.org/Documents/news-resources/statistics/2014-statistics /plastic-surgery-statsitics-full-report.pdf, accessed August 3, 2016.

43. Department of Health, "Review of the Regulation of Cosmetic Interventions: Final Report" (Keogh Review), https://www.gov.uk/government/uploads /system/uploads/attachment_data/file/192028/Review_of_the_Regulation_of _Cosmetic_Interventions.pdf, accessed March 10, 2014, 24.

44. Jeffreys' cites an M&S survey from 2002, which the average women takes twenty-seven minutes a day to get ready, Jeffreys, *Beauty and Misogyny* 118. A recent study suggests the average women in the UK spends 40 minutes a day doing make-up. Bianca London "The Kim Kardashian Effect? Women Today Have 27 STEPS To Their Makeup Routine – Compared to Just Eight a decade ago," *Daily Mail*, November 14, 2016, http://www.dailymail.co.uk/femail/article-3919548 /The-Kim-Kardashian-effect-Women-today-27-STEPS-makeup-routine-com pared-just-eight-decade-ago.html, accessed November 1, 2016. Rhode cites figures that the average American women spends three-quarters of an hour a day on "basic grooming," *The Beauty Bias*, 33.

45. Nancy Etcoff regards "lookism is one of the most pervasive but denied of prejudices," Etcoff, *Survival of the Prettiest*, 39, and Viren Swami and Adrian Furnham argue that "lookism or appearance prejudice should rightly be seen as the latest in a long line of discriminatory acts that includes sexism and racism," Swami and Furnham, *The Psychology of Physical Attraction*, 161.

46. For instance Nancy Etcoff argues that: "beauty is a universal part of human experience, and that it provokes pleasure, rivets attention, and impels actions that help ensure the survival of our genes. Our extreme sensitivity to beauty is hard-wired, that is, governed by circuits in our brain shaped by natural selection. We love to look at smooth skin, thick shinny hair, curved waists, and symmetrical bodies because in the course of evolution the people who notices these signals and desired their possessors had more reproductive success. We are their descendants." *Survival of the Prettiest*, 24.

47. Study cited in Rhode, *The Beauty Bias*, 26.

48. Michael Oliver, *The Politics Of Disablement* (Basingstoke: MacMillian, 1990).

49. Young, *On Female Body Experience*, 71.

50. Ibid., 70.

51. Rachel M. Calogero, Sylvia Herbozo, and J. Kevin Thompson, "Complimentary Weightism: The Potential Costs of Appearance-Related Commentary For Women's Self-Objectification," *Psychology of Women Quarterly* 33, no. 1 (2009): 120–132.

52. Ibid., 129.

53. Ibid., 129.

54. Gimlin, *Body Work*, 71.

55. Ibid., 147.

56. Ann J. Cahill, "Feminist Pleasure and Feminine Beautification," *Hypatia* 18, no. 4 (2003): 42–64, 58.

57. Chambers *Sex, Culture and Justice*, 33.

58. Jeffreys, *Beauty and Misogyny*, 130.

59. Young, *On Female Body Experience*, 70.

Chapter 7. My Body, My Self

1. Heyes, *Self-Transformations*, 87.

2. Wolf, *The Beauty Myth*, 122–123.

3. Bartky, *Femininity and Domination*, 42.

4. For instance in her obituary Sam Roberts reports that "by 2002, responding to critics who said she was too doctrinaire, she acknowledged ambivalently that some women found the pursuit of physical perfection—"turning ourselves into properly feminine women"—to be a more positive experience for them than she had imagined. "It may be the case," she wrote, "that the business of trying to achieve, as near as one can, physical perfection is even more burdensome than my treatment of the topic suggests, or else there is far more pleasure at stake here than I am willing to admit to myself and to my readers.' " Obituary, "Sandra Lee Bartky, at the Vanguard of Feminist Philosophy, Dies at 81," *New York Times*, October 23, 2016, http://www.nytimes.com/2016/10/24/us/sandra-lee-bartky-dead .html?smprod=nytcore-ipad&smid=nytcore-ipad-share&_r=0, accessed November 1, 2016.

5. Jones, *Skintight,* 54.

6. As discussed in the last section of chapter 5, the narrative of transformation to attain the "real" self is less dominant than previously, increasingly replaced
by "to improve" or "to be better."

7. As Heyes rightly states "analysis must begin from the fact that the "natural
body" is an unknowable, fictive entity." *Self-Transformations,* 60.

8. For example, there are parallels between philosophical and psychological
claims about beauty and body image. Fiona MacCallum and Heather Widdows,
"Altered Images: Understanding the Influence
of Unrealistic Images and Beauty Aspirations," *Health Care Analysis,* DOI
10.1007/s10728–016–0327–1.

9. Simone de Beauvoir *The Second Sex* (London: Vintage Classics, 1997, 1949).

10. For example, Susan Heckman, reads de Beauvoir slightly differently, emphasizing De Beauvoir's focus on women not as a fixed reality but situated and
always becoming, and therefore arguably not subject to the essentialist critique
she has so often been associated with (*The Feminine Subject* (Cambridge: Polity
Press, 2014).

11. Bartky, *Femininity and Domination.*

12. Ibid., 27.

13. Ibid., 27.

14. Ibid., 36–37.

15. Ibid., 38.

16. Ibid., 28.

17. For Bartky this is wholly negative and is narcissistic, the "fashion-beauty
complex seeks to glorify the female body and to provide opportunities for narcissistic indulgence. More important than this is its *covert* aim, which is to depreci-
ate women's body and deal a blow to her narcissism." Ibid., 39–40.

18. Ibid., 40.

19. As discussed in the introduction, the topic of sexualization and the increasingly emphasis on looking sexy and hot as beauty is not addressed in detail
in *Perfect Me,* but will be the topic of future work.

20. Immanuel Kant, *The Moral Law: Groundwork of the Metaphysic of Morals,* trans. and analyzed by H. J. Paton (London: Routledge, 1997). Some have
argued that this is not a second formulation of the categorical imperative, but
rather a second injunction. However, for concerns about objectification such discussions are not relevant.

21. Lina Papadaki "What Is Objectification"?" *Journal of Moral Philosophy* 7
(2010) 16–36.

22. Immanuel Kant, *Lectures on Ethics* (Cambridge: Cambridge University
Press, 1997), 156.

23. Given this it is not surprising that Kant is a strong critic of prostitution, and
for him the only way that sex does not lead to sexual objectification is marriage.

24. Linda Papadaki argues that there are more positive readings of Kant's
view to be taken from *The Metaphysics of Morals,* which might suggest that the

harm to humanity does not extend beyond the sex act. Linda Papadaki, "What Is Objectification?" *Journal of Moral Philosophy* 7 (2010): 16–36.

25. Sally Haslanger describes this well in "On Being Objective and Being Objectified," *Resisting Reality: Social Construction and Social Critique* (Oxford and New York: Oxford University Press, 2012), 57–63.

26. Catharine A. MacKinnon, *Feminism Unmodified: Discourses on Life and Law* (Cambridge and London: Harvard University Press, 1987), 6.

27. Haslanger, *Resisting Reality*, 59.

28. Ibid., 59–60.

29. Ibid., 61.

30. It is from these arguments that Dworkin and MacKinnon are able to make arguments about the harms of prostitution and pornography for all women (rather than just for those engaged in the practices).

31. Haslanger, *Resisting Reality*, 62.

32. Ann Cahill argues that we should reject concepts of objectification and instead endorse accounts of "derivation," as the key problem in unethical sexual interactions if not mistaking persons for things but the failure to recognize the distinctiveness of the embodied other. There is much in this argument when it comes to sexual ethics; however, my claim is that objectification and the reduction of persons to things is not inaccurate in beauty, even if it may be in sex. Ann J. Cahill, *Overcoming Objectification: A Carnal Ethics* (New York and London: Routledge, 2011).

33. Gill, *Gender and the Media*, 3.

34. Andrea Dworkin, *Women Hating* (New York: E. P. Dutton, 1974).

35. Martha Nussbaum, "Objectification," *Philosophy and Public Affairs* 24, no. 4 (1995): 249–291, 251.

36. Ibid., 256.

37. Ibid., 253.

38. Ibid., 254–255.

39. Ibid., 285.

40. Indeed she states she supports Kant, MacKinnon, and Dworkin's "central insight: that the instrumental treatment of human beings as tools of the purposes of another, is always morally problematic." Ibid., 289.

41. Ibid., 271.

42. The full quote is: "His blood beat up in waves of desire. He wanted to come to her, to meet her. She was there, if he could reach her. The reality of her who was just beyond him absorbed him. Blind and destroyed, he pressed forward, nearer, nearer to receive the consummation of himself, be received within the darkness which should swallow him and yield him up to himself. If he could come really within the blazing kernel of darkness, if really he could be destroyed, burnt away till he lit with her in one consummation, that were supreme, supreme." D. H. Lawrence, *The Rainbow* cited by Nussbaum, "Objectification," 252.

43. With regard to body parts she argues that "the kind of fungability that is involved in identifying persons with parts of their bodies need not be not be

dehumanizing at all, but can coexist with an intense regard for the person's individuality, which can even be expressed in a personalizing and individualizing of the bodily organs themselves." Nussbaum, "Objectification," 276.

44. Papadaki, "What Is Objectification?" 31.

45. Dworkin, *Women Hating*, 95–117.

46. Ibid., 106.

47. Ibid., 106.

48. "Pain is an essential part of the grooming process, and that is not accidental. Plucking the eyebrows, shaving under the arms, wearing a girdle, learning to walk in high-heeled shoes, having one's nose fixed, straightening or curling one's hair—these things *hurt*." Ibid., 115.

49. Ibid., 115.

50. Bartky, *Femininity and Domination*, 27.

51. She denies any positive reading suggesting this "seems less the spontaneous expression of a healthy eroticism than a ritual of subjugation." Ibid., 27.

52. One other paper, by Kasey Morris and Jamie Goldenberg, seeks to make a distinction between beauty objectification and sexual objectification. This paper posits that beauty objectification presents women as objects, whereas sexual objectification presents women animalistically. This division is very different from the claim I am making where both forms of objectification present women as objects, but one as a sexual object to be sexually used and one as a beauty object to be looked at. While this study makes a similar claim that beauty and sexual objectification might be different, how this difference manifests is different, and a difficult division to make; as the author herself suggests as she recognizes the difficulty of mapping the divide onto the framework. Thus while I have sympathy with the intent and the need to distinguish between beauty and sex I have taken a different route. Kasey Lynn Morris and Jamie L. Goldenberg, "Women, Objects, and Animals: Differentiating between Sex- and Beauty-Based Objectification," *Revue internationale de psychologie sociale* 28, no. 1 (2015): 15–38).

53. This is to slightly caricature both views, which I do not to belittle, but to show that both views equate beauty and sexual desirability.

54. Beauty norms imply sexual norms, but sexual norms and desire are far broader; however, this is a discussion for another book.

55. Thinspiration is the use of images to inspire weight loss, while there are different levels thinspiration content pervades social media and generally promotes an objectified, sexual, and extremely thin depiction of the thin ideal." Ghaznavi and Taylor, "Bones, Body Parts, and Sex Appeal," 60.

56. Current norms, as I will return to in chapter 10 are extreme in their heteronormativity.

57. Rosalind Gill, "Postfeminist Media Culture: Elements of a Sensibility," *European Journal of Cultural Studies* 10 (2): 147–166.

58. Etcoff, *Survival of the Prettiest*, 195.

59. Chambers, *Sex, Culture and Justice*, 40.

60. Gonzo porn "depicts hard-core, body-punishing sex in which women are demeaned and debased." Dines, *Pornland*, x.

Chapter 8. I Will Be Worth It

1. In the next chapter, I will deny the dichotomy between victimized and empowered. Women are sometimes victims and sometimes empowered and usually both.

2. Gill, *Gender and the Media*, 38.

3. Ibid., 112.

4. Ibid., 112.

5. Dines, *Pornland*, xii.

6. Ibid., xiii.

7. Again the conflating of sexiness with beauty is a topic for another book.

8. Gill, *Gender and the Media*, 111.

9. Ibid., 259.

10. Angela McRobbie. *The Aftermath of Feminism: Gender, Culture and Social Change* (London: Sage Publications, 2009), 16–17.

11. Ibid., 18.

12. Tiggemann, Gardiner, and Slater, "I would rather be size 10 than have straight A's," 650.

13. As discussed in chapter 1, the fact that an ideal is unattainable does not necessarily affect adherence to the ideal, indeed unattainability is arguably a feature of any ethical ideal. The end point, what is perfect, *has* to remain beyond if we are to continue to strive for it; see my work on Iris Murdoch and ideals of perfection. Widdows, *The Moral Vision of Iris Murdoch*.

14. Bartky, *Femininity and Domination*, 26.

15. Anthony Elliott makes a similar point when he argues that "the method of coping with and reacting to, anxieties stemming from the new paradigm of self-making in our global age is quite different from previous times." *Making the Cut*, 46.

16. Blum makes a similar point about surgery, arguing that "cosmetic surgery stories are inherently future-oriented, are by their very nature about overcoming obstacles through making a change. In the case of the aging and/or defective body, and operation on the horizon becomes a hope toward which one moves with optimism. It is forward moving, expectation generating." *Flesh Wounds*, 271.

17. Heyes, *Self-Transformations*, 78.

18. For example see Laura Capon's piece on the time taken to make up for a selfie and how it changed her expectations of herself "Is the way we use makeup changing?" *Cosmopolitan*, April 2016, 134–139.

19. Heyes, *Self-Transformations*, 20.

20. Michelle M. Lazar, "The Right to be Beautiful: Postfeminist Identity and Consumer Beauty Advertising," in *New Femininities: Postfeminism, Neoliberalism and Subjectivity*, eds. Rosalind Gill and Christina Scharff (Basingstoke: Palgrave Macmillan, 2011, 2013), 37–51, 43.

21. Ana Elisa and Rosalind Gill, "Beauty Surveillance."

22. Wegenstien, *The Cosmetic Gaze*.

23. Estella Tincknell, "Scourging the Abject Body: *Ten Year Younger and Fragmented Femininity Under Neoliberalism*," in *New Femininities*: *Postfeminism, Neoliberalism and Subjectivity*, eds. Rosalind Gill and Christina Scharff (Basingstoke: Palgrave Macmillan , 2011 2013), 83–95, 86.

24. Gill, *Gender and the Media*, 188.

Chapter 9. I'm Doing it for Me

1. From some perspectives, some aspects of beauty might be wholly wrong: for instance, a justice perspective might condemn the exploitation of poor workers to service the rich; however, this is not a beauty-specific critique.

2. The third of the second of three drivers that Elliott identifies for a rise in cosmetic surgery is consumption, and he argues that "An individualist society requires an especially well-entrenched ideology that the consumer can make her life however she chooses, transforming identity in the very act of such decision-making." *Making the Cut*, 94.

3. Richard Thaler, and Cass Sunstein *Nudge: Improving Decisions about Health, Wealth, and Happiness.* (London: Penguin Books, 2008).

4. Widdows, "Rejecting the Choice Paradigm," 2013.

5. Chambers, *Sex, Culture and Justice*, 4.

6. Ibid., 17.

7. Ibid., 79.

8. Ibid.

9. Ibid., 21; My daughter will always remember this argument: at my Inaugural when she was three, I made this argument with a brightly twinkling Tinkerbell PowerPoint behind me to keep her amused.

10. Widdows, "Rejecting the Choice Paradigm," 2013.

11. As Gimlin points out action does not equate with agency. Gimlin, *Cosmetic Surgery Narratives*, 2012.

12. The Declaration of Helsinki is focused on research rather than clinical practice; however, it is usually regarded as the "gold standard" when it comes to informed consent. It states that, "each potential subject must be adequately informed of the aims, methods, sources of funding, any possible conflicts of interest, institutional affiliations of the researcher, the anticipated benefits and potential risks of the study and the discomfort it may entail, and any other relevant aspects of the study. The potential subject must be informed of the right to refuse to participate in the study or to withdraw consent to participate at any time without reprisal. Special attention should be given to the specific information needs of individual potential subjects as well as to the methods used to deliver the information. After ensuring that the potential subject has understood the information, the physician or another appropriately qualified individual must then seek the potential subject's freely-given informed consent, preferably in writing. WMA Declaration of Helsinki, http://www.wma.net/en/30publications/10policies/b3/17c.pdf, accessed June 27, 2016.

13. As discussed in chapter 6 there have been myriad calls for improvement from reviews and professional bodies, and there is some consensus on where action needs to be taken.

14. Perry points out that this is not always the case: for instance, often labels and warnings are missing on skin-whitening creams in Africa. As such there is nothing approaching informed consent, and "many consumers do not know how to safely use the product or when to discontinue use—that they must protect their skin from the sun while using the product, that if the product is old, it may be stronger than that which is medically safe, that the products with mercury contains poison." Perry, "Buying White Beauty," 600.

15. If this is the case proposals for mandatory counseling at the point of consent are not likely to succeed in getting potential patients to consider alternatives to surgery.

16. Although Jones argues that even if the viewer sees the transformation, it is done away from friends and family and therefore "despite the heavy documentation of the painful procedures, before/after remains secure as a key structuring trope." Jones, *Skintight*, 52.

17. Parallel arguments are made for consent that is never really informed in health—especially when the treatment is the only hope—and here too I think it is hard to think that a fully informed choice is being made (there is really no choice). But what is being weighed and risked, is very different. In the health context the gains are real physical improved quality and perhaps quantity of life.

18. MYA group has clinics in Liverpool, Manchester, Nottingham, Birmingham, Cardiff, London, Leeds, Preston, Newcastle, Cardiff, Chelmsford and Bristol. It has MYA, Make yourself amazing, and the tab which you click on to view what procedures are offered is "MYA forever" (http://www.mya.co.uk/about-us/, accessed 27.06.2016). MYA offers procedures including breast enlargement and uplift, liposuction and "designer vagina," and to access patient stories you click on an image of the patient (all without exception young and "perfect") to read their story.

19. Although there is admittedly some blurring as (from anecdotal reports) surgeons take fat from other places to pad out the breast and, suggest the beauty benefits can be regarded as a silver lining.

20. Ruth Holliday's work suggests that those seeking surgery recognize that testimonials are selective and designed to draw them in and effectively ads, and instead tend to look for stories of those who are ahead of them on the journey. They join on-line groups of those considering surgery (which they may monitor for a number of years, before they engage), and they closely follow progress of those who make the decision before them. Yet while clearly these surgery patients are not unprepared and have given serious attention to the risks, it is still the case that the end point is one they have not yet experienced, and making decisions in this context is not the same as making decisions in a medical context. "Sun, Sea, Sand and Silicone: Mapping Cosmetic Surgery Tourism," ESRC Final Report, http://1nlxkd2jlu702vcxsrlpe3h6.wpengine.netdna-cdn.com/files/2012/11/Sun-Sea-Final-Report.pdf.

21. Department of Health, "Review of the Regulation of Cosmetic Interventions: Final Report" (Keogh Review), https://www.gov.uk/government/uploads/system/uploads/attachment_data/file/192028/Review_of_the_Regulation_of_Cosmetic_Interventions.pdf, accessed March 10, 2014, 35.

22. Cosmetic surgery on Down's Syndrome children is an area of controversy.

23. For instance Keogh states that "people considering cosmetic surgery at times of considerable change in their lives, such as separation or bereavement, are frequently more vulnerable than others." Department of Health, "Review of the Regulation of Cosmetic Interventions: Final Report" (Keogh Review), https://www.gov.uk/government/uploads/system/uploads/attachment_data/file/192028/Review_of_the_Regulation_of_Cosmetic_Interventions.pdf, accessed March 10, 2014, 36.

24. Blum, *Flesh Wounds*.

25. Cynthia Bulik, *Midlife Eating Disorders* (New York: Walker and Company, 2013).

26. Some feminist interviewees reported that they would shave their legs if going to a public event (like a wedding), not because they wanted to (in fact they resented it), but just because it was not easier than to comply with the norm. Presented by Joyce Heckman, "This Is What a Feminist Looks Like: Analysis of Feminist Appearance Negotiations" AHRC network workshop, March, University of Warwick, 2015.

27. Wendy Rodewald-Sulz, "The History of Eyebrows," http://www.beautyblitz.com/history-eyebrows#slide-5, accessed November 1, 2016.

28. As discussed in the introduction, there is less discussion of subcultures and resistance than originally planned, and this is an area where more work is needed.

29. Although even here choice is limited, we cannot simply chose to enter a religious community or academic community; these are often unchosen and the pretence that women can just choose to reject beauty is a particularly heinous one; it is often made by women in privileged positions who do not realize the extent to which it is only their privilege which allows such rejection, as discussed in chapter 2.

30. Heather Widdows, *The Connected Self: The Ethics and Governance of the Genetic Individual* (Cambridge: Cambridge University Press, 2013).

31. Françoise Baylis, "Transnational Commercial Contract Pregnancy in India," *Family-Making: Contemporary Ethical Challenges* (2014): 265–86.

32. Importantly, desperate choice scenarios recognize that an individual can benefit and thus the "desperate choice" can be the "best" choice, but it is not a choice that would be desired if there were other options.

33. The view that more choice equates with more autonomy is a fairly standard liberal view, although one which is critiqued. Thomas Hurka puts this view well when he argues that removing even the worst options, because they are intrinsically bad, does reduce autonomy. He states that to remove bad choices is "limited coercion—forbidding the worst rather than requiring the best—still

violates classical liberalism, and still (somewhat) reduces autonomy." Thomas Hurka, "Why Value Autonomy?" *Social Theory and Practice* 13, no. 3 (1987): 361–382, 363.

34. Widdows, "Rejecting the Choice Paradigm," 2013.

35. For instance I've argued for regulation to prevent some forms of egg sale and paid surrogacy on the grounds that individuals should be protected from exploitative choice precisely because to those in desperate choice scenarios without other options such choices are the best. I argue to allow someone to choose to engage in harmful (exploitative, degrading, or humiliating) practices because they have no other choices extends the injustices that are permitted and so impacts upon what human beings can be and do.

36. In the poorest slum dwellings in South Africa skin-lightening cream is often found (and in preference to food and even antiretrovirals).

37. This should not be read as a suggestion that richer women are at a disadvantage in any general sense, and this claim needs unpacking in context of global justice arguments more broadly.

38. Cressida Heyes also makes this argument, that "ideological captivity in the form of false consciousness cannot explain all of the power of weight-loss dieting as a cultural practice." *Self-Transformations,* 71.

39. Eyerman tracks the development of the concept, from its beginnings in Marx and Engels where it effectively means, "a distorted and limited form of experience in society that could be applied to all social groups and classes" to its definition by the Frankfurt school. Ron Eyerman, "False Consciousness and Ideology in Marxist Theory," *Acta Sociologica* 24 (1981): 43–56, 43.

40. Ibid., 55.

41. Dworkin, *Woman Hating,* 17.

42. Ibid., 21

43. Bartky, *Femininity and Domination,* 2.

44. Ibid., 4.

45. "In sum, feminist consciousness is the consciousness of being radically alienated from her world and often divided against herself, a being who sees herself as victim and whose victimization determines her being-in-the-world resistance, wariness, and suspicion. Raw and exposed much of the time, she suffers from both ethical and ontological shock." Ibid., 21.

46. Chambers *Sex, Culture and Justice,* 193. It is worth noting for Chambers that the harms involved in breast implants, and presumably other surgery carried out for no other reason than complying with a social norm, "are enough at least to make us consider intervention. Ibid., 196.

47. Heyes, *Self-Transformations,* 71.

48. Peiss, *Hope in a Jar,* 269.

49. Holliday and Sanchez Taylor, "Aesthetic Surgery as False Beauty," 192.

50. Holliday and Sanchez Taylor, "Aesthetic Surgery as False Beauty," 184; Fiona Macrae and James Tozer, "Government Adviser Says 50,000 Women SHOULD Have Breast Implants Removed," *Daily Mail,* January 2, 2012.

51. Heyes recognizes that feminist rhetoric has been enabling, but in this form is silencing. *Self-Transformations*, 13.

52. Blum, *Flesh Wounds*, 63.

53. Bartky, *Femininity and Domination*, 78.

54. Following Heyes, "being *held captive* by a picture entails an inability to change one's way of thinking and is thus a form of unfreedom." *Self-Transformations*, 71.

55. Martha Nussbaum, *Women and Human Development: The Capabilities Approach* (Cambridge: University of Cambridge Press, 2000).

56. Ibid. throughout.

57. For instance, Monique Deveaux notes, the "hint of the possibility of false consciousness (wherein the women fail to recognize their own rational self-interest)," ("Political Morality and Culture: What difference does difference make?," *Social Theory and Practice* 28, no. 3 (2002): 503–518, 516; likewise Jaggar describes "adaptive preferences or learned desires for things that are harmful, a phenomenon called "false consciousness" by Western feminists influenced by the Marxist critique of ideology." Jaggar, "Saving Amina," 58.

58. Ibid., 58.

59. Ibid., 69.

60. Jaggar argues that a focus on "illiberal culture" distorts our understanding of women elsewhere, our judgments about and our ability to recognize and challenge the most significant injustices that impact upon poor women. While recognizing local traditions do contribute to injustice, she foregrounds neoliberal globalization, connections between cultures, and critiques the underlying assumptions of such positions; that West is best! Ibid.

61. Natalie Stoljar, "Feminist Perspectives on Autonomy," *The Stanford Encyclopaedia of Philosophy* (Fall 2015 Edition), Edward N. Zalta (ed.), http://plato .stanford.edu/archives/fall2015/entries/feminism-autonomy.

62. Ibid.

63. Stoljar describes the student's situation in a way that adaptive preference looks like false consciousness; "She treats norms about beauty and fashion as important and perhaps overriding reasons for action because she has internalized the idea that appearance is a criterion of self-worth. Due to the effects of the oppressive ideology, the agent treats false stereotypes as 'natural,' and formulates desires and plans based on the stereotype." Ibid.

64. Serene Khader, *Adaptive Preferences and Women's Empowerment* (Oxford and New York: Oxford University Press, 2011), 130ff.

65. Ibid., 14.

66. Ibid., 17.

67. Ibid., 17.

68. Ibid., 18.

69. Ibid., 101.

70. Ibid., 101.

71. Ibid., 105.

72. Widdows, "Rejecting the Choice Paradigm," 2013.

73. Heather Widdows and Herjeet Marway, eds. *Women and Violence: The Agency of Victims and Perpetrators*. (Basingstoke: Palgrave MacMillan, 2015).

74. McRobbie, *The Aftermath of Feminism*, 49.

75. Heather Widdows, "Conceptualising the Self in the Genetic Era," *Health Care Analysis* 15, no. 1 (2007): 5–12.

76. Widdows, "Rejecting the Choice Paradigm," 2013.

77. Graeme Laurie, *Genetic Privacy : A Challenge to Medico-legal Norms* (Cambridge: Cambridge University Press, 2002), 198.

78. Ibid., 195.

79. For instance, one of Gimlin's interviewees, Bonnie, was worried about the politics of cosmetic intervention. *Body Work*, 2002.

80. Fiona Macrae and James Tozer, "Government Adviser Says 50,000 Women SHOULD Have Breast Implants Removed," *Daily Mail*, January 2, 2012, http://www.dailymail.co.uk/health/article-2081089/PIP-breast-implants-Government-adviser-says-50k-women-SHOULD-removed.html, accessed November 22, 2016.

Chapter 10. More Pain, Who Gains?

1. For example, SPANX, which are just updated foundation garments, were an overnight success. Clare O'Connor "Undercover Billionaire: Sara Blakely joins the rich list thanks to Spanx," *Forbes*, March 7, 2012, http://www.forbes.com/sites/clareoconnor/2012/03/07/undercover-billionaire-sara-blakely-joins-the-rich-list-thanks-to-spanx/#275a90ac427e, accessed 11 November 2016.

2. Young, discusses the physical limits in her classic essay, "Throwing Like a Girl" (chapter 2 of *On Female Body Experience*, 27–45).

3. Young, *On Female Body Experience*, 68–69.

4. Jeffreys, *Beauty and Misogyny*, 32.

5. Bartky, *Femininity and Domination*, 71.

6. Ibid., 73.

7. The first shift being paid work, the second housework, and the third body work. Studies suggest that largely the second shift is still a women's shift, but the third shift is not exclusively female. Clare Lyonette and Rosemary Crompton, "Sharing the Load? Partners' Relative Earnings and the Division of Domestic Labour," *Work, Employment & Society* 29, no. 1(2014): 23–40.

8. In a recent chapter, I considered transactional and systematic accounts of exploitation, drawing on arguments from this book. However, they are employed in a different theoretical framework to make different claims. While the chapter also concludes that gender exploitation fails, it does so on more formal grounds and with alternative argumentation. Heather Widdows, "Exploitation and the Global Demands of Beauty," in *Exploitation: From Practice to Theory*, eds. Monique Deveaux and Vida Panitch Rowman & Littlefield International: London (forthcoming).

9. It has not always been the case that beauty ideals have fallen on women more than men. Perhaps most obviously classical culture celebrated the male

body rather than the female body. Further, there are many instances where it was the men—at least as much as the women—that adorned and beautified themselves, with jewelry, fine clothes and make-up. However, such beautifying was limited to the privileged classes and in a time when wealth was scarcer and displayed on male bodies as well as female bodies.

10. See National Eating disorder statistics: https://www.nationaleatingdis orders.org/statistics-males-and-eating-disorders, accessed October 25, 2016; 33 percent figure is also repeated in other studies. Scott Griffiths, Stuart B. Murray, and Stephen Touyz, "Extending the Masculinity Hypothesis: An Investigation of Gender Role Conformity, Body Dissatisfaction, and Disordered Eating in Young Heterosexual Men," *Psychology of Men & Masculinity* 16, no. 1 (2015): 108–113.

11. Linda Papadopoulous, "Sexualisation of Young People: Review," http:// webarchive.nationalarchives.gov.uk/+/http:/www.homeoffice.gov.uk/documents /sexualisation-of-young-people.pdf, accessed November 5, 2016.

12. The Children's Society, "The Good Childhood Report 2016: Summary," http://www.childrenssociety.org.uk/sites/default/files/pcr090_mainreport _web.pdf, accessed November 5, 2016.

13. The trend for large muscled bodies may also contribute to the trend to nakedness, as only when naked can such bodies be clearly distinguished from fat bodies.

14. Peta Stapleton, Timothy McIntyre, and Amy Bannatyne, "Body Image Avoidance, Body Dissatisfaction, and Eating Pathology: Is There a Difference Between Male Gym Users and Non–Gym Users?" *American Journal of Men's Health* 10, no. 2 (2014): 100–109.

15. Grogan, *Body Image*, 30.

16. "Body Image: The Third Edition" Beauty Demands Blog Post. http:// beautydemands.blogspot.co.uk/2016/10/body-image-third-edition.html, accessed October 25, 2016.

17. For example, Samantha Thomas, Timothy Olds, Simone Pettigrew, Melanie Randle, and Sophie Lewis found that both boys and girls regarded thinness as desirable and contributing to happiness, and that boys felt self-conscious if they were too skinny, "Don't Eat That, You'll Get Fat!" Exploring How Parents and Children Conceptualise and Frame Messages about the Causes and Consequences of Obesity," *Social Science & Medicine* 119 (2014): 114–122.

18. Griffiths, Murray and Touyz, "Extending the Masculinity Hypothesis," 2015.

19. British Association of Aesthetic and Plastic Surgeons (BAAPS), "Press Release," http://baaps.org.uk/about-us/audit/2268-super-cuts-daddy-makeovers -and-celeb-confessions-cosmetic-surgery-procedures-soar-in-britain, accessed 1 November 5, 2016.

20. Wolf, *The Beauty Myth*, 242.

21. Edmonds reports that 30 percent of operations are now on men, with common anxieties being losing weight, gaining muscle, hair loss, and virility *Pretty Modern*, 321.

22. Herzig, *Plucked*, 10.

23. Linda Smolak and Sarah K. Murnen, "Gender, Self-Objectification and Pubic Hair Removal," *Sex Roles* 65, no. 7–8 (2011): 506–517.

24. The "sack, back and crack" is one of the fastest growing treatments, ("30–35 Percent Real Men Get Waxed," *The Economist*, 2003, http://www.economist.com.ezproxyd.bham.ac.uk/node/1900122, accessed 27 July 2016.

25. Deepmala Baghel and Parthasarathy, "Pursuing Body Beautiful: Men's Beauty Aesthetics within the Space of the Beauty Parlor," 2013, http://www.inter-disciplinary.net/critical-issues/wp-content/uploads/2013/07/baghelbeapaper.pdf, accessed 27 July 2016.

26. P. Elsner records the dramatic grown in the market: "Overview and Trends in Male Grooming," *British Journal of Dermatology* 166, no. s1 (2012): 2–5.; some studies suggest a 300 percent rise in the male grooming market, http://www.independent.co.uk/life-style/fashion/features/mens-grooming-is-now-a-multi-billion-pound-worldwide-industry-a6813196.html, accessed 16 November.

27. The Statistics Portal, "Size of the Global Male Grooming Market from 2012 to 2023," https://www.statista.com/statistics/287643/global-male-grooming-market-size/, accessed 16 November.

28. Janice Miller, "Making Up Is Masculine: The Increasing Cultural Connections between Masculinity and Make-Up," *Critical Studies in Men's Fashion* 1, no.3 (2014): 241–253; Matthew Hall, *Metrosexual Masculinities* (Basingstoke: Palgrave Macmillan, 2014).

29. Gill, *Gender and the Media,* 32.

30. Brian McNair, *Striptease Culture: Sex, Media and the Democratization of Desire (*London and New York: Routledge, 2002).

31. Cahill argues from a different perspective that objectification of men and women is never the same, neither as degrading nor as harmful. *Overcoming Objectification,* 2011.

32. Wolf, *The Beauty Myth,* 139.

33. Martin Daubney "Men Are Now Objectified More than Women," *The Telegraph* February 9, 2015, http://www.telegraph.co.uk/men/thinking-man/11395576/Men-are-now-objectified-more-than-women.html, accessed June 27, 2016; "Is It Really Ever OK to Objectify Men?" *Marie Claire*, August 2016, http://www.marieclaire.co.uk/uncategorised/objectifying-men-why-saying-a-man-is-hot-is-ok-9702, accessed June 27, 2016.

34. She introduces Linford Christie as an example of the reduction of a black male to his genitals, which she argues is continuous with the treatment of black men under slavery and colonialism. *Black Women's Bodies and the Nation,* 10.

35. It may be that tallness is a global feature, perhaps like youth. It is globally desired, and tall men receive both material and relational goods, as noted in chapter 1, but tallness alone does not make a beauty ideal, but it may be important when it comes to discrimination against short men.

36. In some parts of the gay community, traditionally appearance has mattered more, as has an athletic and toned body type, and there is evidence that the more involved with the gay community men are the more they suffer from body dissatisfaction. Grogan, *Body Image,* 180.

37. Though Trump has perhaps had more appearance comments then most with particular attention to his hair, and speculation, about a possible hair transplant. And Clinton did mock him as an "id with hair." http://www.breitbart.com/big-government/2016/03/31/hillary-clinton-mocks-trump-id-hair-super-lgbt-new-york-fundraiser/, accessed 10 November 2016.

38. Judith Burns, "Body Image 'a Problem for Boys,' Says Advertising Think Tank," *BBC*, http://www.bbc.co.uk/news/education-37010205, accessed November 5, 2016.

39. Lee Kynaston, "Hairy Back? Here's How to Get Rid of It," *Men's Health*, February 2014, http://www.menshealth.co.uk/style/grooming/How-do-I-get-rid-of-back-hair, accessed June 27, 2016.

40. Holliday and Sanchez Taylor, "Aesthetic Surgery as False Beauty," 189.

41. Ibid., 189.

42. Jones, *Skintight*, 29.

43. Heyes, *Self-Transformations*, 97.

44. McRobbie, *The Aftermath of Feminism*, 65–66.

45. Ibid., 60.

46. For instance, Jeffreys argues that, "many men prefer women to look prepubescent and thus hairless. Men are trained by porn to see hairlessness in "women as natural" and to find the hairiness of their girlfriends distasteful or less than exciting." *Beauty and Misogyny*, 79.

47. Cited in Jeffreys, *Beauty and Misogyny*, 3.

48. Ibid., 45.

49. Ibid., 44.

50. MacRobbie, *The Aftermath of Feminism*, 88–89.

51. Gill, *Gender and the Media*, 91.

52. Ibid., 92.

53. Clare Chambers *Sex, Culture and Justice*, 4.

54. Gill in conversation with Meg Barker. Meg Barker and Rosalind Gill, "Sexual Subjectification and Bitchy Jones's Diary," *Psychology & Sexuality* 3, no. 1 (2012): 26–40, 33.

55. Holliday and Sanchez Taylor, "Aesthetic Surgery as False Beauty," 192.

56. Bartky, *Femininity and Domination*, 80.

57. Chambers, *Sex Culture and Justice*, 29.

58. Ibid., 211.

59. Jeffreys, *Beauty and Misogyny*, 30.

Conclusion. Beauty without the Beast

1. Tiggemann, Gardiner and Slater, "I would rather be a size 10 than have straight A's," 651.

2. Thomas et al., "Don't Eat That, You'll Get Fat!" 119.

3. Dhillon, "But I Am Fat," 547.

4. Edmonds, *"Pretty Modern,"* 20.

5. MYA is discussed in chapter 000 note 000 and Meg Matthew's threadlift in chapter 000 note 000.

6. Fiona MacCallum and Heather Widdows, "Altered Images: Understanding the Influence of Unrealistic Images and Beauty Aspirations," *Health Care Analysis* (2016) doi:10.1007/s10728-016-0327-1.

7. We have to escape the (false) divide between "bad old feminists" who are seen as victim creating and blaming and "new feminists" who wholly embrace choice. Bordo, *Twilight Zones*, 36.

8. Tiggemann et al. report that in discussion girls found that hearing the stories of others helped them revaluate their bodies, ("I would rather be size 10 than have straight A's"). This is not a surprising conclusion to anyone who has attempted to find women-friendly and women-loving environments, and such sisterhood approaches are perhaps the best part of the mixed legacy of second wave feminism.

9. For example, Argentina has laws about model size and the clothing sizes that shops need to stock. Gordon B. Forbes, Jaehee Jung, Juan Diego Vaamonde, Alicia Omar, Laura Paris, and Nilton Soares Formiga, "Body Dissatisfaction and Disordered Eating in Three Cultures: Argentina, Brazil, and the US," *Sex Roles* 66, no. 9–10 (2012): 677–694. In addition, and despite some claims by the industry to the contrary, it seems there is public support for more diversity in media imagery. Phillippa C. Diedrichs, Christina Lee, and Marguerite Kelly, "Seeing the Beauty in Everyday People: A Qualitative Study of Young Australians' Opinions on Body Image, the Mass Media and Models," *Body Image* 8, no. 3 (2011): 259–266; Phillippa C. Diedrichs, and Christina Lee, "Waif Goodbye! Average-Size Female Models Promote Positive Body Image and Appeal to Consumers," *Psychology and Health* 26, no. 10 (2011): 1273–1291.

10. Recall the teenager who *imagined* what it was to be a successful business women; see footnote 000.

11. Zali Yager, Phillippa C. Diedrichs, Lina A. Ricciardelli, and Emma Halliwell, "What Works in Secondary Schools? A Systematic Review of Classroom-Based Body Image Programs," *Body Image* 10, no. 3 (2013): 271–281.

12. Etcoff, *Survival of the Prettiest*, 68.

13. Indeed often lookism is used in sexist ways. While I have argued for less gendered exploitation, this should not be read as a claim that sexism is no longer a problem. It is increasingly, as Gill and McCrobbie's work is trailblazing in analyzing this.

BIBLIOGRAPHY

Abraczinskas, Michelle, Brian Fisak, and Rachel D. Barnes. "The Relation between Parental Influence, Body Image, and Eating Behaviors in a Nonclinical Female Sample." *Body Image* 9, no. 1 (2012): 93–100.

Balogun, Oluwakemi M. "Cultural and Cosmopolitan Idealized Femininity and Embodied Nationalism in Nigerian Beauty Pageants." *Gender & Society* 26, no. 3 (2012): 357–381.

Banner, Lois. *Marilyn: The Passion and the Paradox*. London and New York: Bloomsbury, 2012.

Barthel, Diane. *Putting on Appearances: Gender and Advertising*. Philadelphia: Temple University Press, 1989.

Bartky, Sandra Lee. *Femininity and Domination: Studies in the Phenomenology of Oppression*. New York and London: Routledge, 1990.

Baylis, Françoise. "Transnational Commercial Contract Pregnancy in India." *Family-Making: Contemporary Ethical Challenges* (2014): 265–286.

Berkowitz, Dana. *Botox Nation: Changing the Face of America*. New York: New York University Press, 2017.

Bjørn, Hofmann. "Obesity as a Socially Defined Disease: Philosophical Considerations and Implications for Policy and Care." *Health Care Analysis* 24, no. 1 (2016): 86–100.

Blum, Virginia L. *Flesh Wounds: The Culture of Cosmetic Surgery*. Berkeley and London: University of California Press, 2003.

Boniol, Mathiue, Philippe Autier, Peter Boyle, and Sara Gandini. "Cutaneous Melanoma Attributable to Sunbed Use: Systematic Review and Meta-Analysis." *British Medical Journal* 345, no. e4757 (2005). doi 10.1136/bmj.e4757.

Bordo, Susan. *Twilight Zones: The Hidden Life of Cultural Images from Plato to O.J.*. Berkeley, Los Angeles, and London: University of California Press, 1997.

Bordo, Susan. *Unbearable Weight: Feminism, Western Culture and the Body*. Berkeley, Los Angeles, and London: University of California Press, 1993, 2003.

Brand, Peggy. *Beauty Matters*. Bloomington and Indianapolis: Indiana University Press, 2000.

Bromberger, Christian. "Hair: From the West to the Middle East through the Mediterranean (the 2007 AFS Mediterranean Studies Section Address)." *Journal of American Folklore* 121, no. 482 (2008): 379–399.

Brooks, Katie, Daniel Brooks, Zeina Dajani, Susan M. Swetter, Erin Powers, Sherry Pagoto and Alan C. Geller "Use of Artificial Tanning Products among Young Adults." *Journal of the American Academy of Dermatology* 54, no. 6 (2006): 1060–1066.

Bulik, Cynthia. *Midlife Eating Disorders*, New York: Walker and Company, 2013.

Burkley, Melissa, Edward Burkley, S. Paul Stermer, Angela Andrade, Angela C. Bell, and Jessica Curtis. "The Ugly Duckling Effect: Examining Fixed versus Malleable Beliefs about Beauty." *Social Cognition* 32, no. 5 (2014): 466–483.

Cahill, Ann J. "Feminist Pleasure and Feminine Beautification." *Hypatia* 18, no. 4 (2003): 42–64.

Cahill, Ann J. *Overcoming Objectification: A Carnal Ethics*. New York and London: Routledge, 2011.

Calogero, Rachel M., Sylvia Herbozo, and J. Kevin Thompson. "Complimentary Weightism: The Potential Costs of Appearance-Related Commentary for Women's Self-Objectification." *Psychology of Women Quarterly* 33, no. 1 (2009): 120–132.

Calogero, Rachel M., Afroditi Pina, and Robbie M. Sutton. "Cutting Words Priming Self-Objectification Increases Women's Intention to Pursue Cosmetic Surgery." *Psychology of Women Quarterly* 38, no. 2 (2014): 197–207.

Calogero, Rachel M., Stacey Tantleff-Dunn, and J. Thompson. *Self-Objectification in Women: Causes, Consequences, and Counteractions*. Washington, DC: American Psychological Association, 2011.

Chambers, Clare. *Sex, Culture and Justice: The Limits of Choice*. University Park: Pennsylvania State University Press, 2008.

Charles, Christopher A.D. "Skin Bleaching, Self-Hate, and Black Identity in Jamaica." *Journal of Black Studies* 33, no. 6 (2003): 711–728.

Coetzee, Vinet, Stella J. Faerber, Jaco M. Greeff, Carmen E. Lefevre, Daniel E. Re, and David I. Perrett. "African Perceptions of Female Attractiveness." *PloS one* 7, no. 10 (2012): e48116.

Cohen, Rachel, and Alex Blaszczynski. "Comparative Effects of Facebook and Conventional Media on Body Image Dissatisfaction." *Journal of Eating Disorders* 3, no. 23 (2015): 1–11.

Davis, Kathy. *Dubious Equalities and Embodied Differences*. New York and Oxford: Rowman and Littlefield, 2003.

Davis, Kathy. *Reshaping the Female Body: The Dilemma of Cosmetic Surgery*. New York and London: Routledge, 1995.

de Beauvoir, Simone. *The Second Sex*. London: Vintage Classics, 1997 (1949).

Del Giudice, Pascal, and Pinier Yves. "The Widespread Use of Skin Lightening Creams in Senegal: A Persistent Public Health Problem in West Africa." *International Journal of Dermatology* 41, no. 2 (2002): 69–72.

Dellinger, Kirsten, and Christine L. Williams. "Makeup at Work: Negotiating Appearance Rules in the Workplace." *Gender and Society* (1997): 151–177.

DeMaria, Andrea L., and Abbey B. Berenson. "Prevalence and Correlates of Pubic Hair Grooming among Low-Income Hispanic, Black, and White Women." *Body Image* 10, no. 2 (2013): 226–231.

Deveaux, Monique. "Political Morality and Culture: What Difference Does Difference Make?" *Social Theory and Practice* 28, no. 3 (2002): 503–518.

Dhillon Megha, and Priti Dhawan. "But I Am Fat": The Experiences of Weight Dissatisfaction in Indian Adolescent Girls and Young Women." *Women's Studies International Forum* 34, no. 6 (2011) 539–549.

Diedrichs, Phillippa C., and Christina Lee. "Waif goodbye! Average-size Female Models Promote Positive Body Image and Appeal to Consumers." *Psychology and Health* 26, no. 10 (2011): 1273–1291.

Diedrichs, Phillippa C. Christina Lee, and Marguerite Kelly. "Seeing the Beauty in Everyday People: A Qualitative Study of Young Australians' Opinions on Body Image, The Mass Media and Models." *Body Image* 8, no. 3 (2011): 259–266.

Dines, Gail. *Pornland: How Porn Has Hijacked Our Sexuality*. Boston: Beacon Press, 2010.

Dohnt, Hayley K., and Marika Tiggemann. "Peer Influences on Body Dissatisfaction and Dieting Awareness in Young Girls." *British Journal of Developmental Psychology* 23, no. 1 (2005): 103–116.

Dworkin, Andrea. *Women Hating*. New York: E. P. Dutton, 1974.

Dyhouse, Carol. *Glamour: Women, History and Feminism*. London and New York: Zed Books, 2011.

Eagly, Alice H., Richard D. Ashmore, Mona G. Makhijani, and Laura C. Longo. "What Is Beautiful Is Good, But.....: A Meta-Analytic Review of Research on the Physical Attractiveness Stereotype." *Psychological Bulletin* 110, no 1 (1991): 109–128.

Eddy, Kamryn T., Moira Hennessey, and Heather Thompson-Brenner. "Eating Pathology in East African Women: the Role of Media Exposure and Globalization." *Journal of Nervous and Mental Disease* 195, no. 3 (2007): 196–202.

Edgar, Andrew. "The Athletic Body." *Health Care Analysis* (2016): 1–15 (on-line first DOI 10.1007/s10728–016–0332–4).

Edmonds, Alexander. *Pretty Modern: Beauty, Sex, and Plastic Surgery in Brazil*. Durham, NC, and London: Duke University Press, 2010.

Elisa, Ana, and Rosalind Gill. "Beauty Surveillance: The Digital Self-Monitoring Cultures of Neoliberalism (SIDigiplay)." *European Journal of Cultural Studies* (forthcoming).

Elliott, Anthony. *Making the Cut: How Cosmetic Surgery Is Transforming Our Lives*. London: Reaktion Books, 2008.

Elsner, P. "Overview and Trends in Male Grooming." *British Journal of Dermatology* 166, no. 1 (2012): 2–5. DOI 10.1111/j.1365–2133.2011.10782.x.

Elwood, J. Mark, and Janet Jopson. "Melanoma and Sun Exposure: An Overview of Published Studies." *International Journal of Cancer* 73, no. 2 (1997): 198–203.

Etcoff, Nancy. *Survival of the Prettiest*. New York: Anchor Books, 1999.

Eyerman, Ron. "False Consciousness and Ideology in Marxist Theory." *Acta Sociologica* 24 (1981): 43–56.

Fahs, Breanne. "Perilous Patches and Pitstaches: Imagined Versus Lived Experiences of Women's Body Hair Growth." *Psychology of Women Quarterly* 38, no. 2, (2014): 167–180.

Fardouly, Jasmine, Phillippa C. Diedrichs, Lenny R. Vartanian, and Emma Halliwell. "Social Comparisons on Social Media: The Impact of Facebook on Young Women's Body Image Concerns and Mood." *Body Image* 13 (2015): 38–45.

Fardouly, Jasmine, and Lenny R. Vartanian. "Changes in Weight Bias Following Weight Loss: The Impact of Weight-Loss Method." *International Journal of Obesity* 36, no. 2 (2012): 314–319.

Faria, Caroline. "Styling the Nation: Fear and Desire in the South Sudanese Beauty Trade." *Transactions of the Institute of British Geographers* 39, no. 2 (2014): 318–330.

Ferguson, Christopher J. "In the Eye of the Beholder: Thin-Ideal Media Affects Some, but Not Most, Viewers in a Meta-Analytic Review of Body Dissatisfaction in Women and Men." *Psychology of Popular Media Culture* 2, no. 1 (2013): 20–37.

Ferguson, Christopher J., Mónica E. Muñoz, Adolfo Garza, and Mariza Galindo. "Concurrent and Prospective Analyses of Peer, Television and Social Media Influences on Body Dissatisfaction, Eating Disorder Symptoms and Life Satisfaction in Adolescent Girls." *Journal of Youth and Adolescence* 43, no. 1 (2014): 1–14.

Festinger, L. "A Theory of Social Comparison Processes." *Human Relations* 7 (1954): 117–140.

Fiske, Lauren, Elizabeth A. Fallon, Bryan Blissmer, and Colleen A. Redding. "Prevalence of Body Dissatisfaction among United States Adults: Review and Recommendations for Future Research." *Eating Behaviors* 15, no. 3 (2014): 357–365.

Forbes, Gordon B., Jaehee Jung, Juan Diego Vaamonde, Alicia Omar, Laura Paris, and Nilton Soares Formiga. "Body Dissatisfaction and Disordered Eating in Three Cultures: Argentina, Brazil, and the US." *Sex Roles* 66, no. 9–10 (2012): 677–694.

Foucault, Michael. *Discipline and Punish: The Birth of the Prison*. Harmondsworth: Penguin, 1990.

Frevert, Tonya K., and Lisa Slattery Walker. "Physical Attractiveness and Social Status." *Sociology Compass* 8, no. 3 (2014): 313–323.

Frith, Katharine, Ping Shaw, and Hong Cheng. "The Construction of Beauty: A Cross-Cultural Analysis of Women's Magazine Advertising." *Journal of Communication* 55, no. 1 (2005): 56–70.

Ghaznavi, Jannath, and Laramie D. Taylor. "Bones, Body Parts, and Sex Appeal: An Analysis of #thinspiration Images on Popular Social Media." *Body Image* 14 (2015): 54–61.

Gill, Rosalind. *Gender and the Media*. Cambridge: Polity Press, 2007.

Gill, Rosalind. "Postfeminist Media Culture: Elements of a Sensibility." *European Journal of Cultural Studies* 10, no. 2 (2007): 147–166.

Gimlin, Debra L. *Body Work: Beauty and Self-image in American Culture*. Berkeley, Los Angeles, and London: University of California Press, 2002.

Gimlin, Debra. *Cosmetic Surgery Narratives: A Cross-Cultural Analysis of Women's Accounts*. Basingstoke: Palgrave Macmillan, 2012.

Griffiths, Scott, Stuart B. Murray, and Stephen Touyz. "Extending the Masculinity Hypothesis: An Investigation of Gender Role Conformity, Body Dissatisfaction, and Disordered Eating in Young Heterosexual Men." *Psychology of Men and Masculinity* 16, no. 1 (2015): 108–113.

Grogan, Sarah. *Body Image: Understanding Body Dissatisfaction in Men, Women and Children*. 2nd ed. London and New York: Routledge, 2008.

Gupta, M. A., S. K. Chaturvedi, P. C. Chandarana, and A. M. Johnson. "Weight-Related Body Image Concerns among 18–24-Year-Old Women in Canada and India: An Empirical Comparative Study." *Journal of Psychosomatic Research* 50, no. 4 (2001): 193–198.

Haedersdal, M., and H. C. Wulf. "Evidence-Based Review of Hair Removal Using Lasers and Light Sources." *Journal of the European Academy of Dermatology and Venereology* 20, no. 1 (2006): 9–20.

Hall, Matthew. *Metrosexual Masculinities*. Basingstoke: Palgrave Macmillan, 2014.

Hamermesh, Daniel S. *Beauty Pays: Why Attractive People Are More Successful*. Princeton and Oxford: Princeton University Press, 2011.

Harriger, Jennifer. "Age Differences in Body Size Stereotyping in a Sample of Preschool Girls." *Eating Disorders* 23, (2015): 177–190.

Harrison, Kristen. "Television Viewers' Ideal Body Proportions: The Case of the Curvaceously Thin Woman." *Sex Roles* 48, no. 5–6 (2003): 255–264.

Haslanger, Sally. *Resisting Reality: Social Construction and Social Critique*. Oxford and New York: Oxford University Press, 2012.

Heckman, Susan. *The Feminine Subject*. Cambridge: Polity Press, 2014.

Herzig, Rebecca M. *Plucked: A History of Hair Removal*. New York and London: New York University Press, 2015.

Hewamanne, Sandya. "Threading Meaningful Lives: Respectability, Home Businesses and Identity Negotiations among Newly Immigrant South Asian Women." *Identities* 19, no. 3 (2012): 320–338.

Heyes, Cressida. *Self-Transformations: Foucault, Ethics, and Normalised Bodies*. Oxford and New York: Oxford University Press, 2007.

Hobson, Janell. "The "Batty" Politic: Toward an Aesthetic of the Black Female Body." *Hypatia* 18, no. 4 (2003): 87–105.

Holliday, Ruth, David Bell, Olive Cheung, Meredith Jones, and Elspeth Probyn. "Brief Encounters: Assembling Cosmetic Surgery Tourism." *Social Science and Medicine* 124 (2015): 298–304.

Holliday, Ruth, and Joanna Elfving-Hwang "Gender, Globalization and Aesthetic Surgery in South Korea." *Body and Society* 18, no. 2 (2012): 58–81.

Holliday, Ruth, and Jacqueline Sanchez Taylor. "Aesthetic Surgery as False Beauty." *Feminist Theory* 7, no. 2 (2006): 179–195.

hooks, bell. *Black Looks: Race and Representation*. New York and London: Routledge, 2015.

Hunter, Margaret L. "Buying Racial Capital: Skin-Bleaching and Cosmetic Surgery in a Globalized World." *Journal of Pan African Studies* 4, no. 4 (2011): 142–164.

Hunter, Margaret L. *Race Gender and the Politics of Skin Tone*, London and New York: Routledge, 2005.

Hurka, Thomas. "Why Value Autonomy?" *Social Theory and Practice* 13, no. 3 (1987): 361–382.

Hvilsom, Gitte B., Lisbet R. Hölmich, Trine F. Henriksen, Loren Lipworth, Joseph K. McLaughlin, and Søren Friis. "Local Complications after Cosmetic Breast Augmentation: Results from the Danish Registry for Plastic Surgery of the Breast." *Plastic and Reconstructive Surgery* 124, no. 3 (2009): 919–925.

Hwang, Harry S., and Jeffrey H. Spiegel. "The Effect of 'Single' vs 'Double' Eyelids on the Perceived Attractiveness of Chinese women." *Aesthetic Surgery Journal* 34, no. 3 (2014): 374–382.

Jacobs Brumberg, Joan. *The Body Project: An Intimate History of American Girls.* New York: Vintage Books, 1997.

Jaggar, Alison M. "'Saving Amina': Global Justice for Women and Intercultural Dialogue." *Ethics and International Affairs* 19, no. 3 (2005): 55–75.

Jaggar, Alison M. "Transnational Cycles of Gendered Vulnerability." In *Global Gender Justice.* Edited by Alison Jaggar, 18–40. Cambridge: Polity Press, 2014.

Jankowski, Glen S., Phillippa C. Diedrichs, Heidi Williamson, Gary Christopher, and Diana Harcourt. "Looking Age-Appropriate while Growing Old Gracefully: A Qualitative Study of Ageing and Body Image among Older Adults." *Journal of Health Psychology* 21, no. 4 (2016): 550–561.

Jeffreys, Sheila. *Beauty and Misogyny: Harmful Cultural Practices in the West.* London and New York: Routledge, 2005.

Jha, Meeta Rani. *The Global Beauty Industry: Colorism, Racism, and the National Body.* London and New York: Routledge, 2016.

Jones, Meredith. *Skintight: An Anatomy of Cosmetic Surgery.* Oxford and New York: Berg, 2008.

Kaczmarek, Lukasz D., Jolanta Enko, Małgorzata Awdziejczyk, Natalia Hoffmann, Natalia Białobrzeska, Przemysław Mielniczuk, and Stephan U. Dombrowski. "Would You Be Happier if You Looked Better? A Focusing Illusion." *Journal of Happiness Studies* 17, no. 1 (2016): 357–365.

Kant, Immanuel. *Lectures on Ethics.* Cambridge, Cambridge University Press, 1997.

Kant, Immanuel. *The Moral Law: Groundwork of the Metaphysic of Morals.* Trans and analyzed by H. J. Paton. London: Routledge, 1997.

Karupiah, Premalatha. "Have Beauty Ideals Evolved? Reading of Beauty Ideals in Tamil Movies by Malaysian Indian Youths." *Sociological Inquiry* 85, no. 2 (2015): 239–261.

Khader, Serene J. *Adaptive Preferences and Women's Empowerment.* Oxford and New York: Oxford University Press, 2011.

Kilpela, Lisa Smith, Carolyn Black Becker, Nicole Wesley, and Tiffany Stewart. "Body Image in Adult Women: Moving Beyond the Younger Years." *Advances in Eating Disorders: Theory, Research and Practice* 3, no. 2 (2015): 144–164.

Kim, Kyung Bo. "Narratives about the Media, Diet, and Body Image: A Cross-Cultural Comparison between Young Female Adults in the Midwestern United States and South Korea." *Journal of Intercultural Communication Research* 43, no. 4 (2014): 283–303.

Kirchhof, Mark G., and Sheila Au. "Brazilian Waxing and Human Papillomavirus: A Case of Acquired Epidermodysplasia Verruciformis." *Canadian Medical Association Journal* 187, no. 2 (2015): 126–128.

Kubic, Kelly N., and Rebecca M. Chory. "Exposure to Television Makeover Programs and Perceptions of Self." *Communication Research Reports* 24, no. 4 (2007): 283–291.

Kumar, Sameer. "Exploratory Analysis of Global Cosmetic Industry: Major Players, Technology and Market Trends." *Technovation* 25, no. 11 (2005): 1263–1272.

Labre, Megdala Peixoto. "The Brazilian Wax: New Hairlessness Norm for Women?" *Journal of Communication Inquiry* 26, no. 2 (2002): 113–132.

Laurie, Graeme. *Genetic Privacy: A Challenge to Medico-Legal Norms.* Cambridge: Cambridge University Press, 2002.

Lazar, Michelle M. "Discover the Power of Femininity!" Analyzing Global 'Power Femininity' in Local Advertising." *Feminist Media Studies* 6, no. 4 (2006): 505–517.

Lazar, Michelle M. "The Right to be Beautiful: Postfeminist Identity and Consumer Beauty Advertising." In *New Femininities: Postfeminism, Neoliberalism and Subjectivity.* Edited by Rosalind Gill and Christina Scharff, 37–51. Basingstoke: Palgrave Macmillan, 2011.

Lewis, Kelly M., Navit Robkin, Karie Gaska, and Lillian Carol Njoki. "Investigating Motivations for Women's Skin Bleaching in Tanzania," *Psychology of Women Quarterly* 35, no. 1 (2011): 29–37.

Li, Eric P. H., Hyun Jeong Min, and Russell W. Belk. "Skin Lightening and Beauty in Four Asian Cultures." *NA-Advances in Consumer Research* 35 (2008): 444–449.

Lin, Chyong-Ling, and Jin-Tsann Yeh. "Comparing Society's Awareness of Women: Media-Portrayed Idealized Images and Physical Attractiveness." *Journal of Business Ethics* 90, no. 1 (2009): 61–79.

Lipworth, Loren, and Joseph K. McLaughlin. "Excess Suicide Risk and Other External Causes of Death among Women with Cosmetic Breast Implants: A Neglected Research Priority." *Current Psychiatry Reports* 12, no. 3 (2010): 234–238.

Lorenzo, Genevieve L., Jeremy C. Biesanz, and Lauren J. Human. "What Is Beautiful Is Good and More Accurately Understood: Physical Attractiveness in First Impressions of Personality." *Psychological Science* 21, no. 12 (2010): 1777–1782.

Lueck, Jennifer Anette. "Friend-Zone with Benefits: The Parasocial Advertising of Kim Kardashian." *Journal of Marketing Communications* 21, no. 2 (2015): 91–109.

Luo, Wei. "Aching for the Altered Body: Beauty Economy and Chinese Women's Consumption of Cosmetic Surgery." *Women's Studies International Forum* 38 (2013): 1–10.

Luo, Wei. "Selling Cosmetic Surgery and Beauty Ideals: The Female Body in the Web Sites of Chinese Hospitals." *Women's Studies in Communication* 35, no. 1 (2012): 68–95.

Lyonette, Clare, and Rosemary Crompton. "Sharing the Load? Partners' Relative Earnings and the Division of Domestic Labour." *Work, Employment and Society* 29, no. 1 (2014): 23–40.

MacCallum, Fiona, and Heather Widdows. "Altered Images: Understanding the Influence of Unrealistic Images and Beauty Aspirations." *Health Care Analysis*. DOI 10.1007/s10728–016–0327–1 (on-line first, forthcoming).

MacKinnon, Catharine A. *Feminism Unmodified: Discourses on Life and Law.* Cambridge and London: Harvard University Press, 1987.

Makino, Maria, Koji Tsuboi, and Lorraine Dennerstein. "Prevalence of Eating Disorders: A Comparison of Western and Non-Western countries." *Medscape General Medicine* 6, no. 3 (2004): 49.

Mangweth-Matzek, Barbara, Hans W. Hoek, and Harrison G. Pope Jr. "Pathological Eating and Body Dissatisfaction in Middle-aged and Older Women." *Current Opinion in Psychiatry* 27, no. 6 (2014): 431–435.

McCracken, Angela B. V.. *The Beauty Trade: Youth, Gender, and Fashion Globalization.* New York: Oxford University Press, 2014.

McNair, Brian. *Striptease Culture: Sex, Media and the Democratization of Desire.* London and New York: Routledge, 2002.

McRobbie, Angela. *The Aftermath of Feminism: Gender, Culture and Social Change.* London: Sage Publications, 2009.

Meyers, Diana Tietjens. *Gender in the Mirror: Cultural Imagery and Women's Agency.* Oxford and New York: Oxford University Press, 2002.

Miller, Janice. "Making Up Is Masculine: The Increasing Cultural Connections between Masculinity and Make-up." *Critical Studies in Men's Fashion* (2014): 241–253.

Morris, Kasey Lynn, and Jamie L. Goldenberg. "Women, Objects, and Animals: Differentiating between Sex-and Beauty-Based Objectification." *Revue Internationale de Psychologie Sociale* 28, no. 1 (2015): 15–38.

Morris, P. F., and C. P. Szabo. "Meanings of Thinness and Dysfunctional Eating in Black South African Females: A Qualitative Study." *African Journal of Psychiatry* 16, no. 5 (2013): 338–342.

Musaiger, Abdulrahman O., Nora E. Shahbeek, and Maryama Al-Mannai. "The Role of Social Factors and Weight Status in Ideal Body-Shape Preferences as Perceived by Arab Women," *Journal of Biosocial Science* 36, no. 06 (2004): 699–707.

Myers, T. A., and J. H. Crowther. "Social Comparison as a Predictor of Body Dissatisfaction: A Meta-Analytic Review." *Journal of Abnormal Psychology* 118 (2009): 683–698.

Neumark-Sztainer, Dianne, Susan J. Paxton, Peter J. Hannan, Jess Haines, and Mary Story. "Does Body Satisfaction Matter? Five-Year Longitudinal Associations between Body Satisfaction and Health Behaviors in Adolescent Females and Males." *Journal of Adolescent Health* 39, no. 2 (2006): 244–251.

Nicholson, R. M., S. Leinster, and E. M. Sassoon. "A Comparison of the Cosmetic and Psychological Outcome of Breast Reconstruction, Breast Conserving Surgery and Mastectomy without Reconstruction." *The Breast* 16, no. 4 (2007): 396–410.

Nussbaum, Martha. "Objectification." *Philosophy and Public Affairs* 24, no. 4 (1995): 249–291.

Nussbaum, Martha. *Women and Human Development: The Capabilities Approach,* Cambridge: University of Cambridge Press, 2000.

O'Brien Hallstein, Lynn. *Bikini-Ready Moms: Celebrity Profiles, Motherhood, and the Body.* New York: State University of New York Press, 2015.

Ogden, Jane, and Sheriden Russell. "How Black Women Make Sense of 'White' and 'Black' Fashion Magazines: A Qualitative Think Aloud Study." *Journal of Health Psychology* 18, no.12 (2012): 1588–1600.

Okazawa-Rey, Margo, Tracy Robinson, and Janie Victoria Ward. "Black Women and the Politics of Skin Color and Hair." *Women and Therapy* 6, no. 1–2 (1987): 89–102.

Oliver, Michael. *The Politics of Disablement.* Basingstoke: Macmillan, 1990.

Orbach, Susan. *Fat Is a Feminist Issue.* London: Random House and Penguin, 1978.

Papadaki, Lina. "What is objectification?" *Journal of Moral Philosophy* 7 (2010): 16–36.

Patton, Tracey Owens. "Hey girl, am I more than my Hair?: African American Women and their Struggles with Beauty, Body Image, and Hair." *NWSA Journal* 18, no. 2 (2006): 24–51.

Peiss, Kathys. *Hope in a Jar: The Making of America's Beauty Culture.* New York: Henry Holt, 1998.

Perry, Imani. "Buying White Beauty." *Cardozo JL and Gender* 12 (2005): 579–608.

Picton, Oliver. "The Complexities of Complexion: A Cultural Geography of Skin Colour and Beauty Products." *Geography* 98 (2013): 85–92.

Pike, Kathleen M., and Patricia E. Dunne. "The Rise of Eating Disorders in Asia: A Review." *Journal of Eating Disorders* 3, no. 1 (2015): 1–14.

Ponterotto, Diane. "Trivializing the Female Body: A Cross-Cultural Analysis of the Representation of Women in Sports Journalism." *Journal of International Women's Studies* 15, no. 2 (2014): 94–111.

Projansky, Sarah. *Spectacular Girls: Media Fascination and Celebrity Culture.* New York: New York University Press, 2014.

Rguibi, Mohamed, and Rekia Belahsen, "Body Size Preferences and Socio-cultural Influences on Attitudes towards Obesity Among Moroccan Sahraoui Women." *Body Image* 3, no. 4 (2006): 395–400.

Rguibi, Mohamed, and Rekia Belahsen. "Fattening Practices among Moroccan Saharawi Women." *Eastern Mediterranean Health Journal* 12, no. 5 (2006): 619–624.

Rhode, Deborah L. *The Beauty Bias: The Injustice of Appearance in Law and Life.* Oxford and New York: Oxford University Press, 2010.

Rice, Clara. *Becoming Women: The Embodied Self in Image Culture.* Toronto, Buffalo, and London: University of Toronto Press, 2014.

Roberts, Alan, Thomas F. Cash, Alan Feingold, and Blair T. Johnson. "Are Black-White Differences in Females' Body Dissatisfaction Decreasing? A Meta-Analytic Review." *Journal of Consulting and Clinical Psychology* 74, no. 6 (2006): 1121–1131.

Rubenstein, Adam J. "Variation in Perceived Attractiveness Differences between Dynamic and Static Faces." *Psychological Science* 16, no. 10 (2005): 759–762.

Runfola, Cristin D., Ann Von Holle, Christine M. Peat, Danieelle A. Gagne, Kimberly A. Brownley, Sara M, Hofmeier, and Cythia M. Bulik "Characteristics of Women with Body Size Satisfaction at Midlife: Results of the Gender and Body Image Study." *Journal of Women and Aging* 25 (2013): 287–304.

Sarwer, David B., Alison L. Infield, James L. Baker, Laurie A. Casas, Paul M. Glat, Alan H. Gold, Mark L. Jewell, Don LaRossa, Foad Nahai, and V. Leroy Young. "Two-Year Results of a Prospective, Multi-Site Investigation of Patient Satisfaction and Psychosocial Status following Cosmetic Surgery." *Aesthetic Surgery Journal* 28, no. 3 (2008): 245–250.

Schooler, Deborah, L., Monique Ward, Ann Merriwether, and Allison Caruthers. "Who's That Girl: Television's Role in the Body Image Development of Young White and Black Women." *Psychology of Women Quarterly* 28, no. 1 (2004): 38–47.

Smolak, Linda, and Sarah K. Murnen. "Gender, Self-Objectification and Pubic Hair Removal." *Sex Roles* 65, no. 7–8 (2011): 506–517.

Stapleton, Peta, Timothy McIntyre, and Amy Bannatyne. "Body Image Avoidance, Body Dissatisfaction, and Eating Pathology: Is There a Difference Between Male Gym Users and Non–Gym Users?" *American Journal of Men's Health* 10, no.2 (2016): 100–109.

Stewart, K. J., D. A. Stewart, B. Coghlan, D. H. Harrison, B. M. Jones, and N. Waterhouse. "Complications of 278 Consecutive Abdominoplasties." *Journal of Plastic, Reconstructive and Aesthetic Surgery* 59, no. 11 (2006): 1152–1155.

Stice, Eric, Diane Spangler, and W. Stewart Agras. "Exposure to Media-Portrayed Thin-Ideal Images Adversely Affects Vulnerable Girls: A Longitudinal Experiment." *Journal of Social and Clinical Psychology* 20, no. 3 (2001): 270–288.

Stoljar, Natalie. "Feminist Perspectives on Autonomy." In *The Stanford Encyclopaedia of Philosophy.* Edited by Edward N. Zalta. https://stanford.library.sydney.edu.au/archives/fall2013/entries/feminism-autonomy/.

Suhail, Kausar. "Prevalence of Eating Disorders in Pakistan: Relationship with Depression and Body Shape." *Eating and Weight Disorders-Studies on Anorexia, Bulimia and Obesity* 7, no. 2 (2002): 131–138.

Swami, Viren, and Adrian Furnham. *The Psychology of Physical Attraction*. London and New York: Routledge, 2008.

Swami, Viren, Ulrich S. Tran, Stefan Stieger, and Martin Voracek. "Associations between Women's Body Image and Happiness: Results of the YouBeauty.com Body Image Survey (YBIS)." *Journal of Happiness Studies* 16, no. 3 (2015): 705–718.

Talukdar, Jaita. "Thin but Not Skinny: Women Negotiating the 'Never too Thin' Body Ideal in Urban India." *Women's Studies International Forum* 35, no. 2 (2012) 109–111.

Tate, Shirley. *Black Women's Bodies and the Nation: Race, Gender and Culture.* Basingstoke: Palgrave MacMillan, 2015.

Tate, Shirley. "Black Beauty: Shade, Hair and Anti-Racist Aesthetics." *Ethnic and Racial Studies* 30, no. 2 (2007): 300–319.

Thaler, Richard, and Cass Sunstein. *Nudge: Improving Decisions about Health, Wealth, and Happiness.* London: Penguin Books, 2008.

Thomas, Samantha, Timothy Olds, Simone Pettigrew, Melanie Randle, and Sophie Lewis. "Don't Eat That, You'll Get Fat!" Exploring How Parents and Children Conceptualise and Frame Messages about the Causes and Consequences of Obesity." *Social Science and Medicine* 119 (2014): 114–122.

Tiggemann, Marika, Maria Gardiner, and Amy Slater. "'I Would Rather Be Size 10 than Have Straight A's': A Focus Group Study of Adolescent Girls' Wish to Be Thinner." *Journal of Adolescence* 23, no. 6 (2000): 645–659.

Tiggemann, Marika, and Suzanna Hodgson. "The Hairlessness Norm Extended: Reasons for and Predictors of Women's Body Hair Removal at Different Body Sites." *Sex Roles* 59, no. 11–12 (2008): 889–897.

Tiggemann, Marika, and Amy Slater. "NetGirls: The Internet, Facebook, and Body Image Concern in Adolescent Girls." *International Journal of Eating Disorders* 46, no. 6 (2013): 630–633.

Tiggemann. Marika, and Elyse Williams. "The Role of Self-Objectification in Disordered Eating, Depressed Mood, and Sexual Functioning among Women a Comprehensive Test of Objectification Theory." *Psychology of Women Quarterly* 36, no. 1 (2012): 66–75.T

incknell, Estella. "Scourging the Abject Body: *Ten Year Younger* and Fragmented Femininity Under Neoliberalism." In *New Femininities: Postfeminism, Neoliberalism and Subjectivity.* Edited by Rosalind Gill and Christina Scharff, 83–95. Basingstoke: Palgrave Macmillan, 2011.

Toerien, Merran, Sue Wilkinson, and Precilla Y.L. Choi. "Body Hair Removal: The 'Mundane' Production of Normative Femininity." *Sex Roles* 52, no. 5–6 (2005): 399–406.

Trager, Jonathan D. K.. "Pubic Hair Removal—Pearls and Pitfalls." *Journal of Pediatric and Adolescent Gynecology* (2006): 117–123.

Tyler, Imogen. "Pregnant Beauty: Maternal Femininities under Neoliberalism." In *New Femininities: Postfeminism, Neoliberalism and Subjectivity*. Edited by Rosalind Gill and Christina Scharff, 21–36. Basingstoke: Palgrave Macmillan, 2011.

Tyrrell, Jessica, Samuel E. Jones, Robin Beaumont, Christina M. Astley, Rebecca Lovell, Hanieh Yaghootkar, Marcus Tuke, Katherine S. Ruth, Rachel M. Freathy, Joel N. Hirschhorn, Andrew R. Wood, Anna Murray, Michael N. Weedon, and Timothy M. Frayling. "Height, Body Mass Index, and Socioeconomic Status: Mendelian Randomisation Study in UK Biobank." British Medical Journal 352, no. i582 (2016): http://dx.doi.org/10.1136/bmj.i582.

Vantoch, Victoria. *The Jet Set*. Philadelphia: University of Pennsylvania Press, 2013.

Watson, Laurel B., Dawn Robinson, Franco Dispenza, and Negar Nazari. "African American Women's Sexual Objectification Experiences: A Qualitative Study." *Psychology of Women Quarterly* 36, no. 4 (2012): 458–475.

Webb, Jennifer B., Phoebe Butler-Ajibade, and Seronda A. Robinson. "Considering an Affect Regulation Framework for Examining the Association between Body Dissatisfaction and Positive Body Image in Black Older Adolescent Females: Does Body Mass Index Matter?" *Body image* 11, no. 4 (2014): 426–437.

Wegenstien, Bernadette. *The Cosmetic Gaze: Body Modification and the Construction of Beauty*. Cambridge and London: MIT Press, 2012.

Wehner, Mackenzie R., Melissa L. Shive, Mary-Margaret Chren, Jiali Han, Abrar A. Qureshi, and Eleni Linos. "Indoor Tanning and Non-Melanoma Skin Cancer: Systematic Review and Meta-Analysis." *British Medical Journal* 345 (2012): doi: http://dx.doi.org/10.1136/bmj.e5909.

Widdows, Heather. "Conceptualising the Self in the Genetic Era." *Health Care Analysis* 15, no. 1 (2007): 5–12.

Widdows, Heather. *The Connected Self: The Ethics and Governance of the Genetic Individual*. Cambridge: Cambridge University Press, 2013.

Widdows, Heather. "Exploitation and the Global Demands of Beauty." In *Exploitation: From Practice to Theory*. Edited by Monique Deveaux and Vida Panitch. Rowman and Littlefield International: London (forthcoming).

Widdows, Heather. "Global Health Justice and the Right to Health." *Health Care Analysis*, 23, no. 4, (2015): 391–400.

Widdows, Heather. *The Moral Vision of Iris Murdoch*. Aldershot: Ashgate, 2005.

Widdows, Heather. "Rejecting the Choice Paradigm: Rethinking the Ethical Framework in Prostitution and Egg Sale Debates." In *Gender, Agency, and Coercion*. Edited by S. Madhok, A. Phillips, K. Wilson, Clare Hemmings, 157–180. Basingstoke: Palgrave Macmillan, 2013.

Widdows, Heather, and Herjeet Marway, editors. *Women and Violence: The Agency of Victims and Perpetrators*. Basingstoke: Palgrave MacMillan, 2015.

Widdows, Heather, and Peter West Oram. "Revising Global Theories of Justice to Include Public Goods." *Journal of Global Ethics*, 9, no. 2, (2013): 227–243.

Witcomb, Gemma L., Jon Arcelus, and Jue Chen. "Can Cognitive Dissonance Methods Developed in the West for Combatting the 'Thin Ideal' Help Slow the Rapidly Increasing Prevalence of Eating Disorders in Non-Western Cultures?" *Shanghai Archives of Psychiatry* 25, no. 6 (2013): 332–340.

Wolf, Naomi. *The Beauty Myth: How Images of Beauty Are Used Against Women.* London: Vintage Books, 1990.

Yager, Zali, Phillippa C. Diedrichs, Lina A. Ricciardelli, and Emma Halliwell. "What Works in Secondary Schools? A Systematic Review of Classroom-Based Body Image Programs." *Body Image* 10, no. 3 (2013): 271–281.

Yan, Yan, and Kim Bissell. "The Globalization Of Beauty: How Is Ideal Beauty Influenced by Globally Published Fashion and Beauty Magazines?" *Journal of Intercultural Communication Research* 43, no. 3 (2014): 194–214.

Yang, Jie. "Nennu and Shunu: Gender, Body Politics, and the Beauty Economy in China." *Signs* 36, no. 2 (2011): 333–357.

Young, Iris Marion. *On Female Body Experience: "Throwing Like a Girl" and other Essays.* New York: Oxford University Press, 2005.

Zhang, Meng. "A Chinese Beauty Story: How College Women in China Negotiate Beauty, Body Image, and Mass Media." *Chinese Journal of Communication* 5, no. 4 (2012): 437–454.

Zhang, Yuanyuan, Travis L. Dixon, and Kate Conrad. "Female Body Image as a Function of Themes in Rap Music Videos: A Content Analysis." *Sex Roles* 62, no. 11–12 (2010): 787–797.

In addition to the above books, book chapters and journal articles numerous primary sources have been used including magazine and newspaper articles, government and NGO reports (including those by Girlguiding, NSPCC, the YMCA and the Keogh Review), professional association documents (including by the GMC, ISAPS the RCS), and website and social media. All are fully referenced in footnotes, however, key sources include *BBC.co.uk, Beauty Demands Blog, Cosmopolitan, The Economist, The Daily Mail, The Guardian, Huffington Post, The Independent, Marie Claire, The New Yorker, The New York Times, The Sunday Times, The Telegraph*, and *The Sun.*

INDEX

abdominoplasty, 85
ability, versus appearance, 64–65
abortion, 150
academic women, nonconformity to beauty ideal and, 36, 37, 40, 57–58, 134, 211
achievement: of the beauty ideal, 176; beauty versus, 211–212; as reward, 38; weight loss as, 118
actors: aging, 241; beauty ideal for, 242; body shapes of, 239. *See also* names of specific actors
actresses: as beauty objects, 167–168, 176; skin color/tone of, 88–89; thinness of, 94. *See also* names of specific actresses
adaptive preference, 216–217, 220–223, 255
adolescents: body dissatisfaction in, 63–64; breast implants in, 221–222; dieting, 75; eating disorders in, 75; perceptions of beauty ideal, 61
advertising, 217; beauty as pleasure approach of, 194; beauty focus of, 41; ideal body portrayed in, 22; images of women in, 183; Look Good Feel Better campaign, 67–68; of "make yourself amazing" clinics, 258; male sexual objectification in, 239–240; regulation of, 258; sexualized, 185; sexual objectification in, 183, 239–240; of shoes, 48; of skin-care products, 24, 81; of skin-lightening products, 90–91
aerobics, 154
Africa, 79, 92, 303n14
African American men, 78
African American women, 78, 81–82, 284n94; beauty norms and, 219; body dissatisfaction in, 79, 279n27; as models, 88–89; racist constructions of, 90
African college students, 92
African diaspora, 78
African women, 78, 81, 87, 279n30

agelessness look, 65
agency, of women, 182, 185; choice and, 202, 213; denial of, 182; postfeminist interpretation of, 185
aging: aversion to appearance of, 25–26; new beauty criteria for, 65; positive attitude toward, 25–26; shame associated with, 33
air hostesses, 58
Albright, Madeleine, 57
alcohol use, 34
American Society of Plastic Surgeons, 83
amputations, 244
anger, 75, 216, 218
antiaging products, 80, 81, 115
antibeauty norms, 37
antibeauty position, 219
anticellulite creams, 126
antichoice, 227–228
antisex, 166
antiwomen feminist politics, 220
antiwrinkle procedures, 84
anxiety, 7, 60, 68, 255, 258–259, 261
appearance: ability versus, 64–65; historical importance of, 51; as primary value, 61, 64–65; as proxy for character, 30–31; relationship to status, 51
apps, 59, 191
Argentina, 311n9
"Armpits 4 August," 110
artificiality, of beauty, 36
Asia, skin care advertising in, 81
Asian women: blepharoplasty in, 83, 84; eating disorders in, 77–78; skin lightening in, 87
aspiration: of beauty practices, 101; to ideal body shape, 118
athletes, 56–57
attractiveness: assessments of, 41–42, 59; beauty norms and, 176–177

A NOTE ON THE TYPE

This book has been composed in Adobe Text and Gotham. Adobe Text, designed by Robert Slimbach for Adobe, bridges the gap between fifteenth- and sixteenth-century calligraphic and eighteenth-century Modern styles. Gotham, inspired by New York street signs, was designed by Tobias Frere-Jones for Hoefler & Co.